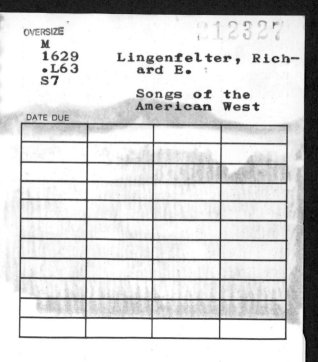

SONGS
OF THE AMERICAN
WEST

SONGS

OF THE

AMERICAN

WEST

Compiled and Edited by

RICHARD E. LINGENFELTER
RICHARD A. DWYER, &
DAVID COHEN

Drawings by
STEVEN M. JOHNSON

UNIVERSITY OF CALIFORNIA PRESS
BERKELEY AND LOS ANGELES
1968

University of California Press
Berkeley and Los Angeles, California

Cambridge University Press
London, England

©1968 by The Regents of the University of California
Library of Congress Catalog Card Number: 67-12220

Designed by W. H. Snyder
Printed in the United States of America

ACKNOWLEDGMENTS

The compilation of this song collection has been made possible through the generous aid of many persons, libraries, historical societies, and state and federal archives. We particularly wish to thank Esther Euler and Ann Hinckley of the University Research Library and Wilbur J. Smith and the staff of the Special Collections Department, University of California, Los Angeles; Helen H. Bretnor and John Barr Tompkins of Bancroft Library and Anne Basart of the Music Library, University of California, Berkeley; F. R. Blackburn and Alberta Pantle of the Kansas State Historical Society Library, Topeka; Mary K. Dempsey of the Library of the Historical Society of Montana, Helena; Fred Folmer and L. Friend of the University of Texas Library, Austin; John James, Jr., of the Utah State Historical Society Library, Salt Lake City; Margaret E. Keillor of the Oregon State Archives, Salem; Irving Lowens of the Music Division, Library of Congress, Washington, D.C.; Harold Merklen of the New York Public Library, New York; Frank Paluka of the Special Collection Library, State University of Iowa, Iowa City; Francine Seders of the Washington State Historical Society Library, Tacoma; and Merle W. Wells of the Idaho Historical Society, Boise.

We would also like to express our appreciation to James de T. Abajian of the California Historical Society Library, San Francisco; Dorothy Anderson of the University of Nebraska Library, Lincoln; Clara S. Beatty of the Nevada Historical Society, Reno; Joyce Bouchard of the Butte Free Public Library, Butte, Montana; L. M. Eldrich of the Yankton College Library, Yankton, South Dakota; Chad J. Flake of the Brigham Young University Library, Provo, Utah; Lorine Garrett of the Sharlot Hall Historical Museum, Prescott, Arizona; Priscilla Knuth of the Oregon Historical Society Library, Portland; Mercedes B. MacKay of the South Dakota State Library, Pierre; Connie Miyamoto of the Wyoming State Library, Cheyenne; Earl E. Olson of the Latter-Day Saints Church Historian's Office Library, Salt Lake City; Allan R. Ottley of the California State Library, Sacramento; Mary S. Pratt of the Los Angeles Public Library, Los Angeles; Margaret Rose of the North Dakota State Historical Society Library, Bismarck; Eleanor B. Sloan of the Arizona Pioneers' Historical Society Library, Tucson; Mrs. Enid T. Thompson of the State Historical Society of Colorado Library, Denver; Edith Thornton of the Denver Public Library, Denver; Marietta Ward of the Music Library, University of Washington, Seattle; Conrad

F. Weitzel of the Ohio State Historical Society Library, Columbus; and Alice Wiren of the Nebraska State Historical Society Library, Lincoln.

In addition we are indebted to the personal generosity of Professors Wayland D. Hand and D. K. Wilgus of the University of California, Los Angeles; Professor Austin E. Fife of Utah State University, Logan; Norman Cohen of Playa Del Rey, California; Professor Ray B. Browne of Purdue University, Lafayette, Indiana; Lester A. Hubbard of Salt Lake City; Professor William E. Koch of Kansas State University, Manhattan; Ethel Moore of Tulsa, Oklahoma; David F. Myrick of San Francisco; Professor D. B. Nunis of University of Southern California, Los Angeles; Mrs. Glen Paris of Dighton, Kansas; Professor Kenneth W. Porter of the University of Oregon, Eugene; James F. Stevens of Seattle; Gerard M. Thomas of Berkeley, California; and Professor Robert C. Wylder of Long Beach State College, Long Beach, California. We would particularly like to thank Sam Chianis, who in the course of preparing the music by hand, goodnaturedly put up with even our most picayunish editorial changes.

Finally we would like to thank the following persons and publishers for permission to use copyrighted material: Beechwood Music Corp., George F. Briegel, Inc., Olive W. Burt, Daughters of Utah Pioneers, Duke University Press, E. P. Dutton & Co., Inc., Fall River Music, Inc., Austin E. Fife, Charles J. Finger Estate, Mrs. Ralph E. Flanders, Barthold Fles, University of Florida Press, Folkways Music Publishers, Inc., Folkways Records & Service Corp., Gail I. Gardner, John Greenway, Harcourt, Brace & World, Inc., Houghton Mifflin Co., Idaho Historical Society, Indiana University Press, Ives Washburn, Inc., Alfred A. Knopf, Inc., Lane Magazine & Book Co., Ludlow Music, Inc., University of Missouri Press, University of Nebraska Press, Noble & Noble Publishers, Inc., Oregon Historical Society, Routledge & Kegan Paul, Ltd., Shawnee Press, Inc., James F. Stevens, Summy-Birchard Co., Tennessee Folklore Society, Texas Folklore Society, Utah State Historical Society, University of Utah Press, *Western Folklore*, and Western Publications.

R. E. L.
R. A. D.
D. C.

CONTENTS

INTRODUCTION, 1

TO THE WEST

COMING AROUND THE HORN

CROSSING THE PLAINS

THE PIONEER STAGE DRIVER

THE RAILROAD CARS ARE COMING

SEEING THE ELEPHANT

WHEN I WENT OFF TO PROSPECT

THE APEX BOARDING HOUSE

WHEN I WAS A MINER, A HARD-ROCK MINER

STAND BY YOUR UNION

COME, COME, YE SAINTS

INTRODUCTION

James Josiah Webb, an adventurer in the early Santa Fe trade, was leading a party back to St. Louis in the winter of 1845. They were camped on an island in the Arkansas River roasting buffalo meat as the snow fell lightly, when, as Webb's journal relates,

Cassius, the cook, began singing "Home, Sweet Home." The camp and all surroundings tended to place us in good spirits, but this was too much. The thought of the comforts of home, and loved friends around the cheerful fireside with no apprehensions of danger from enemies or suffering from cold or hunger, contrasted with our situation (although comfortable compared with what it might have been) was too much. And I called him to order and offered a resolution that any member of the company who, during the balance of the trip, should sing any song of home or speak of the good things of home or of the comforts of home, should be fined a gallon of whiskey payable on our arrival in Westport.

In the interests of any who would understand those huddled pioneers through the kind of gists and piths that only their songs provide, and of any who would probe those songs themselves to learn what subjects came to replace the good things of home, and, finally, of any who would sing a good song and be fined or not, we have made this book. It is a collection of nearly three hundred songs *about* the West selected from the many times that number to be found in manuscript archives, melodion company and political campaign songsters, broadside sheets, and old newspaper clippings, in addition to the published volumes of folk songs recovered from oral tradition by scholars in the field.

The title page of one of the first songsters published in the West recommended the verses within that slim booklet as "giving in a few words what would occupy volumes, detailing the Hopes, Trials and Joys of a Miner's Life." Now, more than a hundred years later, this aim, widened to include most ways of life in the West, is ours too. Not only are the songs more economical in their observations than contemporary journals, they are often the only surviving glimpses of feelings and conditions that were rarely articulated in weightier volumes. And they sometimes show the angular antecedents of later, more comfortable and amorphous attitudes.

The songs are also, in many instances, far more personal visions of life than official documents or commercial reports. Such song makers as John Stone, William Willes, D. J. O'Malley, Joe Hill, and Woodie Guthrie saw in their own experience the reflections of countless silent lives, and they focused them in song. Thus the songs give individual views of the course of Western life with a precision and a spontaneity which have outlasted the local importance of the events they describe.

In addition to recovering neglected songs, we have tried to support our interest in the historical content and personal vision of more popular songs by obtaining their earliest, reasonably complete texts. Thus, the tendency for contextual details and evanescent emotions to become worn away or reshaped to new ends after many years of folk handling should be overcome. For the effects of similar tendencies in songs of reminiscence, we refer the reader to the final selection of songs in this volume.

The time spanned by the subjects of these songs extends from the beginnings of massive American penetration of the West in the 1840's to the Great Depression nearly a hundred years later. They are gathered into occupational categories following the order in which these groups came to some kind of dominance in the West: miners, Mormons, cowboys, homesteaders, organized labor. These distinctions are, of course, arbitrary, for not only could a man do two things at once, he could fail at many before he was through. Moreover, each group had plenty to say about certain others; the cowboys and migrant workers taking on the farmers, and so forth. Within the gaps, the songs of such worthy bodies as the railroaders, Chinese, soldiers, loggers, and hobos are wedged; and within the major headings, the songs are clustered by theme or mood. This organization and our contextual interests have made us heedless of type distinctions among folk songs, art songs, broadsides, and ballads, whether extant or extinct.

Preceding the groups of song texts are commentaries giving brief background notes, generalizations about trends in theme or tone, and occasional opinions about the value or significance of certain songs. For more detailed information, the student is referred to the bibliographic notes printed at the bottom of the last page of the song to which they refer, where he will find references to published texts and variants,* and the commentaries of experts.

Besides encouraging the reader to judge for himself, we might suggest one view of some of the values to be found in Western songs. It has been argued, for example, that the Western frontier nourished the growth of certain traits in the American people, traits that have survived the passing of the answerable conditions: rugged individualism, mobility of place and station, willingness to waste where there was plenty and quickness to invent where there was nothing, a nationalism drifting toward

*In the notes to the songs, the term "variant" refers to all texts of the songs found in the sources given in the bibliography. When the sources themselves include references to additional song texts, the cited pages in these notes are asterisked.

arrogance, reliance on democratic processes—if only as a last resort—and an indifference to, or suspicion of, the intellect.

In estimating the truth of this argument, one can profitably turn to the testimony given by the mass of songs composed in and about the West, songs that have, in many instances, survived the times that made them. The myth of rugged individualism is a good test case, and the many songs on the theme of "seeing the elephant" provide one verdict. The phrase "seeing the elephant" was defined well in 1844 in Kendall's *Santa Fe Expedition:* "When a man is disappointed in anything he undertakes, when he has seen enough, when he gets sick and tired of any job he may have set himself about, he has seen the elephant." An Eastern satire on the gold rush had gone by that name, and in 1850 D. G. Robinson rewrote the play and added a new title song which took a closer look at the truth:

> On the Platte we couldn't agree,
> Because I had the di-a-ree;
> We were split up, I made a break,
> With one old mule for the Great Salt Lake.

As the narrative staggers on, we learn the painful consequences of that theoretically commendable initiative:

> Because I would not pay my bill,
> They kicked me out of Downieville;
> I stole a mule and lost the trail,
> And then fetched up in Hangtown Jail.

After trying various forms of private enterprise, socially sanctioned and not, he tried settling down—and then came the revelation:

> I fell in love with a California girl;
> Her eyes were gray, her hair did curl;
> Her nose turned up to get rid of her chin—
> Says she, "You're a miner, you can't come in."

> When the elephant I had seen,
> I'm damned if I thought I was green;
> And others say, both night and morn,
> They saw him coming round the Horn.

Other seekers of gold encountered the same gray vision on the rush to Pike's Peak, as the song "In the Summer of Sixty" relates. After coming back "flat-busted," the enterprising narrator says:

> 'Twas then I heard farming was a very fine branch,
> So I spent most of my money in buying a ranch;
> And when I got to it, with sorrow and shame,
> I found a big miner had jumped my fine claim.

Denver's life of fashion then summoned him, and he succumbed to gambling fever. The moment of astonished revelation is perfectly captured as he stared at his "winning" card:

> One corner turned down, it's plain to be seen,
> I looked at the fellow and thought he was green,
> Yes I looked at that feller and thought he was green,
> One corner turned down, 'twas so plain to be seen.

That ace, of course, was a trey spot, and the next morning you might have seen,

> In an ox wagon, 'twas me and my wife
> Goin' down the Platte river for death or for life.

As Mart Taylor's narrative reveals in "John Chinaman's Appeal," the imported Oriental laborers were victims of the same desperate fate when they struck out on their own:

> In forty days I reached the Bay,
>   And nearly starved I was, sir.
> I cooked and ate a dog one day—
>   I didn't know the laws, sir—
> But soon I found my dainty meal
>   Was 'gainst the city order.
> The penalty I had to feel—
>   Confound the old Recorder.

John fared no better in the mining camps, where he was beaten and run out by "Know-Nothings" and feuding China agents. His laundry at Yreka brought in only dirty clothes, no money. Finally he cried:

> Oh, now, my friends, I'm going away
> From this infernal place, sir;
>
> . . . .
>
> For Christians all have treated me
> As men should be used never.

A man could perceive the elephant gradually, as did the cowboys whose occupation was eroded away by the railroads and the grangers. The narrator of "Yellowstone Flat" envisions his immediate and distant futures, and neither is rosy:

> But the time for the punchers is now growing slim,
> So down the old cow trail we'll soon split the wind.
> We'll ride to the home ranch, we'll turn the broncs loose;
> For the rope on the saddle there's no future use.

> But as for bronc riding, I've rode broncs enough.
> I'm a-going down East and, like Wild Bill, play tough.
> My hair will grow long and I'll dance on the stage,
> And I'll tell them out West I eat snakes and wild sage.

"The Kansas Farmer's Lament" tells us what those home-steaders who had to fight both the elements and the cattlemen learned of rugged individualism:

> 'Crost crops they'll drive cattle,
> Then turn to fight a battle,
> Their rein in their hand, their guns by their side.
> With quirt they'll make gestures
> And mimic winchesters,
> Then quirting and rowling, on through they ride.

> I'll pick up my knapsack
> And strap on my wife's back,
> And on to the railroad count ties far away.
> My wife and I trudging,
> Our children on budging;
> When we get to Boston, you bet we will stay.

If you think things might have been better in the cities, we point to "The San Francisco Rag-Picker," whose unburdened miseries have all of the features of the seeing-the-elephant narrative about the greased slide downhill:

> When first I went trading upon my own hook,
> I started down South to sell a new book;
> But I got tarred and feathered the very first day,
> Because folks thought I came to run niggers away.

Out West he tried peddling cakes and candy, farming—and spending his profits on quinine—and he even put in a stint oxteaming at Washoe. In fact:

> I've tried everything else other people make pay;
> I've been Methodist preacher, and I've worked by the day;
> Taught school, made bricks, played poker, wrote rhymes,
> But whatever I do, it's always "hard times!"

It would seem, then, if these and many other such songs are an indication, that frontier conditions may have fathered rugged individualism, but they also promptly disinherited it. The songs of men on their own hook are songs of misery and loneliness, despite the comic surfaces. Conversely, one could show that it was not until men on the vanishing frontier organized that they were really able to better their lot. The most hopeful songs are those of the Mormons, the Wobblies, and, occasionally, the grangers. For the influence on rugged individualism of such unlyrical groups as the Pinkerton men, the Wyoming Live Stock Association, and strikebreakers everywhere, the reader is invited within, where he will also find other touchstones to test other notions about the Golden West.

TO THE WEST

In the summer of 1845 an unsigned editorial in the *United States Magazine and Democratic Review* dropped a phrase that became the slogan of American expansion across the continent. It spoke of "the fulfilment of our manifest destiny to overspread the continent allotted by Providence for the free development of our yearly multiplying millions." God's judgment was disputed by various foreign governments and heathen tribes, but an adventurous fraction of those millions kept coming. They had infiltrated eastern Texas and Oregon's Willamette Valley until there were well over 100,000 "gringos" in on the birth of the Republic of Texas, and 5,000 Americans in Oregon ready to fight the English for land clear up to Russian territory above the 54th parallel. One thousand "Bear Flaggers" wrested California from the Mexicans, and 15,000 Mormons occupied land no one wanted. A mere four years after that editorial was printed, the 55,000 "gold rushers" who crossed the plains were on American soil all the way.

Manifest Destiny was not, of course, what Bishop Berkeley had in mind when he wrote that "Westward the course of Empire takes its way," and there were other surprises in store for other naive expectations of the nature of America. Charles McKay, Scots author, journalist, and composer of "To the West," never left the British Isles, but his pleasant beliefs that green waving forests as wide as "all England" and ocean-sized lakes awaited pioneers just across the Mississippi were shared by many Americans. The corrective song, "To the West: A Parody," from a gold rush songster, is no more accurate when it fills those waters with alligators, but it does introduce a point of view that never thereafter disappears from Western song:

> Oh! there's some may exult, but for me, sirs, I'm blest
> If I haven't had as much as I want of the West!

McKay's song was more seriously imitated from the Mormon viewpoint by William Willes in "Deseret":

> 'Tis a land which for ages has been lying waste,
> Where the savage has wandered, by darkness debased.

Further experience of the Great American Desert continued to darken the picture, albeit satirically, in "Hell in Texas," a song that had considerable broadside distribution around the turn of the century.

> The heat in the summer is a hundred and ten,
> Too hot for the Devil and too hot for men;
> The wild boar roams through the black chaparral,—
> It's a hell of a place he has for a hell!

Comparing the actualities of the West with ideas about *Inferno* occurred to a number of visiting journalists, and the image made its way into "The Belmont Stopes," written when the Tonopah mines were booming in the first decade of this century.

> Had Dante lived to ramble
> 'Neath Oddie's old gray slopes,
> He'd found another hades
> In Belmont's burning stopes.

The lurid depictions of the West as hellish above and below ground were no deterrent, of course, to emigration. The prospect of riches from a corner lot outshines all the miseries that the witty author of "Westward Ho" can recall, and the absence of slavery on the free soil of the Golden State attracted the attention of New England abolitionist Jesse Hutchinson in "Ho! For California!" Both of these blandishments surely lie behind the blackface parody of "Oh! Susannah," called "I'm Off for California," a stage song that later cropped up in oral tradition adapted to Boise City.

There are, finally, people who can resist anything, people whose songs rarely appear in this book. "The Rolling Stone" records the persuasiveness of the little woman's arguments against shaking hard times for the hazards of the West, be it the goldfields of California or the rich farms of Wisconsin. Like its subjects, this song never ventured beyond the Ozarks, where it sticks today.

> Dear wife, you've convinced me. I'll argue no more.
> I never once thought of your dying before.
> My dear little children, although they are small,
> And you, my dear wife, more precious than all.
> So we'll stick to our farming, and suffer no loss;
> For the stone that keeps rolling can gather no moss.

TO THE WEST

C. MC KAY   HENRY RUSSELL

To the West! to the West! to the land of the

free, Where might-y Mis-sou-ri rolls down to the

sea, Where a man is a man, if he's will-ing to

toil, And the hum-blest may gath-er the fruits of the

soil. Where chil-dren are bless-ings, and he who hath

most, Has aid for his for-tune and rich-es to

boast, Where the young may ex-ult, and the a-ged may

rest. A-way! far a-way! to the land of the West!

Chorus

To the West! to the West! to the land of the free, Where

might-y Mis-sou-ri rolls down to the sea, Where the

young may ex — ult   and the   a ——— ged may

rest A — way! far a — way!   to the land of the West!

1

To the West! to the West! to the land of the free,
Where mighty Missouri rolls down to the sea,
Where a man is a man, if he's willing to toil,
And the humblest may gather the fruits of the soil.
Where children are blessings, and he who hath most,
Has aid for his fortune and riches to boast,
Where the young may exult, and the aged may rest,
Away! far away! to the land of the West!

CHORUS: To the West! to the West! to the land of the free,
Where mighty Missouri rolls down to the sea,
Where the young may exult, and the aged may rest,
Away! far away! to the land of the West!

2

To the West! to the West! where the rivers that flow,
Run thousands of miles, spreading out as they go;
Where the green waving forests shall echo our call,
As wide as all England, and free to us all!
Where the Prairies like seas, where the billows have roll'd,
Are broad as the kingdoms and empires of old,
And the lakes are like oceans, in storm or in rest—
Away! far away! to the land of the West!

3

To the West! to the West! there is wealth to be won,
The forest to clear is the work to be done;
Where the stars and the stripes, like a banner unfurled,
Invites to its regions the world, all the world.
Where the people are true to the vows that they frame,
And their pride is the honor that's shown to their name;
Away! far away! let us hope for the best,
And build up a home in the land of the West!

TEXT AND MUSIC: Original sheet music reprinted in Jordan and Kessler (1941), pp.
285-288.

VARIANT: Johnson (1858), p. 26.

TO THE WEST: A PARODY

TUNE: To the West

1

To the West! to the West! I once went, do you see,
And one visit, I'm sure, was sufficient for me!
Oh! the things that I saw there, they frightened me quite,
And ever since then, sirs, I've scarcely been right.
My children got sick every day, sirs, almost,
And my wife took the chills, and got deaf as a post!
Oh! there's some may exult, but for me, sirs, I'm blest
If I haven't had as much as I want of the West!

CHORUS: To the West! to the West! I once went, do you see,
And one visit, I'm sure, was sufficient for me!
Oh! there's some may exult, but for me, sirs, I'm blest
If I haven't had as much as I want of the West!

2

To the West! to the West! where the rivers that flow,
Are full of big alligators, you know;
Where the snakes in the forest make you feel precious queer,
And you don't see a bar-room not twice in a year!
And if 'cross the prairie you happen to go,
You're sure to be tossed by some wild buffalo;
Where the lakes are like children—they're never at rest;
'Pon my soul, sirs, I soon had enough of the West!

3

At the West, they told me, there was wealth to be won,
The forest to clear was the work to be done;
I tried it—couldn't do it—guv it up in despair,
And I'm darned if you'll ever again catch me there!
The snug little farm I expected to buy,
I quickly discovered was just all in my eye;
I came back like a streak: you may go, but I'm blest
If you'll ever again, sirs, catch me at the West!

TEXT: Johnson (1858), p. 27.

HELL IN TEXAS

The Dev-il, we're told, in hell was chained, And a thou-sand years he there re-mained; He nev-er com-plained nor did— he groan, But de—ter-mined to start a hell of his own, Where he could tor-ment the souls of men With-out be-ing chained in a pris—on pen. So he asked the Lord if he had on hand An—y-thing left when he made the land.

1

The Devil, we're told, in hell was chained,
And a thousand years he there remained;
He never complained nor did he groan,
But determined to start a hell of his own,
Where he could torment the souls of men
Without being chained in a prison pen.
So he asked the Lord if he had on hand
Anything left when he made the land.

2

The Lord said, "Yes, I had plenty on hand,
But I left it down on the Rio Grande;
The fact is, old boy, the stuff is so poor
I don't think you could use it in hell anymore."
But the Devil went down to look at the truck,
And said if it came as a gift he was stuck;
For after examining it carefully and well,
He concluded the place was too dry for hell.

3

So in order to get it off his hands,
The Lord promised the Devil to water the lands;
For he had some water, or rather some dregs,
A regular cathartic that smelled like bad eggs.
Hence the deal was closed and the deed was given,
And the Lord went back to his home in heaven.
And the Devil then said, "I have all that is needed
To make a good hell," and hence he succeeded.

4

He began to put thorns in all of the trees,
And mixed up the sand with millions of fleas;
And scattered tarantulas along all the roads;
Put thorns on the cactus and horns on the toads.
He lengthened the horns of the Texas steers,
And put an addition on the rabbit's ears;
He put a little devil in the broncho steed,
And poisoned the feet of the centipede.

5

The rattlesnake bites you, the scorpion stings,
The mosquito delights you with buzzing wings;
The sand-burrs prevail, and so do the ants,
And those who sit down need half-soles on their pants.
The Devil then said that throughout the land
He'd managed to keep up the Devil's own brand,
And all would be mavericks unless they bore
The marks of scratches and bites and thorns by the score.

6

The heat in the summer is a hundred and ten,
Too hot for the Devil and too hot for men;
The wild boar roams through the black chaparral,—
It's a hell of a place he has for a hell!
The red pepper grows on the banks of the brooks,
The Mexicans use it in all that they cook.
Just dine with a Greaser, and then you will shout,
"I've hell on the inside as well as the out!"

TEXT: Thorp (1921), pp. 77-79. Used by permission of Houghton Mifflin Co.

MUSIC: Hastings (1931), p. 178. Used by permission of Texas Folklore Society.

VARIANTS: Stanley (1897), pp. 31-32; Lomax (1910), pp. 222-223; Siringo (1919), pp. 40-41; Hastings (1931), pp. 178-181; Lomax and Lomax (1934), pp. 397-402; Lomax and Lomax (1938), pp. 317-319; Boatright (1944), pp. 134-138 (the text is not printed in E. U. Cook's *The First Mortgage* [Chicago: Rhodes & McClure, 1896], as suggested by Boatright); Randolph (1948), pp. 217-219.

J. HUTCHINSON

HO! FOR CALIFORNIA!

D. D. EMMETT

TUNE: De Boatman Dance

1

We've formed our band and are well mann'd,
To journey afar to the promised land,
Where the golden ore is rich in store,
On the banks of the Sacramento shore.

CHORUS: Then, ho! Brothers ho!
    to California go.
There's plenty of gold in the world
    we're told,
On the banks of the Sacramento.
Heigh O, and away we go,
Digging up gold in Francisco.

2

O! don't you cry, nor heave a sigh,
For we'll all come back again, bye and bye,
Don't breathe a fear, nor shed a tear,
But patiently wait for about two year.

3

As the gold is *thar*, most any *whar*,
And they dig it out with an iron bar,
And where 'tis thick, with a spade or pick,
They can take out lumps as *heavy as brick*.

4

As we explore that distant shore,—
We'll fill our pockets with the shining ore;
And how 'twill sound, as the word goes round,
Of our picking up gold by the *dozen pound*.

14

5

We expect our share of the coarsest fare,
And sometimes to sleep in the open air,
Upon the cold ground we shall all sleep sound
Except when the wolves are howling round.

6

As off we roam over the dark sea foam,
We'll never forget our friends at home
For memories kind will bring to mind
The thoughts of those we leave behind.

7

In the days of old, the Prophets told
Of the City to come, all framed in gold,
Peradventure they foresaw the day,
Now dawning in California.

8

O! the land we'll save, for the bold and
   brave—
Have determined there never shall breathe a
   slave;
Let foes recoil, for the sons of toil
Shall make California GOD'S FREE SOIL.

CHORUS: Then, ho! Brothers ho!
     to California go,
No slave shall toil on God's Free
   Soil,
On the banks of the Sacramento.
Heigh O, and away we go,
Chanting our songs of Freedom, O.

TEXT: *Book of Words of the Hutchinson Family* (New York: Baker, Godwin & Co., 1851).

MUSIC: Damon (1936).

VARIANTS: Sandburg (1927), pp. 110-111; Dwyer *et al.* (1964), pp. 15-16.

I'M OFF FOR CALIFORNIA
S. C. FOSTER

TUNE: Oh! Susannah

Now, dark-ies, gath-er round me— I got a thing to tell; 'Twill make you burst your eye—lids, and make your bos-om swell; The white folks all am craz—y wid nuf-fin' in dar mouth, But de mines ob Cal-i—for—nia_ whose a gwan Souff? *Chorus* Oh, Jer—ush—a! whose gwine to go? I'm gwine to Cal-i—forn—ia, so fotch a—long de hoe! hoe!

1

Now, darkies, gather round me—I got a thing to tell;
'Twill make you burst your eyelids, and make your bosom swell;
The white folks all am crazy wid nuffin' in dar mouth,
But de mines ob California—whose a gwan Souff?

CHORUS: Oh, Jerusha! whose gwine to go?
I'm gwine to California, so fotch along de hoe!
Oh, Jerusha! whose gwine to go?
I'm gwine to California, so fotch along de hoe!

2

Now, darkies, just believe me—but you needn't if you like—
I heard from California by de telegraph to-night;
De letter was so heaby, dat dis darkey couldn't hold,
So I took and bust de seal, and found eleben pound of gold.

3

Now, I'll hab a wooden shobel, and I'll hab it made of tin,
And de way I'll scoop de grabel up, it surely am a sin;
And I'll tell de staring white folks, when dey ask us who am we—
We're de famous California Gold Mining Company.

4

Den I'se gwan to work my passage on de telegraph to hire,
'Case dey want a handsome darkie for de greasin' ob de wire;
An' when I get to Mexico, I'll take de charcoal train,
'Till I get to Sally-Gordy, den de telegraph again.

5

Den Daniel Tucker neber want for supper any more;
We'll take de old man back again to old Virginia shore
And dearest Mae, take care yourself, and farewell, Mary Blane—
We're going to California, but we're coming back again.

TEXT: "I'm off for California" (New York: De Marsan, n.d. [broadside]).
MUSIC: Turner *et al.* (1858), p. 18.
VARIANT: Toelken (1962), pp. 16-17.

THE ROLLING STONE

Since times are so hard, I'll tell you, my wife, I've a mind for to shake off this trou-ble and strife And to Cal-i-for-nia my jour-ney pur-sue To dou-ble my for-tune as oth-er men do; For here we may la-bor each day in the field And the win-ters con-sume all that sum-mers do yield.

1

Since times are so hard, I'll tell you, my wife,
I've a mind for to shake off this trouble and strife
And to California my journey pursue
To double my fortune as other men do;
     For here we may labor each day in the field
     And the winters consume all that summers do yield.

2

Dear husband, I've noticed with a sorrowful heart
You've lately neglected your plow and your cart;
Your horses, sheep, cattle disorderly run,
And your new Sunday waistcoat goes every day on.
     Now stick to your farming; you'll suffer no loss,
     For the stone that keeps rolling can gather no moss.

3

Dear wife, let us go, and don't let us wait.
I long to be doing, I long to be great,
And you some great lady, and who knows but I
Some great Governor before we do die.
> For here we may labor each day in the field
> And the winters consume all that summers do yield.

4

Dear husband, remember your land is to clear;
It will cost you the labor of many a year.
Your horses, sheep, cattle will all be to buy,
And before you have got them you are ready to die.
> So stick to your farming; you'll suffer no loss,
> For the stone that keeps rolling can gather no moss.

5

Dear wife, let us go and don't let us stand.
We'll buy us a farm all ready at hand,
And horses, sheep, cattle are not very dear;
And we'll feast on fat buffalo more than half of the year.
> While here we may labor each day in the field
> And the winters consume all that summers do yield.

6

Dear husband, remember your land of delight
Is surrounded by Indians that murder at night;
Your house will be plundered and burned to the ground
And your wife and children lay mangled around.
> So stick to your farming; you'll suffer no loss,
> For the stone that keeps rolling can gather no moss.

7

Dear wife, you've convinced me. I'll argue no more.
I never once thought of your dying before.
My dear little children, although they are small,
And you, my dear wife, more precious than all.
> So we'll stick to our farming, and suffer no loss;
> For the stone that keeps rolling can gather no moss.

TEXT: Belden (1940), pp. 351-352. Used by permission of University of Missouri Press.

MUSIC: *Journal of the American Folklore Society*, XXXV (1922), 409.

VARIANTS: Belden (1940), p. 351*; Randolph (1948), pp. 213-216*; Thompson (1958), pp. 139-141; Hubbard (1961), pp. 307-308; Laws (1964), p. 144*.

WESTWARD HO

1

I love not Colorado
Where the faro table grows,
And down the desperado
The rippling Bourbon flows;

2

Nor seek I fair Montana
Of bowie-lunging fame;
The pistol ring of fair Wyoming
I leave to nobler game.

3

Sweet poker-haunted Kansas
In vain allures the eye;
The Nevada rough has charms enough,
Yet its blandishments I fly.

4

Shall Arizona woo me
Where the meek Apache bides?
Or New Mexico where natives grow
With arrow-proof insides?

5

Nay, 'tis where the grizzlies wander
And the lonely diggers roam,
And the grim Chinese from the squatter flees,
That I'll make my humble home.

6

I'll chase the wild tarantula
And the fierce cayote I'll dare,
And the locust grim, I'll battle him,
In his native wildwood lair.

7

Or I'll seek the gulch deserted,
And dream of the wild red man,
And I'll build a cot on a corner lot
And get rich as soon as I can.

TEXT: Thorp (1921), pp. 161-162. Used by permission of Houghton Mifflin Co.
VARIANTS: Lomax (1910), pp. 37-38; Lomax and Lomax (1938); pp. 415-416.

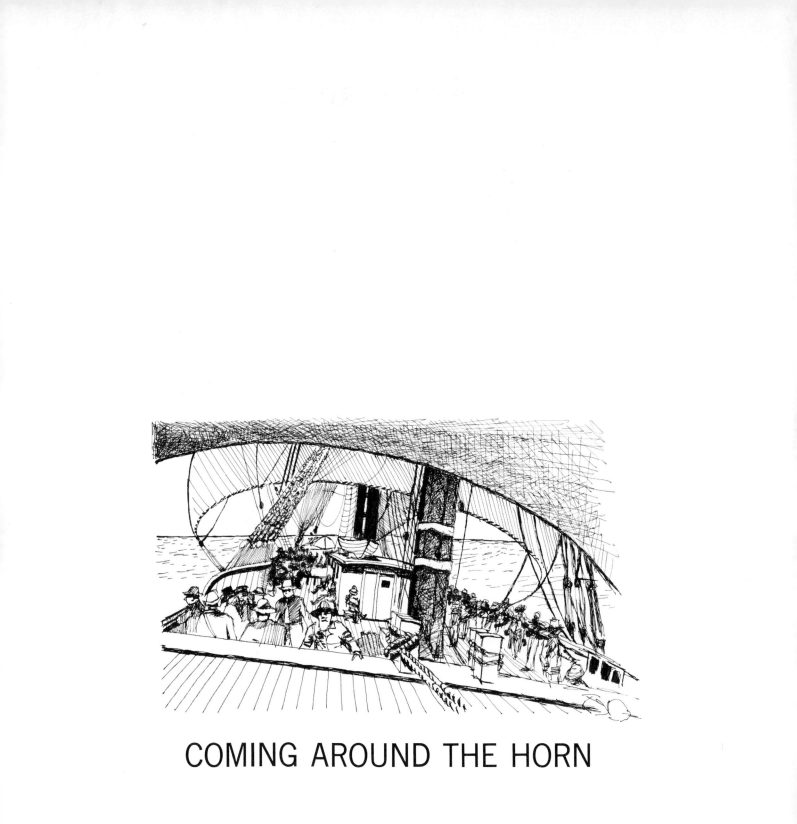

COMING AROUND THE HORN

The first Yankee visitors to the Far West came around Cape Horn in General Washington's ship, the *Columbia*, and that route remained the most fashionable until the completion of the transcontinental railroad. The California goldfields attracted the first massive use of the sea route, best chronicled in the songs of John A. Stone. "Old Put," as he called himself, was the most prolific and successful composer of songs during the gold rush. He had come to California in 1850, struck it rich in '53, and organized a singing troupe—the Sierra Nevada Rangers. He also put together a pocket-sized songster in 1855 which ultimately had a total printing of 25,000 copies. Several more of his songsters appeared before his death in the early '60's. Of his efforts, three are cited here. "Coming Around the Horn" memorializes that pleasant sail:

> We left old New York City, with the weather very thick,
> The second day we puked up boots, oh, wusn't we all sea-sick!

Not only the weather, but the food, the crew, the bugs, and the city of Valparaiso get the same treatment. Stone's "The Fools of '49" recounts the trials of the Panama route from New Orleans by giving first the ideal, "Dear wife don't you cry, I'll send you home the yellow lumps a piano for to buy," followed by the real, "rusty pork and stinking beef, and rotten, wormy bread." His "Humbug Steamship Companies" mentions even darker prospects, for the two ships it names, the *Golden Gate* and the *Yankee Blade*, both sank with a total loss of 253 lives and almost $2 million. The song, "A Ripping Trip," from Stone's *Golden Songster*, continues his visceral preoccupations:

> All about the cabin floor,
>   Passengers lie sea-sick—
> Steamer's bound to go ashore—
>   Rip goes the physic!

The original of this song, "Pop Goes the Weasel," was also parodied in a more favorable, but less interesting, song about the Pike's Peak rush of 1859, "Pop Comes the Rhino."

John Nichols' "Oh, California," another parody of "Oh! Susannah," was probably the first gold rush song, having been written on board the bark *Eliza*, outward bound from New England in November, 1848. For the sailor's point of view on these voyages we turn to "Sacramento," a halyard shanty that celebrates the ninety-day trip and the Dago gals that weren't quite worth all the effort. The last song is "The Dying Californian," which first appeared in the *New England Diadem & Rhode Island Temperance Pledge* in 1850. It purports to be the last words of one Brown Owen who died on the passage to California, and, because of its pious exhortation, became a favorite of the tent camp circuit.

JOHN A. STONE # COMING AROUND THE HORN L. V. H. CROSBY

TUNE: Dearest Mae

1

Now miners, if you'll listen, I'll tell you quite a tale,
About the voyage around Cape Horn, they call a pleasant sail,
We bought a ship, and had her stowed with houses, tools, and grub,
But cursed the day we ever sailed in the poor old rotten tub.

CHORUS: Oh, I remember well the lies they used to tell,
Of gold so bright, it hurt the sight, and made the miners yell.

2

We left old New York City, with the weather very thick,
The second day we puked up boots, oh, wusn't we all sea-sick!
I swallowed pork tied to a string, which made a dreadful shout,
I felt it strike the bottom, but I could not pull it out.

3

We all were owners in the ship, and soon began to growl,
Because we hadn't ham and eggs, and now and then a fowl;
We told the captain what to do, as him we had to pay,
The captain swore that he was boss, and we should him obey.

4

We lived like hogs penned up to fat, our vessel was so small,
We had a "duff" but once a month, and twice a day a squall;
A meeting now and then was held, which kicked up quite a stink,
The captain damned us fore and aft, and wished the box would sink.

5

Off Cape Horn, where we lay becalmed, kind Providence seemed to frown,
We had to stand up night and day, none of us dared sit down;
For some had half a dozen boils, 'twas awful, sure's you're born,
But some would try it on the sly, and got pricked by the Horn.

6

We stopped at Valparaiso, where the women are so loose,
And all got drunk as usual, got shoved in the Calaboose;
Our ragged, rotten sails were patched, the ship made ready for sea,
But every man, except the cook, was up town on a spree.

7

We sobered off, set sail again, on short allowance, of course,
With water thick as castor oil, and stinking beef much worse;
We had the scurvy and the itch, and any amount of lice,
The medicine chest went overboard, with bluemass, cards, and dice.

8

We arrived at San Francisco, and all went to the mines,
We left an agent back to sell our goods of various kinds;
A friend wrote up to let us know our agent, Mr. Gates,
Has sold the ship and cargo, sent the money to the States.

TEXT: Stone (1855), pp. 37-38.

MUSIC: Turner *et al.* (1858), p. 38.

VARIANTS: Grant (1924), pp. 103-104; Sherwin and Katzman (1932), pp. 40-41; Lomax and Lomax (1934), pp. 429-430; Lengyel (1939), pp. 24-25; Black and Robertson (1940), pp. 28-29; Lengyel (1949), pp. 9-10; Dwyer *et al.* (1964), pp. 29-30.

JOHN A. STONE # THE FOOLS OF '49

TUNE: Commence, You Darkies All

1
When gold was found in '48, the people said 'twas gas,
And some were fools enough to think the lumps were only brass;
But soon they all were satisfied, and started off to mine,
They bought their ships, came round the Horn, in the fall of '49.

CHORUS: Then they thought of what they had been told,
When they started after gold,
That they never in the world would make a pile.

2
The people all were crazy then, they didn't know what to do.
They sold their farms for just enough to pay their passage through;
They bid their friends a long farewell; said, "Dear wife, don't you cry,
I'll send you home the yellow lumps a piano for to buy."

3
The poor, the old and rotten scows, were advertised to sail
From New Orleans with passengers, but they must pump and bail;
The ships were crowded more than full, and some hung on behind,
And others dived off from the wharf, and swam till they were blind.

4
With rusty pork and stinking beef, and rotten, wormy bread,
And captains, too, that never were up as high as the main-mast head,
The steerage passengers would rave and swear that they'd paid their
    passage,
And wanted something more to eat besides Bologna sausage.

5
Then they began to cross the plains with oxen, hollowing "haw";
And steamers they began to run as far as Panama,
And there for months the people staid that started after gold,
And some returned disgusted with the lies that had been told.

6
The people died on every route, they sicken'd and died like sheep,
And those at sea, before they were dead, were launched into the deep;
And those that died while crossing the Plains fared not so well as that,
For a hole was dug and they thrown in, along the miserable Platte.

7
The ships at last began to arrive, and the people began to inquire:
"They say that flour is a dollar a pound, do you think it will be any
    higher?"
And then to carry their blankets and sleep out-doors, it seemed so droll,
Both tired and mad, without a cent, they damned the lousy hole.

TEXT: Stone (1855), pp. 7-8.

VARIANTS: Lomax (1916), pp. 404-406; Grant (1924), pp. 77-79; Sandburg (1927), p. 107; Sherwin and Katzman (1932), pp. 16-17; Lomax and Lomax (1938), pp. 381-382; Lengyel (1939), pp. 26 27, and (1949), pp. 41-42; Dwyer *et al.* (1964), p. 33.

J. NICHOLS   # OH, CALIFORNIA   S. C. FOSTER

TUNE: Oh! Susannah

I came from Sa-lem Cit-y, With my wash-bowl on my knee, I'm
go-ing to Cal — i — for-nia, The gold dust for to see. It
rained all night the day I left, The wea-ther it was dry, The
sun so hot I froze to death Oh! bro-thers, don't you
cry! Oh, Cal — i — for-nia, That's the land for me! I'm
bound for San Fran — cis — co With my wash-bowl on my knee.

1

I came from Salem City,
With my washbowl on my knee,
I'm going to California,
The gold dust for to see.
It rained all night the day I left,
The weather it was dry,
The sun so hot I froze to death
Oh, brothers, don't you cry!

CHORUS: Oh, California,
That's the land for me!
I'm bound for San Francisco
With my washbowl on my knee.

2

I jumped aboard the 'Liza ship
And traveled on the sea,
And everytime I thought of home
I wished it wasn't me!
The vessel reared like any horse
That had of oats a wealth;
I found it wouldn't throw me, so
I thought I'd throw myself!

3

I thought of all the pleasant times
We've had together here,
I thought I ought to cry a bit,
But couldn't find a tear.
The pilot's bread was in my mouth,
The gold dust in my eye,
And though I'm going far away,
Dear brothers don't you cry!

4

I soon shall be in Frisco,
And there I'll look around,
And when I see the gold lumps there,
I'll pick them off the ground.
I'll scrape the mountains clean, my boys,
I'll drain the rivers dry,
A pocketful of rocks bring home—
So brothers don't you cry!

TEXT: Lummis (1904), pp. 272-273.

MUSIC: Turner *et al.* (1858), p. 18.

VARIANTS: "California Emigrant" (n.p., n.d., [broadside]); "Two Argonaut Songs," *Land of Sunshine*, XIII (1900), 165-166; Grant (1924), pp. 43-46; Lengyel (1939), p. 16; Lengyel (1949), p. 11; Dwyer *et al.* (1964), pp. 17-18.

A RIPPING TRIP

TUNE: Pop Goes the Weasel

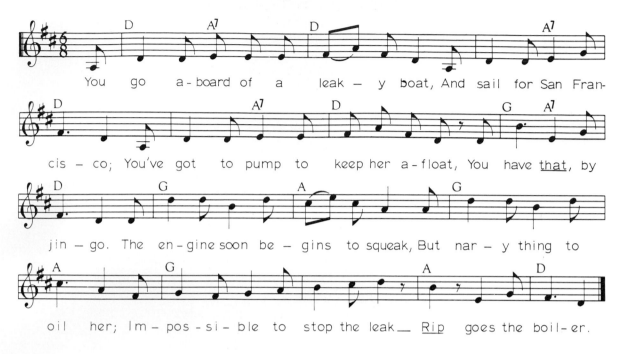

You go a-board of a leak—y boat, And sail for San Fran-cis-co; You've got to pump to keep her a-float, You have *that*, by jin—go. The en-gine soon be—gins to squeak, But nar—y thing to oil her; Im—pos-si—ble to stop the leak__ Rip goes the boil-er.

1

You go aboard of a leaky boat,
    And sail for San Francisco;
You've got to pump to keep her afloat,
    You have *that*, by jingo.
The engine soon begins to squeak,
    But nary thing to oil her;
Impossible to stop the leak
    Rip goes the boiler.

2

The captain on the promenade,
    Looking very savage;
Steward and the cabin maid
    Fighting 'bout a cabbage;
All about the cabin floor,
    Passengers lie sea-sick—
Steamer's bound to go ashore—
    Rip goes the physic!

3

"Pork and beans" they can't afford,
    To second cabin passengers;
The cook has tumbled overboard
    With forty pounds of "sassengers";

The engineer, a little tight,
    Bragging on the Main Line,
Finally gets into a fight—
    Rip goes the engine!

4

Cholera begins to rage.
    A few have got the scurvy;
Chickens dying in their cage—
    Steerage topsy-turvy.
When you get to Panama,
    Greasers want a back-load;
Officers begin to jaw—
    Rip goes the railroad!

5

When home, you'll tell an awful tale,
    And always will be thinking
How long you had to pump and bail,
    To keep the tub from sinking.
Of course, you'll take a glass of gin,
    'Twill make you feel so funny;
Some city sharp will rope you in—
    Rip goes your money!

TEXT: Stone (1858a), p. 46-47.

MUSIC: *The Violin Primer* (*ca.* 1850), p. 27.

VARIANTS: Stone (1858*b*), p. 9; Handy (1908), p. 434; Lomax (1916), pp. 407-408; Grant (1924), pp. 79-80; Sherwin and Katzman (1932), pp. 38-39; Lomax and Lomax (1938), pp. 387-388; Lengyel (1939), p. 19; Black and Robertson (1940), pp. 18-19; Dwyer *et al.* (1964), pp. 31-32.

JOHN A. STONE

HUMBUG STEAMSHIP COMPANIES

TUNE: Uncle Sam's Farm

The great-est im — po — si — tion that the pub-lic ev — er saw, Are the

Cal — i — for — nia steam-ships that run to Pa — na — ma; They're a

per — fect set of rob — bers, and ac — com-plish their de — signs By a

gen — 'ral in — vi — ta — tion of the peo — ple to the mines. Then

come a — long, come a — long, you that want to go, The

best ac — com — mo — da — tions, and the pas — sage ver — y low; Our

boats they are large e — nough, don't be a — fraid, The

Gold — en Gate is go — ing down to beat the Yank — ee Blade. Then

come a — long, don't be a — fraid, The

Gold — en Gate is go — ing down to beat the Yank — ee Blade.

1

The greatest imposition that the public ever saw,
Are the California steamships that run to Panama;
They're a perfect set of robbers, and accomplish their designs
By a gen'ral invitation of the people to the mines.

CHORUS: Then come along, come along, you that want to go,
The best accommodations, and the passage very low;
Our boats they are large enough, don't be afraid,
The *Golden Gate* is going down to beat the *Yankee Blade*.
Then come along, don't be afraid,
The *Golden Gate* is going down to beat the *Yankee Blade*.

2

They have opposition on the route, with cabins very nice,
And advertise to take you for half the usual price;
They get thousands from the mountains, and then deny their bills,
So you have to pay the prices, or go back into the hills.

3

When you start from San Francisco, they treat you like a dog,
The victuals you're compell'd to eat ain't fit to feed a hog;
And a drunken mate a cursing and damning you around,
And wishing that the boat would sink and every one be drowned.

4

The captain goes to dinner and begins to curse the waiter,
Knocks him out of hearing with a thundering big potato;
The cabin maid, half crazy, breaks the meat dish all to smash,
And the steward comes a running with a plate of mouldy hash.

5

You are driven round the steerage like a drove of hungry swine,
And kicked ashore at Panama by the Independent Line;
Your baggage is thrown overboard, the like you never saw,
A trip or two will sicken you of going to Panama.

TEXT: Stone (1855), pp. 43-44.

MUSIC: Turner *et al.* (1858), p. 24.

VARIANTS: Grant (1924), pp. 106-107; Lengyel (1939), pp. 70-71; E Clampus Vitus (1939), p. 18; Black and Robertson (1940), pp. 20-21; Lengyel (1949), p. 13; Dwyer *et al.* (1964), pp. 34-35.

SACRAMENTO

Oh, a - round Cape Horn we are bound for to go, To me
hoo - dah, to me hoo dah! A - round Cape Horn through the
sleet an' the snow, To me hoo - dah, hoo - dah day!

Chorus
Blow, boys, blow for Cal - i - forn - eye - o! There's plen-ty o' gold so
I've bin told, On the banks of the Sac — ra — men — to!

1
Oh, around Cape Horn we are bound for to go,
    To me hoo-dah, to me hoo-dah!
Around Cape Horn through the sleet an' the snow,
    To me hoo-dah, hoo-dah day!

CHORUS: Blow, boys, blow, for Californeye-O!
There's plenty o' gold so I've bin told,
On the banks of the Sacramento!

2
Oh, around the Horn with a mainskys'l set,
    Around Cape Horn an' we're all wringin' wet.

3
Oh, around Cape Horn in the month o' May,
    Oh, around Cape Horn is a very long way.

4
Them Dago gals we do adore,
    They all drink vino an' ask for more.

5
Them Spanish gals ain't got no combs,
    They comb their locks with tunny-fish bones.

6

To the Sacramento we're bound away,
    To the Sacramento's a hell o' a way.

7

We're the buckos for to make 'er go,
    All the way to the Sacramento.

8

We're the bullies for to kick her through,
    Roll down the hill with a hullabaloo.

9

Starvation an' ease in a Yankee ship,
    We're the bullies for to make 'er rip.

10

Santander Jim is a mate from hell,
    With fists o' iron an' feet as well.

11

Breast yer bars an' bend yer backs,
    Heave an' make yer spare ribs crack.

12

Round the Horn an' up to the Line,
    We're the bullies for to make 'er shine.

13

We'll crack it on, on a big skiyoot,
    Ol' Bully Jim is a bloody big brute.

14

Oh, a bully ship wid a bully crew,
    But the mate is a bastard through an' through.

15

Ninety days to 'Frisco Bay,
    Ninety days is damn good pay.

16

Oh, them wuz the days of the good ol' times,
    Back in the days of the Forty-nine.

17

Sing an' heave an' heave an' sing,
    Heave an' make them handspikes spring.

18

An' I wish to God I'd niver bin born,
    To go a-ramblin' round Cape Horn.

TEXT AND MUSIC: Hugill (1961), pp. 109-110.

VARIANTS: Grant (1924), pp. 87-88; Sandburg (1927), p. 112; Smith (1927), p. 25; Gordon (1938), p. 96; Lengyel (1939), p. 20; Lomax and Lomax (1947), pp. 140-141; Lengyel (1949), p. 12; Botkin (1951), p. 734; Doerflinger (1951), pp. 67-70, 351*; Hugill (1961), pp. 105-114.

THE DYING CALIFORNIAN

BALL AND DRINKARD

1. Lay up near-er, broth-er, near-er, For my limbs are grow-ing cold;

2. I am dy-ing, broth-er, dy-ing, Soon you'll miss me in your berth,

3. I am go-ing, sure-ly go-ing, But my hope in God is strong;

And thy pres-ence seem-eth near-er, When thine arms a-round me fold.

For my form will soon be ly-ing 'Neath the o-cean's bri-ny surf.

I am will-ing, broth-er, know-ing That He do-eth noth-ing wrong.

1

Lay up nearer, brother, nearer,
    For my limbs are growing cold;
And thy presence seemeth nearer,
    When thine arms around me fold.

2

I am dying, brother, dying,
    Soon you'll miss me in your berth,
For my form will soon be lying
    'Neath the ocean's briny surf.

3

I am going, surely going,
    But my hope in God is strong;
I am willing, brother, knowing
    That He doth nothing wrong.

4

Tell my father when you greet him,
    That in death I prayed for him,
Prayed that I might only meet him
    In a world that's free from sin.

5

Tell my mother,—God assist her,
    Know that she is growing old,—
That her child would glad have kissed her
    When his lips grew pale and cold.

34

6

Listen, brother, catch each whisper,
    'Tis my wife I'll speak of now!
Tell, O tell her, how I missed her,
    When the fever burned my brow.

7

Tell her she must kiss my children,
    Like the kiss I last impressed,
Hold them as when last I held them,
    Folded closely to my breast.

8

Give them early to their Maker,
    Putting all her trust in God,
And He never will forsake her,
    For He's said so in his word.

9

Oh! my children, Heaven bless them;
    They were all my life to me;
Would I could once more caress them,
    Before I sink beneath the sea.

10

'Twas for them I crossed the ocean,
    What my hopes were I'd not tell,
But they gained an orphan's portion—
    Yet He doeth all things well.

11

Listen, brother, closely listen,
    Don't forget a single word,
That in death my eyes did glisten
    With the tears her memory stored.

12

Tell them I never reached the haven,
    Where I sought the precious dust,
But have gained a port called Heaven
    Where the gold will never rust.

13

Tell my sisters, I remember
    Every kind and parting word,
And my heart has been kept tender,
    By the thoughts its memory stirred.

14

Urge them to secure an entrance
    For they'll find a brother there;
Faith in Jesus and repentance
    Will secure for them a share.

15

Hark! I hear my Saviour speaking,
    'Tis—I know his voice so well,
When I am gone, O don't be weeping
    Brother, hear my last farewell!

TEXT AND MUSIC: B. F. White and E. J. King, *The Sacred Harp* (Philadelphia: S. C. Collins, 1860), p. 410.

VARIANTS: *New England Diadem & Rhode Island Temperance Pledge* (Providence), Feb. 9, 1850; *Los Angeles Star*, June 13, 1857; Johnson (1863), pp. 35-37; A. H. Tolman and M. O. Eddy, *Journal of the American Folklore Society*, XXXV (1922), 364-365*; Pound (1922), pp. 191-193; Grant (1924), pp. 174-176; Daughters of the Utah Pioneers (1932), p. 13; Belden (1940), pp. 350-351*; McMullen (1946), pp. 95-96; Randolph (1948), pp. 181-184*; Thompson (1958), pp. 141-142; Hubbard (1961), p. 219; Moore and Moore (1964), pp. 321-323.

CROSSING THE PLAINS

For those who had neither the purse nor the stomach for the sea, the Oregon Trail along the Platte River and its various cutoffs down to Deseret and on to the Mother Lode offered a dry alternative. And a great many people besides the gold-hungry took those routes across the Great Plains and the deserts of the Great Basin in the 1840's. But trappers and the farmers en route to Oregon's Willamette Valley are unrepresented by songs, and the Mormons have their own sections in this volume. Here, therefore, we find the forty-niners again, and again their best musical representative, John Stone, himself an overlander. His "Crossing the Plains," to the lovely tune of "Caroline of Edinburgh," offers the advice of an old-timer on minute details of the entire trip, with his characteristic observations throughout:

> Your canteens, they should be well filled, with poison alkali,
> So when you get tired of traveling, you can cramp all up and die:
> The best thing in the world to keep your bowels loose and free,
> Is fight and quarrel among yourselves, and seldom if ever agree.

Indeed, songs like this one provide a much-needed honest detail lacking in such works as Lansford Hastings' infamous *Emigrants' Guide*, which showed the Donner Party the way to tragedy.

John Stone's "Sweet Betsey from Pike" has more than entered oral tradition; it is the single best-known piece of literature associated with the westward movement. It not only offers memorable glimpses of the Platte route, but also presents a near-mythic portrait of those hardy pioneers, Long Ike and his Pike County Rose. Stone's two other songs here, "Arrival of the Greenhorn" and "Emigrant from Pike," give first-person accounts of the trip from Chimney Rock, Nebraska, where the grass gives out, to the prison brig on the Sacramento River. A song called here, "O If I Was at Home Again," by John Graham and taken from the diary of forty-niner Palmer C. Tiffany, is another lament from a homesick trudger along the path of empire. And "Johny's Dead," from the repertoire of that ancient and noble order, E Clampus Vitus, is a deadpan, Western look at the "Dying Californian" theme:

> Oh! We gathered round old Johny,
>   Old Johny Wethered;
> And we buried poor old Johny,
>   'Cause he was *dead*.

JOHN A. STONE # CROSSING THE PLAINS

TUNE: Caroline of Edinburgh

Come all you Cal — i — for — nians, I pray o — pen wide your ears.___ If you are go — ing a — cross the Plains with snott — y mules or steers,___ Re — mem — ber beans be — fore you start, like — wise dried beef and ham,___ Be — ware of ven' — son, damn the stuff,. it's of — ten times a ram._

1

Come all you Californians, I pray open wide your ears.
If you are going across the Plains with snotty mules or steers,
Remember beans before you start, likewise dried beef and ham,
Beware of ven'son, damn the stuff, it's oftentimes a ram.

2

You must buy two revolvers, a bowie-knife and belt,
Says you, "Old feller, now stand off, or I will have your pelt";
The greenhorn looks around about, but not a soul can see,
Says he, "There's not a man in town, but what's afraid of me."

3

You shouldn't shave, but cultivate your down, and let it grow,
So when you do return, 'twill be as soft and white as snow;
Your lovely Jane will be surprised, your ma'll begin to cook;
The greenhorn to his mother'll say, "How savage I must look!"

4

"How do you like it overland?" his mother she will say,
"All right, excepting cooking, then the devil is to pay;
For some won't cook, and others can't, and then it's curse and damn,
The coffee-pot's begun to leak, so has the frying-pan."

It's always jaw about the teams, and how we ought to do,
All hands get mad, and each one says, "I own as much as you":
One of them says, "I'll buy or sell, I'm damned if I care which";
Another says, "Let's buy him out, the lousy son of a bitch."

6

You calculate on sixty days to take you over the Plains,
But there you lack for bread and meat, for coffee and for brains;
Your sixty days are a hundred or more, your grub you've got to divide,
Your steers and mules are alkalied, so foot it—you cannot ride.

7

You have to stand a watch at night, to keep the Indians off,
About sundown some heads will ache, and some begin to cough;
To be deprived of health we know is always very hard,
Though every night some one is sick, to get rid of standing guard.

8

Your canteens, they should be well filled, with poison alkali,
So when you get tired of traveling, you can cramp all up and die:
The best thing in the world to keep your bowels loose and free,
Is fight and quarrel among yourselves, and seldom if ever agree.

9

There's not a log to make a seat, along the river Platte,
So when you eat, you've got to stand, or sit down square and flat:
It's fun to cook with buffalo wood, take some that's newly born,
If I knew once what I know now, I'd a gone around the Horn!

10

The desert's nearly death on corns, while walking in the sand,
And drive a jackass by the tail, it's damn this overland;
I'd rather ride a raft at sea, and then at once be lost,
Says Bill, "Let's leave this poor old mule, we can't get him across."

11

The ladies have the hardest, that emigrate by land,
For when they cook with buffalo wood, they often burn a hand;
And when they jaw their husbands round, get mad and spill the tea,
Wish to the Lord they'd be taken down with a turn of the di-a-ree.

12

When you arrive at Placerville, or Sacramento City,
You've nothing in the world to eat, no money—what a pity!
Your striped pants are all worn out, which causes people to laugh,
When they see you gaping round the town like a great big brindle calf.

13

You're lazy, poor, and all broke down, such hardships you endure,
The post-office at Sacramento all such men will cure;
You'll find a line from ma' and pa', and one from lovely Sal,
If that don't physic you every mail, you never will get well.

TEXT: Stone (1855), pp. 13-15.

MUSIC: Brown (1957), p. 207. Used by permission of Duke University Press.

VARIANTS: Thorp (1908), pp. 15-16; Lomax (1916), pp. 375-376; Thorp (1921), pp. 18-20, Grant (1924), pp. 72-73; Sherwin and Katzman (1932), pp. 10-11; Lomax and Lomax (1934), pp. 427-428; Lengyel (1939), pp. 17-18; Black and Robertson (1940), pp. 47-49; Lengyel (1949), pp. 7-8; Dwyer *et al.* (1964), pp. 41-42; Fife and Fife (1966), pp. 58-60.

JOHN P. GRANTHAM   # O IF I WAS AT HOME AGAIN

TUNE: Billy Neal

1

In Mt. Pleasant I once did live and had a happy home;
I was contented with my lot and thought I ne'er should roam.
I did not owe a picayune, nor was I in the lurch.
I did up business all the week; on Sabbath went to Church.
    O happy Johny P. Contented Johny P.
    O if I was at home again,
    How happy I should be.

2

At length strange news was noised about, which took me all aback;
I often times would dream of gold until I had no lack.
My mind was very soon made up, I said that I would go;
My friends said I had better stay, but all I said was "no."
    O crazy Johny P. Unhappy Johny P.
    O if I was home again,
    How happy I should be.

3

My business I had soon arranged, and I was on the way;
I waded mud ofttimes knee deep, and trudged from day to day.
I did endure both heat and cold, was often wet and dry;
My hardships they have been so great, I really thought I'd die.
    O wretched Johny P. Unhappy Johny P.
    O if I was home again,
    How happy I should be.

4

We've had no rain for many a day; the weather is so dry
We snuff up dust from morn till night, enough to make one cry.
I'm out of money—out of clothes, I'm out of shoes and socks;
I'll stand it all and not complain for a pocket full of "rocks."
    O happy Johny P. Contented Johny P.
    If I get home with a pocket full,
    How happy I shall be.

TEXT: "Diary of Palmer C. Tiffany," Aug. 11, 1849 (MS, Yale University Library).

JOHN A. STONE

SWEET BETSEY FROM PIKE

TUNE: Villikins and His Dinah

Oh, don't you re — mem-ber sweet Bet - sey from Pike, Who
crossed the big moun-tains with her lov – er Ike, With two yoke of
cat - tle, a large yel - low dog, A _ tall shang - hai roost-er and
one spot-ted hog. Too - ral lal loo-ral lal loo - ral lal la.

1

Oh, don't you remember sweet Betsey from Pike,
Who crossed the big mountains with her lover Ike,
With two yoke of cattle, a large yellow dog,
A tall shanghai rooster and one spotted hog.
CHORUS: Tooral lal looral lal looral lal la.

2

One evening quite early they camped on the Platte,
'Twas near by the road on a green shady flat,
Where Betsey, sore-footed, lay down to repose—
With wonder Ike gazed on that Pike County rose.

3

Their wagons broke down with a terrible crash,
And out on the prairie rolled all kinds of trash;
A few little baby clothes done up with care—
'Twas rather suspicious, though all on the *square*.

4

The shanghai ran off, and their cattle all died;
That morning the last piece of bacon was fried;
Poor Ike was discouraged, and Betsey got mad,
The dog drooped his tail and looked wondrously sad.

42

5

They stopped at Salt Lake to inquire the way,
When Brigham declared that sweet Betsey should stay;
But Betsey got frightened and ran like a deer,
While Brigham stood pawing the ground like a steer.

6

They soon reached the desert, where Betsey gave out,
And down in the sand she lay rolling about;
While Ike, half distracted, looked on with surprise,
Saying, "Betsey, get up, you'll get sand in your eyes."

7

Sweet Betsey got up in a great deal of pain,
Declared she'd go back to Pike County again;
But Ike gave a sigh, and they fondly embraced,
And they traveled along with his arm round her waist.

8

They suddenly stopped on a very high hill,
With wonder looked down upon old Placerville;
Ike sighed when he said, and he cast his eyes down,
"Sweet Betsey, my darling, we've got to Hangtown."

9

Long Ike and sweet Betsey attended a dance;
Ike wore a pair of his Pike County pants;
Sweet Betsey was covered with ribbons and rings;
Says Ike, "You're an angel, but where are your wings?"

10

A miner said, "Betsey, will you dance with me?"
"I will that, old hoss, if you don't make too free;
But don't dance me hard; do you want to know why?
Dog on you! I'm chock full of strong alkali!"

11

This Pike County couple got married of course,
And Ike became jealous—obtained a divorce;
Sweet Betsey, well satisfied, said with a shout,
"Good bye, you big lummux, I'm glad you've backed out!"

TEXT: Stone (1858a), pp. 50-52.

MUSIC: Turner *et al.* (1858), p.5.

VARIANTS: Stone (1858b), pp. 13-15; Handy (1908), pp. 434-436; Lomax (1916), pp. 258-260; Grant (1924), pp. 64-66; Sandburg (1927), pp. 108-109; Clark (1932), pp. 56-57; Sherwin and Katzman (1932), pp. 42-44; Lomax and Lomax (1934), pp. 424-426; Frey (1936), pp. 90-91; Lomax and Lomax (1938), 388-391; Lengyel (1939), pp. 22-23; E Clampus Vitus (1939), pp. 7-8; Black and Robertson (1940), pp. 10-11; Belden (1940), pp. 343-345*; Lomax and Lomax (1947), pp. 176-179; Randolph (1948), pp. 209-210; Lengyel (1949), pp. 26-27; Lumpkin (1960), pp. 90-91; Lomax (1960), pp. 335-336; Hubbard (1961), pp. 300-301; Dwyer *et al.* (1964), pp. 43-44; Moore and Moore (1964), pp. 319-321; Laws (1964), p. 137*.

JOHN A. STONE

EMIGRANT FROM PIKE

Tunes: Nelly Was a Lady, Old Dan Tucker,
and King of the Cannibal Islands

I have just ar-rived a-cross the Plains, Oh, didn't I have aw-ful
times! It makes the blood run greas-y through my veins___,
I'm so dis-ap-point-ed in the mines. When
I go home with an emp-ty sack, I'll show them where the In-di-ans
shot me in the back, And how my mules laid down and died, And
I near starved to death be-sides. Ho - key, po - key,
wink - er wun, We're all good fel - lows, we'll have some fun, And
all get mar-ried when we go home, So what's the use of talk-ing.

1

I have just arrived across the Plains,
    Oh, didn't I have awful times!
It makes the blood run greasy through my veins,
    I'm so disappointed in the mines.
When I go home with an empty sack,
I'll show them where the Indians shot me in the back,
And how my mules laid down and died,
And I near starved to death beside.

CHORUS: Hokey, pokey, winker wun,
    We're all good fellows, we'll have some fun,
    And all get married when we go home,
    So what's the use of talking.

2

I was taken with the bilious cholera,
    While I was traveling up the Platte;
All my friends they ran away and left me,
    Then, to die contented, down I sat—

    Cramping, twisting, down I sat,
    My inwards all tied up in a knot;
    My old mule he began to bray,
    I, scared to death, began to pray.

3

When I reached the desert, I was starvin',
    Surely thought I'd never get across;
Then I thought of my big brother, Marvin,
    Then the bacon and the mule I'd lost.

    The times to reach the mines were past,
    And I, poor devil, was about the last;
    And when I thought of my big brother,
    I bid farewell to my kind old mother.

4

I got through at last, and went to mining,
    Stole myself a shovel and pick,
But could not raise the color big and shining,
    Swore I'd never strike another lick.

    Then I went round among my friends
    To see if I could raise some tens
    To take me home, for I was scared,
    My hair was all turning into beard.

5

If I get home, I bet my life I'll stay there,
    California'll trouble me no more;
I've tried my luck at everything and everywhere,
    And never have been half so poor before.

    For I've nothing in the world but meat,
    And that I really cannot eat;
    Such times, I never saw the like,
    Oh, Lord, I wish I was back in Pike!

TEXT: Stone (1855), pp. 41-42.

MUSIC: "Nelly Was a Lady," *Minstrel Songs, Old and New* (1882), p. 172; First Chorus: "Old Dan Tucker," Damon (1936); Second Chorus: "King of the Cannibal Islands," Vernon (1927), pp. 156-157.

VARIANT: Dwyer *et al.* (1964), pp. 49-50.

JOHN A. STONE # ARRIVAL OF THE GREENHORN

TUNE: Jeanette and Jeanot

I've just got in a-cross the Plains, I'm poor-er than a
snail, My mules all died, but poor old Clip I pulled in by the
tail; I fed him last at Chim-ney Rock, that's where the grass gave
out, I'm proud to tell, we stood it well, a-long the Truck-ee
route. But I'm ver-y weak and lean, though I start-ed plump and
fat. How I wish I had the gold ma-chine, I left back on the
Platte! And a pair of strip-ed bed-tick pants, my Sal-ly made for
me To wear while dig-ging af-ter gold; and when I left says
she, "Here, take the lauda-num with you Sam, to check the di — a — ree."

1

I've just got in across the Plains, I'm poorer than a snail,
My mules all died, but poor old Clip I pulled in by the tail;
I fed him last at Chimney Rock, that's where the grass gave out,
I'm proud to tell, we stood it well, along the Truckee route.
But I'm very weak and lean, though I started plump and fat.
How I wish I had the gold machine, I left back on the Platte!
And a pair of striped bedtick pants, my Sally made for me
To wear while digging after gold; and when I left says she,
"Here, take the laudanum with you Sam, to check the diaree."

2

When I left Missouri River, with my California rig,
I had a shovel, pick and pan, the tools they used to dig;
My mules gave out along the Platte, where they got alkalied,
And I sick with the "di-a-ree," my laudanum by my side.
When I reached the little Blue, I'd one boot and a shoe,
Which I thought by greasing once or twice, would last me nearly through;
I had needles, thread and pills, which my mammy did prescribe,
And a flint-lock musket full, to shoot the Digger tribe,
But I left them all on Goose Creek where I freely did imbibe.

3

I joined in with a train from Pike; at Independence Rock,
The Indians came in that night, stampeded all their stock;
They laughed at me said, "Go a-foot," but soon they stopped their fun,
For my old mule was left behind so poor he could not run.
So I packed my fancy nag, for the rest I could not wait,
And I traveled up Sweet Water, till I came to Devil's Gate;
When my mule gave out in sight of where I started in the morn,
I'd have given all my boots and shoes if I had not been born,
Or I'd rather stripped at New Orleans, to swim around the Horn.

4

I arrived at Salt Lake City, on the 18th of July,
Old Brigham Young was on a "bust," he swore they'd never die;
I went to see the Jordan, with a lady, God forgive her,
She took me to the water's edge, and shoved me in the river;
I crawled out and started on, and managed very well,
Until I struck the Humboldt, which I thought was nearly hell;
I traveled till I struck the sink where outlet can't be found,
The Lord got through late Saturday night, he'd finished all around,
But would not work on Sunday, so he run it in the ground.

5

The Peyouts stole what grub I had, they left me not a bite,
And now the devil was to pay—the Desert was in sight;
And as the people passed along, they'd say to me, "You fool,
You'll never get through in the world, unless you leave that mule."
But I pushed, pulled and coaxed, till I finally made a start,
And his bones, they squeaked and rattled so, I thought he'd fall apart;
I killed a buzzard now and then, gave Clip the legs and head.
We crossed the Truckee thirty times, but not a tear was shed,
We crossed the summit, took the trail, that to Nevada led.

6

When I got to Sacramento, I got on a little tight,
I lodged aboard the Prison brig, one-half a day and night;
I vamosed when I got ashore, went to the Northern mines,
There found the saying very true, "All is not gold that shines."
I dug, packed and chopped, and have drifted night and day,
But I haven't struck a single lead, that would me wages pay,
At home they think we ought to have gold on our cabin shelves,
Wear high-heeled boots, well blacked, instead of rubbers, No. twelves;
But let them come and try it, 'till they satisfy themselves.

TEXT: Stone (1855), pp. 31-33.

MUSIC: Young and Leonard (1855), p. 32.

VARIANTS: Grant (1924), pp. 107-109; Sherwin and Katzman (1932), pp. 3-5; E Clampus Vitus (1939), pp. 9-10; Black and Robertson (1940), pp. 44-46; Belden (1940), pp. 345-346; Dwyer *et al.* (1964), pp. 45-46.

JOHNNY'S DEAD

1

It was on the banks of the Humboldt
    That old Johny fell;
He was all tuckered out
    And his oxen looked like h——.

Oh! We gathered round old Johny,
    Old John Wethered;
And we buried poor old Johny,
    'Cause he was *dead*.

2

He had left a wife and sweetheart
    And seven little ones;
For gold he'd started hunting,
    Gold and silver by the tons.

Oh! We picked up poor old Johny,
    Old Johny Wethered.
And we buried the poor old devil,
    'Cause he was *dead*.

3

In the valley of the Platte
    The cholera it hit us,
But Johny cured himself
    With a big dose of bitters.

Oh! We hoisted poor old Johny,
    Old Johny Wethered,
He couldn't drink no more bitters
    'Cause he was *dead*.

4

At Fort Laramie he nearly
    Keeled over from the heat
But he hollered, "Jumping Jewsharps,
    They ain't yet got me beat."

Oh! We shrouded poor old Johny,
    Old Johny Wethered,
He was full of gas and liquor,
    And he was *dead*.

5

When he headed toward the Humboldt,
    Old Johny had a stroke,
He was feeling kind of feeble
    And he said he was stone broke.

Oh! We dug a grave for Johny.
    Old Johny Wethered.
We dug it powerful wide and deep,
    'Cause he was *dead*.

6

Coming down into the valley,
    He got an awful itch,
And he seemed a bit downhearted,
    The poor old ——.

They said he was a Clamper,
    Old Johny Wethered;
But that didn't help old Johny,
    'Cause he was *dead*.

7

And now we all must leave him
    Under sagebrush, sun and sand,
While we push on for the diggings,
    And he bakes on Humboldt's strand.

He was always such a humbug,
    Old Johny Wethered,
That we thought he was drunk or fooling,
    'Til he was *dead*.

8

So gather round me brothers,
    And pass the glorious staff,
He could take it, good old Johny,
    Take it even more than half.

So hoist a glass for Johny,
    Old Johny Wethered,
And drink to the poor old cuss,
    'Cause he is *dead*.

9

Now we must leave you, Johny,
    Your whiskey we have drunk,
Into the sand forever,
    Our brother, you have sunk.

Oh! Drink one last drink to Johny,
    Good old Johny Wethered,
Gone to the Clamper heaven,
    'Cause he is *dead*.

10

I wonder if old Johny
    Ever hoists his harp and sings
Of the joys E Clampus Vitus
    To each weary sucker brings.

Oh! I wonder if St. Peter
    And the angels round the throne,
Ever hear old Johny shouting,
    Ever hear old Johny moan—

11

"On the Humboldt bare they left me,
    On the Humboldt far from home;
Passed the Staff and left me lying
    Nevermore abroad to roam."

Nevermore will he the orphan
    Or lonely widow aid
For old Johny's gone to heaven,
    Poor old Johny's dead.

TEXT: E Clampus Vitus (1939), pp. 14-16.

THE PIONEER STAGE DRIVER

Right behind the pioneer on his Conestoga wagon came the professional freighters, stagecoach and celerity wagon drivers. Local operations started in the goldfields immediately, and overland service was not long in waiting. The hazards of each were about equal, it seems, if the story told in "The Pioneer Stage Driver" is representative. Poor George "Baldy" Green drove for the Pioneer Stage Company between Placerville and Virginia City in the mid 1860's. On May 22, 1865, near Silver City, Nevada, three men robbed his stage of $10,000 in gold and greenbacks, and from then on neither highwaymen nor newspapers would let him alone. The *Territorial Enterprise* noted that he narrowly escaped scalping, and someone put up a sign near the spot saying, "Wells, Fargo Distributing Office, Baldy Green, Mgr." Two years later his stage was robbed twice on successive days, and in June, 1868, three more robbers hit him for $5,000. He was discharged, but Charles Rhodes's song about him, sung first in San Francisco's melodion companies, has continued on in oral tradition as a heroic ballad—with consequent extinguishing of its comic lights.

John Stone's "California Stage Company," about a firm that began to monopolize the Sierra trade in 1854, provides the passengers' point of view, although his own, as usual, is irrepressible, "The ladies are compelled to sit With dresses in tobacco spit."

Overland staging began in 1858 after a divided Congress let the Postmaster General choose his own route west. The Butterfield Overland Mail flung stations along a 2,800-mile southern route from Tipton, Missouri, to San Francisco. The following year, the freighting firm of Russell, Majors & Waddell formed the Pike's Peak Express Company running through Denver. To boost their central route, they started a costly ten-day stunt ride called the Pony Express along it in 1860. By the time the Civil War forced Congress to take the central route, R., M. & W. were so broke that Butterfield got the job. The extravagant Ben Holladay then bought out Butterfield and managed the entire network single-handed. "The Overland Stage Driver," written in 1865 by his agent Nat Stein, describes him:

> You ask me for our leader; I'll soon inform you, then;
> It's Holladay they call him, and often only Ben;
> If you can read the papers, it's easy work to scan
> He beats the world on staging now, "or any other man."

On the fringes of these monopolies, dozens of small-timers struggled. "Bill Peters, the Stage Driver," a song Lomax collected, is a heroic piece about a driver on the central Kansas plains, whom the Comanches got,

> And when they bring his body home
> A barrel of tears was shed.

Before the railroad got there in 1898, the chief hauler of coke to the copper smelters of Globe, Arizona Territory, was J. Liberman & Co. of Wilcox, remembered in the song, "Freighting from Wilcox to Globe" as a thieving Livermore. "Pete Orman" tells about the rigors of skinning on the Oregon road between Bend and John Day. "The Bull-Whacker," on the other hand, is a bold, blustery song about the Salt Lake City line and the philosophy it evoked:

> Oh! you've got to take things on the plains as you can,
> They'll never try to please you, "or any other man";
> You go it late and early, and also wet or dry,
> And eat when you can get it—root hog, or die.

CHARLEY RHOADES   # THE PIONEER STAGE DRIVER

1

I'm going to tell a story, and I'll tell it in my song,
I hope that it will please you, and I won't detain you long;
It's about one of the old boys, so gallas and so fine,
He used to carry mails, on the Pioneer line.

2

He was such a favorite wherever he was seen,
He was known about Virginia by the name of Bally Green;
Oh! he swung a whip so graceful, for he was bound to shine,
As a high-toned driver on the Pioneer line.

3

As he was driving up one night, as lively as a coon,
He saw four men jump in the road, by the pale light of the moon;
One sprung for his leaders, while another his gun he cocks,
Saying, "Bally I hate to trouble you, but pass me out that box."

4

When Bally heard him say these words, he opened wide his eyes,
He didn't know what the devil to do, it took him by surprise;
But he reached down in the boot, saying, "Take it sir with pleasure,"
And out into the middle of the road, went Wells & Fargo's treasure.

5

Now when they'd got the treasure-box, they seem'd quite satisfied,—
The man that held the horses, politely stepped aside,
Saying, "Bally, we've got what we want, just drive along your team,"
And he made the quickest time to Silver City ever seen.

6

If you say greenbacks to Bally now, it makes him feel so sore,
It's the first time he was ever stopped, and he's drove that road before;
But they play'd four hands against his one, and shot guns was their game,
And if I had been in Bally's place, I'd have passed it out the same.

TEXT: "The Pioneer Stage Driver," composed and sung by Charley Rhoades (San Francisco: T. C. Boyd, 1865 [broadside]).

VARIANTS: Grant (1924), pp. 152-154; Drury (1931); E Clampus Vitus (1939), p. 17; Lengyel (1939), p. 74; Pound (1942), pp. 121-122; Alderson (1945), pp. 1-11; Lengyel (1949), pp. 36-37; Davidson (1951), pp. 142-143; Burt (1958a), pp. 209-210.

JOHN A. STONE # CALIFORNIA STAGE COMPANY J. R. MYERS

Tune: Dandy Jim of Caroline

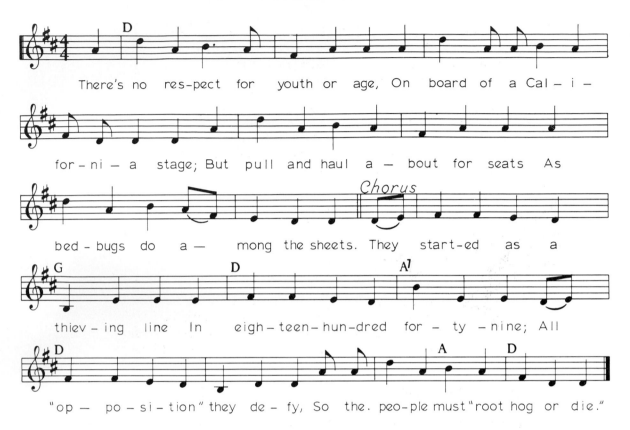

There's no res-pect for youth or age, On board of a Cal-i-

for-ni-a stage; But pull and haul a—bout for seats As

bed-bugs do a—mong the sheets. They start-ed as a

thiev-ing line In eigh-teen-hun-dred for-ty-nine; All

"op—po-si-tion" they de-fy, So the. peo-ple must "root hog or die."

1
There's no respect for youth or age,
On board of a California stage;
But pull and haul about for seats
As bedbugs do among the sheets.

CHORUS: They started as a thieving line
In eighteen hundred forty-nine;
All "opposition" they defy,
So the people must "root hog or
die."

2
You're crowded in with Chinamen,
As fattening hogs are in a pen,
And what will more a man provoke,
Is musty plug tobacco smoke.

3
The ladies are compelled to sit
With dresses in tobacco spit;
The gentlemen don't seem to care,
But talk on politics and swear.

54

4

The dust is deep in summer time,
The mountains very hard to climb;
And drivers often stop and yell,
"Get out, all hands, and push—*up hill!*"

5

The drivers, when they feel inclined.
Will have you walking on behind,
And on your shoulders lug a pole,
To help them through some muddy hole.

6

They promise, when your fare you pay,
"You'll have to walk but *half* the way;"
Then add *aside*, with cunning laugh,
"You'll push and pull the *other half!*"

7

They have and will monopolize
The business, till the *people rise*,
And send them "kiteing" down below,
To start a line with Bates and Rowe!

TEXT: Stone (1858a), pp. 31-32.

MUSIC: Damon (1936).

VARIANTS: Stone (1858*b*), p. 51; Handy (1908), pp. 431-433; Lomax (1916), pp. 411-412; Grant (1924), pp. 70-71; Lomax and Lomax (1938), pp. 393-394; E Clampus Vitus (1939), p. 22; Lengyel (1939), p. 75; Black and Robertson (1940), pp. 34-35; Lengyel (1949), p. 40; Dwyer *et al.* (1964), pp. 140-141.

THE OVERLAND STAGE DRIVER

Tune: The High Salary Driver of the Denver City Line

1

I sing to everybody, in the country and the town,
A song upon a subject that's worthy of renown;
I haven't got a story of fairy-land to broach,
But plead for the cause of sticking to the box seat of a coach.

CHORUS: Statesmen and warriors, traders and the rest,
May boast of their profession and think it is the best;
Their state I'll never envy, I'll have you understand,
Long as I can be a driver on the jolly "Overland."

2

There's a beauty never ending, for me, on the plains,
That's worth a man's beholding, at any cost of pains;
And in the Indian country it offers me a fund
Of glee to see the antelopes and prairie-dogs abscond.

3

The mountains and the canons in turn afford delight,
As often as I pass them, by day or in the night;
That man must be a ninny who'd bury up alive
When all it costs to revel through creation is to drive.

4

Alike are all the seasons and weathers, to my mind;
No heat nor cold can daunt me, or make me lag behind,
In daylight and in darkness, through rain and shine and snow,
It's my confirmed ambition to be up and on the go.

5

You ask me for our leader; I'll soon inform you, then;
It's Holladay they call him, and often only Ben;
If you can read the papers, it's easy work to scan
He beats the world on staging now, "or any other man."

6

And so you must allow me, the agent at his books,
And selling passage tickets, how woebegone he looks!
'T would cause his eyes to twinkle, his drooping heart revive,
Could he but hold the ribbons and obtain a chance to drive.

7

The sup'rintendent, even, though big a chief he be,
Would find it quite a poser to swap off berths with me;
And if division agents, though clever coves and fine,
Should make me such an offer, you can gamble I'd decline.

8

The station-keepers nimble and messengers so gay
Have duties of importance, and please me every way;
But never let them fancy, for anything alive,
I'd take their situations and give up to them my drive.

9

And then the trusty fellows who tend upon the stock,
And do the horses justice, as reg'lar as a clock,
I love them late and early and wish them well to thrive,
But theirs is not my mission, for I'm bound, you see, to drive.

10

A truce to these distinctions, since all the hands incline
To stick up for their business, as I stick up for mine;
And, like a band of brothers, our efforts we unite
To please the traveling public and the mails to expedite.

11

It's thus you're safely carried throughout the mighty West,
Where chances to make fortunes are ever found the best;
And thus the precious pouches of mail are brought to hand
Through the ready hearts that center on the jolly "Overland."

TEXT: *Montana Post* (Virginia City), April 8, 1865.

VARIANTS: Frank A. Root and William E. Connelley, *The Overland Stage to California* (Topeka, Kans.: Root & Connelley, 1901), pp. 464-465; Davidson (1943), pp. 102-103.

THE BULL-WHACKER

Tune: Root Hog, or Die

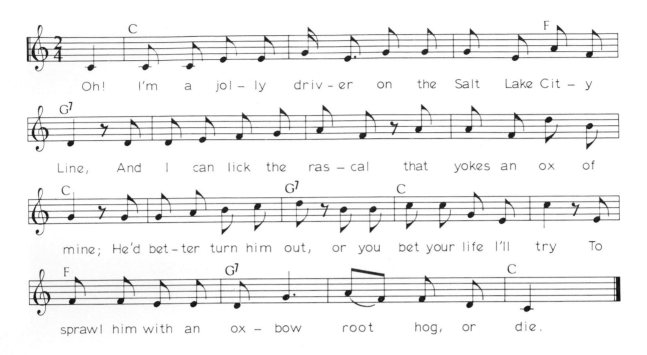

Oh! I'm a jol-ly driv-er on the Salt Lake Cit-y Line, And I can lick the ras-cal that yokes an ox of mine; He'd bet-ter turn him out, or you bet your life I'll try To sprawl him with an ox - bow root hog, or die.

1

Oh! I'm a jolly driver on the Salt Lake City Line,
And I can lick the rascal that yokes an ox of mine;
He'd better turn him out, or you bet your life I'll try
To sprawl him with an ox-bow—root hog, or die.

2

Oh! I'll tell you how it is when you first get on the road:
You've got an awkward team and a very heavy load;
You've got to whip and holler (if you swear, it's on the sly)—
Punch your teams along boys—root hog, or die.

3

Oh! it's every day at noon there is something to do.
If there's nothing else, there will be an ox to shoe;
First with ropes you throw him, and there you make him lie
While you tack on the shoes, boys—root hog, or die.

4

Perhaps you'd like to know what it is we have to eat,
A little bit of bread, and a dirty piece of meat;
A little old molasses, and sugar on the sly,
Potatoes if you've got them—root hog, or die.

5

Oh! there's many strange sights to be seen along the road,
The antelopes and deer and the great big sandy toad,
The buffalo and elk, the rabbits jump so high,
And with all the bloody Injuns—root hog, or die.

6

The prairie dogs in Dog-town, and the prickly pears,
And the buffalo bones that are scattered everywheres;
Now and then dead oxen from vile Alkali,
Are very thick in places, where it's "root hog, or die."

7

Oh! you've got to take things on the plains as you can,
They'll never try to please you, "or any other man";
You go it late and early, and also wet or dry,
And eat when you can get it—root hog, or die.

8

Oh! times on Bitter Creek, they never can be beat,
"Root hog, or die" is on every wagon sheet;
The sand within your throat, the dust within your eye,
Bend your back and stand it, to root hog, or die.

9

When we arrived in Salt Lake, the twenty-fifth of June,
The people were surprised to see us come so soon;
But we are bold bull-whackers on whom you can rely,
We're tough, and we can stand it, to root hog, or die.

TEXT: J. H. Beadle, *Life in Utah: or the Mysteries and Crimes of Mormonism* (Philadelphia: 1870), pp. 227-228.

MUSIC: *Minstrel Songs, Old and New* (1882), pp. 100-101.

VARIANTS: Lomax (1910), pp. 69-71; Lomax and Lomax (1934), pp. 430-432, and (1938), pp. 396-398; Davidson (1943), pp. 99-101, and (1951), pp. 140-141; Lomax (1960), pp. 333-334; Hubbard (1961), pp. 295-296.

BILL PETERS, THE STAGE DRIVER

1

Bill Peters was a hustler
From Independence town;
He warn't a college scholar
Nor man of great renown,
But Bill had a way o' doing things
And doin' 'em up brown.

2

Bill driv the stage from Independence
Up to the Smokey Hill;
And everybody knowed him thar
As Independence Bill,—
Thar warn't no feller on the route
That driv with half the skill.

3

Bill driv four pair of horses,
Same as you'd drive a team,
And you'd think you was a-travelin'
On a railroad driv by steam;
And he'd git thar on time, you bet,
Or Bill 'u'd bust a seam.

4

He carried mail and passengers,
And he started on the dot,
And them teams o'his'n, so they say,
Was never known to trot;
But they went it in a gallop
And kept their axles hot.

5

When Bill's stage 'u'd bust a tire,
Or something 'u'd break down,
He'd hustle round and patch her up
And start off with a bound;
And the wheels o' that old shack o' his
Scarce ever touched the ground.

6

And Bill didn't 'low no foolin',
And when Injuns hove in sight
And bullets rattled at the stage,
He druv with all his might;
He'd holler, "Fellers, give 'em hell,
I ain't got time to fight."

7

Then the way them wheels 'u'd rattle,
And the way the dust 'u'd fly,
You'd think a million cattle,
Had stampeded and gone by;
But the mail 'u'd get thar just the same,
If the horses had to die.

8

He driv that stage for many a year
Along the Smokey Hill,
And a pile o' wild Comanches
Did Bill Peters have to kill,—
And I reckon if he'd had good luck
He'd been a drivin' still.

9

But he chanced one day to run agin
A bullet made o' lead,
Which was harder than he bargained for
And now poor Bill is dead;
And when they brung his body home
A barrel of tears was shed.

TEXT: Lomax (1910), pp. 100-102.
VARIANT: Lomax and Lomax (1938), pp. 391-393.

PETE ORMAN

ASHER

Tune: The Siskiyou Miners

1

I'll tell all you skinners
    From John Day to Bend
That the road south o' Shaniko
    Ain't got no end;
It's rut-holes and boulders,
    It's alkali dust,
But the jerkliners gotta make
    Maupin or bust.

2

They rolled out Pete Orman
    A quarter past three
He never had time
    To get over the spree
That he'd started at noon
    Only two days before;
When the call-boy come 'round,
    Old Pete was right sore.

3

"Now what in the hell
    Are they fixin' for me?"
He wanted to know,
    "Get out, let me be;
Last night my poor side-kick
    Was throwed in the can,
Today we ride jerk-line
    For no God-damn man!"

4

They rolled out Pete Orman
    And bailed out McBee,
They set a stiff price
    With oats and grub free;
The boys had to take it,
    The contract was made,
They watered, fed, harnessed,
    And then hit the grade.

5

The sun was just risin',
    The weather was fine,
They figured clear sailin'
    To the Cow Canyon line;
But while they was startin'
    Up Shaniko Hill,
Orm tickled Old Tommy
    With a porcupine quill.

6

"Put in the oats
    And shovel in the hay,
We're goin' to make it through
    If we can find a way;
We ain't quite as fast
    As the Oregon Trunk,
But we'll pull 'em into Bend
    If we are both drunk."

TEXT: Harold Benjamin, "Case Study in Folk-Song Making," *Tennessee Folklore Society Bulletin*, XIX (1953), 28-30. Used by permission of Tennessee Folklore Society.

FREIGHTING FROM WILCOX TO GLOBE

Tune: Home, Dearie, Home

Come all you jol—ly freight-ers that has freight-ed on the

road, That has hauled a load of freight From Wil—cox To

Globe; We freight-ed on this road____ For six—teen years or

more A—haul-ing freight for Liv—er—more,__ No won-der that I'm

poor. And its home, dear—est home: And its home you ought to

be, O—ver on the Gi—la In the white man's coun—

try, Where the pop—lar and the ash And mes—quite will ev—er

be Grow-ing green down on the Gi—la;__ There's a home for you and me.

1

Come all you jolly freighters
That has freighted on the road,
That has hauled a load of freight
From Wilcox to Globe;
We freighted on this road
For sixteen years or more
A-hauling freight for Livermore,—
No wonder that I'm poor.

CHORUS: And it's home, dearest home:
And it's home you ought to be,
Over on the Gila
In the white man's country,
Where the poplar and the ash
And mesquite will ever be
Growing green down on the Gila;
There's a home for you and me.

2

'Twas in the spring of seventy-three
I started with my team,
Led by false illusion
And those foolish, golden dreams;
The first night out from Wilcox
My best wheel horse was stole,
And it makes me curse a little
To come out in the hole.

3

This then only left me three,—
Kit, Mollie and old Mike;
Mike being the best one of the three
I put him out on spike;
I then took the mountain road
So the people would not smile,
And it took fourteen days
To travel thirteen mile.

4

But I got there all the same
With my little three-up spike;
It's taken all my money, then,
To buy a mate for Mike.
You all know how it is
When once you get behind,
You never get even again
Till you damn steal them blind.

5

I was an honest man
When I first took to the road,
I would not swear an oath,
Nor would I tap a load;
But now you ought to see my mules
When I begin to cuss,
They flop their ears and wiggle their tails
And pull the load or bust.

6

Now I can tap a whiskey barrel
With nothing but a stick,
No one can detect me
I've got it down so slick;
Just fill it up with water,—
Sure, there's no harm in that.

. . . .

7

Now my clothes are not the finest,
Nor are they genteel;
But they will have to do me
Till I can make another steal.
My boots are number elevens,
For I swiped them from a chow,
And my coat cost *dos reals*
From a little Apache squaw.

8

Now I have freighted in the sand,
I have freighted in the rain,
I have bogged my wagons down
And dug them out again;
I have worked both late and early
Till I was almost dead,
And I have spent some nights sleeping
In an Arizona bed.

9

Now barbed wire and bacon
Is all that they will pay,
But you have to show your copper checks
To get your grain and hay;
If you ask them for five dollars,
Old Meyers will scratch his pate,
And the clerks in their white, stiff collars
Say, "Get down and pull your freight."

10

But I want to die and go to hell,
Get there before Livermore and Meyers
And get a job of hauling coke
To keep up the devil's fires;
If I get the job of singeing them,
I'll see they don't get free;
I'll treat them like a yaller dog,
As they have treated me.

TEXT: Lomax (1910), pp. 207-210.

MUSIC: As sung by Abraham John Busby, Library of Congress Recording L 30. Transcribed by David Cohen.

VARIANTS: Lomax and Lomax (1938), pp. 394-396; Library of Congress Recording L 30.

THE RAILROAD CARS ARE COMING

The Southern secession also made it possible for Congress to agree on a route for a transcontinental railroad. Ultimately, the railroads were profoundly to affect all the West, but the choice of the first route created the greatest stir among that distant people whose isolation it threatened, the Mormons. Their ambivalent attitude toward the rails as carriers of both interference and prosperity is expressed in three songs composed before the Union Pacific met the Central Pacific north of Ogden, Utah, in May, 1869. The first of these, "The Railroad Cars Are Coming," expresses a pure enthusiasm, very like McKay's in "To the West," about the trains "dashing flashing, *through* Mormon land." But it was the prospect of their stopping which bothered the Welsh convert, "Ieuan," whose "The Iron Horse" was published in his *Bee Hive Songster* in 1868. Even the implications of the name of the railroad bothered him:

> "Civilized" we shall be;
> Many folks shall we see;
> Lords and nobles, p'raps some bigger;
> Any how we'll see the nigger;
> Saints will come, sinners too;
> We'll have all we can do;
> For this great "Union" Railroad
> Must fetch the devil through.

Referring to a part of the route taken through the Wasatch Mountains by the Mormons, the Argonauts, the Overland Stage and, finally, the Union Pacific Railroad, the song "Echo Canyon" anticipates blessings the U.P. never provided for:

> The great locomotive next season will come,
> To gather the saints from their far distant home,
> And bring them to Utah in peace here to stay,
> While the judgments of God sweep the wicked away.

In order to grease the paths of the railroads west, the federal government and the Western states and territories subsidized the roads with an amount of land nearly equaling the size of Texas. The song "Subsidy: A Goat Island Ballad," composed during an antimonopoly wave that swept through California soon after the completion of the railroad, resentfully alleges abuses in the manipulation of those grants by Leland Stanford and his associates in the Central Pacific: Collis P. Huntington, Mark Hopkins, and Charles Crocker.

Most of the other songs in this section, however, concern the lot of the individual railroader, not the realms of high chicanery. "Bishop Zack, the Mormon Engineer," for example, is a comic piece mingling Mormon polygamy with the motif of the sailor's girl in every port. Zack won't change jobs because the Denver and Rio Grande has better berths than the old U.P. "Way Out in Idaho," very like "Canada-I-O" in story and scansion, is set on the Oregon Short Line, completed across the southern part of the Idaho Territory in 1884. A miscellany of accidental and premeditated violence and wretchedness is cited in "The Wandering Laborer's Song." It alludes to foul play in the Denver and Salt Lake Railroad's Moffat Tunnel, a 6-mile wonder driven through the crest of the Rockies. Begun in 1902 and finished twenty-five years later, it provided plenty of time for plenty of murders.

The turbulent relations between labor and railroad management in the West are glimpsed in Joe Hill's famous "Casey Jones, the Union Scab." Written about a brief and unsuccessful Southern Pacific shopmen's stike in San Pedro, California, in September, 1911, it tells how Casey got a wooden medal and a lot of hell for being good and faithful on the S.P. line.

Finally, from a backwoods Washington newspaper comes "The Peninsula Pike," a song about a delapidated short line that did the "hen wallow shuffle" from Megler, by the Columbia River, up to Ilwaco, Washington, near someplace called Cape Disappointment. It was owned by the Union Pacific, the line that started this whole business in the first place.

ROBERT SNELL

THE RAILROAD CARS ARE COMING

1

The great Pacific Railway,
For California hail!
Bring on the locomotive;
Lay down the iron rail.
Across the rolling prairie,
'Mid mountain peaks so grand,
The railroad cars are steaming, gleaming, through Mormon land;
The railroad cars are speeding, fleeting, through Mormon land.

2
The prairie dogs in Dogtown
Will wag their little tails
When they see cars a–coming,
Just flying down the rails.
Amid the sav'ry sagebrush,
The antelope will stand,
While railroad cars go dashing, flashing, through Mormon land,
While railroad cars go dashing, flashing, through Mormon land.

———————

TEXT AND MUSIC: Briegel (1933), p. 35. Used by permission of George F. Briegel, Inc.
VARIANTS: Sandburg (1927), pp. 358-359; Lengyel (1939), p. 81; Davidson (1945), p. 299.

SUBSIDY: A GOAT ISLAND BALLAD

Tune: A Fine Old English Gentleman

1

There is a corporation within this Golden State,
Which owns a line of railroads for conveying men and freight
To the Mormon town of Ogden, at an elevated rate,
And which began in a very small way *via* the Dutch Flat swindle,
    but by perseverance and bonds, including subsidies,
    became both strong and great,
For this Railroad Corporation is the deuce in subsidies.

2

Now this mighty Corporation had placed its terminus
At Sacramento City, after no small bit of fuss,
Whereat the San Franciscans raved and Oaklanders did cuss,
And tried their best to have a change, so that we of the Bay
    might have all the benefits, profits, and advantages
    come flowing into us,
Of this Railroad Corporation and its heap of subsidies.

3

First, San Francisco said 'twould give all down on Mission Bay,
If the Corporation would but make its terminus that way,
Some sixty acres more or less of finest kind of clay,
Which could be brought to the surface by a dredge with a ten-foot
    stroke or covered over with nice long piles if they wished
      to build a quay,
For this Railroad Corporation from its many subsidies.

4

The Railroad took the handsome gift, but said 'twould wait a while
Before it filled the marsh-land in or drove a single pile,
And then it went to Oakland, and with clever word and smile,
Agreed to make the terminus at that place if the city would donate
    all its waterfront and never expect the cars to stop within a mile,
For this Railroad Corporation is the deuce on subsidies.

5

Next the Corporation bought the old Vallejo route,
And then, before the people could mistrust what 'twas about,
It gobbled all the other roads, and then expressed a doubt
Concerning the permanent location of this remarkable terminus,
    which was as unreliable as a Spanish land title or an old
      black cat with a bad rheumatic gout,
For this Railroad Corporation wanted other subsidies.

6

And then this city rose from sleep, and in a hearty way,
Exclaimed, "If you'll come here we'll build a bridge across the Bay,
We'll raise the funds, you'll have a bridge and not a cent to pay!"
But the Corporation wrote a letter half a yard long, which,
    being interpreted, implied that the Corporation was on another lay;
For this Railroad Corporation has its eye on subsidies.

7

Then the People grew excited, and raised a hue and cry
Of "Anti-Subsidy," and vowed they never more would try
To help the Corporation, but would break its power by
A lot of incorruptible and undefiled Legislators, who had been
    elected for the express purpose of bestowing a black eye
On this Railroad Corporation which is fond of subsidies.

8

But when the Legislature met, the simple People found
That the Corporation's agents had been slyly prowling round,
Till the Legislators one and all had changed their stamping ground,
And voted as the railroad wished on every question, and sent
    Sargent to the Senate with the understanding that he
      should help Jim Nye and his *confreres* to expound
How this Railroad Corporation should have other subsidies.

9

And now that Stanford owns the railroads and the boats,
One half the State and more than half the Legislative votes,
For Frisco or for Oakland he doesn't care two goats,
And has decided to retire to a secluded isle of the sea sometimes
      called Yerba Buena, but more familiarly known as the
      Island of the Goats,
With his terminus, his railroad, and his lots of subsidies.

10

Which little rhyming narrative just shows us that, Whereas,
The Corporation's clever and the Public is an ass—
Resolved, the first must always win, the other go to grass;
Which happy consummation every one who has noted the brilliant efforts
      of a San Francisco community to make a commercial idiot of itself
      hopes soon may come to pass,
As also hopes the Railroad with its wealth of subsidies.

TEXT: *California Mail Bag* (San Francisco) (March–April, 1872), p. 80.

MUSIC: Turner *et al.* (1858), p. 9.

"IEUAN" # THE IRON HORSE

Tune: Caerfilly March

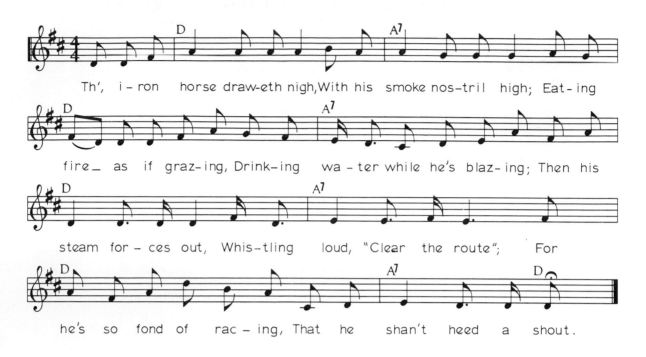

Th', i-ron horse draw-eth nigh, With his smoke nos-tril high; Eat-ing
fire_ as if graz-ing, Drink-ing wa-ter while he's blaz-ing; Then his
steam for-ces out, Whis-tling loud, "Clear the route"; For
he's so fond of rac-ing, That he shan't heed a shout.

1

Th' iron horse draweth nigh,
With his smoke nostril high;
Eating fire as if grazing,
Drinking water while he's blazing;
Then his steam forces out,
Whistling loud, "Clear the route";
For he's so fond of racing,
That he shan't heed a shout.

2

Make him room to come on,
Grade the road he's to run;
Dig tunnels through the mountains,
Turn the currents of the fountains;
Bridges build, stations make,
Lay the track he will take;
For this steam horse is moving,
With a train in his wake;

3

The railroad passes here;
Its iron horse is near:
We'll raise our flags and rally,
With loud shouts, in Salt Lake Valley.
When it comes through our land,
Let us all be on hand,
To mount the cars together,
Like a proud, happy band.

4

We can lead to the Lake;
Little time will it take;
And there enjoy much pleasure—
Bathing, swimming at our leisure.
Then we'll jaunt to the East,
With our friends there to feast,
And west to the Pacific,
With this best iron beast.

5

Mighty horse, iron steed,
O'er the plains let him speed,
Until he links both oceans,
And transport to us all notions:
Then we'll find in Salt Lake
Every thing good to take,
With scores of curious fashions,
Such as pride loves to make.

6

"Civilized" we shall be;
Many folks shall we see;
Lords and nobles, p'raps some bigger;
Any how we'll see the nigger;
Saints will come, sinners too;
We'll have all we can do;
For this great "Union" Railroad
Must fetch the devil through.

7

We've isolated been,
But soon we can be seen;
And round this mountain region,
All can learn of our religion;
Count each man's many wives,
How they're held in their "hives,"
And see those dreadful "Danites,"
Said to lynch many lives!

8

So, make haste, fearless steed,
Make us all one in creed:
We seek to form acquaintance,
And bring people to repentance.
Then, hurrah! come along;
Thro' these high mountains throng:
May th' Iron Horse and Mormons
Always right every wrong.

———

TEXT: *Bee Hive Songster* (1868), pp. 11-13.

MUSIC: As sung by Joseph H. Watkins, Library of Congress Recording L 30. Transcribed by David Cohen.

VARIANTS: Briegel (1933), p. 52; Carter (1944), p. 521; Davidson (1945), pp. 299-300; Fife and Fife (1947), pp. 51-52, and (1956), pp. 329-330; Hubbard (1961), pp. 452-455.

ECHO CANYON

1

At the head of great Echo, there's a railroad begun,
And the Mormons are cutting and grading like fun;
They say they'll stick to it until it's complete,
For friends and relations are longing to meet.

CHORUS: Hurrah! hurrah! the railroad's begun;
Three cheers for our contractor—his name's Brigham Young.
Hurrah! hurrah! we're honest and true;
And if we stick to it, it's bound to go through.

74

2

Now there's Mister Reed, he's a gentleman too,
He knows very well what the Mormons can do;
He knows in their work they are lively and gay,
And just the right boys to build a railway.

3

Our camp is united, we all labor hard,
And if we work faithfully, we'll get our reward;
Our leader is wise and industrious too,
And all things he tells us we're willing to do.

4

The boys in our camp are light-hearted and gay,
We work on the railroad ten hours a day;
We're thinking of the good times we'll have in the fall,
When we'll take our ladies and off for the ball.

5

We surely must live in a very fast age,
We've travelled by ox teams and then took the stage,
But when such conveyance is all done away,
We'll travel in steam cars upon the railway.

6

The great locomotive next season will come,
To gather the saints from their far distant home,
And bring them to Utah in peace here to stay,
While the judgments of God sweep the wicked away.

TEXT AND MUSIC: Daughters of Utah Pioneers (1932), pp. 196-197. Used by permission of Daughters of Utah Pioneers.

VARIANTS: Briegel (1933), pp. 2-3; Carter (1944), p. 520; Davidson (1945), pp. 298-299; Botkin (1951), pp. 752-753; Hubbard (1961), pp. 451-452.

S. L. SAMSON

BISHOP ZACK, THE MORMON ENGINEER

Zack Black came to U—tah back in Eigh—ty three, A right good Mor—mon and a Bish—op, too, was he, He ran a lo—co—mo—tive on the "D'n' R. G.," And Zack was aw—ful pop—u—lar, as you will see____.

Chorus

Hear him whis—tle! Hear him whis—tle! He ran a lo—co—mo—tive on the "D'n' R. G____."

1

Zack Black came to Utah in Eighty-three,
A right good Mormon and a Bishop, too, was he,
He ran a locomotive on the "D'n' R. G.,"
And Zack was awful popular, as you will see.

CHORUS: Hear him whistle! Hear him whistle!
He ran a locomotive on the "D'n' R. G."

2

Zack he had a wife in ev'ry railroad town,
He numbered them from twelve 'way down to number two,
Oh, in his locomotive he'd go steaming 'round,
And when he'd pass each wifie's home his whistle blew.

3

Zack he always said he loved 'em all the same,
But wifie number twelve he loved her mighty well,
He had her picture mounted in his engine cab,
And when he passed her home he'd always ring the bell.

4

Listen, ev'rybody, 'cause this story's true,
Zack had a wife in ev'ry town his train passed through,
They tried to shift Zack over to the old "U.P.,"
But Zack demurred, 'cause he preferred the "D'n' R. G."

———

TEXT AND MUSIC: Briegel (1933), pp. 38-39. Used by permission of George F. Briegel, Inc.
VARIANTS: Davidson (1945), p. 293; Botkin and Harlow (1953), p. 444.

WAY OUT IN IDAHO

TUNE: Sam Bass

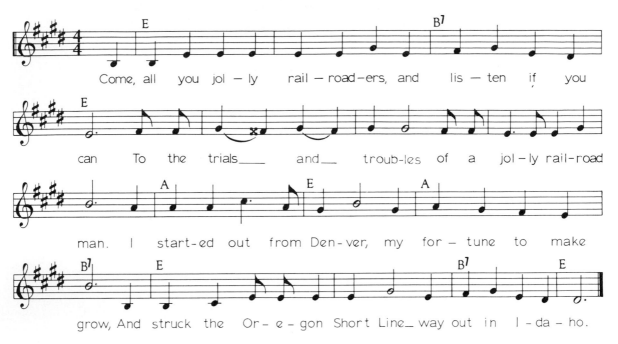

Come, all you jol—ly rail—road-ers, and lis—ten if you can To the trials____ and__ troub-les of a jol—ly rail-road man. I start-ed out from Den-ver, my for—tune to make grow, And struck the Or—e—gon Short Line_ way out in I—da—ho.

1

Come, all you jolly railroaders, and listen if you can
To the trials and troubles of a jolly railroad man.
I started out from Denver, my fortune to make grow,
And struck the Oregon Short Line—way out in Idaho.

2

As I was walking around in Denver, one lucky April day,
A Kilpatrick man stepped up to me and these words he did say:
"Lay me down five dollars as quickly as you can
And hurry and catch the train—she's startin' for Cheyenne.

3

"When you get to Cheyenne, to Ogden you must go,
And there you'll take the narrow gauge and go to Idaho."
But when I got to Pocatello, my troubles began to grow
Asleeping in the sage brush, through frost and hail and snow.

4

So cold and wet and hungry, my blankets on my back,
I started for American Falls and there I met "Fat Jack."
Says he: "You're a stranger and perhaps your funds are low
And yonder stands my hotel, 'tis the best in Idaho!"

5

I followed my conductor to his hotel tent,
And for a square and hearty meal—I paid him my last cent.
"Fat Jack's" a jolly and happy fellow and you'll always find him so,
And I had the squarest meal since I struck Idaho.

6

Next morning I started out for Kilpatrick's camp
And thought myself quite fortunate, like any other tramp,
But when I struck the wretched spot, my heart was filled with woe,
For it was a dirty, lousy camp—the worst in Idaho.

7

My heart was filled with pity, as I walked along the track,
To see so many bummers with their blankets on their back.
They said the task was heavy and the grub they couldn't go
Around Kilpatrick's table—way out in Idaho.

8

Next morning went to work for a cuss called "Cranky Bill";
He gave me a ten-pound hammer to pound upon a drill
And said if I didn't like it I could take my shirts and go
And leave my blankets for my board—way out in Idaho.

9

But now I'm well and working in O'Brien's camp,
And think I shall continue until I raise a stamp,
Then go back to Kansas and marry the one I know
And bid farewell to the O.S.L. and the hills of Idaho.

TEXT: Idaho State Historical Society, *18th Biennial Report* (1940), pp. 72-74.

MUSIC: As sung by Lannis F. Sutton, Library of Congress Recording L 30. Transcribed by David Cohen.

VARIANTS: Lomax and Lomax (1941), pp. 269-270; Emrich (1942c), pp. 229-230; Botkin and Harlow (1953), pp. 440-441.

THE WANDERING LABORER'S SONG

1

It was up on the Moffat Tunnel,
    In Colorado's snowy clime,
Two buddies while working together
    Quarreled over a jug of wine.
One with remorse is bitten
    And below on the rocks lies dead;
The other above lies groaning,
    A pick buried in his head.

CHORUS: I love my pick and shovel,
I'll paint its handles red,
For without my pick and shovel
I couldn't earn my bread.

2

It was on the Denver–Salt Lake Line,
    A Mexican section gang
Met a light engine in a tunnel,
    And the grave made loud harangue.
Arms and feet lay thrown about,
    And spattered blood around,
And Death, in its grimness grinning,
    Lay stark upon the ground.

3

It's pay day around Mount Shasta,
    And the prostitutes are gay,
For they're coming down with their gambling
      pimps
    To take our checks away.
You'll be in despair when you wake,
    Tomorrow in the morn,
But few days of labor left
    And your winter's stake all gone.

———

TEXT: Milburn (1930), pp. 278-279. Used by permission of Ives Washburn, Inc.

CHARLEY L. GRANT   # THE PENINSULA PIKE

1

There's a railroad they call the Peninsula Pike—
    Go get me the Bible and read it—
Just two streaks of rust on top of a dyke—
    O, where is salvation? I need it.
From Megler this railroad goes winding about,
    Like two streaks of rust in an alley,
On low joints and high joints we're jostled about,
    Till the doctor can scarcely make us rally.

2

From Megler to Holman there's 900 pains
    To scourge your anatomy's function;
In fact, those who ride are near void of their brains
    When they get down to Ilwaco Junction.
You ache in your feet and you ache in your legs,
    You ache in your arms and your shoulders;
In fact, one can scarcely stand on his pegs
    As he bounds over split logs and boulders.

3

There is no place to stop when you wait for a train,
    If raining, if sunshine or storming;
If chilled to the core you may struggle in vain,
    You'll surely find no way of warming.
It's the hen wallow shuffle you get every mile,
    The half Nelson hold and the strangle;
And agony lurks where there should be a smile,
    And the trip is a terrible wrangle.

4

This railroad was built just after the flood—
    No effort's been made to improve it;
Just two streaks of rust in the weeds and the mud,
    And nothing, it seems, will behoove it.
Thousands of ties nearly rotten today,
    Bridges unsafe as the devil,
The rails were aged when laid, they say,
    But the roadbed is not on the level.

5

The spikes are all rusted and loose as old teeth,
    The fish plates have passed all redemption;
The whole thing is dead; so I am weaving this wreath—
    As a railroad it's surely an exemption.
This railroad is owned by the famous U.P.,
    The same as the Southern Pacific,
And the way the whole looks now to me
    Is something most damnably terrific.

TEXT: *Ilwaco Tribune* (Ilwaco, Wash.) (Sept., 1914), quoted in Thomas E. Jessett, "The Ilwaco Railroad," *Oregon Historical Quarterly*, LVIII (1957), 157.

JOE HILL # CASEY JONES, THE UNION SCAB

TUNE: Casey Jones

The work-ers on the S. P. line to strike sent out a call, But

Ca — sey Jones, the En — gin-eer, he would-n't strike at all; His

boil — er it was leak-ing and his driv-ers on the bum, And his

en — gine and his bear-ings, they were all out o' plumb.

Chorus

Ca — sey Jones kept his junk pile run — ning,——

Ca — sey Jones was work — ing dou — ble time,

Ca — sey Jones got a wood — en med — al For

be — ing good and faith — ful on the S. P. line——.

1

The workers on the S.P. line, to strike sent out a call,
But Casey Jones, the Engineer, he wouldn't strike at all;
His boiler it was leaking and his drivers on the bum,
And his engine and his bearings, they were all out o' plumb.
  Casey Jones kept his junk pile running,
  Casey Jones was working double time,
  Casey Jones got a wooden medal
  For being good and faithful on the S.P. line.

82

The workers said to Casey: "Won't you help us win the strike?"
But Casey said: "Let me alone, you'd better take a hike."
Then someone put a bunch of railroad ties across the track,
And Casey hit the river with an awful crack.

     Casey Jones hit the river bottom,
     Casey Jones broke his blooming spine,
     Casey Jones was an Angeleno;
     He took a trip to heaven on the S.P. line.

3

When Casey Jones got up to heaven to the pearly gate,
He said: "I'm Casey Jones, the guy that pulled the S.P. freight."
"You're just the man," said Peter, "Our musicians went on strike,
So you'll get a job a-scabbin' any time you like."

     Casey Jones got a job in heaven,
     Casey Jones was doing mighty fine,
     Casey Jones went scabbing on the angels,
     Just like he did the workers on the S.P. line.

4

The angels got together, and they said it wasn't fair
For Casey Jones to go around a-scabbin' everywhere.
The Angels Union, No. 23, they sure "were there,"
And they promptly fired Casey down the golden stair.

     Casey Jones went to hell a-flying,
     "Casey Jones," the Devil said, "Oh, fine!
     Casey Jones, get busy shoveling sulphur;
     That's what you get for scabbing on the S.P. line."

TEXT: IWW (1912a), p. 16.

MUSIC: "The Original Talking Union and Other Union Songs," Pete Seeger and the Almanac Singers, Folkway Record FH 5285. Transcribed by David Cohen. Used by permission of Folkways Records & Service Corp.

VARIANTS: IWW (1912b-1932); Alderson (1942), pp. 373-374; Emrich (1942 e), pp. 292-293; Greenway (1953), p. 186; Stavis and Harmon (1955), pp. 8-10; Fowke and Glazer (1960), p. 43; Kornbluh (1964), pp. 133-134.

SEEING THE ELEPHANT

The gold rush of '49 is full of ironies. It is clear now that the mere presence of those pioneers in the Far West was to be much more significant to the development of America than any metals they washed from the placers, and it readily became clear to them that they would discover a great many things besides gold during their lives in the West. These songs comprise the nicely discriminated varieties of disillusionment suffered by the forty-niners; and their experience with disease, vermin, larceny, women, and politicians must have become familiar to many more persons in the early West than those who crowded the foothills of the Sierra.

The title song, by D. G. Robinson, a New England road-show trouper who opened one of San Francisco's first theaters, expresses the immense disenchantment of one who failed at a little bit of everything on the way from Marysville to the southern mines. John Stone's "Hunting after Gold" and "Prospecting Dream" worsen the picture by showing that it included both high and low estates:

> The first man I saw in Sacramento Valley,
> Was His Honor lying drunk on a ten-pin alley.

> I then took up a little farm, and got a senorita,
> Grey-eyed, hump-backed, and black as tar—her name was Marguerita.

The author of "The Gold Digger's Lament" was probably more fatigued by the work he did on his dismal pun than by any he did at mining:

> I went up to the mines and help'd to turn a stream,
> Got trusted on the strength of that delusive golden dream;
> But when the river we turn'd, we found it would not do,
> And we who damn'd the river, our creditors did sue.

Three songs, the last quite famous, portray the more familiar kind of gold digger. Although there were some attempts, notably by Eliza Farnham, to introduce ladies into the West, John Stone's "California Bloomer" exhibits the probable product of that acclimation:

> Miss Ella is a gallus nag,
> Miss Ella she is neat;
> Her eyes look like a saffron bag,
> And, Lord, what awful feet!

Stone's "California Ball" extravagantly describes one of those well-lubricated functions:

> "Old Alky" makes their bowels yearn,
> They stagger round and fall;
> And ladies say when they return,
> "Oh, what a splendid ball!"

"Joe Bowers," whose gal's baby's hair, like the butcher's, "was inclined to be red," has been ascribed to Mark Twain, Squibob, John Woodward and John Stone, someone named English and an anonymous Missourian in Doniphan's expedition. The question is as moot as the song is ubiquitous, although we have elsewhere cast our lot for Woodward.

"The Lousy Miner," another of Stone's songs which has entered oral tradition, makes food the subject of its complaint. While this miner, like Joe Bowers, left a gal behind who deserted him, he is troubled by his stomach rather than his heart, and most vividly complains that "I've lived on swine till I grunt and squeal." "California As It Is," from the New York music halls of 1849, is a marvelously detailed gritch:

> I was shot, and stabbed, and kicked, and remarkably well licked,
> And compell'd to eat poll parrots which were roasted but not picked,
> And I slept beneath a tent which hadn't got a top,
> With a ragged blanket round me and the ground all of a sop.

Finally, we offer "California Joe," Hector Stuart's parody of a lengthy tearjerker of the same name by Captain Jack Crawford, the poet-scout of the Black Hills of South Dakota. It recounts, to an audience seemingly familiar with it, the story of how the narrator was knocked insane by a lump of gravel at his digs, and how, after being penned up for ten years in Stockton Asylum, he returned home to find his family had all died. Now back in California, he roams the gulches waiting to reach another "golden shore."

D. G. ROBINSON
SEEING THE ELEPHANT
D. D. EMMETT
TUNE: De Boatman Dance

When I left the States for gold, Ev-ery-thing I had I sold: A

stove and bed, a fat old sow, Six - teen chick-ens and a cow.

Chorus

So leave, you min - ers, leave, oh, leave, you min-ers, leave, Take

my ad - vice, kill off your lice, or else go up in the moun-tains;

Oh no, lots of dust, I'm go-ing to the cit - y to get on a "bust."

1
When I left the States for gold,
Everything I had I sold:
A stove and bed, a fat old sow,
Sixteen chickens and a cow.

CHORUS: So leave, you miners, leave, oh,
    leave you miners, leave,
Take my advice, kill off your lice,
    or else go up in the mountains;
Oh no, lots of dust, I'm going to
    the city to get on a "bust."
Oh no, lots of dust, I'm going to
    the city to get on a "bust."

2
Off I started, Yankee-like,
I soon fell in with a lot from Pike;
The next was, "Damn you, back, wo-haw,"
A right smart chance from Arkansaw.

3
On the Platte we couldn't agree,
Because I had the di-a-ree;
We were split up, I made a break,
With one old mule for the Great Salt Lake.

4

The Mormon girls were fat as hogs,
The chief production, cats and dogs;
Some had ten wives, others none,
Thirty-six had Brigham Young.

5

The damn fool, like all the rest,
Supposed the thirty-six the best;
He soon found out his virgin dears
Had all been Mormons thirteen years.

6

Being brave, I cut and carved,
On the desert nearly starved;
My old mule laid down and died,
I had no blanket, took his hide.

7

The poor coyotes stole my meat,
Then I had nought but bread to eat;
It was not long till that gave out,
Then how I cursed the Truckee route!

8

On I traveled through the pines,
At last I found the northern mines;
I stole a dog, got whipt like hell,
Then away I went to Marysville.

9

There I filled the town with lice,
And robbed the Chinese of their rice;
The people say, "You've got the itch,
Leave here, you lousy son of a bitch."

10

Because I would not pay my bill,
They kicked me out of Downieville;
I stole a mule and lost the trail,
And then fetched up in Hangtown Jail.

11

Canvas roof and paper walls,
Twenty horse-thieves in the stalls;
I did as I had done before,
Coyoted out from 'neath the floor.

12

I robbed a nigger of a dollar,
And bought unguent to grease my collar;
I tried a pint, not one had gone,
Then it beat the devil how I daubed it on.

13

The people threatened hard my life,
Because I stole a miner's wife;
They showed me a rope, to give me signs,
Then off I went to the southern mines.

14

I mined a while, got lean and lank,
And lastly stole a monte-bank;
Went to the city, got a gambler's name
And lost my bank at the thimble game.

15

I fell in love with a California girl;
Her eyes were gray, her hair did curl;
Her nose turned up to get rid of her chin—
Says she, "You're a miner, you can't come in."

16

When the elephant I had seen,
I'm damned if I thought I was green;
And others say, both night and morn,
They saw him coming round the Horn.

17

If I should make another raise,
In New York sure I'll spend my days;
I'll be a merchant, buy a saw,
So good-bye, mines and Panama.

TEXT: Stone (1855), pp. 19-21.

MUSIC: Damon (1936).

VARIANTS: Sherwin and Katzman (1932), pp. 27-29; Lengyel (1939), pp. 34-36; Belden (1940), p. 347; Black and Robertson (1940), pp. 50-52; Davidson (1941a), p. 212; Lengyel (1949), pp. 14-15; Dwyer *et al.* (1964), pp. 53-55.

JOHN A. STONE # HUNTING AFTER GOLD

TUNE: Combo

1

When I left old New York, to go hunting after gold,
Chunks bigger than my head I could pick up, I was told;
I stopped at Sacramento, on a devil of expense,
And they sent me to the mountains, where I've not been sober since.

CHORUS: Tang de di, de ding, de dang;
de diddle al de da.

2

The first man I saw in Sacramento Valley,
Was His Honor lying drunk on a ten-pin alley,
With half a dozen more, some whose names I dare not call;
If you'd rolled for the center, you'd been sure to got them all.

3

The people in the mountains, they were all on a bust,
They were going through at Monte, though they pungled down
       the dust.
I went into a temperance house to get a bit segar,
And there laid the landlord drunk behind the bar.

4

I went to eat some oysters, along with Captain Sutter,
And he reared up on the table, and sat down in the butter;
The Mayor and Recorder, they were both drunk as ever,
So the next day they sent me fluming on the river.

5

The river of a sudden, then began to rise,
But the devil was coming, which did me surprise;
'Twas a big pine log, coming neat as a pin,
Which stove both ends of my long tom in.

6

I looked up the river, and the next thing I saw
Was a rocker and a pail floating down towards me,
And when they got abreast of me, says I,
"Old rocker, you've earned me a pile, good bye."

7

It seemed too bad, 'twas a devil of a shame,
To work all summer, and then to lose a claim,
With a bully little pick, and a long handled shovel,
And a chance for a flume left to go to the devil.

8

So those that had money, they were bound to have a spree,
But they that hadn't any, said, "You can't fool me;
We know where you're going, or at least we mistrust,
You are going to Nevada, to get on another 'bust.'"

9

I bucked awhile at Monte, at a half dollar bank,
And the dealer he got trusted for the whisky that I drank;
I drank till my throat got so sore I couldn't swallow,
So I tapp'd him on the Jack, and I won half a dollar.

10

I haven't had a cent since I failed on the river,
Nor I haven't had clothes enough my nakedness to cover;
These breeches I got trusted for, but now I cannot pay;
This is the only shirt I've had since the 23d of May.

11

My hair pulled like the devil, I was troubled with the shorts,
So, without a cent of money, I went hunting after quartz;
And I found as rich a lead as ever had been seen,
But the devil of it was, I had no machine.

12

The people were surprised; when we told them, how they laughed,
That a dozen of our company had gone to sink a shaft,
And we'd all make a pile, around the Horn have a sail,
When the Sheriff took the dozen who were digging off to jail.

13

The stories they were going, going very fast indeed,
And the miners going faster, to stake off the lead;
Among the rest a-coming that was going to make a strike,
On a spike-tail mule, was a man from Pike.

14

The excitement died away; there was nothing in the lead,
So those that bought an interest, among themselves agreed,
For the flour they had bought, and a little gnarly ham,
They would never pay a cent, for the lead warn't worth a damn.

TEXT: Stone (1855), pp. 23-25.

VARIANTS: Grant (1924), pp. 118-120; Sherwin and Katzman (1932), pp. 20-21; Dwyer *et al.* (1964), pp. 60-61.

THE GOLD DIGGER'S LAMENT

TUNE: Jeanette and Jeanot

1

I am going far away from my creditors just now,
I ain't got the tin to pay 'em, and they're kicking up a row;
There's the sheriff running after me with pockets full of writs,
And my tailor's vowing vengeance, he swears he'll give me fits.
There's no room for speculation, and the mines ain't worth a flam,
And I ain't one of those lucky coves that works for Uncle Sam;
Whichever way I turn, I am sure to meet a dun,
"So I think the best thing I can do is just to cut and run."

2

I wish those "tarnal critters" that wrote home about the gold
Was in the place the Scriptures say is never very cold:
They told you of the heaps of dust and lumps so very big,
But they never said a single word how hard you had to dig.
I went up to the mines and help'd to turn a stream,
Got trusted on the strength of that delusive golden dream;
But when the river we turn'd, we found it would not do,
And we who damn'd the river, our creditors did sue.

3

I am going far away, but I don't know where I'll go;
'Twont do to turn homeward now, they'd laugh at me I know,
For I told them when I left I was going to make my pile,
But if they could only see mine now I rather guess they'd smile.
If of these United States I was the President,
No man who owed another should ever pay a cent;
And he who dunn'd another should be banish'd far away,
For attention to the pretty girls is all a man should pay.

TEXT: "The Gold-Digger's Lament" (New York: J. Wrigley, n.d. [broadside]).

VARIANTS: George Hunter, *Reminiscences of an Old Timer* (4th ed.; Battle Creek, Mich.: Review & Herald, 1889), p. 57.

JOHN A. STONE PROSPECTING DREAM S. C. FOSTER

TUNE: Oh! Susannah

I dreamed a dream the oth-er night, when ev-ery-thing was still, I dreamed that I was car-ry-ing my long-tom down a hill; My feet slipp'd out and I fell down, oh, how I jarr'd my liv-er, I watched my long-tom till I saw it fetch up in the riv-er. Oh, what a min-er, what a min-er was I, All swelled up with the scur—vy, so I real-ly thought I'd die.

1
I dreamed a dream the other night, when everything was still,
I dreamed that I was carrying my longtom down a hill;
My feet slipp'd out and I fell down, oh, how I jarr'd my liver,
I watched my longtom till I saw it fetch up in the river.

CHORUS: Oh, what a miner, what a miner was I,
All swelled up with the scurvy, so I really thought I'd die.

2
My matches, flour, and chili beans, lay scattered all around,
I felt so bad I wished to die, as I lay on the ground;
My coffee rolled down by a rock, my pepper I could not find,
'Twas then I thought of Angeline, the girl I left behind.

3

I took my shovel, pick and pan, to try a piece of ground,
I dream'd I struck the richest lead that ever had been found;
Then I wrote home that I had found a solid lead of gold,
And I'd be home in just a month, but what a lie I told!

4

I dug, I panned and tommed awhile, till I had but a dollar,
I struck it here, and right down there, I could not raise the color;
John Chinaman he bought me out, and pungled down the dust,
Then I had just an ounce in change to start out on a "bust."

5

I went to town and got drunk; in the morning, to my surprise,
I found that I had got a pair of roaring big black eyes,
And I was strapp'd, had not a cent, not even pick or shovel,
My hair snarled up, my breeches torn, looked like the very devil.

6

I then took up a little farm, and got a senorita,
Grey-eyed, hump-backed, and black as tar—her name was Marguerita,
My pigs all died, hens flew away, Joaquin he stole my mules,
My ranch burnt "down," my blankets "up," likewise my farming tools.

7

I left my farm, and hired out to be a hardware clerk,
I got kicked out, "cos" couldn't write, so again I went to work;
But when they caught me stealing grub, a few went in to boot him,
And others round were singing out, "Hang him, hang him, shoot him!"

TEXT: Stone (1855), pp. 11-12.

MUSIC: Turner *et al.* (1858), p. 18.

VARIANTS: Grant (1924), pp. 114-115; Sherwin and Katzman (1932), pp. 34-35; E Clampus Vitus (1939), p. 11; Lengyel (1939), pp. 52-53; Black and Robertson (1940), pp. 42-43; Lengyel (1949), pp. 18-19; Dwyer *et al.* (1964), pp. 74-75.

JOHN A. STONE # CALIFORNIA BALL G. P. KNAUFF

TUNE: Wait for the Wagon

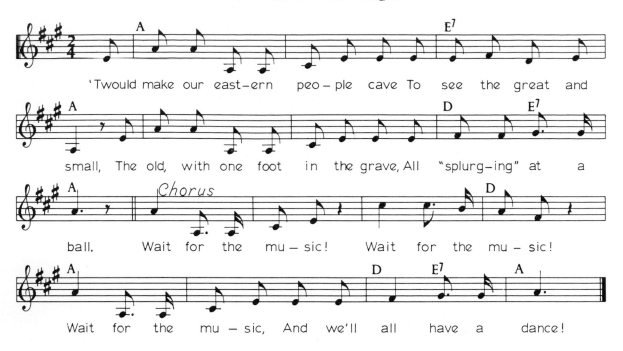

'Twould make our east-ern peo-ple cave To see the great and small, The old, with one foot in the grave, All "splurg-ing" at a ball.

Chorus

Wait for the mu-sic! Wait for the mu-sic! Wait for the mu-sic, And we'll all have a dance!

1

'Twould make our eastern people cave
To see the great and small,
The old, with one foot in the grave,
All "splurging" at a ball.

CHORUS: Wait for the music!
Wait for the music!
Wait for the music,
And we'll all have a dance!

2

On foot they through the diggings wind,
And over mountains tall,
With young ones tagging on behind,
"Flat-footed" for the ball!

3

A dozen babies on the bed,
And all begin to squall;
The mothers wish the brats were dead,
For crying at the ball!

4

The manager begins to curse,
And swaggers through the hall,
For mothers they've gone out to nurse
Their babies at the ball!

94

5

Old women in their Bloomer rigs
    Are fond of "balance all!"
And "weighty" when it comes to jigs,
    And so on, at the ball!

6

A yearling miss fills out the sett,
    Although not very tall;
"I'm anxious now," she says, "you bet,
    To proceed with the ball!"

7

A married woman—gentle dove—
    With nary tooth at all,
Sits in the corner making love
    To some "pimp" at the ball!

8

A drunken loafer at the dance
    Informs them one and all,
With bowie knife stuck in his pants,
    "The best man at the ball!"

9

The Spanish hags of ill repute
    For brandy loudly call,
And no one dares their right dispute
    To freedom at the ball!

10

The gambler all the money wins,
    To bed the drunkest crawl;
And fighting then of course begins
    With rowdies at the ball!

11

They rush it like a rail-road car;
    And often is the call
Of, "Promenade up to the bar,"
    For whisky at the ball!

12

"Old Alky" makes their bowels yearn,
    They stagger round and fall;
And ladies say when they return,
    "Oh, what a splendid ball!"

TEXT: Stone (1858a), pp. 13-15.

MUSIC: *The Violin Primer* (ca. 1850), p. 28.

VARIANTS: Stone (1858b), pp. 21-22; *Los Angeles Star*, April 7, 1860; Grant (1924), pp. 156-157; Sherwin and Katzman (1932), pp. 6-7; Lengyel (1939), pp. 50-51; Black and Robertson (1940), pp. 30-31; Lengyel (1949), pp. 43-44; Dwyer *et al.* (1964), pp. 127-128.

JOHN WOODWARD # JOE BOWERS J. E. JOHNSON

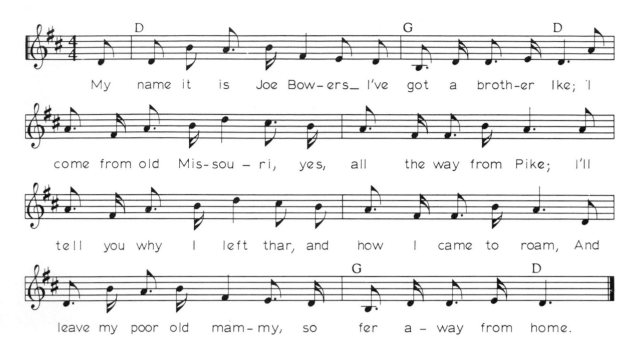

My name it is Joe Bow-ers_ I've got a broth-er Ike; I
come from old Mis-sou – ri, yes, all the way from Pike; I'll
tell you why I left thar, and how I came to roam, And
leave my poor old mam-my, so fer a – way from home.

1

My name it is Joe Bowers, I've got a brother Ike;
I come from old Missouri, yes, all the way from Pike;
I'll tell you why I left thar, and how I came to roam,
And leave my poor old mammy, so fer away from home.

2

I used to love a gal thar, they call'd her Sally Black;
I axed her for to marry me, she said it was a whack;
"But," says she to me, "Joe Bowers, before we hitch for life,
You'd orter have a little home to keep your little wife."

3

Says I, "My dearest Sally, oh! Sally, for your sake,
I'll go to Californy, and try to raise a stake."
Says she to me, "Joe Bowers, oh, you're the chap to win,
Guv me a buss to seal the bargain," and she threw a dozen in!

4

I shall ne'er forgit my feelins when I bid adieu to all;
Sally cotched me round the neck, then I began to bawl;
When I sot in, they all commenced—you ne'er did hear the like,
How they all took on and cried, the day I left old Pike.

5

When I got to this 'ere country, I hadn't nary red,
I had sich wolfish feelings, I wish'd myself most dead;
But the thoughts of my dear Sally soon made these feelins git,
And whispered hopes to Bowers—Lord, I wish I had 'em yit!

6

At length I went to minin', put in my biggest licks,
Come down upon the boulders jist like a thousand bricks;
I worked both late and airly, in rain, and sun, and snow,
But I was working for my Sally, so 'twas all the same to Joe.

7

I made a very lucky strike, as the gold itself did tell,
And saved it for my Sally, the gal I loved so well;
I saved it for my Sally, that I might pour it at her feet,
That she might kiss and hug me, and call me something sweet.

8

But one day I got a letter from my dear, kind brother, Ike—
It come from old Missouri, sent all the way from Pike;
It brought me the gol-darn'dest news as ever you did hear—
My heart is almost bustin', so, pray, excuse this tear.

9

It said my Sal was fickle, that her love for me had fled;
That she'd married with a butcher, whose *har* was orful red!
It told me more than that—oh! it's enough to make one swar,
It said Sally had a baby, and the baby had red *har!*

10

Now, I've told you all I could tell about this sad affar,
'Bout Sally marryin' the butcher, and the butcher had red *har*.
Whether 'twas a boy or gal child, the letter never said,
It only said its cussed *har* was inclined to be a *red!*

TEXT: Johnson (1858), pp. 45-46.

MUSIC: J. T. Hughes, *Doniphan's Expedition* (Topeka, Kans.: Connelley, 1907), p. 10.

VARIANTS: Allan (1874), pp. 36-37; Lomax (1910), pp. 15-17; Pound (1915), pp. 32-33, and (1922), pp. 186-188; Dean (1922), pp. 98-99; Grant (1924), pp. 34-36; Drury (1931); Lomax and Lomax (1934), pp. 421-423, and (1938), pp. 375-377; Pound (1937), pp. 13-15; E Clampus Vitus (1939), p. 12; Lengyel (1939), pp. 37-38; Belden (1940), pp. 341-343*; Black and Robertson (1940), pp. 22-23; McMullen (1946), p. 140; Randolph (1948), pp. 191-195*; Lengyel (1949), pp. 23-25; Owens (1950), pp. 107-109; Botkin (1951), pp. 736-737; Pound (1957), pp. 111-120*; Lomax (1960), pp. 336-338; Hubbard (1961), pp. 302-303; Dwyer *et al.* (1964), pp. 56-57; Moore and Moore (1964), pp. 323-325; Laws (1964), pp. 139-140*.

JOHN A. STONE

THE LOUSY MINER

TUNE: Dark-eyed Sailor

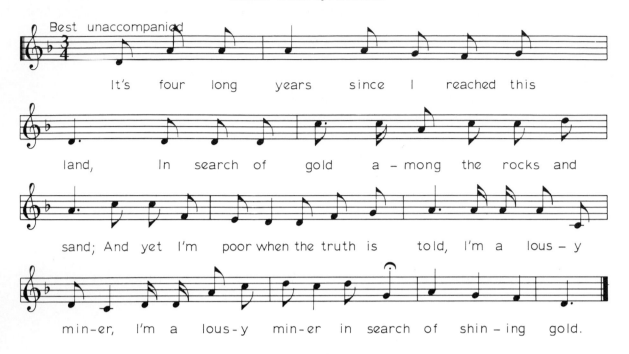

It's four long years since I reached this land, In search of gold a-mong the rocks and sand; And yet I'm poor when the truth is told, I'm a lous-y min-er, I'm a lous-y min-er in search of shin-ing gold.

1

It's four long years since I reached this land,
In search of gold among the rocks and sand;
    And yet I'm poor when the truth is told.
        I'm a lousy miner,
    I'm a lousy miner in search of shining gold.

2

I've lived on swine till I grunt and squeal,
No one can tell how my bowels feel,
    With slapjacks swimming round in bacon grease.
        I'm a lousy miner,
    I'm a lousy miner; when will my troubles cease?

3

I was covered with lice coming on the boat,
I threw away my fancy swallow-tailed coat,
    And now they crawl up and down my back;
        I'm a lousy miner,
    I'm a lousy miner, a pile is all I lack.

4

My sweetheart vowed she'd wait for me
Till I returned; but don't you see
    She's married now, sure, so I am told,
        Left her lousy miner,
    Left her lousy miner, in search of shining gold.

5

Oh, land of gold, you did me deceive,
And I intend in thee my bones to leave;
So farewell, home, now my friends grow cold.
I'm a lousy miner,
I'm a lousy miner in search of shining gold.

TEXT: Stone (1855), p. 48.

MUSIC: Flander *et al.*, (1939), p. 36. Used by permission of Helen Hartness Flanders.

VARIANTS: Grant (1924), pp. 122-123; Sandburg (1927), p. 107; Sherwin and Katzman (1932), pp. 14-15; E Clampus Vitus (1939), p. 23, Lengyel (1939), p. 56; Black and Robertson (1940), pp. 24-25; Botkin (1944), p. 863; Lomax (1960), p. 338; Dwyer *et al.* (1964), p. 155.

THADDEUS W. MEIGHAN

CALIFORNIA AS IT IS

TUNE: Jeanette and Jeanot

I've been to Cal - i - for-nia and I have-n't got a
dime; I've lost my health, my strength,my hope, and
I have lost my time, I've on - ly got a
spade and pick; and if I felt quite brave, I'd
use the two of them 'ere things to scoop me out a
grave. This— dig - ging hard for gold may be
pol - i - tic and bold, But you could not make me
think so; but you may if you are told. Oh! I've
been to Cal - i - for-nia, and I'm mi - nus all the

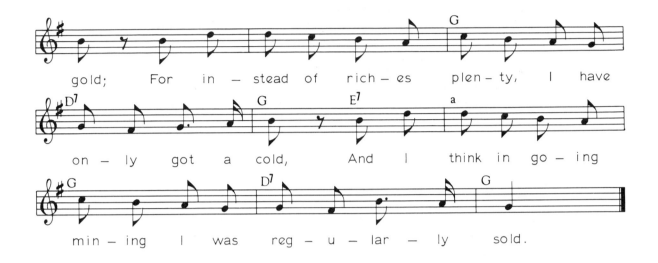

gold; For in — stead of rich — es plen — ty, I have on — ly got a cold, And I think in go — ing min — ing I was reg — u — lar — ly sold.

1

I've been to California and I haven't got a dime;
> I've lost my health, my strength, my hope, and I have lost my time.
I've only got a spade and pick; and if I felt quite brave,
> I'd use the two of them 'ere things to scoop me out a grave.
This digging hard for gold may be politic and bold,
> But you could not make *me* think so; but *you* may if you are told.
Oh! I've been to California, and I'm minus all the gold;
> For instead of riches plenty, I have only got a cold,
> > And I think in going mining I was regularly sold.

2

I left this precious city with two suits of gallus rig;
> My boots though India-rubber, were sufficiently big
For to keep the water out, as well as alligators,
> And I tell you now my other traps were very small potatoes.
I had a great machine, the greatest ever seen
> To wash the sands of value and to get the gold out clean,
And I had a fancy knapsack fill'd with sausages and ham,
> And of California diggers, I went out "the great I am,"
> > But I found the expedition was a most confounded flam.

3

Now only listen to me, and I'll tell you in a trice
> That poking in the dirt for gold ain't more than very nice;
You're starved, stewed, and frozen, and the strongest man he says he's
> Bound to have your money or he'll wallup you like blazes.
I was shot, and stabbed, and kicked, and remarkably well licked,
> And compell'd to eat poll parrots which were roasted but not picked,
And I slept beneath a tent which hadn't got a top,
> With a ragged blanket round me and the ground all of a sop.
> > And for all this horrid suffering, I haven't got a *cop!*

4

So here I am without a home, without a cent to spend,
  No toggery, no wittles, and not a single friend;
With lizards, parrots, spiders, snakes, and other things unclean,
  All crowded in my stomach, and I'm very weak and lean.
But I ain't the only one that's got tired of this 'ere fun,
  For about a dozen thousand chaps are ready now to run
As hard as they can possibly, from there to kingdom come,
  For there they ain't nobody, sir, but here they might be *some,*
    And enjoy their cakes and coffee and now and then some *rum.*

5

MORAL

If you've enough to eat and drink and buy your Sunday clothes,
  Don't listen to the gammon that from California blows;
But stay at home and thank your stars for every hard-earned cent,
  And if the greenhorns go to dig, why cooly let 'em went.
If you go, why you will see the *elephant,* yes siree,
  And some little grains of gold that are no bigger than a flea;
I've just come from California, and if any here there be
  Who is got that yellow fever, they need only look at me,
    And I think New York will suit 'em, yes, exactly to a T.

———————

TEXT AND MUSIC: Thaddeus W. Meighan, "California As It Is" (New York: Wm. Hall & Son, 1849).

VARIANT: *The Pioneer* (San Jose, Calif.), Nov. 17, 1877.

JOHN A. STONE   # CALIFORNIA BLOOMER   W. WHITLOCK

TUNE: Lucy Long

Miss El — la she is twen-ty- nine, Has tak-en two' de-

grees, And tore her shirt-tail off be-hind, So she can show her

Chorus

knees.   So   take your time, Miss El - la,   take your time, Miss El - la,

do,   And   I will rock the cra-dle, give the or - o all to you.

1
Miss Ella she is twenty-nine,
    Has taken two degrees,
And tore her shirt tail off behind,
    So she can show her knees.

CHORUS: So take your time, Miss Ella, take
    your time, Miss Ella, do,
And I will rock the cradle, give the
    oro all to you.

2
Miss Ella is a gallus nag,
    Miss Ella she is neat;
Her eyes look like a saffron bag,
    And, Lord, what awful feet;

3
I saw Miss Ella on the Platte
    Where she got alkalied;
Her jackass he was rolling fat,
    And straddle she would ride.

4
She's from Lumpkin County, Georgia,
    I know her like a book;
I used to see her wash her feet
    In Johnson's saw-mill brook.

5
Miss Ella has a claim, they say,
    She works it all the while;
She creviced round the other day,
    Panned out a little pile.

6
She'll get it all after awhile,
    If patiently she waits;
I'll leave her when I make a pile,
    And vamose for the States.

TEXT: Stone (1855), p. 34.

MUSIC: Damon (1936).

VARIANTS: Grant (1924), pp. 159-160; E Clampus Vitus (1939), p. 10; Black and Robertson (1940), pp. 36-37; Dwyer *et al.* (1964), p. 125.

HECTOR A. STUART # CALIFORNIA JOE

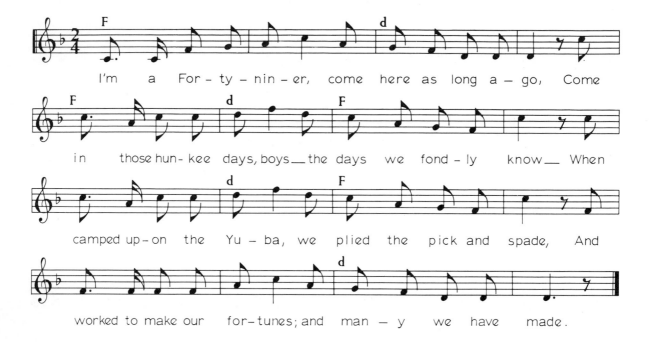

I'm a For-ty-nin-er, come here as long a-go, Come
in those hun-kee days, boys—the days we fond-ly know— When
camped up-on the Yu-ba, we plied the pick and spade, And
worked to make our for-tunes; and man—y we have made.

1
I am a Forty-niner, come here as long ago,
Come in those hunkee days, boys—the days we fondly know—
When camped upon the Yuba, we plied the pick and spade,
And worked to make our fortunes; and many we have made.

2
I left my home one noontime in the Green Mountain State,
To seek the Golden Land, boys, with youth and hope elate;
I crossed the plains in safety, and with my good ox team,
Wo-hawed upon the Yuba, that famous mining stream.

3
I struck the diggins richly—I yanked a heap of dust—
No man than I worked harder, I warn't the blade to rust;
I worked as you all know, pards, to gain a hefty pile
To give my pretty babies and keep the folks in style.

4
But time crawled on and often—yes, nearly every mail—
Wife asked me to come back soon, as maw began to fail;
As gran-paw, too, was going, was weaker than afore—
But I still kept a-digging—still wished a little more.

5
At last I thought I'd travel—pulled up my cabin stakes,
Took all the dust I'd gathered for my dear babies' sakes;
But as I cleaned the riffle, there came a sudden cave,
And I was quickly buried as if within a grave.

6

You know what followed then pards—know more than I can
    tell—
Know how on this poor gray-head the lump of gravel fell,
How long I lay a-suffering, and how I went insane;
And ten long years in Stockton was forced to wear a chain.

7

You know the hull sad story—know all that since occurred,
When first from that dark prison the voice of friends I heard;
And shaking off my fetters, went to Varmount again
To see if still alive thar my babies did remain.

8

Forgive these salty drops, pards, this heart is full of woe;
You can't tell how I suffer—I hope will never know—
Will never feel the anguish that fell my soul upon
When I found all my loved ones had to the churchyard gone.

9

I saw whar they were buried—saw whar gran-paw was laid,
Whar my dear mother rested, beneath a maple's shade;
Saw whar my lovely babies slept in their little graves
Nigh whar above my wife's head a weeping-willow waves.

10

And now I'm back again, pards, in California; here
I roam the lonely gulches—a crazy man appear;
But I am only waiting to reach the other shore,
To meet the ones departed, where sorrow is no more.

TEXT: *The Pioneer* (San Jose, Calif.), June 16, 1877.

MUSIC: Larkin (1931), pp. 134-135. Used by permission of Alfred A. Knopf, Inc.

WHEN I WENT OFF TO PROSPECT

In the years after the California gold rush, a milling body of impoverished prospectors began to press into the less hospitable interior of the continent in search of shining gold. Ultimately, they opened all the land from the Sierra to the Rockies and from Mexico to the Klondike, but the musical chronicle of their progress given here shows that it was tough going. Life in the boom camps seems to get worse and worse as we move from lice-infested Sutter's Mill to the sub-zero rigors of Dawson. Stone's "When I Went Off To Prospect" depicts the teeming camps of Michigan Bluff and Iowa Hill and rightly demonstrates that more money was to be made in them than in the mines:

> And now I'm loafing around dead broke,
> My pistol and tools are all in soak,
> And whisky bills at me they poke—
> But I'll make it right in the morning.

There are not many memorable prospectors, but at Placerville—nee Hangtown—Mark Hopkins peddled groceries, Philip Armour had a butcher shop, and John Studebaker made wheelbarrows, and just up the American River at Michigan Bluff, Leland Stanford kept a store. Consequently, when gold was struck in placers near Pike's Peak in 1858, and at the same time silver turned up in fabulous quantities in Nevada's Comstock, slightly wiser "miners" dealt more in paper speculation, leaving the digging to the big companies. Here, three songs commemorate the Pike's Peak rush. "Cherry Creek Emigrant's Song," like many of the prospectors themselves, was made over from the rush of '49. It is an adaptation of Jesse Hutchinson's "Ho! For California!" "A Hit at the Times," written by A. O. McGrew for a Christmas fest near Denver in 1858, is a much closer look at the actualities of the Colorado scene:

> Speculation is the fashion, even at this early stage,
> And corner lots and big hotels appear to be the rage;
> The emigration's bound to come, and to greet them we will try.
> Big pig, little pig, root hog, or die.

"In the Summer of Sixty," collected by Louise Pound, is a vision of the elephant in the Rockies. Its narrator tries everything—gambling mostly—and ends up going down the Platte for death or for life.

In the early 1860's gold was discovered along the Snake River and its tributaries. the Clearwater and the Salmon rivers, in Idaho. The song "A Trip to Salmon," written by returned miner Max Irwin, records, to the tune of "Jordan Is a Hard Road To Trabel," the difficulties of even getting there. It still survives in the Willamette Valley, once part of the route there. "Idaho," written from the perspective of Chicago by Frank French in 1864, retains the enthusiasm of one who only contemplates the trip. This song, too, is extant, but in the Ozarks it praises Arkansas.

The gold rush to the Black Hills of South Dakota in 1876 led to a temporary stalemate in the battle between General George Crook and Crazy Horse at Slim Buttes; to the opening wide of Deadwood, where Wild Bill Hickok held his aces and eights; and to the western hemisphere's largest gold mine, the Homestake, a small investment of George Hearst's which paid many millions in bullion. Dick Brown, the composer of "The Dreary Black Hills," sampled only the first of these fruits. "A Trip to Rapid River" alludes to one of those obscure but numerous diggings, unassociated with any great lode, at which loners hoped to strike it rich. This one, located in 1892, is on a short tributary of the middle fork of the Salmon in central Idaho.

Barney Riley's "San Juan," written at the turn of the century, records a progress from the rich heights of Creede and Cripple Creek down to the arid valley of the San Juan River, a stream three-quarters silt by volume. His imagery is hallucinatory:

> By the skin of our scattered teeth,
> We hung to the thread of life;
> Like a livid beam from a deadly gleam
> Were those terrible days of strife.

Finally, a song about one of America's last and most hazardous mineral frontiers, the Yukon, which experienced its own '49 in '98. "Just from Dawson" compounds the accounts of the miseries of the earlier tales. Even the merchants gouged better, since the Canadian Mounties would not let anyone enter the Yukon who did not carry a year's supply of food—some 1,200 pounds. The dying miner advises:

> "Tell the fellows in the homeland to remain and have a cinch,
> That the price of patent pork chops here is 80 cents an inch."

JOHN A. STONE

WHEN I WENT OFF TO PROSPECT

J. BROUGHAM

TUNE: King of the Cannibal Islands

1

I heard of gold at Sutter's Mill,
At Michigan Bluff and Iowa Hill,
But never thought it was rich until
I started off to prospect.
At Yankee Jim's I bought a purse,
Inquired for Iowa Hill, of course,
And traveled on, but what was worse,
Fetched up in Shirttail Canon.

CHORUS: A sicker miner every way
Had not been seen for many a day;
The devil it always was to pay,
When I went off to prospect.

2

When I got there, the mining ground
Was staked and claimed for miles around,
And not a bed was to be found,
When I went off to prospect.
The town was crowded full of folks,
Which made me think 'twas not a hoax;
At my expense they cracked their jokes,
When I went off to prospect.

3

I left my jackass on the road,
Because he wouldn't carry the load;
I'd sooner pick a big horn toad,
When I went off to prospect.
My fancy shirt, with collar so nice,
I found was covered with body-lice;
I used unguentum once or twice,
But could not kill the grey-backs.

4

At Deadwood I got on a tight—
At Groundhog Glory I had a fight;
They drove me away from Hell's Delight,
When I went off to prospect.
From Bogus-Thunder I ran away—
At Devil's Basin I wouldn't stay;
My lousy shirt crawled off one day,
Which left me nearly naked.

5

Now all I got for running about,
Was two black eyes, and a bloody snout;
And that's the way it did turn out,
When I went off to prospect.
And now I'm loafing around dead broke,
My pistol and tools are all in soak,
And whisky bills at me they poke—
But I'll make it right in the morning.

———————————

TEXT: Stone (1855), pp. 46-47.

MUSIC: Vernon (1927), pp. 156-157.

VARIANTS: Grant (1924), pp. 116-118; Black and Robertson (1940), pp. 26-27; Lengyel
(1949), p. 21; Dwyer *et al.* (1964), pp. 71-72.

BARNEY RILEY # SAN JUAN

1

I located a claim in Creede,
 And my title did not stick:
I sold my traps to some Eastern chaps,
 And I got to Cripple Creek.
I was doing fairly well,
 For an unprofessional man,
Till I heard of the luck that had been struck
 'Way out in the San Juan.

2

'Twas enough to unsettle a man,
 Or rather unsettle his mind,
So I sold my stake and made a break
 For that wonderful placer find.
In the rush that was heading there,
 I was squarely in the run;
There was joy in store and fun galore
 On the way to the San Juan.

3

We went by the Rio Grande
 And outfitted at Dolores;
Our grub was sacked and our mules were
  packed
 With a good supply of stores.
We footed it up the road,
 As a prospector only can;
We pushed ahead and was damn near dead,
 Going up to the San Juan.

4

There was miles and miles of rock
 And a waste of barren sand,
But never a trace of gold in place
 In that God-forsaken land.
Our scattered hopes had fled,
 And every well laid plan
Had melted away in a single day,
 While there in the San Juan.

5

We struck the homeward trail
 With many a bitter sigh,
And the coyotes flew, for well they knew
 There was blood in the miner's eye.
There were redskins on the way,
 But a greater danger than
A Navajo's hand we had to stand
 Coming home from the San Juan.

6

By the skin of our scattered teeth,
 We hung to the thread of life;
Like a livid beam from a deadly gleam
 Were those terrible days of strife.
Home we find the old boys,
 Trot around with that beer when you
  can;
I'm as dry as a fish, and from my heart I wish
 Good luck to the San Juan.

TEXT: *Miners' Magazine* (Denver), Aug., 1901, pp. 15-16.

III

CHERRY CREEK EMIGRANT'S SONG

D. D. EMMETT

TUNE: De Boatman Dance

We ex—pect hard times, we ex—pect hard fare, Some-times sleep in the o—pen air; We'll lay on the ground and sleep ver—y sound, Ex—cept when In—dians are howl—ing a—round. Then ho boys ho, to Cher-ry Creek we'll go. There's plen-ty of gold in the West, we are told, In the new El—dor—a—do.

1
We expect hard times, we expect hard fare,
Sometimes sleep in the open air;
We'll lay on the ground and sleep very sound,
Except when Indians are howling around.

CHORUS: Then ho boys ho, to Cherry Creek we'll go.
There's plenty of gold
In the West, we are told,
In the new Eldorado.

2
We'll rock our cradles around Pike's Peak
In search of the dust, and for nuggets seek;
If the Indians ask us why we are there,
We'll tell them we're made as free as the air.

3
The gold is there, 'most anywhere.
You can take it out rich with an iron crowbar,
And where it is thick, with a shovel and pick
You can pick it out in lumps as big as a brick.

4

At Cherry Creek if the dirt don't pay,
    We can strike our tents most any day.
We know we are bound to strike a streak
    Of very rich quartz among the mountain peaks.

5

Oh dear girls, now don't you cry,
    We are coming back by and by;
Don't you fret nor shed a tear,
    Be patient wait about one year.

———

TEXT: *Rocky Mountain News* (Denver), June 18, 1859.

MUSIC: Damon (1936).

VARIANTS: Davidson (1943), p. 96.

A. O. McGrew

A HIT AT THE TIMES

TUNE: Root Hog, or Die

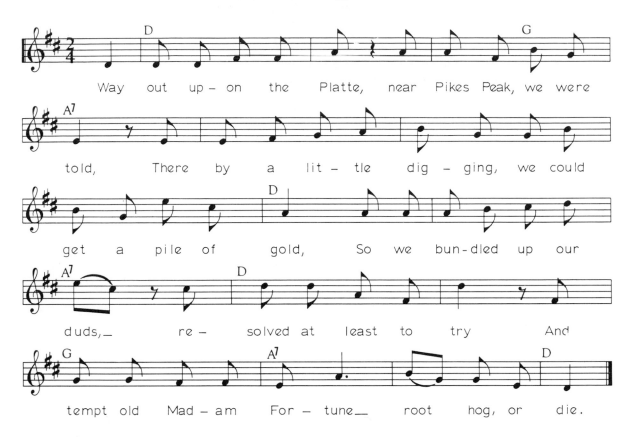

Way out up-on the Platte, near Pikes Peak, we were told, There by a lit-tle dig-ging, we could get a pile of gold, So we bun-dled up our duds,__ re-solved at least to try And tempt old Mad-am For-tune__ root hog, or die.

1
Way out upon the Platte, near Pikes Peak, we were told,
There by a little digging, we could get a pile of gold,
So we bundled up our duds, resolved at least to try
And tempt old Madam Fortune—root hog, or die.

2
So we traveled across the country, and we got upon the ground,
But cold weather was ahead, the first thing we found.
We built our shanties on the ground, resolved in spring to try,
To gather up the dust and slugs—root hog, or die.

3
Speculation is the fashion, even at this early stage,
And corner lots and big hotels appear to be the rage;
The emigration's bound to come, and to greet them we will try.
Big pig, little pig, root hog, or die.

4
Let shouts resound, the cup pass 'round, we all came for gold,
The politicians are all gas, the speculators sold,
The "scads" are all we want, and to get them we will try.
Big pig, little pig, root hog, or die.

5

Surveyors now are at their work, laying off the towns,
And some will be of low degree, and some of high renown.
They don't care a jot nor tittle who do buy
The corner lots, or any lots—root hog, or die.

6

The doctors are among us, you can find them where you will,
They say their trade it is to cure, I say it is to kill.
They'll dose you, and they'll physic you, until they make you sigh,
And their powders and their lotions make you root hog, or die.

7

The next in turn comes lawyers, a precious set are they;
In the public dairy they drink the milk, their clients drink the whey.
A cunning set these fellows are; they'll sap you 'til you're dry,
And never leave you 'til you have to root hog, or die.

8

A preacher now is all we want, to make us all do good;
But at present, there's no lack of *spiritual* food.
The kind I refer to, will make you laugh or cry,
And its real name is Taos—root hog, or die.

9

I have finished now my song, or, if you please, my ditty;
And that it was not shorter, is about the only pity.
And now, that I have had my say, don't say I've told a lie;
For the subject I've touched will make us root hog, or die.

TEXT: *Omaha Times*, Feb. 17, 1859.
MUSIC: *Minstrel Songs, Old and New* (1882), pp. 100-101.
VARIANTS: Davidson (1943), p. 92, and (1951), pp. 16-17.

IN THE SUMMER OF SIXTY

1

In the summer of sixty, as you very well know,
The excitement at Pike's Peak was then all the go;
Many went there with fortunes and spent what they had
And came back flat-busted and looking quite sad.

2

'Twas then I heard farming was a very fine branch,
So I spent most of my money in buying a ranch;
And when I got to it, with sorrow and shame,
I found a big miner had jumped my fine claim.

3

So I bought a revolver and swore I'd lay low
The very next fellow that treated me so;
I then went to Denver and cut quite a dash
And took extra pains to show off my cash.

4

With a fine span of horses, my wife by my side,
I drove through the streets with my hat on one side;
As we were a-goin' past the old "Denver Hall,"
Sweet music came out that did charm us all.

5

Says I, "Let's go in and see what's the muss,
For I feel right now like having a fuss."
There were tables strung over the hall,
Some was a-whirling a wheel with a ball.

6

Some playin' cards and some shakin' dice
And lots of half dollars that looked very nice;
I finally strayed to a table at last
Where all the poor suckers did seem to stick fast.

7

And there stood a man with cards in his hand,
And these were the words which he did command,
"Now, gents, the winning card is the ace,
I guess you will know it if I show you its face."

8

One corner turned down, it's plain to be seen,
I looked at that fellow and thought he was green,
Yes I looked at that feller and thought he was green,
One corner turned down, 'twas so plain to be seen.

9

So I bet all my money and lo and behold
'Twas a trey spot of clubs and he took all my gold.
Then I went home and crawled into bed
And the devil a word to my wife ever said.

10

'Twas early next morning I felt for my purse
Biting my lips to keep down a curse;
Yes, 'twas early next morning as the sun did rise
You might have seen with your two blessed eyes,

11

In an ox wagon, 'twas me and my wife
Goin' down the Platte river for death or for life.

TEXT: Pound (1915), pp. 23-24.

VARIANTS: Pound (1922), pp. 189-190; Lomax and Lomax (1938), pp. 386-387; Davidson (1951), pp. 18-19; Koch and Koch (1961), pp. 15-16.

A TRIP TO SALMON

MAX IRWIN   D. D. EMMETT

Tune: Jordan Is a Hard Road To Trabel

(Lyrics under the music:)

I looked to the North and I looked to the South, And I

saw the Cal-i-for-nians a-com-ing With their picks and

pans and shov-els on their backs. They were trav-el-ing their

way up to Sal-mon. *Chorus* Then save your mon-ey boys to

pay your way thro, Two to one on Sal-mon a-

gainst Car-i-boo; Don't be too has-ty and get in-to a

fe-ver, For you'll all make a for-tune up in Sal-mon Riv-er.

1

I looked to the North and I looked to the South,
    And I saw the Californians a-coming
With their picks and pans and shovels on their backs.
    They were traveling their way up the Salmon.

CHORUS: Then save your money boys to pay your way thro',
    Two to one on Salmon against Cariboo,
Don't be too hasty and get into a fever,
    For you'll all make a fortune up in Salmon River.

2

We left California with a hundred pound pack,
 And rested on the Siskiyou Mountains;
We took a drink of red eye and started on the track,
 For its a hard road to travel up to Salmon.

3

We traveled through Rogue River all complete,
 Till we got away out to the Canyon,
When the Umpqua country stuck to our feet,
 But we shook it off on the Callapoola Mountains.

4

We camped that night and all climbed a tree
 To look for the land of promise,
But away to the North as far as we could see,
 There was nothing but the river Long Thomas.

5

I asked a Long Tom man to loan me a hoss,
 I will return him again next Summer,
"By the flood already I have suffered great loss,
 So you had better git, you California bummer."

6

We called a miners' meeting right on the spot,
 For President we elected old Higgins,
We agreed one and all to fill our pockets full of rocks
 And foot it to the Salmon River Diggings.

TEXT: *Los Angeles Star*, May 12, 1862, quoted from *Portland Times* (Portland, Ore.).

MUSIC: Turner *et al.* (1858), p. 19.

VARIANTS: "Ballad of the Territorial Road," *Oregon Historical Quarterly*, XLIII (1942), 149; Brunvand (1965), pp. 246-247.

FRANK FRENCH # IDAHO FRANK FRENCH

1
They say there is a land,
  Where crystal waters flow,
O'er beds of quartz and purest gold,
  Way out in Idaho.

CHORUS: O! wait, Idaho!
  We're coming, Idaho;
Our four "hoss" team
  Will soon be seen
Way out in Idaho.

2
We're bound to cross the plains
  And up the mountains go;
We're bound to seek our fortunes there,
  Way out in Idaho.

3

We'll need no pick or spade,
    No shovel, pan, or hoe;
The largest chunks are 'top of ground,
    Way out in Idaho.

4

We'll see hard times no more,
    And want we'll never know,
When once we've filled our sacks with *gold*,
    Way out in Idaho.

TEXT AND MUSIC: "Idaho," by Frank French (Chicago: H. M. Higgins, 1864). 6 pp.

VARIANT: Larkin (1931), pp. 78-81; Lomax and Lomax (1938), pp. 265-266; Randolph (1949), pp. 14-17; Owens (1950), pp. 237-238; Lomax (1960), pp. 309-310; Brunvand (1965), pp. 247-248.

DICK BROWN
THE DREARY BLACK HILLS

1

Kind folks, you will pity my horrible tale;
I'm an object that's needy and looking quite stale;
I gave up my trade, selling Wright's Patent Pills,
To go digging for gold in the dreary Black Hills.

CHORUS: So don't go away, stay home if you can,
Far away from that city, they call it Cheyenne,
For old Sitting Bull and Commanche Bill
Will raise up your hair in the dreary Black Hills

2

In Cheyenne the Round House is filled up ev'ry night
With Pilgrims of every description in sight;
No clothes on their backs, in their pockets no bills,
And yet they are striking out for the Black Hills.

3

When I came to the Black Hills, no gold could I find;
I thought of the free lunch I left far behind;
Through rain, hail and sleet, nearly froze to the gills—
They call me the orphan boy of the Black Hills.

4

Oh, I wish that the man who first started this sell
Was a captive, and Crazy Horse had him in—well,
There is no use in grieving, or swearing like pitch,
But the man who would stay here is a son of a bitch.

5

So now to conclude, this advice I'll unfold:
Don't come to the Black Hills a-looking for gold,
For Big Wallapie and Commanche Bill
Are scouting, I'm told, in the dreary Black Hills.

TEXT: "The Black Hills," as Sung by Dick Brown (San Francisco: Bell & Co., *ca.* 1876 [broadside]).

MUSIC: Larkin (1931), pp. 88-89. Used by permission of Alfred A. Knopf, Inc.

VARIANTS: Lomax (1910), pp. 177-181; Pound (1915), pp. 22-23, and (1922), pp. 185-186; Sandburg (1927), pp. 264-265; Larkin (1931), pp. 88-90; Clark (1932), p. 23; Lomax and Lomax (1934), pp. 438-440; Frey (1936), p. 48; Lomax and Lomax (1938), pp. 372-374; Belden (1940), pp. 349-350; Botkin (1951), p. 739; Lomax (1960), pp. 339-340; Hubbard (1961), pp. 304-305.

HANNIBAL F. JOHNSON   # A TRIP TO RAPID RIVER

1

It was on the twenty-fifth of March, eighteen hundred and ninety-two,
There met in Council Valley a jolly mining crew;
Three of them from the Webfoot State, the other three we know
Had lived for many years within the state of Idaho.

CHORUS: You hear of Rapid River! You take the golden fever!
Got a pretty girl at home? Go right away and leave her.
Saddle up your old cayuse and through the valley go it;
And if you strike a good thing, let everybody know it.

2

We were bound for Rapid River, we scarcely had a dime;
It was just before the rush began, the weather was sublime;
But now the snow is melting fast, the mud is to our knees;
Before we reached the camp that night, I thought we'd surely freeze.

3

We reached the Salmon Meadows, the snow was very deep;
The Webfooters took a cutoff, which almost made them weep;
They'd traveled many hundred miles and at great expense,
And in the Salmon Meadows had to coon a barbed wire fence.

4

Then down the Salmon Meadows, through mud, ice and snow;
The road turned out so very bad we had to travel slow.
We reached a Mr. Campbell's, a place we all admire;
We found a spot where we could squat and build a small campfire.

5

Early in the morning, the earth was white with snow;
But soon the rain began to fall and that was forced to go.
The drizzling rain and chilling blasts made every member shiver,
But nothing could our zeal surpass; hurrah for Rapid River!

6

Early after breakfast, we loaded up our train;
In disregard of wind and storm, we hit the road again;
We crossed the Little Salmon from east to western side;
We crossed Round Valley on a charge and hit the mountain side.

7

Before we reached the summit, we had a small mishap;
Though nothing very serious, 'twas strange to Webfoot chaps;
The snow was four to six feet deep; with all our care and skill,
One pack horse slipped upon the trail and tumbled down the hill.

8

At last we crossed the summit; we did not this regret,
For still the rain was falling fast and everything was wet.
We reached the Little Salmon, we left the snow behind;
Here wood and water's plenty, but grass we could not find.

9

Our ponies all seemed restless, they did not like the camp;
The grass so short and very scarce, they thought they'd take a tramp:
They waked us from our slumbers before the break of day;
We had to tie the leaders up and feed them on stake hay.

10

We packed up in the morning and left that camp with speed;
We had to camp quite early to let our ponies feed;
The wind and snow and rain that night made every muscle quiver,
But still we kept the music up; hurrah for Rapid River!

11

But still some distance we must go before we reached the camp,
Across the mountain through the snow, ten miles we had to tramp;
But courage boys, the end is near, and fortune will deliver
All those who scale the mountain peaks that border Rapid River.

12

And now we've reached the golden shore; the mines are rich, no doubt.
We'll run our tunnels, sink our shafts, and take the ore out,
Then when we make our fortunes, we'll end this toil and strife;
We'll go back home, we'll wed our girls, and live a happy life.

TEXT: Hannibal F. Johnson, *Poems of Idaho* (Weiser, Idaho: Signal Job House, 1895), pp. 32-35.

JUST FROM DAWSON

Tune: Bingen on the Rhine

1

A Dawson City mining man lay dying on the ice.
He didn't have a woman nurse—he didn't have the price;
But a comrade kneeled beside him, as the sun sank in repose,
To listen to his dying words and watch him while he froze.
The dying man propped up his head above four rods of snow,
And said: "I never saw it thaw at ninety-eight below.
Send this little pin-head nugget that I swiped from Jason Dills
To my home, you know, at Deadwood, at Deadwood in the hills.

2

"Tell my friends and tell my enemies, if you ever reach the East,
That this Dawson City region is no place for man or beast;
That the land's too elevated and the wind too awful cold,
And the hills of South Dakota yield as good a grade of gold;
Tell my sweetheart not to worry with sorrow too intense,
For I'm going to a warmer and far more cheery hence.
Oh! the air is growing thicker and those breezes give me chills;
Gee, I wish I was in Deadwood, in Deadwood in the hills.

3

"Tell the fellows in the homeland to remain and have a cinch,
That the price of patent pork chops here is 80 cents an inch.
That I speak as one who's been here scratching 'round to find the gold,
And at ten per cent of discount I could not buy up a cold.
Now, so long," he faintly whispered, "I have told you what to do."
And he closed his weary eyelids and froze solid p. d. q.
His friends procured an organ box and c. o. d. the bills,
And sent the miner home that night to Deadwood in the hills.

TEXT: *Miners' Magazine* (Denver), Nov., 1901, 20, quoted from *Deadwood Pioneer* (Deadwood, S.D.).

MUSIC: Johnson (1881), pp. 537-541.

VARIANTS: Dean (1922), pp. 132-133; Lomax and Lomax (1934) pp. 440-441.

THE APEX BOARDING HOUSE

This section might have been titled "Bedding Down with the Elephant," for those miners who held out through the initial trouble and disillusionment of each new rush found only more of the same awaiting them in the daily routine of mining. A look at that routine begins with "The Apex Boarding House," a hair-raising menu of the hostelry at the Apex Copper Mine near St. George in southwestern Utah. One marvelous line anticipates Joe Hill's influence: "The pudding had the jimjams; the pies was in disguise." John Stone's "An Honest Miner" not only recalls the more familiar kinds of skulduggery among camp types, but also introduces a character to become famous in labor lore, the scissorbill. The song describes him perfectly as he exits from the equivalent of a Chinese whorehouse:

> An honest miner's often seen crawling out of a Spanish corral,
> And pretend to respectable be,
> Will damn them from A to Z;
> They're the first in the shout of "Let's run 'em out,"
> And the first to get round where they be.

Stone's "The Happy Miner," now living among the Michigan shantyboys and singing their praises, was an idle, saucy, scheming fellow, tough as Spanish beef, who made the dark-eyed senoritas run to him "head and tail up like a steer rushing through the corn." "A Miners' Meeting," to the tune of "The Raging Canal," shows that Sierra litigation did not follow the *Jarndyce v. Jarndyce* precedent:

> Now "Bob" brings up a man and proves "he has not been unwell,
> But since the date of bill of sale has been as drunk as hell."
> The friends of "Bob" begin to howl, and "Jake's" begin to swear,
> A few go in and fight it out, or "try it on the square."

Three songs from the camps of the interior confirm the earlier portraits of the individual miner's lot. "I Want To Make the Riffle," from the Sweetwater, Wyoming, rush of 1868, sketches the prospector's unflagging ability to down beer and fantasy:

> Plans I've laid out for life straight as a line—
> They've been laying out, I guess, since "Forty-nine."
> I'm getting in the yellow leaf—I'm an old fellow I fear;
> But if I can make the riffle, you'll find me all here.

"Colorado Home," once considered to be the original of "Home on the Range," was a parody of it written by prospectors at Leadville, Colorado, in 1885. The "Glenwood below Where the one-lungers go" was a rest camp, laid out as "Defiance" in 1883 and wisely renamed later. "We Came to Tamichi," composed by Scott Judy and "Doc" Hammond in a now defunct camp near White Pine, Colorado, is thick with good-fellowship and suggests that other values take over when the "yellow fever" wanes: " 'We've struck it!' says the Judge, 'Won't you take something wet?' "

Finally, there is H. F. Johnson's "The Seven Devil Mines" from his *Poems of Idaho*, published in 1895. In verse that is not very good, it makes the shrewd point that miners were troubled with a variety of devils, both within and without:

> Then when we're down a hundred feet,
> With ore on the dump,
> The money kings will all take hold
> And make the Devils hump.
> . . . .
>
> For when a man has wealthy grown,
> The past is all forgot;
> He's honored, petted, loved, and praised,
> Although a drunken sot.
> And as our wealth accumulates,
> The ladies all will smile;
> We'll bid the Devils all good-bye,
> And live in splendid style.

THE APEX BOARDING HOUSE

If you'll give your at - ten - tion   and   lis - ten   to   my   rhyme,   I'll

sing a - bout   the   board - ing house up   to   the   A - pex Mine, Where they

make   us   Zi - on   bis - cuits just   as   hard   as   an - y   slug;   You

would   of   died   had   you   of   tried old Cur - ly's aw - ful   grub.

1
If you'll give your attention and listen to my rhyme,
I'll sing about the boarding house up to the Apex Mine,
Where they make us Zion biscuits just as hard as any slug;
You would of died had you of tried old Curly's awful grub.

2
The coffee has the dropsy; the tea it has the grippe.
The butter was consumptive, and the slapjacks they had fits;
The beef was strong as jubilant; it walked upon the floor.
The spuds got on their dignity and rolled right out the door.

3
The pudding had the jimjams; the pies was in disguise.
The beans came to the table with five hundred thousand flies.
The hash was simply murdered, just as hard as dobe mud.
We howl, we wail, our muscles fail on Baxter's awful grub.

4
A stranger came to our camp who was off to St. George bend.
We invited him to share a meal and ably intend.
We blew him out, we filled his tank plumb up to the mug
On acrobatic, paralatic, democratic grub.

5
On a stretcher he arrived in town, well now I've heard it said,
With sympathetic friends arrived around his dying bed.
Doc. Affleck came and shook his head while gazing at his mug;
He said it was not suicide, but Curly's awful grub.

TEXT AND MUSIC: Hubbard (1961), p. 435. Used by permission of University of Utah
Press.

AN HONEST MINER

TUNE: Low Backed Car

When first I went to min-ing, I was un-com-mon green, With a "gal-lus" rig I went to dig, and claimed a whole ra-vine; But when I could not make my grub, with im-ple-ments to gag, An hon-est min-er might have been seen at night with a pig in a bag.___ As he lugged it a-way from the pen,___ Was think-ing how luck-y he'd been;___ Went in-to a hole, dug deep af-ter gold, With pig in the bag tum-bled in.___

1

When first I went to mining, I was uncommon green,
With a "gallus" rig I went to dig, and claimed a whole ravine;
But when I could not make my grub, with implements to gag,
An honest miner might have been seen at night with a pig in a bag.

> As he lugged it away from the pen,
> Was thinking how lucky he'd been;
> Went into a hole, dug deep after gold,
> With pig in the bag tumbled in.

2

I wandered round from place to place, and no one did mistrust,
But what an honest miner had—most any amount of dust;
It seems a gang of thieves had robbed a hen-roost neat and clean,
An honest miner wringing their necks, might possibly have been seen.

> As he thought of the elegant stew,
> The rooster would make—but he flew;
> But he'd cook up the hens and invite in his friends,
> As the dog run him out of the roost.

3

No matter who was robbed or killed, 'twas all laid to Joaquin,
His band out in the chaparral not long ago was seen;
With pick and shovel on his back, as though out on a tramp,
An honest miner might have been seen, robbing a Chinese camp.

> As he pulled them around by the tails,
> They scratched with their long finger nails;
> A tom iron round his body was bound,
> So of course it must be Joaquin.

4

A certain class will drink and fight, and gamble all the while,
And live among the prostitutes, in low, degraded style;
The people think it's with the few, but I for one will tell,
An honest miner's often seen crawling out of a Spanish corral.

> And pretend to respectable be
> Will damn them from A to Z;
> They're first in the shout of "Let's run 'em out,"
> And the first to get round where they be.

5

An honest miner's like a pile—almighty hard to find;
So, what's a chicken among so few, when they are chicken inclined?
But if you'll give the devil his due, there's not a cent to choose,
An honest miner's often round when pigs and chickens you lose.

> Though it's always a gang of thieves,
> The lucky one laughs in his sleeves;
> He looks with surprise, and seems to despise
> Anything like a pig in a bag.

6

An honest miner'll drink and fight, and raise the very devil;
But that's all right, if once a week he's seen with pick and shovel.
Of course he'll starve before he'll steal, but, try him a trip and see,
I've mined too long to be deceived, I have that, yes-sir-ree.

  But we're all of us bound to live,
  By mining though, without or with;
  Though after awhile we'll make a pile,
  So, remember the pig in a bag.

TEXT: Stone (1855), pp. 29-30.

MUSIC: Alfred Moffat, *The Minstrelsy of Ireland: 200 Irish Songs* (London: Augener & Co., 1897), p. 304.

VARIANTS: Grant (1924), pp. 134-136; Sherwin and Katzman (1932), pp. 24-26; Black and Robertson (1940), pp. 12-14; Dwyer *et al.* (1964), pp. 83-84.

JOHN A. STONE # THE HAPPY MINER

TUNE: I Get in a Weaving Way

1

I am a happy miner, I love to sing and dance;
    I wonder what my love would say, if she could see my pants
With canvas patches on the knees, and one upon the stern;
    I'll wear them while I'm digging here, and home when I return.

CHORUS: So I get in a jovial way, I spend my money free,
And I've got plenty, will you drink lager beer with me?

2

She writes about her poodle dog, but never thinks to say,
    "O, do come home, my honey dear, I'm pining all away."
I'll write her half a letter, then give the ink a tip;
    If that don't bring her to her milk, I'll coolly "let her rip."

3

They wish to know if I can cook, and what I have to eat,
    And tell me should I take a cold be sure to soak my feet;
But when they talk of cooking, I'm mighty hard to beat—
    I've made ten thousand loaves of bread the devil could not eat.

4

I like a lazy partner, so I can take my ease,
    Lay down and talk of going home, as happy as you please;
Without a thing to eat or drink, away from care and grief,
    I'm fat and saucy, ragged too, and tough as Spanish beef.

5

The dark-eyed senoritas are very fond of me;
    You ought to see us throw ourselves when we get on a spree;
We are saucy as a clipper ship dashing round the horn,
    Head and tail up like a steer rushing through the corn.

6

I never changed my fancy shirt, the one I wore away,
    Until it got so rotten I finally had to say,
"Farewell old standing collar, in all thy pride of starch,
    I've worn thee from December til the seventeenth of March."

7

No matter whether rich or poor, I'm happy as a clam;
    I wish my friends at home could look and see me as I am,
With woolen shirt and rubber boots, in mud up to my knees,
    And lice as large as Chili beans fighting with the fleas.

8

I'll mine for half an ounce a day, perhaps a little less;
    But when it comes to China pay, I cannot stand the press;
Like thousands here, I'll make a pile, if I make one at all,
    About the time the allied forces take Sebastopol.

TEXT: Stone (1858a), pp. 43-45.

VARIANTS: Stone (1858b), pp. 34-36; Handy (1908), pp. 433-434; Lomax (1916), pp. 409-410; Grant (1924), pp. 68-69; Lomax and Lomax (1938), pp. 383-384; Lengyel (1939), pp. 54-55, and (1949), pp. 16-17; E. C. Beck, *Songs of the Michigan Lumberjacks* (Ann Arbor: University of Michigan, 1942), pp. 62-63 (a shantyboy variant); Dwyer *et al.* (1964), p. 87.

JOHN A. STONE   # A MINERS' MEETING

Tune: The Raging Canal

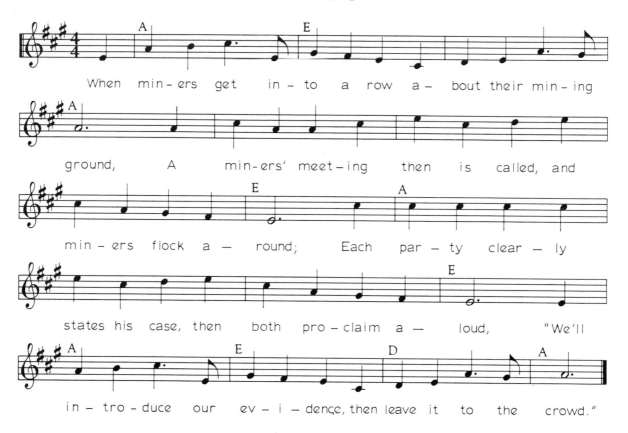

When min-ers get in-to a row a-bout their min-ing
ground, A min-ers' meet-ing then is called, and
min-ers flock a-round; Each par-ty clear-ly
states his case, then both pro-claim a-loud, "We'll
in-tro-duce our ev-i-dence, then leave it to the crowd."

1

When miners get into a row about their mining ground,
A miners' meeting then is called, and miners flock around;
Each party clearly states his case, then both proclaim aloud,
"We'll introduce our evidence, then leave it to the crowd."

2

A witness then is called upon, who tells a crooked yarn,
Declares the diggings "jumpable," so far as he can "larn,"
Is positive they've not been worked as mining laws require;
And any man that says they have, he'll tell him *he's a liar!*

3

A witness on the other side tells quite another tale.
An interested party then presents a bill of sale,
And proves it clear, and furthermore, that he's been very sick,
Not able since he bought the claims to strike a single lick.

4

Now "Bob" brings up a man and proves "he has not been unwell,
But since the date of bill of sale has been as drunk as hell."
The friends of "Bob" begin to howl, and "Jake's" begin to swear,
A few go in and fight it out, or "try it on the square."

136

5

A call is made from either side to hear the ayes and noes—
By this time half the crowd is drunk, and care not how it goes;
And all begin to curse and swear, and out with bowie knives,
All ready, should it come to blows, to take each other's lives.

6

A drunken bully in the crowd throws off his hat and coat,
And right or wrong, no matter which, he thus demands the vote—
"Now all in favor of OLD BOB will please to hollow AYE,
And all who vote the other way shall leave the diggings dry."

7

The crowd send forth a hideous howl, and "Bob" has won the day,
Who now invites all hands to drink before they go away,
"Old Jake" concludes he's badly beat, and quietly retires,
Well satisfied that "Bob" has raised *the largest crowd of liars!*

TEXT: Stone (1858a), pp. 23-24.

MUSIC: Flander *et al.* (1939), p. 79. Used by permission of Helen Hartness Flanders.

VARIANTS: Stone (1858b), pp. 58-59; Grant (1924), pp. 125-126; Dwyer *et al.* (1964), pp. 77-78.

I WANT TO MAKE THE RIFFLE

1

It was an old miner—pick upon his shoulder,
Sat upon a rock, looking at a boulder.
Hello! old fellow, what's the good cheer?
"I want to make the riffle, and I think I'll make it here."
Same old miner sat at a table—
Played poker all night as long as he was able.
Got dead broke, drank all the beer.
"I'm Bound to make the riffle, but I can't make it here."

2

"I've been in good luck, I've been in bad,O—
All through from Mexico up to Colorado.
Chawed raw dog when I couldn't chaw deer
'Cause I couldn't make the riffle, and starvation was near.
Old woman far away waits for my coming,
Doesn't think her old man goes around bumming.
Wait a while, old lass, its panning out clear;
And when I can make the riffle, I will soon quit here.

3

I've got a claim here, prospects fair.
I've got a castle gay, high up in air,
Waiting to be furnished for more than twenty year—
But if I can make the riffle, it'll all come out clear.
If I can make the riffle, I'll buy a new hat.
If I can make the riffle, I'll have a good suit of clothes on my back.
I'll go into business that'll pay me a hundred percent clear,
And I'll walk in the best society For other twenty year.

4

Plans I've laid out for life straight as a line—
They've been laying out, I guess, since "Forty-nine."
I'm getting in the yellow leaf—I'm an old fellow I fear;
But if I can make the riffle, you'll find me all here.
I've got a son at home able to stand up and preach.
I've got a grown up daughter, gay as a peach.
They have not seen their daddy for many and many a year,
'Cause I couldn't make the riffle and had to stay out here.

5

I drink my beer among the boys; I sit down with them to play;
And sometimes I go it blind for a whole night and a day.
I look a rough old specimen, and I've had a rough career
Trying to make the riffle for more than twenty year.
Now I've struck a big thing, and yet—who can tell—
Before another season goes, it may be all in.
So let's be jolly while we may, and pass round the beer;
There's many a riffle made and lost in less than twenty year.

TEXT: *South Pass 1868: James Chisholm's Journal of the Wyoming Gold Rush* (Lincoln: University of Nebraska, 1960), pp. 156-159.

SCOTT JUDY AND
DOC HAMMOND # WE CAME TO TAMICHI

1

We came to Tamichi in 1880
Looking for mineral all the hills o'er;
We travelled the valleys and climbed the steep mountains
Till our feet were all blistered, our legs were all sore.

2

We packed from the wagons the crooked trail over;
We held a big meeting and voted free roads;
But Boone and Jess Davis they downed old Judge Tucker,
And now all us boys will have to pay toll.

3

We lived on sow-belly, baked beans, and strong coffee;
We done our own cooking and washed our own clothes;
We polished the drill like any old-timer,
And put on the rocks our good honest blows.

4

The mail to our camp it came on the jack-train;
Ol' jolly Tom Allen, the chief engineer,
He carried our chuck for Chick and the miners,
And to the Windsor brought moonshine and beer.

5

We drank at Ed Dyart's, the solid old duffer.
We'd wink and say, "Ed, mark her down on the slate,
When we strike it, we'll ante and then you can rub it."
He'd smile and say, "Boys, you are rather too late."

6

There is Thomas O'Riley, who lives in Creede City,
A jolly old bummer, you can bet your last cent;
For punishing booze, he can beat any baby;
They say that for women, old Tom is hell bent.

7

There's old Judge and Ben, who live in the Buckhorn,
They struck a big thing in their own Sleepy Pet;
They were solid for Hancock 'til they heard from Indiana.
"We've struck it!" says the Judge, "Won't you take something wet?"

8

Oh, yes, there's another; you may count him a winner;
'Tis said that they struck him while boring for oil;
He runs the Strawberry and works on the Free Road;
'Tis nobody else but our own Andy Boil.

9

Goodbye, old pards, we are going to leave you;
The blanket's rolled up, and the pick's laid away;
We are going home, to eat Christmas turkey;
We'll meet you again, when the snow melts away.

TEXT: Collected by the Colorado Writers' Project from Margaret Flick, Gunnison County,
Colo., March 15, 1934 in State Historical Society of Colorado Library.

VARIANTS: Davidson (1943), pp. 97-98, and (1951), pp. 25-26.

H. F. JOHNSON
THE SEVEN DEVIL MINES
TUNE: Oh! Susannah

Come all ye bold ad — ven — tur — ers And lis — ten to my song A — bout the Sev — en Dev — il mines__ I will not keep you long; Those mines of wealth that's late — ly found Dis — play the ore — bright, And mil — lions yet be — neath the ground Is bound to see the light. *Chorus* Then dig boys, dig, let us the ore — find, And o — pen up in hand — some style the Sev — en Dev — il mines.

1

Come all ye bold adventurers
And listen to my song
About the Seven Devil mines—
I will not keep you long;
Those mines of wealth that's lately found
Display the ore bright,
And millions yet beneath the ground
Is bound to see the light.

CHORUS: Then dig boys, dig, let us the ore
find,
And open up in handsome style the
Seven Devil mines.

2

And when you pack your old cayuse
    And start to make a raise,
And stop upon a grassy plot
    To let the equine graze,
You're liable at any time
    To meet a rattle bug,
Then don't forget the snake bite cure,
    Corked up in the brown jug.

3

Then when you reach the Devil mines,
    All filled with wind and gush,
Don't mope about and hang your head—
    You'd make the Devils blush;
But shoulder up your pick and pan
    And take your shovel too,
Then when you strike an ore vein,
    Just pop the Devils through.

4

And when the rock becomes so hard
    You can no longer pick,
Don't hang your head and look so sour—
    You'd make the Devils sick;
But seize your drill and hammer too,
    Put down a four-foot hole,
Then charge it well with dynamite,
    And let the thunder roll.

5

Then when we're down a hundred feet,
    With ore on the dump,
The money kings will all take hold
    And make the Devils hump.
Then when we sell our mines of wealth,
    We'll money have to spend;
We'll put our plated harness on
    And visit all our friends.

6

For when a man has wealthy grown,
    The past is all forgot;
He's honored, petted, loved and praised,
    Although a drunken sot.
And as our wealth accumulates,
    The ladies all will smile;
We'll bid the Devils a good-bye,
    And live in splendid style.

LAST CHORUS:

Then laugh boys, laugh, we have the ore
    found.
We'll make our pile, we'll live in style,
    Then pass the lager round.

TEXT: H. F. Johnson, *Poems of Idaho* (Weiser, Idaho: Signal Job House, 1895), pp. 76-77.

MUSIC: Turner *et al.* (1858), p. 18.

VARIANT: Brunvand (1965), pp. 244-245.

COLORADO HOME

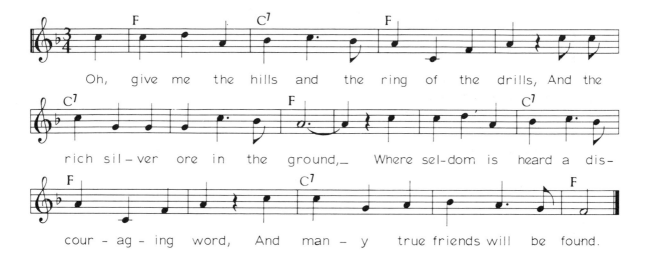

1

Oh, give me the hills
And the ring of the drills,
And the rich silver ore in the ground,
Where seldom is heard
A discouraging word,
And many true friends will be found.

2

Oh, give me the camp
Where the prospectors tramp,
And business is always alive,
Where dance halls come first
And the faro banks burst
And every saloon is a dive.

3

Oh, give me the steed
And the gun that I need,
Shoot game from my own cabin door,
With Glenwood below
Where the one-lungers go,
And we'll camp on the banks of the Grand.

4

Oh, give me the wife,
The pride of my life,
She can ride, she can shoot like a man;
She's a fond and true heart,
And we never will part—
Together we'll roam through the land.

5

Oh, give me the hills
And the roaring stamp mills,
And the riches that in the hills lie;
We'll work and we'll play
All the livelong day,
Oh, there let me live till I die.

TEXT AND MUSIC: Emrich (1942c), p. 225. Used by permission of California Folklore Society.

VARIANTS: Clark (1932), p. 38; Emrich (1942a), p. 64. *See also* "Home on the Range."

WHEN I WAS A MINER, A HARD-ROCK MINER

With a pan, rocker, or long tom, anyone could wash gold from a placer; but much more was required to wrest it from the deep, elusive quartz veins. By the late 1850's the importance of placer mining had passed, and the bulk of mineral production in the West came from highly capitalized hard rock mining. With that passing went much of the miner's independence and the larger share of the fruit of his labor. In exchange, he got the increased hazards of underground work and an ever-decreasing paycheck. In short, mining became an industry.

"When I Was a Miner, a Hard-Rock Miner," to the tune of "When You Wore a Tulip," shows that, first, the new miner needed a body built to dodge the undertaker. If he was one of those holdouts who probed a claim single-handed (like "The Broken-Hearted Leaser," from Charles Winter's *Grandon of Sierra*), he needed considerable ingenuity to trace the wandering vein, and not a little larcenous fortitude when it slipped over into the next property: "Our gold has us forsaken, some other path it's taken, But I still believe you'll strike it just the same."

Most miners, however, drilled, loaded, and blasted for hire—and their complaints are seldom against the parsimonious rocks. In "Bisbee's Queen," about Phelps Dodge's Copper Queen mine in Bisbee, Arizona, the complaints are about the speedup and the pay—harder to extract than copper in a company town:

> And about the time you're limbering up on that sulphide pyramid,
>   And imagine that you're moving dirt as mortal never did,
> The jigger gently whispers, in a voice so soft and low,
>   "Do you think you'll get a measure in half an hour or so?"

The Tonopah, Nevada, silver mines were booming in 1910 when "The Belmont Stopes" appeared in the *Miners' Magazine*. It was hazardous transferring the metal to George Wingfield's vaults from those red-hot stopes,

> Where the gas it hangs in halos
>   'Round the candle's sickly glare,
> And the mucker goes a-gasping
>   For a breath of com-pressed air.
> And the timber stands in forests
>   To hold the slabby ground,
> And the stulls they fall like ten-pins,
>   And lie broken all around.

"Casey Jones, the Miner," one of many adaptations of "Casey Jones," discusses the technical problems arising from drilling with a Burleigh machine into a previously unignited powder hole. There is a hint of criticism in Casey's being a "ten day man," a migrant.

"I Wandered Today up the Hill, Maggie" is one of many good parodies of popular songs sung by the miners of Butte, Montana. That region supplies the majority of our remaining miners' songs for several reasons: it is one of the oldest, continuously operating mining communities; its working population was not only stable, but highly organized; and its first songs were printed early, and the surviving ones were professionally collected and studied. Besides complaining of the gas, falling rock, and water in the drifts, the miners commented on one another. "The Rustling Song" merely mentions the variety of their origins. The numbers from France and Germany were insignificant, but of miners from Cork, Wales, and Cornwall, there were plenty. "Cousin Jacks," they were called; and, as Charley Tregonning's song says, "for singing and for mining, They have somehow got the knack." "I Once Was a Carman in the Big Mountain Con," like "The Cowboy's Lament," is another version of "The Unfortunate Rake," although in it most of the traditional lament pattern is cast aside in order to salute the Irish influx.

For both comic and tragic views of their working conditions, we offer a late Butte parody called "Drill, Ye Miners, Drill!" It enshrines in song a bit of folksay about the miner who was buried,

> Next time payday came around,
> A dollar short by his wife was found.
> When asked, "What for?" came this reply,
> "They lost time digging him out of the ground."

Is one of the ironies that it was only a dollar? "Only a Miner Killed in the Breast" is further evidence that native American song consists in link after link of adaptation: parodic, occupational, topical. The pathetic subject of this song, like the cowboy and the brakeman in their own versions, is one more nameless victim of forces beyond any individual's control. The songs of the next section suggest one of his recourses.

WHEN I WAS A MINER, A HARD-ROCK MINER

TUNE: When You Wore a Tulip

1

When I was a miner, a hard-rock miner,
Down in a deep, deep mine,
The hashers all caressed me,
The chambermaids blessed me;
My contract drift was paying fine.
But I soon grew weary,
My eyes got getting bleary;
My lungs they wheezed most all the time.
So to dodge the undertaker,
I turned a moonshine maker,
And gave up the deep, dark mine.

TEXT: Hand *et al.* (1950), p. 44.
Used by permission of California Folklore Society.

CASEY JONES, THE MINER

TUNE: Casey Jones

1

Come all you muckers and gather here,
    If you want to hear the story of a miner dear.
Casey Jones was the miner's name;
    On a Burleigh machine he won his fame.

CHORUS: Casey Jones was a ten day miner,
Casey Jones was a ten day man;
Casey Jones took a chance too many,
And now he's mining in the promised land.

2

The story I am about to tell
    Happened at a mine called the Liberty Bell;
They went into a crosscut and mucked her out
    And Casey said, "We'd better step about."

3

Casey said, "We'd better dig in
    Before that damned old shift boss comes in;
If he finds out we've been taking five,
    He'll send us to the office to get our time."

4

They went to the crosscut, put up the bar,
    Placed the machine up on the arm,
Put in a starting drill with its bit toward the ground,
    Turned on the air, and she began to pound.

5

Casey said, "If I haven't lied,
    There is a missed hole on that right hand side."
His partner said, "Oh gracious me!
    If it ever went off, where would we be."

6

They went into the crosscut to drill some more;
    The powder exploded with a hell of a roar.
It scorched poor Casey just as flat as a pan,
    And now he's mining in the promised land.

7

Casey said, just before he died,
    "There's one more machine I would like to have tried."
His partner said, "What can it be?'
    "An Ingersoll jackhammer, don't you see?"

TEXT AND MUSIC: Emrich (1942*b*), pp. 104-105. Used by permission of Southern Folklore Quarterly.

VARIANTS: Emrich (1942*a*), p. 382, (1942*c*), pp. 217-218, and (1942*d*), pp. 7-8; Hand *et al.* (1950), pp. 33-34.

CHARLES E. WINTER # THE BROKEN-HEARTED LEASER

1

In a rusty, wornout cabin sat a broken-hearted leaser;
His singlejack was resting on his knee.
His old "buggy" in the corner told the same old plaintive tale—
His ore had left in all his poverty.
He lifted his old singlejack, gazed on its battered face,
And said: "Old boy, I know we're not to blame;
Our gold has us forsaken, some other path it's taken,
But I still believe you'll strike it just the same.

CHORUS: "We'll strike it, yes, we'll strike it just the same,
Although it's gone into some other's claim.
My dear old boy, don't mind it; we won't starve if we don't find it—
And we'll drill and shoot and strike it just the same.

2

"For forty years I've hammered steel and tried to make it strike;
I've burned twice the powder Dewey ever saw.
I've made just coin enough to keep poorer than a snake;
My jack's ate all my books on mining law.
I've worn gunnysacks for overalls, and 'California socks,'
I've burned candles that would reach from here to Maine,
I've lived on powder smoke and bacon, that's no lie, boy, I'm not fakin';
But I still believe I'll strike it just the same.

3

"Last night as I lay sleeping in the midst of all my dream,
My assay ran six ounces clear in gold,
And the silver it ran clean sixteen ounces to the seam,
And the poor old miner's joy could scarce be told.
I lay there, boy, I could not sleep, I had a feverish brow,
Got up, went back and put in six holes more.
And then, boy, I was chokin', just to see the ground I'd broken;
But alas! alas! The miner's dream was o'er.

LAST CHORUS: "We'll strike it, yes, we'll strike it just the same,
Although it's gone into some other's claim.
My dear old boy, don't mind it; we won't starve if we don't find it—
And I still believe I'll strike it just the same."

TEXT: Charles E. Winter, *Grandon of Sierra* (New York: Little and Ives Co., 1907), pp. 176-177.

VARIANTS: Lomax (1910), pp. 25-26; Sherwin and Katzman (1932), pp. 45-47; Hand *et al.* (1950), pp. 17-18.

THE BELMONT STOPES

1

To all you rustlin' miners,
    Who for a job have hopes,
Just hear this little story
    Of life in the Belmont Stopes.

2

Perhaps you'll think I am joshing
    Or handing you some dope—
Just take a muck-stick and go down
    Into a red hot stope.

3

Where the gas it hangs in halos
    'Round the candle's sickly glare,
And the mucker goes a-gasping
    For a breath of com-pressed air.

4

And the timber stands in forests
    To hold the slabby ground,
And the stulls they fall like ten-pins,
    And lie broken all around.

5

You will have no time for loafing
    Or any chance to mope,
For you'll rustle for air and water
    In a Belmont Stope.

6

And the mucker to the shift boss
    Of his troubles must be mute,
As he's mucking down the high-grade
    Into a hungry shoot.

7

When he knows with Death he's playing,
    As the slabs they fall about,
That he's taking desperate chances
    That life's candle will snuff out.

8

Yet he knows he'll get what's coming,
    However bold or brave,
A ticket to the hospital—
    A free pass to the grave.

9

And the poet who sung of hades
    And wrote with a jeweled pen
Of a future place called Inferno
    For the souls of all bad men.

10

Had Dante lived to ramble
    'Neath Oddie's old gray slopes,
He'd found another hades
    In Belmont's burning stopes.

11

I know I have been sinful,
    And for them all must pay,
Down in the hell with Pluto
    Where I'll go some future day.

12

But whether dead or living,
    I'll cherish fondest hopes
That I will not suffer the torments
    As I did in the Belmont Stopes.

TEXT: *Miners' Magazine* (Denver), June 9, 1910.

I WANDERED TODAY
UP THE HILL, MAGGIE

J. A. BUTTERFIELD

TUNE: When You and I Were Young, Maggie

1

I wandered today up the Hill, Maggie;
I applied for a rustling card;
I got both the card and the job, Maggie,
But the job it was too damned hard.

Oh, the stope it was filled with gas, Maggie,
And the ground it was fitchery as well;
The rock it came a-tumbling down on me, Maggie,
And the shifter was crazier than hell.

2

Oh, there was time in Butte, Maggie,
When you could take five and hold your job;
But now it's put the rock in the box, Maggie,
And then put the waste in the gob.
Oh, my blond hair has turned to green, Maggie,
From the water that drips from the back;
I'm the homeliest plug in the town, Maggie,
And you'll soon want your maiden name back.

TEXT: Hand *et al.* (1950), p. 37. Used by permission of California Folklore Society.

MUSIC: *Home Songs* (Boston: Oliver Ditson Co., 1906), p. 102.

THE RUSTLING SONG

Well now, I've rus—tled the High Ore, I've rus—tled the Bell, I've

rus—tled the Dia—mond, I've rus—tled like hell; I've rus—tled the Moun—tain Con,

Moun tain View, too, And I land—ed a job in the El—ler—mer—loo,

Too—ra—lay,___ Too ra lee,___ For how would ya, how would ya,

like to be me? There were min—ers from Bis—pee and

some came from Cork; Some from New Jer—sey, and

some from New York; And a big—bel—lied Dutch—man from

o—ver the Rhine Got a job sling—ing muck in the Moun—tain Con Mine.

Too—ra—lay,___ Too—ra—lee,___ For how would ya, how would ya,

like to be me? There were min—ers from Eng—land, And

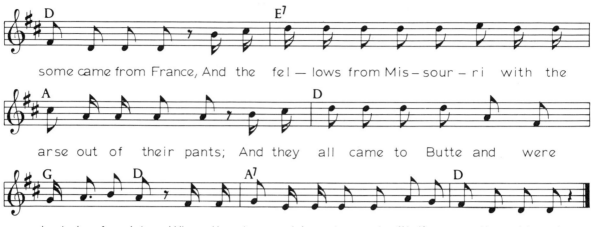

some came from France, And the fel — lows from Mis – sour – ri with the

arse out of their pants; And they all came to Butte and were

look-ing for jobs, When the boss put 'em to work fil–ling up the old gob.

1

Well now, I've rustled the High Ore, I've rustled the Bell;
I've rustled the Diamond, I've rustled like hell;
I've rustled the Mountain Con, Mountain View, too,
And I landed a job in the Ellermerloo,
CHORUS: Too-ra-lay, Too-ra-lee,
For how would ya, how would ya, like to be me?

2

There were miners from Bisbee and some came from Cork;
Some from New Jersey, and some from New York;
And a big-bellied Dutchman from over the Rhine
Got a job slinging muck in the Mountain Con Mine.

3

There were miners from England, and some came from France,
And the fellows from Missouri, with the arse out of their pants;
And they all came to Butte and were looking for jobs,
When the boss put 'em to work filling up the old gob.

TEXT AND MUSIC: Hand *et al.* (1950), p. 22. Used by permission of California Folklore Society.

VARIANTS: Emrich (1942*c*), pp. 226-227, and (1942*d*), p. 10; Hand *et al.* (1950), p. 23.

BISBEE'S QUEEN

1

Say, pal, which way are you drifting; how's the cutting down the line?
 I hear the camps are booming and are working overtime.
I've never worked the border, so I'm wandering down to see
 If that great camp of Bisbee will seem a paradise to me;
For I hear that work's a plenty, and the wages are all right,
 And if you're working night shift, you don't have to work all night.
Say, pal, do tell me truly, are my fancies all a dream?
 For I've sure heard wondrous stories of Bisbee's Copper Queen.

2

Well, neighbor, since you've asked me, I'll peddle out to you
 The wondrous things in Bisbee that I saw when I came through.
You're right, the jobs are plenty, you may get on any time;
 And if it's work you're out for, neighbor, they'll suit you in that line.
I'll not blast the hopes you've builded, nor wreck your castles bright,
 For the wisdom that you'll gather in that camp is worth a sight.
So mosey down and get your card, and if your record's clean
 For eleven years before your birth, you'll get in on Bisbee's Queen.

3

They'll hand you to a jigger, who will escort you down below,
 And introduce you to a sweatbox where breezes never blow.
He'll hunt you up a muck pile that fills the set in square,
 Then present you with a square-point fan, with which to fan the air.
And about the time you're limbering up on that sulphide pyramid,
 And imagine that you're moving dirt as mortal never did,
The jigger gently whispers, in a voice so soft and low,
 "Do you think you'll get a measure in half an hour or so?"

4

But the jiggers are good fellows, they really earn more pay;
 Think of the weight they carry on their shoulders every day!
They must carefully watch the shift boss, and get busy when he's due,
 And hold the stope from caving until each shift's work is through.
Then it's up to them to hold the watch and keep the men in line,
 For you must not reach the station until after tally time.
You are hired for eight hours, and they pull you out in nine,
 For they seem to love your presence and long to hold you in the mine.

5

Yes, they pay the swellest money—but mostly in hot air,
 For you drag down chucker's wages when you run machines down
  there.
And the miner blocks the timbers for the same three, six-bits per,
 Oh yes, she's generous, very, is Bisbee's Queen; that's her!
She's a weakness for the welfare of the man that's underground;
 You can tell it in the manner that she hands the good things round.
But when the C. Q. she gets hers, and your pay-day statement's clean,
 You're a lucky man if you're not in debt to Bisbee's Copper Queen!

6

They raised the wages, just to show the people they're all right;
    But for several weeks beforehand, they laid awake all night
Manipulating figures and adjusting prices so
    The miner gets a con game, and the Queen, she gets the dough.
All dreams of easy fortune for the man who digs the mud
    Are gone with the awakening, for she's nipped them in the bud.
And she smiles to see him frisk himself to find his pockets clean,
    In this game between the miners and Bisbee's noble Queen.

7

They had a scheme of reclamation to save the erring soul:
    You do not break the Sabbath by laboring in the hole,
But copper, she went skyward and raised all copper stock;
    Now they desecrate the Sabbath because the smelter needs the rock!
She's the Queen of all hypocrites; 'tis her main stock and trade,
    As she barters for the dollars that her willing dupes have made.
For she truly loves her neighbor, she'll agree to any scheme
    That will net for him *un peso* and *dos pesos* for the Queen.

TEXT: *Miner's Magazine* (Denver), April 11, 1907, quoted from the *Douglas Examiner* (Douglas, Ariz.).

COUSIN JACK

You ask me for a song, folks, And I'll try to please you all; Don't blame me if I do not suit, For na-ture had its call.

Chorus

But for sing-ing and for min-ing, They have some-how got the knack; It's a sec-ond na-ture to that class Of lads called "Cous-in Jacks."

1
You ask me for a song, folks,
 And I'll try to please you all;
Don't blame me if I do not suit,
 For nature has its call.

CHORUS: But for singing and for mining,
 They have somehow got the knack;
It's a second nature to that class
 Of lads called "Cousin Jacks."

2
You'll find them on the mountain top,
 You'll find them on the plains;
You'll find those boys wher'er you go,
 And you'll find their mining claims.

3
They come from distant Tombstone
 And Virginia on the hill;
You ne'er can beat a Cousin Jack
 For hammering on the drill.

4
Amongst you other Irishmen,
 Do justice if you can;
For there's none that can compete
 With the good old Cornishman.

TEXT AND MUSIC: Emrich (1942b), pp. 103-104. Used by permission of Southern Folklore Quarterly.

VARIANTS: Emrich (1942a), p. 220, and (1942d), p. 9; Botkin (1951), p. 738.

I ONCE WAS A CARMAN
IN THE BIG MOUNTAIN CON

TUNE: Cowboy's Lament

1

'Twas once in the saddle I used to go dashing;
'Twas once as a cowboy I used to be brave;
But ain't it a pity, I came to Butte City
To work for Jim Brennan and now to my grave.

CHORUS: Oh beat your drums loudly; Sound your fifes merrily;
Play the bagpipe as ye carry me on;
Lay a square pointed fan on the lid of my coffin,
So I'll be known as I go along.
Get six jolly ladies to come and dance o'er me;
Get six husky carmen to carry me on;
Take me to the Flat boys, and throw the soil o'er me,
For I once was a carman in the Big Mountain Con.

2

There's Big Jack O'Neill—we call him "The Rimmer";
To a hard-working miner, he never was mean;
If you h'aint a "big wheeler" when first you come over,
You'll have to go muckin' behind a machine.

3

There's Big Tim O'Malley, just over from Kerry,
The greenest young chaw that a man ever seen;
It was his ambition to gain a position,
So he had to go muckin' behind a machine.

4

Come all ye Corkonians, Fardowns, and Kerryonians;
Come all ye good people from the Land of the Green.
Come all ye "big wheelers" who ain't got your papers,
You'll have to go muckin' behind a machine.

5

Then hurrah for Old Ireland, the land of good miners,
The dear little isle that I see in my dreams;
I'll go back to Old Ireland to the girl who waits for me,
To hell with your mines and your mining machines.

TEXT: Hand *et al.* (1950), pp. 31-32. Used by permission of California Folklore Society.

DRILL, YE MINERS, DRILL!

THOMAS F. CASEY

TUNE: Drill, Ye Tarriers, Drill!

1

Every morning after the Con's whistle blows,
There are thousands of miners working underground;
And the shifters come through, and they say, "Hey! Mick!
Better come down heavy on that mucking stick!
And drill, ye miners, drill!!'

CHORUS: And drill, ye miners, drill!
For it's work all day for food, they say,
Down inside the Hill,
And drill, ye miners, drill!
And load! and blast!

158

2

Now the new foreman was the tough Turk;
By God, his face was one fat smirk.
Past week some heavy ground came down
And buried a young miner up to his crown,
Oh, muck, ye miners, muck!

3

Next time payday came around,
A dollar short by his wife was found.
When asked, "What for?" came this reply,
"They lost time digging him out of the ground."
And timber, ye miners, timber!

4

The men looked at the "weedgie board" sign
And saw no notice of that cave-in.
They were not surprised, because they said,
"'Twas no accident, he was just done in."
So drill, ye miners, drill!

5

Then two young miners started a new drift
And barred down as much as they possibly could;
But pretty soon the assistant came
And fired both for the unnoticed slab way back.
So take five, ye miners, take five!

6

A couple of old-timers went into a raise
That was so hot they were soon all wet.
When the shifter came through he said, "Put on the hose,"
But the miners told him, "It's just plain sweat."
So wet 'er down, miners, wet 'er down!

7

Now mining is tough, everyone does say,
And the speedup is tougher in many a way;
There are more and tougher shifters than ever before,
And the workers must fight more and more.
So fight, ye workers, fight.

TEXT: *Miners' Voice* (Butte, Mont.) (Sept., 1939), reprinted in Hand *et al.* (1950), pp. 35-36.

MUSIC: "Drill, Ye Tarriers," an Irish comic song by Thomas Casey (New York: Frank Harding's Music House, 1888).

ONLY A MINER KILLED IN THE BREAST

Down in the mine, in the dark, dis — mal drift, Two

min-ers were work-ing their long mid-night shift, With mus-cles of steel and a

heart of good-will, The mu — sic kept time with the ham-mer and drill.

Chorus

On — ly a min — er killed in the breast, On — ly a work-ing man

gone to his rest, Read on his grave 'neath the whis-per-ing pines: "Our

Joe, aged just twen — ty, was killed in the mines."

1
Down in the mine, in the dark, dismal drift,
Two miners were working their long midnight shift,
With muscles of steel and a heart of goodwill,
The music kept time with the hammer and drill.

CHORUS: Only a miner killed in the breast,
Only a workingman gone to his rest,
Read on his grave 'neath the whispering pines:
"Our Joe, aged just twenty, was killed in the
mines."

2
Unconscious of danger, the mid-hour had fled,
They heard not the crash of the rock overhead,
Till it fell like a bolt to the death blow of one,
At the feet of his comrade, he sank with a moan.

3

"Partner, goodbye!" then he sank in the clay,
The candle's dim light on his dim vision lay.
His partner bent o'er him, his life was all gone;
Death ended his shift, and his mercy was done.

4

"Mother, Joe's dead, he was killed in the mine:"
This telegram trembles along o'er the line;
The fate she had feared had taken her boy,
Cut down in his manhood her pride and her joy.

———————————

TEXT AND MUSIC: Emrich (1942c), pp. 220-221. Used by permission of California Folklore Society.

STAND BY YOUR UNION

Miners in Virginia City had organized as early as the mid-1860's, followed by the copper miners of Butte in 1878 and the silver-lead miners of Idaho's Coeur d'Alene district soon after. The Western Federation of Miners was formed in 1893, withdrew from association with the American Federation of Labor in 1897, became the backbone of the Industrial Workers of the World—the Wobblies—when they organized in 1905, withdrew from the IWW in 1908, and rejoined the AFL in 1911. This continual realigning of ranks is only an organizational mirror of the bloody turbulence experienced by the workers themselves as they sought protection from the exactions of management and the disputing theorists of revolutionary, craft, and industrial unionism in the decades before World War I.

"Stand by Your Union" was written in 1908, the year following the unsuccessful prosecution of "Big Bill" Haywood and other WFM officers for conspiracy in the bombing of ex-Governor Steunenberg of Idaho. The song came from the *Miners' Magazine* published by the WFM in Colorado, where the imposition of martial law during the Cripple Creek strike of 1903 brought the forced deportation of hundreds of strikers. And six years after it was written, the clash between militia and strikers during the United Mine Workers' recruitment resulted in the "Ludlow massacre." Standing by one's union was to be, for more than a while, as hazardous as working in the West.

Scottie's "The Miner" expresses typical discontent with conditions in the Montana mines where

> The only birds that warble there
> Are "buzzies" and "jackhammers";
> Their song is death in every note,
> For human life they clamour.

The answer to the "clamour" was a nearly industry-wide walkout beginning in the fall of 1916. Miners from Bisbee, Arizona, to Butte, Montana, joined to protest a variety of grievances. In Arizona 1,200 of the strikers were rounded up by the army and held in a desert detention camp for three months. On June 12, 1917, the Butte miners struck, and the story is told in detail in Joe Kennedy's "The Copper Strike of '17." It mentions one of the Wobbly trio of Martyrs, Frank Little. A chairman of the IWW General Executive Board, he made a speech in Butte on July 31, 1917. In the middle of that night, he was taken from his hotel room, dragged behind an automobile, and hanged outside town. The song also mentions, as many others do, the miners' complaint against the "rustling card." This company-granted clearance card was comparable to those currently required of Bantu workers in the Union of South Africa to permit easy check against official blacklists.

A new complaint in consequence of the strike was that against scabs. "The Scab's Lament" is a pathetic parody of that pathetic song, "After the Ball." It is an old miner's explanation to his daughter of how he lost all friends and hope when he deserted the Butte Metal Mine Workers Union. "A Scabby Cousin Jack" is another Joe Kennedy song from *New Songs for Butte Mining Camp* (1918), and it threatens aliens who scab with a little growl from the Wob's favorite paper tiger, "Old Sabo Tabby"—otherwise known as the "conscious withdrawal of efficiency."

Management replied on the scab's behalf with the "goon." "The Strike-Breaker's Lament" was written in 1902 after a decade of bitter and tragic striking in the Coeur d'Alene district ending with the imprisonment of hundreds of strikers in "bull pens" and the reign of martial law imposed by federal troops. The song relates the astonishment of an imported scab from the lead mines of Joplin, Missouri, that the pay, grub, booze, and funeral accommodations are not what he anticipated.

We end with Scottie's Butte adaptation of Wobbly Ralph Chaplin's "Solidarity Forever." Such borrowing emphasizes the sharing of grievances and hopes between the Montana hard-rock miners and the West Virginia coal miners for whom the original was written in 1915. In spite of its songs and its solidarity, however, organized labor was crushed all over the West during World War I by the companies, federal troops, and "loyalty leagues" charging pro-German sedition. Butte did not win back the closed shop until 1934.

STAND BY YOUR UNION

TUNE: The Hard Working Miner

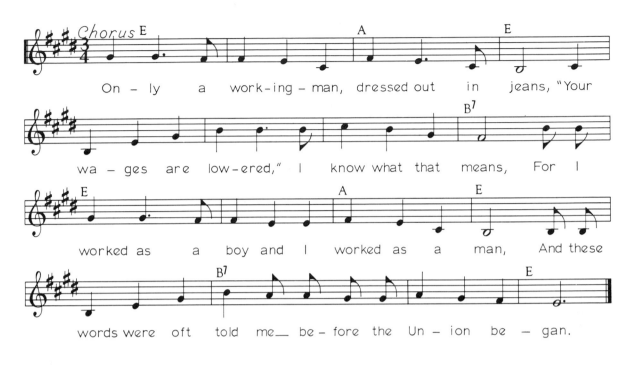

On - ly a work-ing-man, dressed out in jeans, "Your
wa - ges are low-ered," I know what that means, For I
worked as a boy and I worked as a man, And these
words were oft told me— be - fore the Un - ion be - gan.

1
My form is all bent and my hands are hard worn,
 And often I wished I had never been born.
Like a ship without rudder, at random, I ran,
 All this was before the Union began.

CHORUS: Only a workingman, dressed out in jeans,
   "Your wages are lowered," I know what that means,
For I worked as a boy and I worked as a man,
  And these words were oft told me—before the Union
   began.

2
Father and mother died when I was a tot;
 I was the oldest one in the whole lot,
And I got boy's wages—did the work of a man—
 This was before the grand Union began.

3
I loved, as God bade me, a working lass;
 I longed to get married, no home could amass;
When I spoke that I'd marry, they said: "Don't see how you can!"
 And this was before our Union began.

4
Yes, I wear the jeans, and my form is bent;
 I'm crippled and old, and my strength is near spent;
I look back in sorrow at Life's narrow span,
 'Cause they broke me down e'er the Union began.

5

Young man, you lion, in God's given strength,
  Take an old man's advice and go your whole length
In support of your Union; stand together as one,
  For now, praise the Lord! The Union's begun.

6

The newspapers here bow down to pelf,
  They lie about us; this you know yourself.
Be firm and true, we'll yet make them run,
  We're a power on earth since the Union's begun.

TEXT: *Miners' Magazine* (Denver), May 14, 1908.

MUSIC: Hand *et al.* (1950), p. 16. Used by permission of California Folklore Society.

THE COPPER STRIKE OF '17

1

On the twelfth of June we called a strike
Which filled the miners with delight;
In union strong we did unite,
On the rustling card to make a fight.

2

The Bisbee miners fell in line,
And, believe me, Miami was not far behind;
In Globe they surely were on time
To join their striking brothers.

3

The companies were money mad;
This strike made dividends look sad.
The men to Con these words did say,
"They'll be twice as short before next May."

4

The local press it came out bold
And said it must be German gold,
Although we did not have a dime
The morn we hit the firing line.

5

Although we're classed as an outlaw band,
We've surely made a noble stand;
Our fight is just for liberty,
And make Butte safe for democracy.

6

Six hundred gunmen came to town
And tried to keep the strikers down.
In spite of all, we're full of vim;
Our password is, "We're bound to win!"

7

The old war-horse is in the game;
I know all rebels heard his name;
For thirty years and more, I'm told,
His fellow-workers never sold.

8

The A.C.M., they tried their skill,
When Fellow-Worker Little's blood did spill.
The day will come when union men
Will have a voice in Butte again.

9

Fellow-Worker Campbell, true and bold,
His comrades would not sell for gold;
He said to Con, "Why, I'll get mine
By standing on the firing line."

10

Now respect to all true union men,
Who have courage to fight until the end;
To copper barons we will say,
"The rustling card has gone to stay."

TEXT: *New Songs for Butte Mining Camp* (Butte, Mont.: Century Printing Co., *ca.* 1918), pp. 14-15.

VARIANTS: Kornbluh (1964), pp. 304-305.

SCOTTIE
THE MINER
TUNE: Standard on the Braes O'Mar

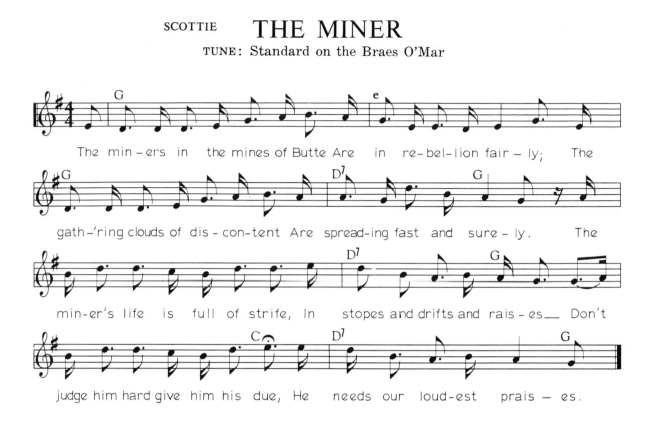

The min-ers in the mines of Butte Are in re-bel-lion fair-ly; The
gath-'ring clouds of dis-con-tent Are spread-ing fast and sure-ly. The
min-er's life is full of strife, In stopes and drifts and rais-es— Don't
judge him hard give him his due, He needs our loud-est prais-es.

1

The miners in the mines of Butte
Are in rebellion fairly;
The gathering clouds of discontent
Are spreading fast and surely.
The miner's life is full of strife,
In stopes and drifts and raises—
Don't judge him hard, give him his due,
He needs our loudest praises.

2

Down in these holes each shift he goes
And works mid dangers many,
And gets the "miner's con" to boot,
The worst disease of any.
In hot-boxes he drills his rounds,
Midst floods of perspiration,
And clogs his lungs with copper dust—
A hellish occupation.

3

The merry breezes never blow
Down in these awful places;
The sun's rays are one-candle power
That shines on pallid faces.
The only birds that warble there
Are "buzzies" and "jack hammers";
Their song is death in every note,
For human life they clamour.

4
Conditions such as these, my friends,
Have made the miners rebels;
The under-current is gaining strength,
The mighty system trembles.
The revolution's coming fast;
Old institutions vanish.
The tyrant-rule from off the earth
For evermore 'twill banish.

TEXT: *New Songs for Butte Mining Camp* (Butte, Mont.: Century Printing Co., *ca.* 1918), pp. 2-3.

MUSIC: John Greig, *Scots Minstrelsie* (London: Caxton Publishing Co., n.d.), VI, 361-363.

VARIANT: Kornbluh (1964), pp. 302-303.

THE SCAB'S LAMENT

CHARLES K. HARRIS

TUNE: After the Ball

Once a lit - tle maid - en climbed an old man's

knee_____ And asked, "A_____ stor - y,

pa - pa, please tell me._____ Why are you

lone - ly, why are you sad,_____ Why

do the min — ers call you a scab?"_____

"I had man — y friends, pet, long, long a -

go,_____ And how I lost them, you

soon shall know._____ I'll tell it all,

pet, tell all my shame;_____ I was a

scab, pet, I was to blame.

Chorus

Af — ter the strike was o — ver, af — ter the men had won,_____ Af — ter the mines were run — ning, af — ter the gun — men were gone,_____ The chil — dren who were or — phaned in the 'Spec' fire that night_____ Still tell of Camp - bell who led that ter — ri — ble fight._____

1

Once a little maiden climbed an old man's knee
And asked, "A story, papa, please tell me.
Why are you lonely, why are you sad,
Why do the miners call you a scab?"
"I had many friends, pet, long long ago,
And how I lost them, you soon shall know.
I'll tell it all, pet, tell all my shame;
I was a scab, pet, I was to blame.

CHORUS: "After the strike was over, after the men had won,
After the mines were running, after the gunmen were
gone,
The children who were orphaned in the 'Spec' fire that
night
Still tell of Campbell who led that terrible fight.

"Brave men were striking and fighting hard
For better conditions and no rustling card.
First I was with them, whole heart and soul;
But when the raise came, I left them cold.
I thought it best, pet, to turn a scab,
And go back to the old job I had;
That's why I'm lonely, that's why I'm sad,
That's why the miners call me a scab.

3

"Many years have passed, pet, since I won that name,
And in song and story they have told my shame.
Everywhere I wander, everywhere I roam,
The story of my shame is sure to find my home.
I'd give my life, pet, yes, I'd give it all,
If I'd not turned traitor or scabbed at all;
If I'd my life to live again, I know what I would do,
Job or no job, I'd stay with the M.M.W.U."

TEXT: *New Songs for Butte Mining Camp* (Butte, Mont.: Century Printing Co., *ca.* 1918), p. 19.

MUSIC: "After the Ball," by Charles K. Harris (Milwaukee: Chas. K. Harris & Co., 1892).

VARIANT: *Miners' Magazine* (Denver), Jan. 7, 1904.

JOE KENNEDY   # A SCABBY COUSIN JACK

TUNE: Auld Lang Syne

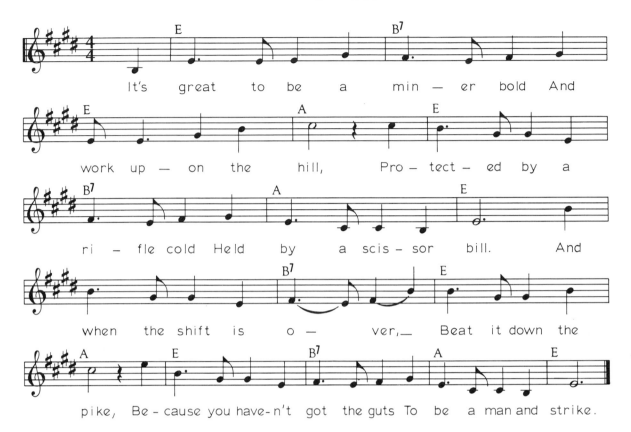

It's great to be a min — er bold And work up — on the hill, Pro — tect — ed by a ri — fle cold Held by a scis — sor bill. And when the shift is o — ver,— Beat it down the pike, Be - cause you have-n't got the guts To be a man and strike.

1

It's great to be a miner bold
    And work upon the hill,
Protected by a rifle cold
    Held by a scissor bill.
And when the shift is over,
    Beat it down the pike,
Because you haven't got the guts
    To be a man and strike.

2

Oh, fellow-worker, Cousin Jack,
    On you we're keeping tab;
Your first name may be Tussie,
    But your middle name is SCAB.
And when the strike is over
    And we've killed the rustling card,
You'd better hit the high spots,
    For the sliding will be hard.

3

You'd better beat it down the pike,
    And strike right straight 'ome;
A rock might slip (I hope it does)
    And crack your solid dome.
Or, perhaps, a lagging may be cut
    And laid across the chute,
Because Old Sabo Tabby
    Might be on the job in Butte.

4

So hurry up and catch the boat
    For dear old Hengland's shore;
Real working men are wise to you—
    You're rotten to the core.
The principles of unionism,
    Certainly you lack;
But what can be expected
    From a scabby Cousin Jack!

TEXT: *New Songs for Butte Mining Camp* (Butte, Mont.: Century Printing Co., *ca.* 1918), pp. 15-16.

MUSIC: *The Good Old Songs We Used To Sing,* (Boston: Oliver Ditson Co., 1887), I, 113.

STRIKE BREAKER'S LAMENT

TUNE: Bingen on the Rhine

A min — er from Mis — sou — ri lay
dy — ing in the hills___ He was sick with moun — tain
fe — ver and var — i — ous oth — er ills___ He ___
called his part — ner to him and mur — mured soft and
low; "I wish I was in Jop — lin,____ in
Jop — lin down in Mo. They shipped me here to
Mul — lan and gave me a per — mit.____ The
men who worked be — fore me got or — ders then to
quit.____ They all were first-class min — ers, but
then they had to go;____ Their jobs were filled with

green-horns who came from Jop — lin, Mo."_____

1

A miner from Missouri lay dying in the hills—
He was sick with mountain fever and various other ills—
He called his partner to him and murmured soft and low:
"I wish I was in Joplin, in Joplin down in Mo.
They shipped me here to Mullan and gave me a permit.
The men who worked before me got orders then to quit.
They all were first-class miners, but then they had to go;
Their jobs were filled with greenhorns who came from Joplin, Mo.

2

"They told us that our wages would be three to four a day,
And that, you know, in Joplin is more than double pay;
The thought of such great riches, it made my heart to glow,
For I'd felt the rack of poverty in Joplin, Joplin, Mo.
The grub we get to chew on is something I can't eat—
They give us beef and mutton, but never salted meat;
We never get no hoe-cake, or biscuits of sour dough,
The same as what we live on in Joplin, Joplin, Mo.

3

"Whene'er I start to licker, it makes me weep to think
How, everywhere in Mullan, it's 15 cents a drink;
While gin, beer, rum or whisky is only 5 a throw
At that dear place I come from, in Joplin, Joplin, Mo.
I wish I was in Joplin, where burros sing so sweet,
But then I couldn't walk there; I'm weak upon my feet.
Don't bury me in Mullan—that land of ice and snow—
But ship me back to Joplin, to Joplin, down in Mo.

4

"Please write and tell the old folks I'm sorry that I left
And came to work in Mullan, for I've lost my heft—"
Just then his voice it faltered, he ceased to murmur low,
His soul it went a-scooting to Joplin, Joplin, Mo.
His partner wept above him, and sadly fell his tears,
Then tried to drown his sorrow by drinking many beers;
He boxed the stiff and shipped him, as fast as he could go,
To the land of scabbing miners in Joplin, Joplin, Mo.

TEXT: *Miners' Magazine* (Denver), Feb., 1902, p. 15.

MUSIC: Johnson (1881), pp. 537-541.

VARIANT: *Miners' Magazine* (Denver), March 3, 1910, quoted from the *Black Hills Daily Register* (Lead City, S.D.).

SCOTTIE # SOLIDARITY FOREVER

TUNE: Battle Hymn of the Republic

On the twelfth of June in sev — en — teen, one
bright mid-sum mer's day, The work-ers in the mines of Butte, they
took a hol — i — day; Con — di — tions sure were rot — ten, and they
want — ed bet — ter pay, So they made a un — ion strong.

Chorus
Sol — i — dar — i — ty for — e — ver, sol — i — dar — i — ty for —
e _____ ver, Sol — i — dar — i — ty for —
e _____ ver, for the un — ion makes us strong. __

1

On the twelfth of June in '17, one bright mid-summer's day,
The workers in the mines of Butte, they took a holiday;
Conditions sure were rotten, and they wanted better pay,
    So they made a union strong.

CHORUS: Solidarity forever, solidarity forever,
Solidarity forever, for the union makes us strong.

2

The owners of the mines in Butte are called the A.C.M.,
A dirty bunch of parasites whose place is in the pen,
So we call upon all workers, all good, red-blooded men,
    To join the union strong.

3

It is we who sunk the shafts, drove drifts and contract raises too;
It is we who work in hot-box 'til the sweat runs out our shoe.
Is there anything left for us but to organize and brew
    A great big union strong?

4

The master class is organized in one big union strong;
The workers are disorganized, a weak and motley throng;
But now they are awakening and the time will not be long,
    For the union makes us strong.

5

The rustling card has got to go—it ne'er shall see New Year.
It's kept the working class of Butte in misery and fear,
But its days are nearly ended and its funeral is near,
    For the union makes us strong.

6

Now we call upon all workers, no matter what your creed,
Your color, nationality—to that we pay no heed;
We're workers all and nothing more, so hurry up and speed
    The one big union strong.

TEXT: *New Songs for Butte Mining Camp* (Butte, Mont.: Century Printing Co., *ca.* 1918), p. 5.

MUSIC: *Franklin Square Song Collection* (1884), II, 117.

COME, COME, YE SAINTS

The Mormons were, and still may be, the singingest people in the West, possibly because their earlier, Eastern experience had given them so little to be tuneful about. If William Clayton's hymn "Come, Come, Ye Saints," said to have been written at Brigham Young's request in 1846 at the start of the Mormons' great migration, cries with such vigor, "We'll make the air with music ring—Shout praises to our God and King," it is because they saw a respite from the persecution that had dogged them from Palmyra, New York in the 1820's to Kirtland, Ohio, and on to Nauvoo, Illinois. These first songs exhibit the variety of expectations the Mormons had of the West and the sort of beliefs that sustained them there.

"Upper California," from the early missionary's hymnbook published in Liverpool, England, refers to the entire area west of the Rockies where the Mormons foresaw such varied triumphs as lifting Jacob's yoke and spreading "abroad our curtains throughout fair Zion's land." This same enthusiasm is present in the several songs by William Willes printed here. Willes was an elder from England who had helped establish a mission in Calcutta in 1851 and had come to Utah around 1853. His *Mountain Warbler* (1872) is the source of such songs as "There Is a People in the West," which proclaims, slightly ambiguously, the Mormons' forceful convictions:

> The truth in many lands is known; in power, the Lord rolls forth the stone,
> Which from the mountains has gone forth, and will, in time, fill all the earth.

His "Deseret" not only compares the pre-Mormon West to hell, as noted earlier, but also reveals what the Mormons thought they were leaving and what they hoped to build:

> Deseret, Deseret shows the pattern to all,
> That all may take warning ere Babylon shall fall,
> And flee to the mountains when trouble shall come,
> To be free from the plagues in this beautiful home.
>
> Where labor is honored, nor workmen opprest,
> Where youth is instructed and age finds a rest,
> Where society frowns upon vice and deceit,
> And adulterers find heaven's laws they must meet.

Willes's "They Cry 'Deluded Mormons' " further illumines the apocalyptic tinge in the motives for their migration:

> The world is tied in bundles before the burning day,
> The stone it swiftly trundles, and does its power display;
>
> Tho' wicked men among us, the Lord will trot them through,
> He will not leave a grease-spot to mark the place they trod.

The Saints even appropriated secular songs for their religious purposes, as in "A Church Without a Prophet," which, like "Upper California," is set to the tune of "The Rose That All Are Praising." Written before 1852, it shows the role played in the Mormon church polity by such concepts as a bountiful Nature, a physical God, theocratic rule, and a mild anti-intellectualism. Finally, Willes's "In the Hive of Deseret" alludes to the many mundane triumphs of the Mormons to complement the erection of their theology: the introduction of irrigation, the God-sent gulls and crickets, the arrival of the "Battalion Boys," their Phoenix-like survival of a punitive expedition, and the welcoming of thousands of foreign converts, sought from the very beginning of their organized church activity.

WILLIAM CLAYTON
COME, COME, YE SAINTS
J. T. WHITE

TUNE: All Is Well

1. Come, come, ye Saints, no toil nor la-bor fear, But with joy wend your way;

Tho' hard to you this jour-ney may ap-pear, Grace shall be as your day.

'Tis bet-ter far for us to strive Our use-less cares from

us to drive; Do this, and joy your hearts will swell— All is well! All is well!

1

Come, come, ye Saints, no toil nor labor fear,
But with joy wend your way;
Tho' hard to you this journey may appear,
Grace shall be as your day.
'Tis better far for us to strive
Our useless cares from us to drive;
Do this, and joy your hearts will swell—
All is well! All is well!

2

Why should we mourn, or think our lot is hard?
'Tis not so; all is right!
Why should we think to earn a great reward,
If we now shun the fight?
Gird up your loins, fresh courage take,
Our God will never us forsake;
And soon we'll have this truth to tell—
All is well! All is well!

3

We'll find the place which God for us prepared,
Far away in the West,
Where none shall come to hurt or make afraid;
There the Saints will be blessed.
We'll make the air with music ring—
Shout praises to our God and King;
Above the rest each tongue will tell—
All is well! All is well!

4

And should we die before our journey's through,
Happy day! All is well!
We then are free from toil and sorrow, too;
With the just we shall dwell.
But if our lives are spared again
To see the Saints their rest obtain,
O how we'll make this chorus swell—
All is well! All is well!

TEXT: *Sacred Hymns and Spiritual Songs* (Salt Lake City: George Q. Cannon, 1871), no. 47.

MUSIC: *Deseret Sunday School Song Book* (Salt Lake City: G. Q. Cannon & Sons, 1892), pp. 188-189.

VARIANTS: Daughters of Utah Pioneers (1932), p. 1; Carter (1944), pp. 499-500.

WILLIAM WILLES
THERE IS A PEOPLE IN THE WEST

TUNE: So Early in the Morning

1

There is a people in the West, the world call Mormonites in jest,
The only people who can say, "We have the truth, and own its sway."
Away in Utah's valleys, away in Utah's valleys,
Away in Utah's valleys, the chambers of the Lord.

2

The world in darkness long has lain, since Jesus and the Saints were
    slain,
Until these glorious latter days, when Joseph did the standard raise,
And brought the Book of Mormon, and brought the Book of Mormon,
And brought the Book of Mormon, to cheer our souls with light.

3

The truth in many lands is known; in power, the Lord rolls forth the
    stone,
Which from the mountains has gone forth, and will, in time, fill all
    the earth.
Go forth from Utah's valleys, go forth from Utah's valleys,
Go forth from Utah's valleys, the chambers of the Lord.

4

And all ye Saints where'er you be, from bondage try to be set free,
Escape unto fair Zion's land, and thus fulfill the Lord's command,
And help to build up Zion, and help to build up Zion,
And help to build up Zion, before the Lord appear.

TEXT: Willes (1872), pp. 60-61.
VARIANT: Marshall (1882), pp. 208-209.

JOHN TAYLOR   UPPER CALIFORNIA   EDWARD J. LODER

TUNE: The Rose That All Are Praising

The Up — per Cal — i — for — nia_ Oh, that's the land for

me!_____ It lies be — tween the moun — tains and the

great Pa — cif — ic Sea:_____ The Saints can be sup —

port — ed there, And taste the sweets of lib — er — ty In

Up — per Cal — i — for — nia_ Oh, that's the land for me!_ Oh,

that's the land for me,_ Oh, that's the land for me!_

1

The Upper California—Oh, that's the land for me!
It lies between the mountains and the great Pacific Sea:
    The Saints can be supported there,
    And taste the sweets of liberty
In Upper California—Oh, that's the land for me!
    Oh, that's the land for me,
    Oh, that's the land for me!

2

We'll go and lift our standard, we'll go there and be free;
We'll go to California and have our jubliee—
    A land that blooms with beauty rare,
    A land of life and liberty,
With flocks and herds abounding—Oh, that's the land for me!
    Oh, that's the land for me,
    Oh, that's the land for me!

3

We'll burst off all our fetters and break the Gentile yoke,
For long it has beset us, but now it shall be broke:
    No more shall Jacob bow his neck;
    Henceforth he shall be great and free
In Upper California—Oh, that's the land for me!
    Oh, that's the land for me,
    Oh, that's the land for me!

4

We'll reign, we'll rule and triumph, and God shall be our King;
The plains, the hills and valleys shall with hosannas ring;
    Our towers and temples there shall rise
    Along the great Pacific Sea,
In Upper California—Oh, that's the land for me!
    Oh, that's the land for me,
    Oh, that's the land for me!

5

We'll ask our cousin Lemuel to join us heart and hand,
And spread abroad our curtains throughout fair Zion's land;
    Till this is done, we'll pitch our tents
    Along the great Pacific Sea
In Upper California—Oh, that's the land for me!
    Oh, that's the land for me,
    Oh, that's the land for me!

6

Then join with me, my brethren, and let us hasten there;
We'll lift our glorious standard and raise our house of prayer;
    We'll call on all the nations round
    To join our standard and be free
In Upper California—Oh, that's the land for me!
    Oh, that's the land for me,
    Oh, that's the land for me!

TEXT: *Sacred Hymns and Spiritual Songs* (12th ed.; Liverpool, 1863), p. 352.
MUSIC: Johnson (1881), pp. 276-277.
VARIANTS: Daughters of Utah Pioneers (1940), p. 306; Carter (1944), p. 510; Davidson (1945), pp. 282-283.

WILLIAM WILLES # DESERET HENRY RUSSELL

TUNE: To the West

De — ser — et, De — ser — et, 'tis the home __ of the
free, And dear — er than all oth — er lands 'tis to
me, Where the Saints are se — cure from op — pres — sion and
strife, And en — joy to the full, the rich bles — sings of
life. 'Tis a land which for a — ges has
been ly — ing waste, Where the sav — age has
wan — dered, by dark — ness de — based, Where the
wolf and the bear un — mo — lest — ed did
roam, A — way! far a — way! De — ser —

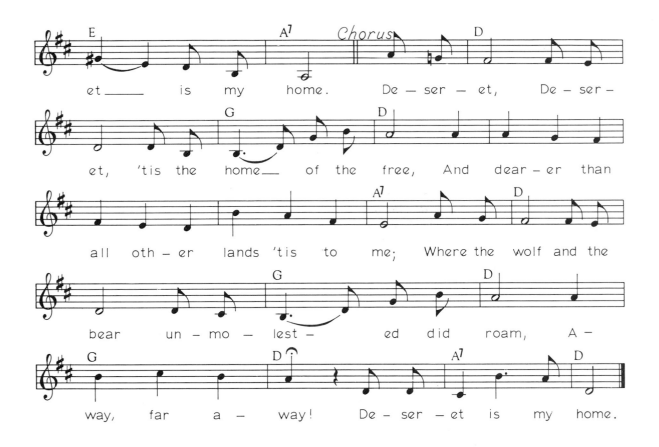

et ____ is my home. De — ser — et, De — ser —
et, 'tis the home__ of the free, And dear — er than
all oth — er lands 'tis to me; Where the wolf and the
bear un — mo — lest — ed did roam, A —
way, far a — way! De — ser — et is my home.

1

Deseret, Deseret, 'tis the home of the free,
And dearer than all other lands 'tis to me,
Where the Saints are secure from oppression and strife,
And enjoy to the full, the rich blessings of life.
'Tis a land which for ages has been lying waste,
Where the savage has wandered, by darkness debased,
Where the wolf and the bear unmolested did roam,
Away, far away! Deseret is my home.

CHORUS: Deseret, Deseret, 'tis the home of the free,
And dearer than all other lands 'tis to me;
Where the wolf and the bear unmolested did roam,
Away, far away! Deseret is my home.

2

Deseret, Deseret, she long has been opprest,
But now for a while she is taking her rest;
She feels like a giant refreshed with new wine,
And enjoys from Jehovah, his blessings benign.
Here are hearts that can feel for another's deep woe,
And with charity, blessings on others bestow,
Return good for evil to those who oppress,
And await the time coming to give them redress.

3

Deseret, Deseret, O! I love to be here
With my brethren and sisters each blessing to share,
Nor regret I've forsaken the land of my birth
To dwell on this sweet favored spot of the earth,
Where Brigham and George A. and Daniel preside
With all the full quorums of priesthood beside,
Where the Law of the Lord is the standard of life,
Apart from foul Babylon's darkness and strife.

4

Deseret, Deseret, she's the pride of the world,
Where the banner of freedom is widely unfurled,
Where oppression is hated and liberty loved,
And truth and sincerity highly approved,
Where labor is honored, nor workmen opprest,
Where youth is instructed and age finds a rest,
Where society frowns upon vice and deceit,
And adulterers find heaven's laws they must meet.

5

Deseret, Deseret shows the pattern to all,
That all may take warning ere Babylon shall fall,
And flee to the mountains when trouble shall come,
To be free from the plagues in this beautiful home.
O, how my heart yearns for the time to draw near
When earth will be freed from oppression and fear,
And the truth rule triumphant o'er sea and o'er land,
And Jesus as King of the Nations will stand.

TEXT: Willes (1872), pp. 18-19.

MUSIC: Jordan and Kessler (1941), pp. 285-288.

WILLIAM WILLES   # THEY CRY "DELUDED MORMONS"

TUNE: Aunt Sally

1

They cry "deluded Mormons" in all the world around,
And the reason why they do is very far from sound;
It's only just a cry that is echoed from tongue to tongue,
Of these awful wicked Mormons, and their leader, Brigham
    Young.

CHORUS: True Saints rally, around the standard come,
Away in Utah's valleys, our lovely mountain home.

2

The world is tied in bundles before the burning day,
The stone it swiftly trundles, and does its power display:
It never has stood still, and will ever be rolling on,
While the doings of the wicked shall all be past and gone.

3

While all the world is fretting about the future time,
At loggerheads are getting, the sight is quite sublime;
The Mormons, they are growing in everything that's good,
And Babylon is going down as they did in Noah's flood.

4

There's nothing can destroy us if we are firm and true,
Tho' wicked men among us, the Lord will trot them through,
He will not leave a grease-spot to mark the place they trod,
But hurl them to destruction beneath the Iron Rod.

5

We'll make this earth an Eden, just as it was before,
And many blessings hidden, the Priesthood will restore;
And truth and virtue triumph, and peace and love abound,
And happiness and glory fill all the world around.

———

TEXT: Willes (1872), pp. 11-12.

A CHURCH WITHOUT A PROPHET

EDWARD L. LODER

TUNE: The Rose That All Are Praising

1

A church without a prophet is not the church for me;
It has no head to lead it, in it I would not be;
  But I've a church not built by man,
  Cut from the mountain without hand,
A church with gifts and blessings—oh, that's the church for me,
Oh, that's the church for me, oh, that's the church for me.

2

The God that others worship is not the God for me;
He has no parts nor body, and cannot hear nor see;
  But I've a God that lives above,
  A God of Power and of Love,
A God of Revelation—oh, that's the God for me,
Oh, that's the God for me, oh, that's the God for me.

3

A church without apostles is not the church for me;
It's like a ship dismasted afloat upon the sea;
    But I've a church that's always led
    By the twelve stars around its head,
A church with good foundations—oh, that's the church for me,
Oh, that's the church for me, oh, that's the church for me.

4

The hope that Gentiles cherish is not the hope for me;
It has no hope for knowledge, far from it I would be;
    But I've a hope that will not fail,
    That reaches safe within the veil,
Which hope is like an anchor—oh, that's the hope for me,
Oh, that's the hope for me, oh, that's the hope for me.

TEXT: *Sacred Hymns and Spiritual Songs* (Salt Lake City: George Q. Cannon, 1871), no. 297.

MUSIC: Johnson (1881), pp. 276-277.

VARIANTS: Marshall (1882), pp. 195-196; Davidson (1945), p. 275; Hubbard (1959), pp. 121-122, and (1961), p. 392.

WILLIAM WILLES   # IN THE HIVE OF DESERET   JOHN DAVY

TUNE: Bay of Biscay

When the Saints first reached the moun-tains From off the des-ert plains, Be-side the crys-tal foun-tains, They swell'd their joy-ful strains; Here reigned but sol-i-tude A-mong these moun-tains rude.

Chorus Here we thrive in the hive, In the hive of De-ser-et.

1

When the Saints first reached the mountains
   From off the desert plains,
Beside the crystal fountains,
   They swell'd their joyful strains;
Here, reigned but solitude
   Among these mountains rude.

CHORUS: Here we thrive in the hive,
   In the hive of Deseret.

2

Not e'en an ear of corn
   Had graced these vales forlorn;
No wheat nor pulse was sown;
   The Indian roamed alone;
The Saints' good works and faith
   Disarmed the power of death.

3

They plow'd, they sow'd, they watered;
    The rain did seldom fall.
They persevered and conquered,
    Altho' their means were small.
Their crops the crickets ate;
    At this they did not fret.

4

The Pioneers united
    With the Battalion Boys;
And they the Saints invited,
    To share with them their joys.
The gulls, as friends appeared,
    And saved their second crop.

5

The blood-stained, wicked nation
    From whence the Saints had fled,
Express'd their approbation,
    And wished that they were dead;
But Phoenix-like they rose
    Above their angry foes.

6

But soon they're famed in story,
    Among the nations round;
Became a territory,
    And blessings did abound,
Their delegates sent forth
    To the nations of the earth.

7

And now her teeming thousands,
    Throughout these valleys fair,
From Europe's favor'd islands
    Do annually repair.
From all the world around,
    The Saints of God abound.

8

This is the stone the builders
    Did scornfully reject.
The truth the world bewilders;
    Salvation they neglect.
Their fearful doom draws nigh,
    Then put your trust on High;
LAST CHORUS: All ye Saints in the hive,
In the hive of Deseret.

TEXT: Willes (1872), pp. 36-37.
MUSIC: Johnson (1881), pp. 175-178.

THE HANDCARTS

If Joseph Smith received a divine revelation on golden plates. Brigham Young had a vision of a wooden cart that could be built for 10 dollars, carry several hundred pounds of provisions, and be pulled by a man across the plains in two weeks less time than the wagon trains took. A start too late in the season did bring disaster; but before the scheme was abandoned in 1860, 3,000 people had pulled their way across the prairie. William Hobbs's "The Handcarts, I" asserts the appeal to Europeans, those who could least afford covered wagons:

> The lands that boast of modern light
> We know are all as dark as night,
> Where poor men toil and want for bread,
> Where peasant hosts are blindly led.
> These lands that boast of liberty
> You ne'er again would wish to see
> When you from Europe make a start
> To cross the plains with your handcart.

That appeal had started in the fall of 1849 from Scandinavia to Polynesia and soon spread elsewhere. So effective was it that the 1870 census reveals that of the adult population of Utah, only 15,000 were born in the United States while 31,000 came from abroad. The remaining 41,000 were children born in Utah, giving substance to the claim that babies were Utah's principal crop. "Handcarts, III" is a cheerful song showing that these vehicles went both ways. Its author, Philip Margetts, had come to Utah from England in 1850. Seven years later he accompanied missionaries hauling handcarts back across the plains on their way to duty abroad.

The Mormons' first migration across the Mississippi had been more forced than freely sought. "Early This Spring We'll Leave Nauvoo" scourges a town in Illinois which was the site of more than one idealistic, communal failure. It was founded in the 1830's by Connecticut speculators as Commerce City, and renamed in 1840 by Joseph Smith and his band under special charter. As the Mormons increased in number, so did faction and Gentile fear of Mormon political power until violence erupted in 1844 when Smith announced his candidacy for the presidency of the United States and attempted to suppress an opposition newspaper, the *Expositor*. A mob killed him and his brother Hyrum as they lay in the nearby Carthage jail on June 27, 1844. Within two years the Mormons had moved west, but Nauvoo was reoccupied by a colony of French communists called the Icarians, led by Etienne Cabet. Faction split this group too, one part of which ended as the Icaria-Speranza community in Sonoma County, California, in 1884.

Bernard White's "In 1864" is a balled narrating the mild harassment suffered by an emigrating wagon train along the Platte. William Willes's "The Way They Emigrate" notes the addition of the iron horse to earlier modes of travel and the tendency of many newcomers to be dissatisfied. If they too often "hop the twig," one needn't fear that of the best emigrants of all, the new "arrivals from behind the veil."

WILLIAM HOBBS # THE HANDCARTS, I

TUNE: King of the Cannibal Islands

Ye   Saints who dwell on Eu – rope's shore, Pre-pare your-selves, for man-y more, To

leave be-hind your na-tive land, For   sure God's judg-ments are   at   hand; For

you must cross the   rag – ing main Be – fore the pro-mised land you gain, And

with the faith–ful make a start To   cross the plains with your hand – cart.

Chorus

For   some must push and some must pull, As   we   go march-ing up   the hill; So

mer – ri – ly   on   the way we   go   Un – til we reach the   Val – ley.

1

Ye Saints who dwell on Europe's shore,
Prepare yourselves, for many more,
To leave behind your native land,
For sure God's judgments are at hand;
For you must cross the raging main
Before the promised land you gain,
And with the faithful make a start
To cross the plains with your handcart.

CHORUS: For some must push and some must pull,
As we go marching up the hill;
So merrily on the way we go
Until we reach the Valley.

2

The lands that boast of modern light
We know are all as dark as night,
Where poor men toil and want for bread,
Where peasant hosts are blindly led.
These lands that boast of liberty
You ne'er again would wish to see
When you from Europe make a start
To cross the plains with your handcart.

3

As on the road the carts are pulled,
'Twould very much surprise the world
To see the old and feeble dame
Thus lend a hand to pull the same.
And maidens fair will dance and sing—
Young men more happy than a king,
And children, too, will laugh and play,
Their strength increasing day by day.

4

But some will say, "It is too bad
The Saints upon the foot to pad
And more than that, to pull a load,
As they go marching o'er the road."
But then we say, "It is the plan
To gather up the best of men—
And women too, for none but they
Will ever travel in this way."

5

And long before the Valley's gained,
We will be met upon the plains
With music sweet and friends so dear,
And fresh supplies our hearts to cheer.
And then with music and with song,
How cheerfully we'll march along,
And thank the day we made a start
To cross the plains with our handcart.

6

When you get there, among the rest
Obedient be and you'll be blest;
And in God's chambers be shut in
While judgments cleanse the earth from sin.
For we do know, it will be so;
God's servants spoke it long ago.
We say it is high time to start
To cross the plains with our handcart.

TEXT: Daughters of Utah Pioneers (1932), p. 21. Used by permission of Daughters of Utah Pioneers.

MUSIC: Vernon (1927), pp. 156-157.

VARIANTS: Carter (1944), pp. 513-514; Davidson (1945), pp. 278-279; Botkin (1951), pp. 753-754; Fife and Fife (1956), pp. 67-70; Hubbard (1961), pp. 399-402.

THE HANDCARTS, II

A. HART

TUNE: A Little More Cider

Oh, our faith goes with the hand-carts, And they have our hearts' best love;___ 'Tis a nov — el mode of trav — el — ling, De — vised by God a — bove. Hur — rah for the camp of Is — ra — el! Hur — rah for the hand-cart scheme! Hur — rah! hur — rah! 'tis bet — ter far Than the wag — on and ox — team.

1

Oh, our faith goes with the handcarts
    And they have our hearts' best love;
'Tis a novel mode of travelling,
    Devised by the God above.

CHORUS: Hurrah for the Camp of Israel!
    Hurrah for the handcart
        scheme!
Hurrah! hurrah! 'tis better far
    Than the wagon and ox-team.

2

And Brigham's their executive;
    He told us the design;
And the Saints are proudly marching on,
    Along the handcart line.

3

Who cares to go with the wagons?
    Not we who are free and strong;
Our faith and arms, with right good will,
    Shall pull our carts along.

TEXT: T. B. H. Stenhouse, *Rocky Mountain Saints* (New York, 1873), p. 333n.

MUSIC: *Heart Songs Dear to the American People* (1909), pp. 372-373.

VARIANTS: J. H. Beadle, *Polygamy* (Philadelphia: National Publishing Co., 1904), pp. 137-138; Davidson (1945), p. 279.

PHILIP MARGETTS   # THE HANDCARTS, III   S. C. FOSTER

TUNE: Oh! Susannah

No purse, no script they bear with them, but cheer-ful-ly they start And cross the plains a thou-sand miles, and draw with them a cart. Ye na-tions list, the men of God, from Zi — on now they come, Clothed with the Priest-hood and the power to gath-er Is — rael home.

Chorus Then cheer up, ye El-ders, you to the world will show That Is — rael will be gath-ered soon, and ox — en are too slow.

1

No purse, no script they bear with them, but cheerfully they start
And cross the plains a thousand miles, and draw with them a cart.
Ye nations list, the men of God, from Zion now they come,
Clothed with the Priesthood and the power to gather Israel home.

CHORUS: Then cheer up, ye Elders, you to the world will show
That Israel will be gathered soon, and oxen are too slow.

2

Ye pious men whose sympathy is touched for fallen man,
A pattern now is set for you; just beat it if you can!
Here's men who're called to go abroad, the Gospel to impart;
They leave their friends and homes so dear and start with their
    handcart.

3

Now competition is the rage, throughout the world 'tis true;
To head the Mormons they must rise far earlier than they do.
For Mormonism it is sound, without a crack or flaw;
They know the arts and sciences, and we're learning how to *draw*.

4

Some folks would ask, "Why do you start with carts, come tell I pray?"
We answer, "When our Prophet speaks, the Elders all obey;
Since Brigham has the way laid out that's best for us, we'll try;
Stand off ye sympathetic fools, the handcarts now or die—"

5

Then come ye faithful ministers, with blessings now we'll go
To gather out the honest hearts from darkness and from woe;
Our strength increasing day by day, as from this land we part,
We'll bless the day that we were called to go with our handcart.

TEXT: *Millennial Star* (Manchester, Eng.), Aug. 15, 1857.

MUSIC: Turner *et al.* (1858), p. 18.

VARIANTS: Daughters of Utah Pioneers (1940), p. 309; Carter (1944), pp. 514-515; Davidson (1945), pp. 280-281.

EARLY THIS SPRING WE'LL LEAVE NAUVOO

TUNE: Old Dan Tucker

Ear—ly this spring we'll leave Nau-voo, and on our jour—ney we'll pur-sue; We'll go and bid the mob fare-well, and let them go to heav-en or hell. So on the way to Cal-i—for—nia in the spring we'll take our jour-ney, Far a—bove Ar—kan—sas foun-tains, pass be—tween the Rock—y Moun—tains.

1

Early this spring we'll leave Nauvoo, and on our journey we'll pursue;
We'll go and bid the mob farewell, and let them go to heaven or hell.

CHORUS: So on the way to California in the spring we'll take our journey,
Far above Arkansas fountains, pass between the Rocky Mountains.

2

The mobocrats have done their best, old Sharp and Williams with the rest,
They've burnt our houses and our goods and left our sick folks in the
woods.

3

Below Nauvoo on the green plains, they burnt our houses and our grains;
And if fought, they were hell-bent to raise for help the government.

4

The old settlers that first claimed the soil, they thought that they would
take a spoil,
And a fuss they did begin, but not much money did bring in.

5

Old Governor Ford, his mind so small, has got no room for soul at all;
If heaven and hell should do their best, he neither could be damned or
blessed.

6

Backenstos, his mind so large, upon the mob he made a charge;
Some three or four he did shoot down, and left them lying on the ground.

7

The old State Marshal came to town and searched our temple up and down.
He told the Saints that he had come, and brought a writ for Brigham
    Young.
SECOND CHORUS: So out of the way old Major Warren, you can't come it
    over the Mormons,
Far above Arkansas fountains, pass between the Rocky Mountains.

8

Now since it's so we have to go and leave the City of Nauvoo,
I hope you'll all be strong and stout, and then no mob can back you out.

9

The temple shining silver bright, and Christ's own glory gives the light,
High on the mountains we will rear a standard to the nations far.

TEXT: Fife and Fife (1956), pp. 317-318. Used by permission of Indiana University Press.
MUSIC: Damon (1936).
VARIANT: Daughters of Utah Pioneers (1932), pp. 192-193.

BARNARD WHITE # IN 1864

1

In eighteen-hundred-sixty-four
We started out to meet the poor;
We left our families and our friends
To help to gather Israel in.
Four yoke of cattle to each team,
But some of them were rather lean;
Our teams did number fifty-three
And on we rolled so merrily.

CHORUS: Hurrah, my boys, chain up your
gaps;
The cattle are a-coming in.
Fifteen minutes to yoke up in,
And then, my boys, we're off again.

2

With captain Preston at our head,
The Mormons' train he nobly led
Thru rivers, over rocks, thru sand,
To bring the Saints to Zion's land.
But nothing happened to relate
Until we came to devil's gate;
The devil thot he'd lay a snare
To try to keep our cattle there.

3

Next morning early we rose up
Our cattle soon drove in from feed;
And when we'd get them all corralled,
All at once they did stampede.
The yokes and chains flew round and round;
A wagon was turned up-side down;
Some bloody noses, shirts were torn,
As we went out to meet the poor.

4

On the fourth of June we crossed the Platte;
Some places the water was over our back;
Five wagons went in a little too low
And rolling down the stream did go.
The wagon boxes left the wheels;
The boys soon followed at their heels;
"My greenbacks are inside," they cried
As they went down the rolling tide.

5

When all the teams had come to land,
The Captain did refreshments hand
Saying, "Drink my boys it's very cold
And that will make your hearts feel bold.
These wagons must and shall come out
Now who is in for going out?"
"I am," a dozen voices cried.
We soon jumped in the rolling tide.

6

Three yoke of cattle we took in.
Sometimes we all did have to swim;
But the Mormon boys, they know no fear.
We soon snaked out the running gears
And thru the water we did dash,
Some ropes on to the boxes lashed.
Four wagons we got out that night;
The other one left until daylight.

7

Next morning we rose up in haste,
And soon we did our breakfast take;
In the river, looked and saw in sight
The wagon we'd left over night.
The Captain started on a trot
And very soon refreshments got.
Toasts were drunk, the cup went round,
And soon we in the tide did bound.

8

Then thru the waters we did dash,
Some ropes onto the box we lashed;
Then up and down the stream did feel
But soon found out we had lost one wheel.
And soon we towed the box to shore;
Refreshments went around once more,
Which cheered our hearts and spirits bold,
And soon the train in motion rolled.

9

We are as jolly a Mormon band
As ever traveled over land,
And what I have told you is a fact;
It happened when we crossed the Platte.
On this or any other trip,
Our duty we will not forget;
In the water, on the land
We'll always by our Captain stand.

TEXT: Carter (1944), pp. 517-519. Used by permission of Daughters of Utah Pioneers.

WILLIAM WILLES # THE WAY THEY EMIGRATE

TUNE: Female Auctioneer

1

Of all the systems I can name
　　Within our bee hive State,
Is that which much concerns us all,
　　The way they emigrate.
Some chose the wagon and ox team,
　　And said it was the best;
With some the handcarts were supreme,
　　And pull'd them with a zest.
　　　　To swell the mighty throng
　　　　In the Valleys of the West,
　　　　They come, etc., to be blest.

2

Some pad the hoof with patience rare
　　Across the plains of sage,
And sturdy men and maidens fair,
　　And youth and tottering age;
But many, when they reach our home,
　　Dissatisfied appear,
And say they wish they ne'er had come,
　　And think their lot severe;
　　　　And soon they hop the twig.
　　　　From the valleys of the west,
　　　　They come, etc., but not to be blest.

3

The best of all the plans to swell
　　The emigration here
Are arrivals from behind the vail,
　　When the babies do appear.
God bless the little babies dear.
　　I hail them with delight;
Of them, there's very little fear.
　　They'll ever take their flight,
　　　　But be faithful to the end
　　　　In the valleys of the West.
　　　　They come, etc., to be blest.

4

And, now the iron horse doth snort,
　　And brings the Saints along.
With lightning speed they now are brought
　　To swell the mighty throng.
And many strangers will come up
　　To visit Zion's stake
And ask to join our standard
　　And of our light partake,
　　　　And make them happy homes
　　　　In the valleys of the West.
　　　　They come, etc., to be blest.

TEXT: Willes (1872), pp. 38-39.

WISH I WAS A MORMONITE

The Saints have generated much music in Gentiles, too, although there is plenty of testimony that Mormons themselves may be the most vigorous, if circumspect, singers of anti-Mormon songs. Here, we present some of those songs making fun, neither always clean nor good, of various Mormon beliefs and practices. The most tapped source of humor was the doctrine of polygamy—publically denied until the church resorted to Utah, and officially condemned by it in 1890. Johnson's San Francisco Minstrels' "Wish I Was a Mormonite" puzzles over the rare abilities of "the man Who'd bring another woman home To my wife, Sarah Ann." A typical complementary argument would be like the scrap of doggerel run in an 1866 issue of the *Union Vedette*. The aim of that organ, founded by Colonel Patrick Connor of the volunteer California occupation force in Salt Lake City during the Civil War, was to "educate the Mormons in American views":

> 'Tis strange, I vow—if we have to believe
>   In the truth of the Lion's revelation—
> That God, when He fashioned fair Eve
>   For Adam's express delectation,
> Did not—still further these "Saints" to console—
>   Place *more* of the "Dears" under Adam's control.

On the other side, William Willes's "The Mormon Creed" was a cautionary reminder to his people to mind their own business and ignore the criticisms of those whose "false systems of the day Shall melt into thin air."

Scholars have noted the existence of a Brigham Young cycle, a nascent epic with components scattered at the folk level; and there is an anti-Brigham Young cycle, too, some bits of which are gathered here. "Brigham Young, I," from *Conner's Irish Song Book*, is a dialect piece bemoaning Uncle Sam's interruption of his difficult domesticity. "Brigham Young, II," begins with a barnyard atmosphere—the roaring ram among his fine tub sheep and pretty little lambs—but more relevant here is its backhanded recognition of Mormon tunefulness:

Now his boys they all sing songs all day, and his girls they all sing psalms;
And among such a crowd he has it pretty loud, for they're as musical as a Chinee gong.

"The Mormon King" by G. W. Anderson, a parody of the popular stage song "King of the Cannibal Islands," was written about 1857, the time of the Mormon "War." It is rather abusive:

> If we get old Brigham in our paws,
> We'll make him close his heavenly jaws,
> And let him know that we've got laws
>   For old Salt Lake City.

The "Mormon Love Serenade," possibly quite recent, passionately pledges a freely given sixteenth of its narrator's love. Where such mathematics reign, one wonders what the other fifteen wives thought of their hubby's request, "Then wilt thou not thy fraction yield To make complete my perfect bliss?"

Satirizing not only polygamy but evangelism, the husband-narrator of "My Wife Has Become a Mormonite" laments her daily strolls with a sanctified young chap and the subsequent loss of the family furniture.

William Willes parodied all these critics with "In the Midst of These Awful Mormons," also set to their favorite tune, "King of the Cannibal Islands." It mocks the idea that the Mormons threatened the serenity of the Union and, incidentally, mentions a custom infrequently attacked by outsiders:

> And Brigham Young, he is their king;
> To him, they tithes and offerings bring.

Finally, and again to the same tune, "The Cohabs," by the devout George Hicks, describes the indignities awaiting those arrested under the antipolygamy Edmunds Act of 1882. Five hundred individuals were taken into custody, but the real effect of the act was to delay statehood and withhold the vote and public office from all those whom a presidential commission judged "unfit."

WISH I WAS A MORMONITE

1

I wish I was a Mormonite,
    And lived in Utah State,
In the shadow of the Temple,
    Close beside its "holy gate";
That I might see the Prophet pass,
    That good and gracious man,
More wondrous than false Mahomet,
    Tamerlane, or Ghengis Khan.

2

I'd like to be a Deacon bold—
    They lead such pious lives—
With lots of "tin" and real estate,
    And half a hundred wives.
If *one* is here considered right,
    Then no one can deny
That fifty wives are just the thing
    The flesh to mortify.

3

I don't know how they manage there,
    But I'd like to see the man
Who'd bring another woman home
    To my wife, Sarah Ann;
There'd be the tallest kind of row
    That ever you heard tell—
The other gal would have to clear,
    Or else be sent to——Well.

4

I s'pose old Brigham knows the way
    The womenkind to please:
I scarce can manage one, while he
    Takes fifty at his ease.
If this great man should die, and he
    To make a will should fail,
I wonder if his heir at law
    Would all his wives entail?

TEXT: Johnson (1863), pp. 30-31.
VARIANT: Fife and Fife (1956), p. 125.

J. W. CONNER

BRIGHAM YOUNG, I

TUNE: Villikins and His Dinah

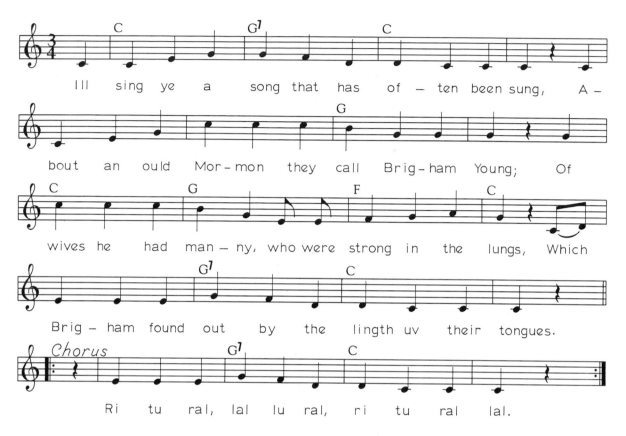

I'll sing ye a song that has of-ten been sung, A-
bout an ould Mor-mon they call Brig-ham Young; Of
wives he had man-ny, who were strong in the lungs, Which
Brig-ham found out by the lingth uv their tongues.

Chorus

Ri tu ral, lal lu ral, ri tu ral lal.

1
I'll sing ye a song that has often been sung,
About an ould Mormon they call Brigham Young;
Of wives he had manny, who were strong in the lungs,
Which Brigham found out by the lingth uv their tongues.

CHORUS: Ri tu ral, lal lu ral, ri tu ral lal.

2
Oh, sad was the life of a Mormon to lade,
Yet Brigham adhered all his life to his crade;
He said 'twas sich fun, and thrue, widout doubt,
Jist to see the young wives knock the ould ones about.

3
One day, as ould Brigham sat down to his dinner,
He saw a young wife who was not getting thinner;
Whin the elders cried out, one afther the udther,
"By the holy, she wants to go home to her mudther!"

4
Ould Brigham replied (which can't be denied)
He cudn't afford to lose sich a bride!
"Thin do not be jealous, but banish yer fears,
For the tree is well known by the fruit which it bears.

5

"That I love one and all, ye very well know,
Thin, do not provoke me, or my anger I'll show.
What wud be our fate, if found here in a row,
Should Uncle Sam come wid his row de dow dow?

6

"Thin cease all yer quarrels, an' do not deshpair;
To meet Uncle Sam, I'll quickly prepare.
Hark! I hear Yankee Doodle playing over the hills!
Och! here's the innemy, come wid their cannon and pills!"

7

Whin the both armies met and the fusht gun was fired,
Ould Brigham was shot, an' he quickly expired!
But, ere life had vanished, he said; "If I'd manes,
I'd smather ivvery woman that gave me my——*green corn!*"

TEXT: Conner (1868), p. 23.

MUSIC: Turner *et al.* (1858), p. 5.

VARIANTS: *Marching Through Georgia and the Wearing of the Green Songster* (San Francisco: Appleton & Co., 1867), pp. 24-25; Lomax (1916), pp. 399-400; Lomax and Lomax (1938), pp. 399-400; Fife and Fife (1956), p. 123.

BRIGHAM YOUNG, II

Old Brig—ham Young was a Mor—mon bold and a

lead—er of the roar—ing rams, And a

shep—herd of a heap of pret—ty lit—tle sheep and a

nice fold of pret—ty lit—tle lambs. And he

lived with five and for—ty wives in the

cit—y of the Great Salt Lake, Where they

woo and coo as pret—ty doves do, and

cack—le like ducks to a drake.

Chorus

Brig—ham, Brig—ham Young,'tis a mir—a—cle he sur—vives, With his

roar—ing rams,his pret—ty lit—tle lambs,and his five and for—ty wives.

1

Old Brigham Young was a Mormon bold and a leader of the roaring rams,
And a shepherd of a heap of pretty little sheep and a nice fold of pretty
little lambs.
And he lived with five and forty wives in the city of the Great Salt Lake,
Where they woo and coo as pretty doves do, and cackle like ducks to a
drake.

CHORUS: Brigham Young, 'tis a miracle he survives,
With his roaring rams, his pretty little lambs, and his five and
forty wives.

2

Number forty-five was about sixteen, number one was sixty-three,
And among such a riot, how he ever keeps them quiet is a right-down mystery to me;
For they clatter and they claw and they jaw, jaw, jaw; each one has a
different desire.
It would aid the renown of the best shop in town to supply them with half
what they require.

3

Oh, Brigham Young was a stout man once, but now he is thin and old,
And I love to state there's no hair on his pate, which once wore a covering
of gold;
For his youngest wives won't have white wool, and his old ones won't take
red,
So tearing it out they have taken turn about, till they've pulled all the wool
from his head.

4

Now his boys they all sing songs all day, and his girls they all sing psalms;
And among such a crowd he has it pretty loud, for they're as musical as a
Chinee gong.
And when they advance for a Mormon dance, he is filled with the greatest
surprise,
For they're sure to end the night with a tabernacle fight and scratch out
one another's eyes.

5

There never was a home like Brigham Young's, so curious and so queer,
For if his joys are double he has a terrible lot of trouble, for it gains on
him year by year.
He sets in his state and bears his fate in a sanctified sort of way,
He has one wife to bury, and one wife to marry, and a new kid born every
day.

6

Now if anybody envies Brigham Young, let them go to Great Salt Lake;
And if they have leisure to examine at their pleasure, they'll find it's a
great mistake.
One wife at a time, so says my rhyme, is enough for the proudest don,
So ere you strive to live lord of forty-five, live happy if you can with one.

TEXT AND MUSIC: Fife and Fife (1956), pp. 121-123. Used by permission of Indiana University Press.

VARIANTS: Lomax (1916), pp. 401-402; Lomax and Lomax (1934), pp. 432-433, and
(1938), pp. 400-401; Fife and Fife (1947), pp. 49-51, and (1956), pp. 121-123; Hubbard
(1961), pp. 408-409.

G. W. ANDERSON

THE MORMON KING

TUNE: King of the Cannibal Islands

Oh hark, kind friends, while I do sing A — bout Brig–ham Young, the Mor — mon King. Who swears that he'll do ev — ery–thing Out in Salt Lake Cit — y. He al — so says we'll rue the day That e'er we came in — to his way, For all of us he'll sure — ly slay Out in Salt Lake Cit — y. Old Brig — ham, mind your P's and Q's, Or we will show you what to do, If we get our hands on you Out in Salt Lake Cit — y.

1

Oh hark kind friends while I do sing
About Brigham Young, the Mormon King
Who swears that he'll do everything
    Out in Salt Lake City.
He also says we'll rue the day
That e'er we came into his way,
For all of us he'll surely slay
    Out in Salt Lake City.

CHORUS: Old Brigham, mind your P's and Q's
Or we will show you what to do,
If we get our hands on you
    Out in Salt Lake City.

2

Poor Brigham's mind, it can't be right,
Or else he's surely lost his sight,
To think he'd a Yankee 'fright
    Away from Salt Lake City.
Old Brigham he has somewhere's near
About seventy wives and children dear.
Oh Lor' they must be very queer
    Out in Salt Lake City.

3

They say their children are quite tall,
And like their father loudly squall,
And often make old Brigham bawl—
    Out in Salt Lake City.
If that's the case, some future day
We'll make him bawl another way,
For his motley crew we'll surely slay,
    Out in Salt Lake City.

4

Old Brigham mustn't think we are fools,
To be knocked about like wooden stools,
But we will let him know our rules,
    Out in Salt Lake City.
If any fuss he goes to make,
The whole of his city we will take,
And then fasten him unto a stake
    Out in Salt Lake City.

5

If we get old Brigham in our paws,
We'll make him close his heavenly jaws,
And let him know that we've got laws
    For old Salt Lake City.

TEXT: *The Mormon King*, words by G. W. Anderson, Irish vocalist (New York: Andrews, n.d.).

MUSIC: Vernon (1927), pp. 156-157.

WILLIAM WILLES   # THE MORMON CREED

TUNE: The Days That We Went Gipsying

1

The Mormon Creed I'll now explain,
    Which you may quickly learn:
'Tis "mind your own business,"
    And that's no small concern.
For all the people in the world
    That I have ever known,
Are apt to mind their neighbors',
    And oft forget their own.

CHORUS: So let us mind the Mormon Creed,
    And then we all shall thrive,
Shall hide a multitude of sins,
    And save our souls alive.

2

The Mormons oft forget their creed,
    Altho' it is so plain,
And meddle where they have no need,
    And cause much grief and pain.
Whereas, if they would only heed
    The Spirit's warning voice,
They'd find that this is just the creed
    That's worthy of their choice.

3

The Mormon Creed is built upon
    The rock of ages sure,
With prophets and apostles too,
    It ever shall endure;
And all false systems of the day
    Shall melt into thin air,
And all the evils sin has caused,
    King Jesus will repair.

4

The Mormon Creed we've learned from
    The prophet of the Lord,
For he came forth to lead us home,
    And gives to us God's word;
And all who will obedient be,
    And to the end endure,
From sin and death they will be free,
    Eternal life secure.

TEXT: Willes (1872), pp. 42-43.

ALFRED NORTON # MORMON LOVE SERENADE # S. RIGGS

Say, Su-san, wilt thou come with me, In sweet com—mun—i—ty to live? Of heart and hand and home to thee, A six—teenth part I'll free—ly give, Of all the love that swells my breast, Of all the hon—or of my name, Of world-ly wealth by me pos-sessed, A six—teenth por—tion thou shalt claim.

1

Say, Susan, wilt thou come with me,
In sweet community to live?
Of heart and hand and home to thee,
A sixteenth part I'll freely give,
Of all the love that swells my breast,
Of all the honor of my name,
Of worldly wealth by me possessed,
A sixteenth portion thou shalt claim.

2

Nay, tell me not too many share
The blessings that I offer thee;
Thou'lt find but fifteen others there,
A household happy, gay and free.
A mod'rate household, I may say,
My neighbor has as many more
And Brother Brigham, o'er the way,
Luxuriates in forty-four.

3

I'll give thee whatso'er thou wilt,
So it but be a sixteenth part;
'Twould be the deepest depth of guilt,
To slight the rest who share my heart.
Then wilt thou not thy fraction yield
To make complete my perfect bliss?
Say "yes" and let our joy be sealed
With just the sixteenth of a kiss.

TEXT AND MUSIC: Briegel (1933), p. 45. Used by permission of George F. Briegel, Inc.
VARIANTS: Davidson (1945), pp. 293-294; Hubbard (1961), p. 415.

MY WIFE HAS BECOME A MORMONITE

Be - hold in me a bro-ken man, all bro-ken down with woe; I've

lost my wife and can-not find her wher - ev - er I may go. At

first she robbed me of my love, and now she's gone from me. And

tak — en all my fur - ni - ture. Wher - ev - er can she be?

Chorus

Per — haps she's on the rail — way with a swell so fair; Per-

haps she's up in a bal-loon rid — ing through the air; Per-

haps she's dead, per — haps she's a - live, per — haps she's gone to sea; Per-

haps she's gone to Brig — ham Young, a Mor-mon - ite to be.

1

Behold in me a broken man, all broken down with woe;
I've lost my wife and cannot find her wherever I may go.
At first she robbed me of my love, and now she's gone from me
And taken all my furniture. Wherever can she be?

CHORUS: Perhaps she's on the railway with a swell so fair;
Perhaps she's up in a balloon riding through the air;
Perhaps she's dead, perhaps she's alive, perhaps she's gone to
    sea;
Perhaps she's gone to Brigham Young, a Mormonite to be.

She read so much of Mormonites, so nothing else she'd talk;
And with a sanctified young chap, each day she used to walk.
She said he was a Mormonite from far across the sea;
She's taken all my furniture. Wherever can she be?

TEXT AND MUSIC: Hubbard (1961), pp. 416-417. Used by permission of University of Utah Press.

VARIANTS: Hubbard (1947), p. 92; Randolph (1949), p. 266.

IN THE MIDST OF
THESE AWFUL MORMONS

WILLIAM WILLES

TUNE: King of the Cannibal Islands

Oh dear, I'm sad, I've got the blues; I've late-ly heard some
dread-ful news; I real-ly trem-ble in my shoes__ 'Tis
all a-bout the Mor-mons! For sure, they are the
stran-gest set That ev—er in this world were met; They
live in a place called Des—er—et In the midst of the Rock-y
Moun-tains. And Brig—ham Young, he is their king; To
him, they tithes and of-fer-ings bring, And he con-trols in
ev—ery-thing, In the midst of these aw—ful Mor—mons.

1

Oh dear, I'm sad, I've got the blues;
I've lately heard some dreadful news;
I really tremble in my shoes—
    'Tis all about the Mormons!
For sure, they are the strangest set
That ever in this world were met;
They live in a place called Deseret
    In the midst of the Rocky Mountains.

CHORUS: And Brigham Young, he is their
    king;
To him they tithes and offerings
    bring,
And he controls in everything,
    In the midst of these awful
    Mormons.

2

These poor deluded people say
O'er all the world they'll soon bear sway,
And sweep the Gentiles all away,
    And "send them to hell across lots,"
For none but Mormons there can stay.
I'm sure there'll be the devil to pay
Unless there's something quickly done
    To put these saucy Mormons down.

3

In all the nations of the world,
These Mormons have their flag unfurled,
And sent their missionaries round
    To spread their awful doctrines.
It matters not which way we turn,
Nothing but Mormons we discern.
I wonder how there came to be
    "So many beastly Mormons."

4

These Mormons marry many wives,
And every man among them strives
To raise the greatest crowd of boys,
    To thrash the wicked Gentiles.
And men and women all agree
To Brigham they'll obedient be;
And at his little finger's crook,
    They'll bring outsiders all to book.

5

So now I think you'll all agree
It is a shocking thing to see
So many people led astray
    By their "beastly abominations."
I wish that Uncle Sam would send
The troops—and make these Mormons
    quickly bend
    To Christian institutions.

6

For, if he don't we're all undone,
As sure as light is in the sun;
The Mormons they will take away
    Our glorious state and nation.
For sure they are the strangest set
That ever in this world were met;
They live in a place called Deseret
    In the midst of the Rocky Mountains.

———————

TEXT: Willes (1872), pp. 49-50.

MUSIC: Vernon (1927), pp. 156-157.

VARIANTS: Fife and Fife (1956), pp. 123-124; Hubbard (1961), pp. 410-411.

GEORGE HICKS   # THE COHABS

TUNE: King of the Cannibal Islands

1
Now, you cohabs, still dodging round,
You'd better keep on underground,
For if with number two you're found,
They'll put you into limbo.

2
Some gent will meet you at the gate,
And with complexion, height and weight,
The contents of your pockets take
When you get into limbo.

3
They'll shave your face and mow your hair,
And give you striped clothes to wear,
And see that you have the best of care
When you get into limbo.

4
O when you pass the double door
The coons within begin to roar:
"Fresh fish, fresh fish is all the go
When you get into limbo."

5
On Friday, fish, on Sunday, beans;
The bread is fit for kings and queens;
All you lack is cabbage and greens
When you get into limbo.

6
Here you see both men and boys
Making different kinds of toys,
And bridles, whips, and walking sticks
When you get into limbo.

7
And if you do not fall in line,
They'll put you into fifty-nine
And take away your toffer time
When you get into limbo.

TEXT: Hubbard (1961), p. 418. Used by permission of University of Utah Press.
VARIANT: Fife and Fife (1956), p. 332.

BRIGHAM YOUNG

THE MORMON QUESTION

The "Mormon question" was raised in the national mind by the reports and diatribes of returning federal officers who found there was little they could or had to do in the way of administration among the proud, self-governing Mormons. President Buchanan gave credence to the reports of licentiousness and anarchy, and in 1857 dispatched 2,500 troops, ultimately under Albert Sidney Johnston, to settle the question. Although the song "The Mormon Question" does not betray it, the people of Utah panicked. Hurried preparations for evacuation, "scorched earth," and guerrilla warfare were made as Brigham Young violently denounced the invasion. "The Mormon Du Dah Song" shouts down the "Missouri ass" (Federal Governor Alfred Cumming) and "Squaw-Killer Harney" (the general replaced en route by Johnston). What Mormon delaying tactics there were, were sufficient to halt Johnston on the eastern side of the Wasatch Range over the winter; and by the time his army entered Salt Lake City the following June, all parties on the scene had cooled off.

William Willes's "The Mormons in the Mountains" looks back on those days and at the continuing but less imminent threats to Mormon sovereignty. Among those were the harsh criticisms of polygamists recorded in John Davies' "Uncle Sam and the Mormons." Another song from the *Bee Hive Songster* (1868), "All Are Talking of Utah," lists among its topics one that we have noted as provoking as much talk, song, and change as any, "Whatever may be coming, we cannot well foresee; For it may be the railroad, or some great prodigy."

Had they been able to take a train, the Fancher party of some 140 Ozark emigrants on their way through southern Utah in that difficult year of 1857 might have made it. As it was, they were the victims of what the broadside version printed here called "The Utah Horror! Darkest Deed of the 19th Century! Mountain Meadows Massacre!" On Sunday evening, September 6, a meeting of Nauvoo Legion and Mormon Church leaders at Cedar City vowed to finish the job of exterminating the party begun by Indians whom the Missourians had provoked. On September 10 the Mormons approached the embattled party and gave assurances of protection as they escorted them to Cedar City. After separating eighteen children from the others, the Mormons and Indians fell upon the group and slaughtered them. Confusion surrounding the extent of Mormon culpability caused the Johnston command to regard the affair as another of the misfortunes their military presence would henceforth prevent, and the preoccupations of the Civil War silenced the issue in the 1860's. In the early 1870's, however, renewed Gentile indignation in Utah and elsewhere provoked a vigorous prosecution of the case, with the result that John D. Lee, commander of the Mormon band at the massacre, was captured, tried, brought back to the Meadows, and shot by a firing squad on March 23, 1877. Several versions of the ballad exist, assigning various degrees of guilt to Brigham Young and Lee. The version given here, from a San Francisco broadside (*ca.* 1875-1877), is complete and blames them both.

We conclude this section with two songs showing the alternative attitudes with which the Mormons could face a future in the Union. "The Mormon Bishop's Lament" is the purported first-person confession of a wretched churchman. After admitting a part in a variety of atrocities, including Mountain Meadows, he sighs for a restful pit in hell. "The Mormon Car," on the other hand, sporting a timely metaphor, embraces the future:

> We've been long enough in leading-strings and can't with patience wait,
> But we'll make our bow to Uncle Sam and ask to be a State;
> And then with Brigham at the head, and Jed' and Heber too,
> We'll all unite, with one consent, and pop her quickly through.

THE MORMON QUESTION

1

When Uncle Sam, he first set out his army to destroy us,
Says he, "The Mormons we will rout, they shall no longer annoy us."
The force he sent was competent to "try" and "hang" for treason;
That is, I mean it would have been, but don't you know the reason?

CHORUS: There's great commotion in the East about the Mormon question;
The problem is, to say the least, too much for their digestion.

2

As we were going up the Platte singing many a lusty ditty,
Saying we'll do this and we'll do that when we get to Salt Lake City,
And sure enough when they got there, they made the Mormons stir, Sir;
That is, I mean they would have done, but oh, they didn't get there.

When they got within two hundred miles, the old boys they were saying,
"It will be but a little while, till the Mormons he'll be slaying.
We'll hang each man who has two wives, we've plenty of rope quite handy";
That is, I mean they would have had, but Smith burned it on "Sandy."

4

Then they returned with awful tales, saying "The Mormons beat the devil:
They ride up hill, and over rocks as fast as on the level;
And if perchance you shoot one down, and surely think he's dead, Sir,
The first you know he's on his horse and pushing on ahead, Sir!"

5

Then on "Ham's Fork" they camped awhile, saying, "We'll wait a little
     longer,
'Till Johnson and his crew come up, and make us a little stronger.
Then we'll go on, take Brigham Young, and Heber, his companion;"
That is, I mean they would have done, but were afraid of Echo Canyon.

6

Now Uncle Sam, take my advice; you'd better stay at home, Sir!
You need your money and your men to defend your rights at home, Sir!
But if, perchance, you need some help, the Mormons will be kind, Sir.
They've helped you once, and will again, that is, if you've a mind, Sir!

TEXT AND MUSIC: Daughters of Utah Pioneers (1932), pp. 84-85. Used by permission of Daughters of Utah Pioneers.

VARIANTS: Briegel (1933), pp. 20-21; Carter (1944), p. 515; Davidson (1945), p. 286; Hubbard (1959), pp. 125-126, and (1961), pp. 436-439.

WILLIAM WILLES   # THE MORMONS IN THE MOUNTAINS

TUNE: The Captain with His Whiskers

1

Many people in the nations
    Are very much afraid
Of the Mormons in the mountains,
    Who, they fear, will make a raid;
For they tremble in their shoes,
    And they don't know what to do,
And they swear in their anger
    They will surely pop us through.
They firstly cut us off,
    And anon we are annexed;
They think that we're a hard case
    And all are sorely vexed.

2

While the Saints were in their borders,
    They could not let them rest;
We've suffered from marauders,
    Who, to kill us, did their best.
They drove us to the mountains,
    As they thought, quite out of sight,
Hop'd the Indians would kill us,
    And annihilate us quite.
But they're very much deceiv'd,
    For, we didn't die just then:
Our deliverance God achieved
    From the hands of wicked men.

3

And now that they find
    We are thriving in the West,
They all are combining
    To disturb us from our rest.
They hate those they've injured,
    And they overflow with gall,
For their conscience is disturbed,
    And made cowards of them all.
So if they swallow us,
    They'll find a heavy load,
Like the sorrow-stricken snake,
    When he gulped the horny-toad.

TEXT: Willes (1872), pp. 119-120.

THE MORMON DU DAH SONG

S. C. FOSTER

TUNE: De Camptown Races

There's sev-en hun-dred wag-ons on the way, Du – dah!

Du – dah! And their cat-tle are nu-mer-ous, so they say,

Du – dah! Du – dah day! Now, to let them per-ish would

be a sin, Du – dah! Du–dah! So we'll take all they've got for

bring-ing them in, Du – dah! Du – dah day!

Chorus

Then let us be on hand, By Brig-ham Young to stand; And

if our en – e-mies do ap-pear, We'll sweep them off the land.

1

There's seven hundred wagons on the way,
 Du dah! Du dah!
And their cattle are numerous, so they say,
 Du dah! Du dah day!
Now, to let them perish would be sin,
 Du dah! Du dah!
So we'll take all they've got for bringing them in,
 Du dah! Du dah day!

CHORUS: Then let us be on hand,
 By Brigham Young to stand;
 And if our enemies do appear,
 We'll sweep them off the land.

2

Old Sam has sent, I understand,
    Du dah! Du dah!
A Missouri ass to rule our land,
    Du dah! Du dah day!
But if he comes, we'll have some fun,
    Du dah! Du dah!
To see him and his juries run,
    Du dah! Du dah day!

3

Old Squaw-Killer Harney is on his way,
    Du dah! Du dah!
The Mormon people for to slay,
    Du dah! Du dah day!
Now if he comes, the truth I'll tell,
    Du dah! Du dah!
Our boys will drive him down to hell,
    Du dah! Du dah day!

TEXT: T. B. H. Stenhouse, *The Rocky Mountain Saints* (New York, 1873), pp. 370, 372.

MUSIC: *Minstrel Songs, Old and New* (1882), pp. 94-95.

VARIANTS: Marshall (1882), pp. 206-207; J. H. Beadle, *Polygamy* (Philadelphia: National Publishing Co., 1904), pp. 159-160; Daughters of Utah Pioneers (1932), pp. 188-189; Briegel (1933), p. 47; Davidson (1945), pp. 286-287; Hubbard (1959), p. 124, and (1961), p. 441.

ALL ARE TALKING OF UTAH

H. C. WORK

Tune: Marching Through Georgia

1

Who'd ever think that Utah would stir the world so much?
Who'd ever think the Mormons were widely known as such?
I hardly dare to scribble, or such a subject touch;
For all are talking of Utah.

CHORUS: Hurrah! hurrah! The Mormons have the name;
Hurrah! hurrah! They're on the road to fame.
Don't matter what they style us; it's all about the same;
For all are talking of Utah.

2

'Tis Utah and the Mormons in Congress, pulpit, press.
'Tis Utah and the Mormons in every place, I guess.
We must be growing greater: we can't be growing less;
For all are talking of Utah.

3

They say they'll send an army to set the Mormons right,
Regenerate all Utah, and show us Christian light,
Release our wives and daughters, and put us men to flight;
For all are talking of Utah.

4

They say that Utah cannot be numbered as a State.
They wish our lands divided, but left it rather late.
It's hard to tell of Mormons what yet may be their fate;
For all are talking of Utah.

5

Whatever may be coming, we cannot well foresee;
For it may be the railroad, or some great prodigy.
At least the noted Mormons are watching what's to be;
For all are talking of Utah.

6

I now will tell you something you never thought of yet:
We bees are nearly filling the hive of Desert.
If hurt, we'll sting together, and gather all we get;
For all are talking of Utah.

TEXT: *Deseret News* (Salt Lake City), Jan. 30, 1867.

MUSIC: *War Songs* (1883), p. 30.

VARIANTS: *Bee Hive Songster* (1868), pp. 18-19; Willes (1872), pp. 66-67; Carter (1944), pp. 521-522; Hubbard (1947), pp. 77-78, (1959), p. 127, and (1961), p. 450.

THE MOUNTAIN MEADOWS MASSACRE

Come all ye Sons of Free____ dom, Un—
to my rhyme give ear. 'Tis of an aw—ful
mas—sa—cre You pre—sent—ly shall hear. In
splen-dor o'er the moun__ tains, Some thir—ty wag-ons came, At—
tacked by a wretch-ed band: Oh! U—tah, blush for shame.

1
Come all ye Sons of Freedom,
Unto my rhyme give ear,
'Tis of an awful massacre
You presently shall hear.

2
In splendor o'er the mountains
Some thirty wagons came,
Attacked by a wretched band:
Oh! Utah, blush for shame.

3
It was in Indian garb and colors,
Those bloody hounds were seen
To flock around that little train
All on the meadows green.

4
Attacked in the morning
As the train was under way,
They forthwith corralled their wagons
And fought in blood all day.

5

Till Lee, the Captain of the band,
This word to them he gave,
Saying, "If you will give up your arms,
We surely will let you live."

6

With this request they did comply,
Thinking their lives to save;
Lee's words were broken like the rest,
Which sent them to their grave

7

When once their arms they did give up
And started for Cedar City,
They rushed on them, Indian style:
Oh! what a human pity.

8

They melted down with one accord,
Like wax before the flame,
Both men and women, old and young:
Oh! Utah blush for shame.

9

To see mothers and their children
Lying bleeding in their gore,
Oh! such an awful sight, I think,
Was never seen before.

10

It was by orders of the President
This bloody deed was done,
The leader of the Mormon Church,
Whose name is Brigham Young.

11

Their property being divided
Among the bloody crew,
And Uncle Sam is trying
To see the matter through.

TEXT: *The Utah Horror!* (San Francisco: Bruce's Printing House, *ca.* 1875-1877 [broadside]).

MUSIC: Fife (1953), p. 234. Used by permission of California Folklore Society.

VARIANTS: Fife (1953), pp. 229-241*; Fife and Fife (1956), pp. 72-73; Burt (1958a), pp. 118-119, and (1959), pp. 150-151; Toelken (1959), pp. 169-171; Hubbard (1961), pp. 445-446; Laws (1964), p. 142*.

JOHN J. DAVIES   # UNCLE SAM AND THE MORMONS

1

Yes, Uncle Sam is trying his best
To drive the Mormons from the West.
I hope that we shall stand the test,
Brigham at the head.

CHORUS: Sing, let us sing,
Brigham Young shall be our King;
Sing, sing, let us sing,
Sing for the Priesthood, sing.

2

Colfax, he was in fret
When he was here in Deseret:
He said, "The Mormons we'll upset;
Brigham ain't the man."

3

And Cragin thought that he was wise,
Yet Mormonism he despised;
But he, with all the others, lies
About the Mormon boys.

4

Bill Collum also with the rest
Said in Congress he knew best:
"We'll rout the Mormons from the West;
Brigham ain't the man."

5

The Editors, they've tried their best
To publish lies on Deseret,
And some of them proclaimed we'll fight,
Brigham at the head.

6

Sectarians, they do all they can
To stop the Savior's glorious plan,
But Mormonism goes on:
Brigham is the man.

7

They say that we're an awful set
Away out here in Deseret,
But we don't care and let them sweat:
Brigham is the man.

8

Minister Foote, I understand,
Is coming back to the Mormon land
With twenty thousand dollars on hand
To civilize the Saints.

9

Minister Foote must be a fool
To think the Mormons he can rule,
And we don't want Gentile schools:
We can do without them.

10

The next comes in is Judge McKean.
He thought the Saints were very green.
He soon found out a different scene.
Brigham is the man.

11

And Doctor Newman came to test
Plural marriage in Deseret,
But Orson Pratt made him to sweat:
Orson was the man.

12

Prince Edmunds thought that he did well.
His proclamation he did tell.
He must repent or go to hell:
Brigham is the man.

13

Come, faithful Saints, and be on hand
To obey the Lord's command
That we may go on hand in hand:
Brigham is the man.

14

My friends, the truth I must unfold
That Brigham Young was called of God
As Abraham in days of old:
God is at the helm.

TEXT: "Diary of John J. Davies," *Utah Historical Quarterly*, IX (1941), 166-167.
VARIANT: Davidson (1945), pp. 289-290.

THE MORMON BISHOP'S LAMENT

I am a Mormon bishop, and I will tell you what I know.
I joined the confraternity some forty years ago.
I then had youth upon my brow and eloquence, my tongue;
But I had the sad misfortune then to meet with Brigham Young.

He said, "Young man, come join our band and bid hard work farewell.
You are too smart to waste your time in toil by hill and dell.
There is a ripening harvest, and our hooks shall find the fool;
And in the distant nations, we shall train them in our school."

I listened to his preaching, and I learned all the role;
And the truth of Mormon doctrines burned deep within my soul.
I married sixteen women, and I spread my new belief.
I was sent to preach the gospel to the pauper and the thief.

'Twas in the glorious days when Brigham was our only Lord and King,
And his wild cry of defiance from the Wasatch tops did ring.
'Twas when that bold Bill Hickman and that Porter Rockwell led,
And in the blood atonements the pits received the dead.

They took in Dr. Robertson and left him in his gore,
And the Aiken brothers sleep in peace on Nephi's distant shore.
We marched to Mountain Meadows; and on that glorious field,
With rifle and with hatchet, we made man and woman yield.

'Twas there we were victorious with our legions fierce and brave.
We left the butched victims on the ground without a grave.
We slew the load of emigrants on Sublet's lonely road
And plundered many a trader of his then most precious load.

Alas, for, all the powers that were in the by-gone time!
What we did as deeds of glory are condemned as bloody crime.
No more the blood atonements keep the doubting one in fear,
While the faithful were rewarded with a wedding once a year.

As the nation's chieftain President says, "Our days of rule are o'er,"
And his marshals with their warrants are on watch at every door,
Old John he now goes skulking on the by-roads of our land,
Or, unknown, he keeps in hiding with the faithful of our band.

Old Brigham now is stretched beneath the cold and silent clay,
And the chieftains now are fallen that were mighty in their day.
Of the six and twenty women that I wedded long ago,
There are two now left to cheer me in these awful hours of woe.
The rest are scattered where the Gentile's flag's unfurled,
And two score of my daughters are now numbered with the world.

Oh, my poor old bones are aching and my head is turning gray.
Oh, the scenes were black and awful that I've witnessed in my day.
Let my spirit seek the mansion where old Brigham's gone to dwell,
For there's no place for Mormons but the lowest pits of hell.

TEXT: Lomax (1910), pp. 47-50.

VARIANT: Lomax and Lomax (1938), pp. 401-403.

THE MORMON CAR

TUNE: Jeanette and Jeanot

1

The Mormon Car is moving and has been in motion long.
At first her pow'r was feeble, but now it's getting strong;
And having started on the track, the best that we can do
Is to keep the car in motion, and to pop her quickly through.
We have a good Conductor and a Brakesman with his force,
Who, when a danger threatens, can stop the Iron Horse.
We've an Engineer and Fireman, and an Engine good and true;
Then let's keep the car in motion, and pop her quickly through.

She has had a few collisions as she's mov'd along her track,
And been jostled, crush'd, and splinter'd but she never would go back;
And though oppos'd by every power, she's ne'er collapsed a flue,
But let on steam, and clear'd the track, and popp'd her quickly through.
She's had stations with the Buckeyes, and with Pukes and Suckers, too,
Who prophesied the Mormon Car could never travel through;
But on solid track, and fired up, with Deseret in view,
She disappointed all their hopes, and popp'd her quickly through.

3

She's friends around in every land, in nations near and far,
Who're calling for the pure in heart to step into the Car.
They will station them, and ticket them—what more, then, can they do
Than to tell them all to step aboard, and she will pop them through?
And to thousands now in every clime who're hastening to their home,
Who, like "doves unto their windows," or in "ships of Tarshish come,"
There's a place for all, a home for all, in Deseret for you.
Then never faint, but go ahead, and pop her quickly through.

4

We have tried her on Religion, and she's distanc'd every clan.
We're running now with Politics, and soon we'll take the van.
Our Banner floats for all men who do the right pursue,
Who vice despise and virtue love, we'll pop them quickly through.
We've been long enough in leading-strings and can't with patience wait,
But we'll make our bow to Uncle Sam and ask to be a State;
And then with Brigham at the head, and Jed' and Heber too,
We'll all unite, with one consent, and pop her quickly through.

TEXT: Fife (1947), p. 298. Used by permission of Austin E. Fife.
MUSIC: Young and Leonard (1855), p. 32.
VARIANT: Anderson (1947), pp. 188-189.

THE MERRY MORMONS

If Mormon theology is a questionable advance in the history of metaphysics, and if Mormon villainy is too rare to be efficient, it suggests only that Mormons, like other Americans, are far better at other things, such as making an abundant life out of unpromising materials. This last selection of Mormon songs illustrates the resolution and, at times, the fervor with which the Mormons faced the more mundane threats of aridity, locusts, economic competition, flood, and spiritual women.

"The Merry Mormons," by Matthew Rowan, is sometimes called "Daddy, I'm a Mormon." Although it continues the appeals to the Deity to

> Celestialize and purify
> This earth for perfect Mormons,

it also exhibits the quieter confidence under discussion:

> At night the Mormons do convene
> To chat awhile and sing a hymn;
> And one, perchance, repeat a rhyme
> He made about the Mormons.

"Sea Gulls and Crickets" commemorates, as does a monument in Salt Lake City, the seemingly miraculous arrival of "sea gulls feathered in angel-white" to deliver Mormon crops from the ravages of crickets. No hint of Egyptian parallels darkens the simile,

> Black crickets by tens of millions came
> Like fog on a British coast.

William Willes's "Home Manufactures," like the songs about the Mormons' foreign missionary work, demonstrates their competitive and persistently international outlook:

> We will vie with old Birmingham, Sheffield and Leeds,
> And Manchester, too, with its marvellous deeds,
>   For home manufacture will meet all our needs.
> We'll produce cotton cloth without cotton lords
> And employ spinning-jennies in every place.
> We'll make knives and scissors, and trusty good swords,
>   And in broadcloth, be never behind in the race.

"Once I lived in Cottonwood," popular in folk tradition, is another song written by George Hicks. Born in Canada in 1830, he had been in Nauvoo with his parents in 1843, and arrived in Zion in 1852. Several years later he moved to the settlements in southern Utah—Dixie—where, for a while, the production of cotton and molasses was important. This thickly detailed song is a kind of imitation of "Sweet Betsey from Pike," although its tone is more desperate than comic.

"Early Life in Dixie" is a good narrative which starts off in seeing-the-elephant fashion with complaints about the excessive demands on the resources of the colonist. The "ditch" especially required a large share of every man's efforts, but the water it provided made the land fruitful: "Wild sagebrush has yielded its place to the vine, And foul stinking whisky gave way to good wine." "St. George" tells the same story with less narrative and more folksay:

> The wind with fury here doth blow, that when we plant or sow, sir,
> We place one foot upon the seeds and hold them till they grow, sir.

Continual resolution in the face of continual adversity can, obviously, bring tragedy. "The Boys of Sanpete County" relates the drowning of six young members of Captain W. S. Seeley's rescue party in the Green River in June, 1868. The song was popular and was sung to the tune of "Just Before the Battle, Mother." To compensate, we end with a lively, pleasant song, unpretentiously titled "Tittery-irie-aye."

MATTHEW ROWAN

THE MERRY MORMONS

TUNE: Bonny Breast Knots

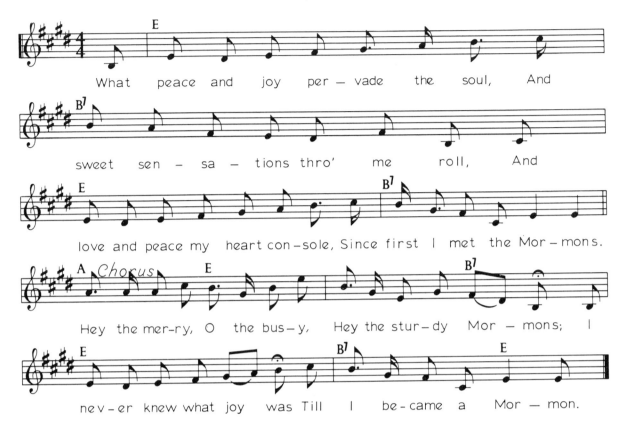

What peace and joy per — vade the soul, And
sweet sen — sa — tions thro' me roll, And
love and peace my heart con — sole, Since first I met the Mor — mons.

Hey the mer-ry, O the bus—y, Hey the stur—dy Mor — mons; I
nev—er knew what joy was Till I be-came a Mor — mon.

1

What peace and joy pervade the soul
And sweet sensations thro' me roll,
And love and peace my heart console,
Since first I met the Mormons.

CHORUS: Hey the merry,
O the busy,
Hey the sturdy Mormons;
I never knew what joy was
Till I became a Mormon.

2

They sing the folly of the wise;
Sectarian precepts they despise:
A heaven far beyond the skies,
Is never sought by Mormons.

3

To Sabbath meetings they repair;
Both old and young assemble there,
The words of inspiration share—
No less can suit the Mormons.

4

At night the Mormons do convene
To chat awhile and sing a hymn;
And one, perchance, repeat a rhyme
He made about the Mormons.

5

The Mormon fathers love to see
Their Mormon families all agree;
The prattling infant on the knee
Cries, "Daddy, I'm a Mormon."

6

As youth in Israel once decried
To wed with those that heaven denied,
So youth among us now have cried,
"We'll marry none but Mormons."

7

High be our heaven, the Mormons cry,
Our place of birth and where we die;
Celestialize and purify
This earth for perfect Mormons.

8

So, while we tread our foeman's ground,
We'll make the trump of freedom sound,
And scatter blessings all around,
Like free and happy Mormons.

TEXT: Willes (1872), pp. 74-75.

MUSIC: Hubbard (1961), p. 405. Used by permission of University of Utah Press.

VARIANTS: Marshall (1882), pp. 212-213; Davidson (1945), pp. 294-295; Hubbard (1961), p. 405.

SEA GULLS AND CRICKETS

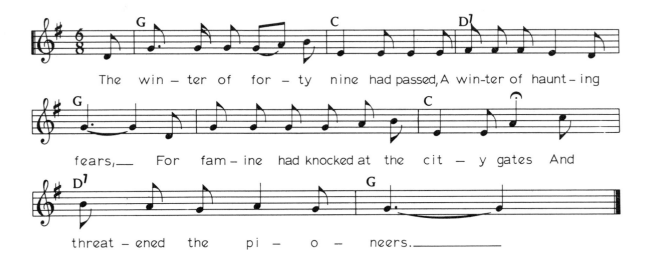

The win-ter of for-ty nine had passed, A win-ter of haunt-ing fears,__ For fam-ine had knocked at the cit-y gates And threat-ened the pi-o-neers.__

1

The winter of '49 had passed,
　　A winter of haunting fears,
For famine had knocked at the city gates
　　And threatened the pioneers.

2

But spring with its smiling skies lent grace
　　And cheer to the hosts within,
And they tilled their fields with a new-born
　　　trust
　　And the courage to fight and win.

3

With the thrill of life, the tender shoots
　　Burst forth from the virgin plain,
And each day added its ray of hope
　　For a blessing of ripened grain.

4

But lo in the east strange clouds appeared
　　And dark became the sun,
And down from the mountainsides there
　　　swept
　　A scourge that the boldest shunned.

5

Black crickets by tens of millions came
　　Like fog on a British coast,
And the finger of devastation marked
　　Its course on the Mormon host.

6

With a vigor that desperation fanned,
　　They battled and smote and slew,
But the clouds still gathered and broke afresh
　　'Til the fields that waved were few.

7

With visions of famine and want and woe,
　　They prayed from their hearts sincere,
When lo from the west came other clouds
　　To succor the pioneers.

8

'Twas sea gulls feathered in angel-white,
　　And angels they were forsooth.
These sea gulls there by the thousands came
　　To battle in very truth.

9

They charged down upon the cricket hordes;
　　And gorging them day and night,
They routed the devastating foe,
　　And the crickets were put to flight.

10

All heads were bowed as they thanked their
　　　God
　　And they reaped while the devil raved.
The harvest was garnered to songs of praise,
　　And the pioneers were saved.

TEXT AND MUSIC: Sung by L. M. Hilton, Ogden, Utah; reproduced in Fife and Fife (1956), pp. 322-324. Used by permission of Indiana University Press.

WILLIAM WILLES

HOME MANUFACTURES

TUNE: Sprig of Shillaleh

Let home man—u—fac—tures en—gage our at—ten—tion, For

for—eign pro—duc—tions must suf—fer de—clen—sion: Here

home man—u—fac—tures must car—ry the day. 'Tis

here in the val—leys the pow—er of in—ven—tion Will

nev—er die out, but will ev—er in—crease. We're

learn—ing the les—son of co—op—er—a—tion, In—

creas—ing in un—ion, and dwel—ling in peace.

1

Let home manufactures engage our attention,
For foreign productions must suffer declension:
     Here home manufactures must carry the day.
'Tis here in the valleys the power of invention
Will never die out, but will ever increase.
We're learning the lesson of co-operation,
Increasing in union, and dwelling in peace.

2

The mountains around us abound with productions
Our mechanics can use in endless constructions,
     In home manufactures in every way.

Here are timber and iron and coal in abundance,
With nitre and sulphur, and other choice things;
And we are the boys that possess the assurance
To cope with the world with its nobles and kings.

3

The Saints have been preaching to many a nation,
And building the kingdom 'mid much agitation,
        In poverty, hunger and suffering dire;
But very few people have cared for the warning,
Nor yet for the Saints' distant gathering place.
To gather with us doth provoke them to scorning:
They think that it is such a dreadful disgrace.

4

The first on the list of our wants I will mention
Are the boys and the girls that most claim our attention,
        For building up Zion in these, the last days;
And these must be raised on the old fashioned plan
Which Abraham and Isaac and Jacob pursued,
To give many women to every good man,
And raise up a host from our own mountain brood.

5

We've tinkers and tailors and soldiers and sailors
And farmers and blacksmiths, shoemakers and nailers—
        The bone and the sinew in mighty array—
And founders and printers and weavers and hatters,
With carpenters, masons and all other trades.
With these, we'll control manufacturing matters
And make foreign aid disappear in the shades.

6

We will vie with old Birmingham, Sheffield and Leeds,
And Manchester, too, with its marvelous deeds,
        For home manufacture will meet all our needs.
We'll produce cotton cloth without cotton lords
And employ spinning-jennies in every place.
We'll make knives and scissors, and trusty good swords,
And in broadcloth, be never behind in the race.

7

We'll get up the steam, and the railway lay down,
And the telegraph working in every town,
        And spread information to every clime.
We'll never stand still till success we've attained.
Independence and home manufactures combined
To go right ahead, nothing e'er can restrain,
Or crush the bright germ of the great Mormon mind.

TEXT: Willes (1872), pp. 24-25.
MUSIC: *Franklin Square Song Collection.* VII.

GEORGE A. HICKS

ONCE I LIVED IN COTTONWOOD

TUNE: Georgia Volunteers

Oh, once I lived in "Cot-ton-wood," and owned a lit-tle farm, But
I was called to Dix-ie, which gave me much a-larm. To
raise the cane and cot-ton, I right a-way must go, But the
rea-son why they sent me, I'm sure I do not know.

1

Oh, once I lived in "Cottonwood," and owned a little farm,
But I was called to Dixie, which gave me much alarm.
To raise the cane and cotton, I right away must go,
But the reason why they sent me, I'm sure I do not know.

2

I yoked old Jim and Bally up, all for to make my start;
To leave my house and garden, it almost broke my heart.
We moved along quite slowly, and often looked behind,
For the sands and rocks of Dixie, kept running through my mind.

3

At length we reached the "Black Ridge," where I broke my wagon down.
I could not find a carpenter—we were twenty miles from town—
So with a clumsy cedar pole, I fixed an awkward slide.
My wagon pulled so heavy then that Betsy could not ride.

4

While Betsy was a walking, I told her to take care,
When all upon a sudden, she struck a prickly pear.
Then she began to blubber out as loud as she could bawl,
"If I was back in 'Cottonwood,' I wouldn't come at all."

5

And when we reached the Sandy, we could not move at all,
For poor old Jim and Bally began to puff and bawl.
I whipped and swore a little, but could not make the rout,
For myself, the team and Betsy, were all of us give out.

248

6

And next we got to Washington, where we stayed a little while
To see if April showers would make the verdure smile;
But, Oh, I was mistaken, and so I went away,
For the red hills of November, looked just the same in May.

7

I feel so sad and lonely now, there's nothing here to cheer,
Except prophetic sermons, which we very often hear.
They will hand them out by dozens, and prove them by the Book;
I'd rather have some roasting ears to stay at home and cook.

8

I feel so weak and hungry now, I think I'm nearly dead;
'Tis seven weeks next Sunday, since I have tasted bread.
Of carrot tops and lucerne greens, we have enough to eat;
But I'd like to change my diet off for buckwheat cakes and meat.

9

I brought this old coat with me, and about two years ago,
And how I'll get another one, I'm sure I do not know.
May Providence protect me against the wind and wet,
And I think myself and Betsy, these times will ne'er forget.

10

My shirt is dyed with wild dockroot, with greasewood for a set;
I fear the colors all will fade when once it does get wet.
They said we could raise madder, and indigo so blue,
But that turned out a humbug: the story was not true.

11

The hot winds whirl around me and take away my breath.
I've had the chills and fever till I'm nearly shook to death.
"All earthly tribulations are but a moment here,"
And, Oh, if I proved faithful, a righteous crown shall wear.

12

My wagon's sold for sorghum seed to make a little bread,
And poor old Jim and Bally, long, long ago were dead.
There's only me and Betsy left to hoe the cotton tree—
May heaven help the Dixieite, wherever he may be.

TEXT: *Keepapitchinin* (Salt Lake City), May 1, 1870.

MUSIC: Daughters of Utah Pioneers (1932), p. 94. Used by permission of Daughters of Utah Pioneers.

VARIANTS: *Utah Indian War Veterans' Songster* (n.p., n.d.), pp. 62-63; Lomax (1910), pp. 182-184; Daughters of Utah Pioneers (1932), pp. 94-95; Lomax and Lomax (1938), pp. 403-404; Carter (1944), pp. 524-525; Davidson (1945), pp. 297-298; Hubbard (1961), pp. 429-431.

SAMUEL KENNER # EARLY LIFE IN DIXIE

1

As I was loafing on Main Street one day,
A comrade came to me and thus he did say,
"Prepare yourself, Doc., for the favor is thine
To go to the south and raise cotton, make wine."

2

I packed up my blankets; my hopes they ran high
With thoughts of enjoying fair Dixie's soft sky
And inhaling the breeze of Pacific's broad shore—
A blessing I never had enjoyed before.

3

Arriving in Dixie, the scenery was grand,
With its high towering mountains and red rocky land.
A lofty crowned cactus resided along
In mockery unto the Imperial throne.

4

My thoughts they were pleasing from night until morn;
They presented the rose, yet secreted the thorn.
I built me air castles, not counting the cost;
In the language of Shakespeare, "There came a sad frost."

5

It nipped all my hopes, the unmerciful lout.
My Camp Floyd bacon began to give out.
My wife, she came to me one morning and said,
"I'll tell you the truth, Doc., we're quite out of bread."

6

"Then get me a sack," I replied with a frown,
"I think I can borrow some corn meal in town."
"Oh, Doc., you well know I cut up the last sack
To patch up the holes in your sun-stricken back."

7

The bishop stepped in—'twas no time to reflect—
Saying, "Come along, Doc., you're behind in the sect.
Our ditch must be made." I had nothing to say.
I started but was stopped by a friend on the way

8

Saying, "Doc, you well know your fence is not up.
The stock will get in and away goes your crop."
Says I to this man, "I'm aware of the fact.
I'll go just as soon as—hello, who is that?

9

"Some neighbor is calling, I'll just step and see;
I know from the tone that he's calling for me."
"Hello there, friend Doc., just allow me to say
'Tis your turn to herd our milch cows today."

10

I start for the bishop's to make an excuse,
But stopped to receive a sweet strain of abuse
From old sister W., who lives over the way;
She says I've not paid for my last washing day.

11

I start off for Cedar some grub to obtain,
When outside the canyon it sets into rain.
While crossing the Black Ridge with hurry and dash,
My wagon came down with a terrible crash.

12

And thus ends the first year of sweet Dixie life,
Confusion and bother and all kinds of strife.
I can't make a movement to plow, sow or stitch,
But the water boss calls me to work on the ditch.

13

I tried one dark morning to lie down and die
And pay my last homage to Dixie's fair sky;
But the water boss came in and told me quite flat
To come to the ditch, for there's no time for that.

14

We'll now turn the tables and look for awhile
On the side of the picture that beams with a smile.
Just five years have passed since that terrible day,
And the scenes of hard trials are fast fading away.

15

Wild sagebrush has yielded its place to the vine,
And foul stinking whisky gave way to good wine.
Every low bench and small valley looks fair;
The rose and the lily perfumes the soft air.

16

The sweet-flavored apricot smiles from the tree.
The blush of the peach everywhere I can see,
And here stands the fig tree of ancient renoun
That decked the fair garden of Eden around.

17

Oh, who could behold such favors so fair
And not lift their voice filled with praises and prayer
To God, the great framer of earth, sea and sky,
Who hears the young ravens in their lonely cry!

TEXT: Hubbard (1961), pp. 432-433. Used by permission of University of Utah Press.

ST. GEORGE

1

Oh, what a dreary place this was when first the Mormons found it.
They said no white men here could live, and Indians prowled around it.
They said the land it was no good, and the water was no gooder,
And the bare idea of living here was enough to make men shudder.

CHORUS: Mesquite, soap root, prickly pears and briars;
St. George ere long will be a place that everyone admires.

Now green lucerne in verdant spots redeems our thriving city,
Whilst vines and fruit trees grace our lots with flowers sweet and
    pretty,
Where once the grass in single blades grew a mile apart in distance,
And it kept the crickets on the hop to pick up their subsistence.

3

The sun it is so scorching hot it makes the water sizz, sir,
And the reason that it is so hot is just because it is, sir.
The wind with fury here doth blow, that when we plant or sow, sir,
We place one foot upon the seeds and hold them till they grow, sir.

———————

TEXT AND MUSIC: Fife and Fife (1956), pp. 330-331. Used by permission of Indiana University Press.

THE BOYS OF SANPETE COUNTY

G. F. ROOT

TUNE: Just Before the Battle, Mother

We, the boys of San-pete Coun-ty, In o-be-dience to the
call, Start-ed out with for-ty wag-ons
To bring em-i-grants that fall. With-out fear or thot of
dan-ger, Light-ly on our way we sped,
Ev—ery heart with joy a—bound-ing,
Cap—tain See—ly at our head.

Chorus

To ac—com-plish our great mis—sion
We were call'd to fill be-low, We left our friends and dear re-
la—tions, O'er the drear-y plains to go.

1

We, the boys of Sanpete County,
In obedience to the call,
Started out with forty wagons
To bring emigrants that fall.
Without fear or thot of danger,
Lightly on our way we sped,
Every heart with joy abounding,
Captain Seely at our head.

CHORUS: To accomplish our great mission
We were call'd to fill below,
We left our friends and dear
    relations,
O'er the dreary plains to go.

2

Over hills and by the fountain,
Thro' the mud and in the dust,
Slowly climb'd the lofty mountains,
Far above the snow's white crust.
With the sun to us declining,
Glad, we welcomed close of day;
By some stream or gushing fountain,
To refresh at night we'd stay.

3

When we reach'd Green River Ferry,
On her banks all night we stayed.
Morning ferried our wagons over,
Thinking soon to roll away.
Next to drive our cattle over,
But we found they would not swim,
Though the boys were in the water
Many hours up to their chin.

4

Thus we tried from morn till evening,
Weather most severe and cold,
For the water and the labor
Brought us low, tho' we were bold.
And the mighty winds were blowing,
All the day and night before,
And the gurgling, rushing waters
Drove our cattle back to shore.

6

As the boys were passing over,
Water in the boat did pour.
Captain cried, "Boys we're gone under,
We shall die this very hour."
Down they went and crushed the tackling,
'Neath those waters all went down,
And that mighty rushing current
Swept them off with haughty frown.

6

Some to oxen horns were clinging,
'Till with them life was all o'er.
Boys and cattle all went under,
Ne'er again to step on shore.
Some to planks and boards were clinging,
Down the swelling tide did float;
Some by Heaven seemed protected,
Driven to shore upon the boat.

7

One had landed on an island,
Clinging to the willows green;
But to him life was extinguished,
He fell backward in the stream.
These six boys from parents taken,
And from friends whom they did love,
But we soon again shall meet them
In that better land above.

TEXT AND MUSIC: Daughters of Utah Pioneers (1932), pp. 150-151. Used by permission of Daughters of Utah Pioneers.
VARIANTS: Carter (1944), p. 517; Hubbard (1961), p. 404; Laws (1964), pp. 144-145*.

255

TITTERY-IRIE-AYE

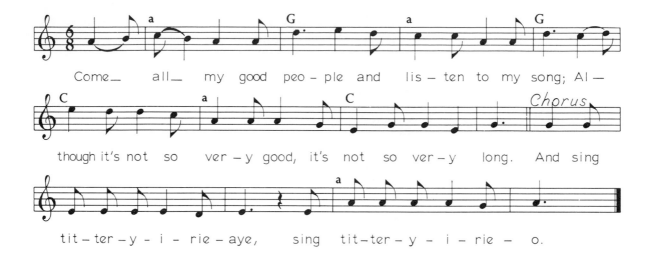

Come all my good people and listen to my song;
Although it's not so very good it's not so very long.

CHORUS: And sing tittery-irie-aye, sing tittery-irie-o.

Now concerning this strange people I'm now a-going to sing,
For the way they have been treated, I think it is a sin.

They've been driven from their homes and away from Nauvoo
For to seek another home in the wilderness anew.

Oh, they stopped among the Indians, but there don't mean to stay,
And they'll soon be a-packing up and jogging on their way.

They made a halt at Council Bluffs but there don't mean to stay;
Some feed their cattle rushes and some prairie hay.

Oh, of logs we've built our houses, of dirt we have for floors;
Of sods we've built our chimneys, and shakes we have for doors.

There is another item, to mention it I must,
Concerning spiritual women that make a hell-uv-a fuss.

Some men have got a dozen wives, and others have a score;
And the man that's got but one wife is a-looking out for more.

Now young men, don't get discouraged. Get married if you can,
But take care; don't get a woman that belongs to another man.

Now concerning this strange people, I have nothing more to say
Until we all get settled in some future day.

———

TEXT AND MUSIC: As sung by L. M. Hinton, Library of Congress Recording L 30. Transcribed by David Cohen.

VARIANTS: Fife and Fife (1947), pp. 46-47, and (1956), pp. 318-319.

THE SIOUX INDIANS

Intended to be a "final solution" to the Indian problem, the line of forts snaking down from Upper Michigan to the Red River of Texas in the 1840's fenced out of White America a great many people who had not before thought of themselves as Plains Indians. The fence did not hold back the Whites, and when they met the real Plains Indians—Sioux, Cheyenne, Arapahoe, and Comanches—the encounter was long and bloody. Had there been more such Indians, Americans might not have tried a military solution first, or they might have mobilized more men and broken the Indians sooner. As it was, a seasoned force, averaging 20,000 soldiers, roamed the vast plains for fifty years subduing, relocating, and supressing resistance among a hundred thousand nomads.

"The Sioux Indians," a widely distributed song, records a depredation against an overland wagon train, accounting for less than a dozen dead and giving such curious details as "We sprang to our rifles with a flash in each eye." No less popular or odd, "Plantonio, the Pride of the Plain," is about a horse that saved New Mexico by outrunning the redskins, although he couldn't elude their weapons:

> The arrow you see
> Hanging there on the wall
> Had passed through my foot,
> Stirrup, saddle and all.

The first determined resistance to the Indians came from the Texas Rangers. Legally organized in 1835, they became the only early consumers of Sam Colt's six-shooter, a weapon perfected for killing Comanches and Mexicans from horseback at high speed. The song, "The Texas Rangers," alludes to no pistols, which may help to confirm Belden's suspicion that it echoed the fight at the Alamo, March 6, 1835. Here, the enemy is Indian, but there are versions that call him Mexican or Yankee. "The Disheartened Ranger," from Francis Allen's *Lone Star Ballads* (1874), scourges the Comanches less than it does "Those great alligators—the State Legislators—" who don't elect to pay for the protection they praise. "The Dying Ranger" commends his sister to his troop and expires under a palmetto far away from northwest Texas.

Eben Rexford, who wrote dime novels and "Silver Threads among the Gold," also composed a verse narrative in Poe's *Raven* rhythm called "The Ride of Paul Venarez." It concerns the hero's attempt to warn his sweetheart's frontier village of an impending attack by "Red Plume's warriors." Curiously, the song became very popular at the folk level, usually under the name "Bill Venaro." Less romantically unreal is "A Fair Lady of the Plains." She herded cattle, loved red liquor, used "a six-shooter in both of her hands," and "in come a bullet and dashed out her brain."

Blond, brilliant George Armstrong Custer was graduated from West Point directly into the Civil War and fought handsomely. The Cheyenne whipped him on the Washita in 1868, after which he begat a book. On June 25, 1876, he found himself leading a meager charge into an encampment of thousands of Sioux and Cheyenne warriors. The song, "Custer's Last Charge," well-feathered with adjectives, indicates the baroque nature of the fray.

Having tried show business for a year with Buffalo Bill, Sitting Bull retired in exile to Canada; but when the messianic, anti-White craze swept the Sioux in 1890, he returned to South Dakota to agitate and organize rebellion. He was killed in a scuffle with the Indian police, but Yellow Bird continued the movement. It ended on December 29, 1890, when 200 Indians were machinegunned and left along two miles of Wounded Knee Creek. Later, after their frozen bodies were put into a common grave, W. H. Prather, a Negro private in the 9th Cavalry, wrote "The Indian Ghost Dance and War," a verse about the affair to be distributed to soldiers in the campaign.

THE SIOUX INDIANS

I will sing you a song___ it may be a sad one___ Of tri-als and trou-bles when they first be-gun. I left my own coun-try, my friends and my home, O'er plains___ and des-erts to the moun-tains to roam.

1

I will sing you a song—it may be a sad one—
Of trials and troubles when they first begun.
I left my own country, my friends and my home,
O'er plains and deserts to the mountains to roam.

2

We crossed the Missouri and joined the large train,
Which bore me o'er deserts, o'er mountains and plains;
And while crossing, out hunting we'd go
To kill the fleet antelope and the wild buffalo.

3

We traveled two weeks till we came to the Platte.
We formed our corral on the end of the flat.
We spread our blankets down on the green grassy ground.
Our mules and our horses were grazing around.

4

While taking refreshments, we heard a low wail,
And a band of Sioux Indians coming up from the dale.
We sprang to our rifles with a flash in each eye.
"Brave boys," cried our leader, "we will fight till we die."

5

We got on our horses all ready to fight
When a band of Sioux Indians then came up in sight.
The Indians came on us with a whoop and a yell,
At the crack of our rifles, there were six of them fell.

259

6

They, seeing their brave comrades lying dead on the ground,
They whooped and they yelled and they circled around.
They made a bold dash and come near to our train;
Their arrows fell around us like hail and like rain.

7

We killed their bold chief at the head of his band.
He died like a warrior with his gun in his hand.
They, seeing their bold chief lying dead in his gore,
They whooped and they yelled and we saw them no more.

8

We hitched up our horses and started the train.
We had three bloody battles that trip on the plain,
And the last one, which there were three brave men fell.
We laid them to rest in the green, shady dell,
In the green, shady dell.

TEXT AND MUSIC: Hubbard (1961), pp. 293-294. Used by permission of University of Utah Press.

VARIANTS: Lomax (1910), pp. 56-57; Lomax and Lomax (1938), pp. 344-346; Fife and Fife (1947), pp. 43-44; Randolph (1948), pp. 216-217; Botkin (1951), pp. 743-744; Burt (1958a), pp. 142-143; Moore and Moore (1964), pp. 293-294; Laws (1964), p. 138*.

THE INDIAN
W. H. PRATHER, GHOST DANCE AND WAR

The Red Skins left their Agency, the Soldiers left their Post,
All on the strength of an Indian tale about Messiah's ghost
Got up by savage chieftains to lead their tribes astray;
But Uncle Sam wouldn't have it so, for he ain't built that way.
They swore that this Messiah came to them in visions sleep
And promised to restore their game and Buffalos a heap,
So they must start a big ghost dance, then all would join their band,
And may be so we lead the way into the great Bad Land.

CHORUS: They claimed the shirt Messiah gave, no bullet could go through;
But when the Soldiers fired at them, they saw this was not true.
The Medicine man supplied them with their great Messiah's
    grace;
And he, too, pulled his freight and swore the 7th hard to face.

About their tents the Soldiers stood, awaiting one and all,
That they might hear the trumpet clear when sounding General call,
Or Boots and Saddles in a rush, that each and every man
Might mount in haste, ride soon and fast to stop this devilish band;
But Generals great like Miles and Brooke don't do things up that way,
For they know an Indian like a book, and let him have his way
Until they think him far enough and then to John they'll say,
"You had better stop your fooling or we'll bring our guns to play."

The 9th marched out with splendid cheer the Bad Lands to explo'e—
With Col. Henry at their head, they never fear the foe;
So on they rode from Xmas eve 'till dawn of Xmas day;
The Red Skins heard the 9th was near and fled in great dismay.
The 7th is of courage bold, both officers and men;
But bad luck seems to follow them and twice has took them in.
They came in contact with Big Foot's warriors in their fierce might;
This chief made sure he had a chance of vantage in the fight.

A fight took place; 'twas hand to hand, unwarned by trumpet call.
While the Sioux were dropping man by man, the 7th killed them all.
And to that regiment be said, "Ye noble braves, well done.
Although you lost some gallant men, a glorious fight you've won."
The 8th was there, the 6th rode miles to swell that great command
And waited orders night and day to round up Short Bull's band.
The Infantry marched up in mass the Cavalry's support,
And while the latter rounded up, the former held the fort.

E battery of the 1st stood by and did their duty well,
For every time the Hotchkiss barked, they say a hostile fell.
Some Indian soldiers chipped in too and helped to quell the fray,
And now the campaign's ended and the soldiers marched away.
So all have done their share, you see, whether it was thick or thin,
And all helped break the ghost dance up and drive the hostiles in.
The settlers in that region now can breathe with better grace;
They only ask and pray to God to make John hold his base.

TEXT: *Bureau of American Ethnology, 14th Annual Report* (1892-93), II, 883.
VARIANTS: *Davidson* (1943), p. 111, and (1951), pp. 131-132.

EBEN E. REXFORD

THE RIDE OF PAUL VENAREZ

Paul Ve – nar – ez heard them say, in a

fron – tier town that day, That a

band of. Red Plume's war–riors was up–on the trail of death;

Heard them tell of mur – der done

three men killed at Rock — y Run. "They're in

dan – ger up at Craw–ford 's," said Ve – nar – ez un – der breath.

1
Paul Venarez heard them say, in the frontier town that day,
  That a band of Red Plume's warriors was upon the trail of death;
Heard them tell of murder done—three men killed at Rocky Run.
  "They're in danger up at Crawford's," said Venarez under breath.

2
"Crawford's"—thirty miles away—was a settlement that lay
  In a green and pleasant valley of the mighty wilderness;
Half a score of homes was there, and in one a maiden fair
  Held the heart of Paul Venarez—"Paul Venarez' little Bess."

3
So no wonder he grew pale when he heard the settler's tale
  Of the men he had seen murdered yesterday at Rocky Run.
"Not a soul will dream," he said, "of the danger that's ahead;
  By my love for little Bessie, I must see that something's done."

4
Not a moment he delayed when his brave resolve was made.
  "Why, my man," his comrades told him when they knew his daring
    plan,
"You are going straight to death." But he answered, "Save your breath;
  I may fail to get to Crawford's, but I'll do the best I can."

O'er the forest trail he sped, and his thoughts flew on ahead
    To the little band at Crawford's, thinking not of danger near.
"Oh, God help me save," cried he, "little Bess!" And fast and free,
    Trusty Nell bore on the hero of the far-away frontier.

6

Low and lower sank the sun. He drew rein at Rocky Run;
    "Here these men met death, my Nellie," and he stroked his horse's
        mane.
"So will they we go to warn, ere the breaking of the morn,
    If we fail. God help us, Nellie!" Then he gave his horse the rein.

7

Sharp and keen a rifle-shot woke the echoes of the spot.
    "Oh, my Nellie, I am wounded," cried Venarez, with a moan,
And the warm blood from his side spurted out in a red tide,
    And he trembled in the saddle, and his face had ashy grown.

8

"I will save them yet," he cried. "Bessie Lee shall know I died
    For her sake." And then he halted in the shelter of a hill.
From his buckskin shirt he took, with weak hands a little book;
    And he tore a blank leaf from it." This," said he, "shall be my will."

9

From a branch a twig he broke, and he dipped his pen of oak
    In the red blood that was dripping from the wound below the heart.
"Rouse," he wrote, "before too late. Red Plume's warriors lie in wait.
    Good-by, Bess! God bless you always." Then he felt the warm tears
        start.

10

Then he made his message fast, love's first letter, and its last;
    To his saddle-bow he tied it, while his lips were white with pain.
"Bear my message, if not me, safe to little Bess," said he.
    Then he leaned down in the saddle, and clutched hard the sweaty
        mane.

11

Just at dusk, a horse of brown, flecked with foam, came panting down
    To the settlement at Crawford, and she stopped at Bessie's door.
But her rider seemed asleep. Ah, his slumber was so deep
    Bessie's voice could never wake him, if she called forever more.

12

You will hear the story told by the young and by the old
    In the settlement at Crawford's, of the night when Red Plume came;
Of the sharp and bloody fight; how the chief fell, and the flight
    Of the panic-stricken warriors. Then they speak Venarez' name

13

In an awed and reverent way, as men utter "Let us pray,"
    As we speak the name of heroes, thinking how they lived and died;
So his memory is kept green, while his face and heaven between
    Grow the flowers Bessie planted, ere they laid her by his side.

TEXT: *One Hundred Choice Selections No. 21*, ed. Phineas Garrett (Philadelphia: Garrett, n.d.), pp. 99-101.

    MUSIC: Larkin (1931), pp. 27-28. Used by permission of Alfred A. Knopf, Inc.

VARIANTS: Lomax (1910), pp. 299-302; German (1929); Larkin (1931), pp. 25-29; Clark (1932), pp. 60-61; Frey (1936), pp. 44-45; Coolidge (1937), pp. 119-122; Lomax and Lomax (1938), pp. 197-200; Pound (1939), pp. 25-26; Randolph (1948), pp. 222-227*; Botkin (1951), pp. 759-760; Laws (1964), p. 136*.

PLANTONIO, THE PRIDE OF THE PLAIN

I'll tell you a sto—ry: There is one I know Of a
horse I once owned —— In New Mex – i – co.

1
I'll tell you a story:
There is one I know
Of a horse I once owned
In New Mexico.

2
Swift as an antelope,
Black as a crow,
Star on his forehead
Was whiter than snow.

3
His arched neck was hidden
By a long flow of mane
They called him Plantonio,
The Pride of the Plain.

4
The country was new,
And the settlers were scarce,
And the Indians on the warpath
Were savage and fierce.

5
The captain stepped up,
Said someone must go
For the aid and protection
Of New Mexico.

6
A dozen young fellows
Straightforward said "Here!"
But the captain saw me—
I was standing quite near.

7
"You're good for the ride,
You're the lightest one here
On the back of that mustang,
You've nothing to fear."

8
They all shook my hand
As I nodded my head,
Rode down the dark pathway,
And north turned his head.

9
The black struck a trot,
And he kept it all night;
And just as the east
Was beginning to light,

10
Not a great ways behind
There arose a fierce yell,
And I knew that the redskins
Were hot on my trail.

11
I jingled the bells
At the end of his rein,
Spoke his name softly,
And struck his dark mane.

12
He answered my call
With a toss of his head.
His dark body lengthened
And faster he sped.

13

The arrows fell 'round us
Like torrents of rain.
Plantonio, Plantonio,
The Pride of the Plain.

14

I delivered my message
And tried to dismount,
But the pain in my foot
Was so sharp I could not.

15

The arrow you see
Hanging there on the wall
Had passed through my foot,
Stirrup, saddle and all.

16

With New Mexico saved,
We'd not ridden in vain,
Plantonio, Plantonio,
The Pride of the Plain.

TEXT AND MUSIC: Larkin (1931), pp. 112-113. Used by permission of Alfred A. Knopf, Inc.

VARIANTS: Lomax and Lomax (1938), pp. 356-358; Randolph (1948), pp. 242-243; Malone (1961), pp. 155-157; Fowke (1962), p. 249; Laws (1964), pp. 138-139*.

THE TEXAS RANGERS

(Best unaccompanied)

Come all you Tex-as Rang-ers, wher-ev — er you may be,— And lis-ten to some trou— bles that hap-pened un — to me; And know the things we suf-fered in that ear — ly bor-der day When In–dians hid on ev–ery trail, the Rang-ers brave to slay.

1

Come all you Texas Rangers, wherever you may be,
And listen to some troubles that happened unto me;
And know the things we suffered in that early border day
When Indians hid on every trail, the Rangers brave to slay.

2

I was but sixteen years of age when I joined this roving band.
We marched from San Antonio down to the Rio Grande;
And there our Captain ordered, "Look sharp, my boys, tonight.
Before we reach our station, we'll have a bloody fight."

3

When I saw the Indians coming and heard their awful yell,
My feelings at that moment no tongue can ever tell.
I saw their glittering lances, the arrows seemed to fly;
And I thought unto my sorrow, "Now is my time to die."

4

Our Captain called upon us to meet them hand to hand,
And every man stood ready, obeying his command.
First emptying our rifles, and then with sabres drawn,
We fought the redskins right and left until the early dawn.

5

We fought them full five hours before the fight was o'er.
Such sights I saw that morning, I never saw before;
And when the sun was rising and the Indians they had fled,
We loaded up our rifles and counted up our dead.

6

And all of us were wounded, our noble Captain slain;
And when the moon shone sadly across the bloody plain,
Sixteen as noble rangers as ever saw the West
Were buried by their comrades—Sweet be their peaceful rest!

7

Now, perhaps you have a mother, likewise a sister, too;
Perhaps you have a sweetheart that would weep and mourn for
   you.
If that be your condition, I advise you not to roam;
And I tell you from experience you had better stay at home.

8

My old mother's voice was trembling as she to me did say,
"They all are strangers to you—with me you had better stay."
But I thought that she was childish, the best she did not know;
My mind was bent on ranging, and I was bound to go.

9

I have seen the fruits of rambling, I know its hardships well.
I crossed the Rocky Mountains when many a brave man fell.
I have been in the great Southwest, where the wild Apaches roam,
And I tell you from experience you had better stay at home.

TEXT: Hall (1908), pp. 220-221.

MUSIC: As sung by Sloan Matthews, Library of Congress Recording L 28. Transcribed by David Cohen.

VARIANTS: Allan (1874), p. 38; Andrew J. Sowell, *Rangers and Pioneers of Texas* (San Antonio, (1884), pp. 231-232; Lomax (1910), pp. 44-46; Will (1913), p. 186; Pound (1915), pp. 28-29, and (1922), pp. 163-164; Siringo (1919), pp. 9-11; Clark (1932), pp. 59-60; Federal Writers' Project (1937a), pp. 6-7; Lomax and Lomax (1938), pp. 359-361; Hull (1939), p. 43; Belden (1940), pp. 336-339*; Lomax and Lomax (1941), pp. 245-247; Davidson (1943), p. 102; Randolph (1948), pp. 169-173*; Botkin (1951), pp. 774-775; Lomax (1960), pp. 331-332; Hubbard (1961), pp. 291-292*; Moore and Moore (1964), pp. 312-314; Laws (1964), p. 123*.

M. B. SMITH

THE DISHEARTENED RANGER

Come, list to a Ran-ger, you kind-heart-ed stran-ger. A
song, tho' a sad one, you are wel-come to hear. He
kept the Co-man-ches a-way from your ranch-es And
fol-low'd them far on the Tex-as fron-tier.

1

Come, list to a Ranger, you kind-hearted stranger.
A song, tho' a sad one, you are welcome to hear.
He kept the *Comanches* away from your ranches
And follow'd them far on the Texas frontier.

2

He's weary of scouting, of riding, and routing
The blood-thirsty brutes thro' the prairies and woods.
No rest for the sinner, no breakfast or dinner,
No rest for a Ranger but a bed in the mud.

3

No corn nor potatoes, nor beets, nor tomatoes;
The jerk beef as dry as the sole of your shoe;
All day without drinking, all night without winking—
I tell you, kind stranger, this never will do.

4

Those great alligators—the State Legislators—
Are puffing and blowing two-thirds of their time,
But windy orations about Rangers and rations
Never put in our pockets one-tenth of a dime.

5

They do not regard us; they will not reward us,
Tho' hungry and haggard, with holes in our coats.
But Election is coming when they will be running
And praising our valor to purchase our votes.

6

Altho' it may grieve you, the Ranger must leave you
Expos'd to the arrow and knife of the foe.
So guard your own cattle and fight your own battles,
For home to the States I'm determin'd to go.

7

Where churches have steeples and things are more equal,
Where churches have people and ladies more kind,
Where worth is regarded, and work is rewarded,
Where pumpkins are plenty, and pockets lined!

———

TEXT: Allan (1874), p. 92.

MUSIC: As sung by Carl T. Sprague, Victor Record V-40066. Transcribed by David Cohen.

VARIANTS: Lomax (1910), pp. 261-262; J. Evetts Haley, *Charles Goodnight* (Boston: Houghton Mifflin, 1936), pp. 97-98; Lomax and Lomax (1938), pp. 369-370; Randolph (1948), pp. 178-179*; Moore and Moore (1964), pp. 315-316.

THE DYING RANGER

The sun was set-ting in the west and fell with ling-'ring ray Through the branch-es of a for-est where a wound-ed rang-er lay. In the shade of a palm-et-to, 'neath the sum-mer's sul-try sky, Far a-way from his home in Tex-as, they laid him down to die.

1

The sun was setting in the west and fell with a ling'ring ray
Through the branches of a forest where a wounded ranger lay.
In the shade of a palmetto, 'neath the summer's sultry sky,
Far away from his home in Texas, they laid him down to die.

2

A group had gathered round him, his comrades in the fight.
The tears rolled down each manly cheek as he bade his last good night.
One tried and true companion was kneeling by his side
To stop his life-blood flowing, but all in vain he tried.

3

When in despair and anguish he saw it was in vain,
While down his loved companion's cheek, the tears poured like rain,
Up spoke the dying ranger, "Boys, do not weep for me.
I am crossing the dark river to a country that is free.

4

"Draw nearer to me, comrades, and listen to what I say;
I am going to tell a story as my spirit hastes away.
Way back in northwest Texas, that good old Lone Star State,
There is one who for my coming with an anxious heart will wait,

5

"A little girl, my sister, my only joy and pride.
I've loved her since her childhood for I've had no one beside.
I've loved her as a brother and with a brother's care,
I've tried through grief and sorrow her little heart to cheer.

6

"Our country was invaded; they called for volunteers.
She threw her arms about me and bursting into tears,
Saying, 'Go, my darling brother. Drive the traitors from our shore.
My heart may need your presence, but our country needs you more!'

7

"'Tis true I love my country; to it I've given my all.
If it was not for my sister, boys, I'd be content to fall.
Oh comrades, I am dying; she'll never see me more,
Though she'll vainly wait my coming by our little cabin door.

8

"My mother, she lies sleeping beneath the churchyard sod,
And many a day has passed away since her spirit went to God.
My father, he lies sleeping beneath the deep blue sea.
We have no other kindred, there is only Nell and me.

9

"Draw nearer to me, comrades, and listen to my dying prayer.
Who'll be to her a brother and protect her with his care?"
Up spoke those noble rangers; they answered one and all:
"We will be to her a brother till the last of us does fall."

10

One happy smile of pleasure o'er the ranger's face was spread.
One dark, convulsive shudder, and the ranger boy was dead.
Far from his darling sister, they laid him down to rest
With his saddle for a pillow and his rifle across his breast.

TEXT: Coolidge (1912), pp. 507-508.

MUSIC: Lomax (1910), pp. 214-218.

VARIANTS: Lomax (1910), pp. 214-218; Siringo (1919), pp. 24-26; Barnes (1925), p. 125;
Finger (1927), pp. 170-173; Clark (1932), p. 30; Allen (1933), pp. 80-83; Frey (1936),
pp. 36-37; Coolidge (1937), pp. 110-113; Lomax and Lomax (1938), pp. 366-368; Belden
(1940), pp. 397-398; Randolph (1948), pp. 196-199*; Moore and Moore (1964), pp.
316-319; Laws (1964), p. 125*.

A FAIR LADY OF THE PLAINS

There was a fair la — dy who lived on the plains. She

helped me herd cat — tle through hard, storm-y rains. She

helped me one sea — son through all the round-up;

She would drink with me from the cold, bit — ter cup. She

loved her red liq — uor which served a man so; She

was a fair la — dy, as white as the snow.

1

There was a fair lady who lived on the plains.
She helped me herd cattle through hard, stormy rains.
She helped me one season through all the round-up;
She would drink with me from the cold, bitter cup.
She loved her red liquor which served a man so;
She was a fair lady, as white as the snow.

2

She loved her red liquor which served a man so;
She was a fair lady as white as the snow.
I taught her as a cowboy when the Rangers come 'round
To use a six-shooter in both of her hands,
To use a six-shooter and never to run
As long as loads lasted in either gun.

3

We was going down the canyon in the Spring one year
To camp there a season with a herd of wild steers.
The Injuns charged on us at the dead hour of the night.
She rose from her slumber the battle to fight.
'Mid lightning and thunder and the downpour of rain,
It's in come a bullet and dashed out her brain.

4

'Mid lightning and thunder and the downpour of rain,
It's in come a bullet and dashed out her brain.
I sprung to my saddle with a gun in each hand
Saying, "Come all you cowboys, let's fight for our band,"
Saying, "Come all you cowboys, let's fight for our life.
These redskins has murdered my darling young wife!"

———

TEXT AND MUSIC: Arcadian Magazine (Eminence, Mo.) (June, 1930), p. 30.

VARIANTS: B. E. Denton, *A Two-Gun Cyclone* (Dallas, Tex., 1927), p. 142; *Journal of American Folklore*, XLV (1932), 153-154; Larkin (1931), pp. 147-149; Randolph (1948), pp. 199-203; Laws (1964), pp. 136-137*.

CUSTER'S LAST CHARGE

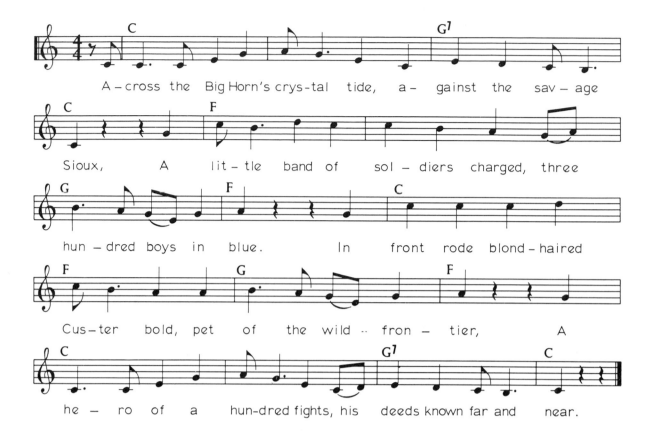

A-cross the Big Horn's crys-tal tide, a- gainst the sav-age
Sioux, A lit-tle band of sol-diers charged, three
hun-dred boys in blue. In front rode blond-haired
Cus-ter bold, pet of the wild fron-tier, A
he-ro of a hun-dred fights, his deeds known far and near.

1

Across the Big Horn's crystal tide, against the savage Sioux,
A little band of soldiers charged, three hundred boys in blue.
In front rode blond-haired Custer bold, pet of the wild frontier,
A hero of a hundred fights, his deeds known far and near.

2

"Charge, comrades, charge! There's death ahead, disgrace lurks in our rear!
Drive rowels deep! Come on, come on!" came his yells with ringing cheer.
And on the foe those heroes charged. There rose an awful yell:
It seemed as though those soldiers stormed the lowest gates of hell.

3

Three hundred rifles rattled forth, and torn was human form.
The black smoke rose in rolling waves above the leaden storm.
The death groans of the dying braves, their wounded piercing cries,
The hurling of the arrows fleet did cloud the noonday skies.

4

The snorting steeds with shrieks of fright, the firearms' deafening roar,
The war song sung by the dying braves who fell to rise no more;
O'er hill and dale the war song waved 'round craggy mountain side.
Along down death's dark valley ran a cruel crimson tide.

5

Our blond-haired chief was everywhere 'mid showers of hurling lead.
The starry banner waved above the dying and the dead.
With bridle rein in firm-set teeth, revolver in each hand,
He hoped with his few gallant boys to quell the great Sioux band.

6

Again they charged: three thousand guns poured forth their last-sent ball;
Three thousand war whoops rent the air; Gallant Custer then did fall;
And all around where Custer fell ran pools and streams of gore,
Heaped bodies of both red and white whose last great fight was o'er.

7

The boys in blue and their savage foe lay huddled in one mass,
Their life's blood ran a trickling through the trampled prairie grass,
While fiendish yells did rend the air, and then a sudden hush,
While cries of anguish rise again as on the mad Sioux rush.

8

O'er those strewn and bloodstained fields those goading redskins fly.
Our gang went down three hundred souls, three hundred doomed to die.
Those blood-drunk braves sprang on the dead and wounded boys in blue;
Three hundred bleeding scalps ran high above the fiendish crew.

9

Then night came on with sable veil and hid those sights from view;
The Big Horn's crystal tide was red as she wound her valleys through;
And quickly from the fields of slain, those gloating redskins fled,
But blond-haired Custer held the field, a hero with his dead.

TEXT AND MUSIC: As sung by Warde H. Ford in Central Valley, California, 1938, Library of Congress Recording L 30. Transcribed by David Cohen.

VARIANT: Botkin (1951), pp. 745-746.

THE REGULAR ARMY, O!

The Western army was kept in the saddle by more than redskin uprisings. The Mexican border, in particular, supplied a variety of motives for continuous military presence there. The mineral-rich Gadsden Purchase attracted covetous attention from many outsiders, including Maximilian, the puppet emperor of Mexico, and Colonel Sibley's Confederate Brigade. It was the home of Cochise, Geronimo, and many other Apaches. It was the base of filibuster agitation to annex Sonora, Mexico. And, as mentioned earlier, the troops there during World War I drew the duty of maintaining detention camps for striking copper miners. It is not surprising, then, that the first post of the Irish narrator of "The Regular Army, O!" was Arizona. Later, his successors also saw duty with General George "Rosebud" Crook, whose firm policy had stabilized the border until he was transferred north in 1875.

The nearly universal military complaints uttered in "The Regular Army, O!" were elicited only after serious provocation from one Western unit, the Mormon Battalion. The songs "The Mormon Battalion" and "The Desert Route" tell how this hardy group of Mormon volunteers, responding to President Polk's call-up for the Mexican War, marched from Council Bluffs, Iowa, to Santa Fe, New Mexico, where General Kearney sent them on a blistering trek across the deserts to arrive in San Diego, California, in early 1847.

> A "Mormon" soldier band we are;
> May our great Father's watchful care
> In safety kindly guide our feet,
> Till we again our friends shall meet,
> In these hard times.

The Mexican War produced many more songs in the West than did the Civil War. In J. Frank Dobie's opinion, both "Mustang Gray" and "The Maid of Monterrey" may be by the same author, one James T. Lytel, a participant in the Battle of Monterrey, September, 1846, and in the occupation of Puebla the following year. He contributed such verses regularly to a weekly published there, the *Flag of Freedom*.

"The Sonora Filibusters," from John Stone's *Original California Songster*, recalls the petty imperialism of William Walker, who sought to establish a "Republic of Lower California" through a private military expedition there in 1853. Walker surrendered to United States authorities, but did not give up the principle. He was killed not long afterward during a similar attempt to seize Nicaragua.

"Our Leaky Tents" was composed in the late 1860's by volunteers for what Mormon scholars like to call "the Black Hawk War." No one was to prevent a chief from taking the name of a famous warrior, but the volunteers were apparently successful in keeping him from further rustling in Sanpete County.

"There Is No Work in the Army" and "Old Arizona Again" are two more songs about the rigors of border duty. The first makes the interesting point that it is better to be fighting than scraping, painting, and overdrilling in the coast artillery, while the second remarks wittily of the Mexican predators: "They don't know the Boston dip, But they shoot you from the hip."

In response to one of those southern bands, "Blackjack" Pershing's cavalry rattled around the border in 1916; but the terrorist Francisco "Pancho" Villa was not stopped until July, 1923, when seven Mexicans whom he had variously dishonored riddled his automobile, him, and three companions. "It's a Long, Long Way To Capture Villa" is a truthful jingle, and it shares with "When We Go Marching Home" a certain tartness we have observed before:

> To hell, to hell with dear old Texas,
> To hell, to hell with all the cactus,
> To hell, to hell with all the "Mexs."
> Three cheers for New York town!

ED HARRIGAN # THE REGULAR ARMY, O!

Three years a - go this ver - y day, we went to Gov'- nor's Isle To stand for - inst the can - non in true mil - i - tar - y style. Sev - en - teen A - mer - i - can dol - lars each month we'd sure - ly get____ For lug - gin' a gun in the red hot sun to a mil - i - tar - y step____. We had our choice of go - ing to the arm - y or to jail____, Or up the Hud - son Riv - er, with a cop to take a sail____; So we puck-ered up our cour - age and brave-ly we did go____. We curse the day we went a - way in the

279

reg – u – lar arm – y, O___! There was Ser – geant John Mc –
Caf – fer – y and Cap – tain Don – o – hue__. They made us march and
toe the mark in gal – lant Com–pany 2___. The drums would roll, up–
on me soul, and this is the way we'd go___: Fort –y
miles a day on beans and hay in the reg – u – lar Arm – y O___!

1

Three years ago this very day, we went to Gov'nor's Isle
To stand forinst the cannon in true military style.
Seventeen American dollars each month we'd surely get
For luggin' a gun in the red hot sun to a military step.
We had our choice of going to the army or to jail,
Or up the Hudson River with a cop to take a sail;
So we puckered up our courage and bravely we did go.
We curse the day we went away in the regular army, O!

CHORUS: There was Sergeant John McCaffery and Captain Donohue.
They made us march and toe the mark in gallant Company 2.
The drums would roll, upon me soul, and this is the way we'd go:
Forty miles a day on beans and hay in the regular army, O!

2

We went to Arizona for to fight the Indians there.
They did their best to raise our scalps, but couldn't raise a hair.
We lay about in ditches in the dirty yellow mud,
And we never saw an onion, a turnip, or a spud.
Then we was taken prisoners, and brought before the chafe.
He saw we'd make an Irish stew, the dirty Indian thafe.
On the Telegraph wire, me boys, we walked to Mexico.
We bless the day we skipped away from the regular army, O!

3

We've been dry as army herrings and as hungry as a Turk,
And the boys along the streets would shout, "Oh, soger go to work."
We skipped into the Navy for to plow the raging sea;
Cowld water sure we couldn't endure—it would never do for me.
We'll join the politicians and then we'll be well fed:
No more we'll sleep upon the ground, but in a feather bed.
And if a war, it should break out and we are called to go,
We'll get Italian substitutes for the regular army, O!

4

We've got corns upon our heels, me boys, and bunions on our toes;
Through luggin' a gun in the red hot sun, put freckles on our nose.
Ould England has her Grenadiers and Frances has her Zoo zoos,
But the U.S.A. never change they say, but continually stick to blues.
And when we go upon parade, our muskets must be bright,
Or they'll put us in the Guard House to pass away the night.
And if we want a furlough, to the Colonel we must go.
He says, "Go to bed and sleep till you're dead, in the regular army, O!"

5

But 'twas out upon the Yellowstone we had the damndest time:
Faix, we made the trip wid Rosebud George, six months without a dime.
Some eighteen hundred miles we went through hunger, mud, and rain,
Wid backs all bare, and rations rare, no chance for grass or grain;
Wid bunkies starvin by our side, no rations was the rule;
Shure 'twas ate your boots and saddles, you brutes, but feed the packer
  and mule.
But you know full well that in your fights no soldier lad was slow,
And it wasn't the packer that won ye a star in the regular army, O!

TEXT: "The Regular Army, O!," sung with great success by the California Minstrels (San Francisco: Bell & Co., n.d. [broadside]); last stanza: Charles King, *Campaigning With Crook* (New York: Harpers, 1890), pp. 158-159.

MUSIC: Dolph (1929), pp. 6-8.

VARIANTS: Dean (1922), p. 67; Botkin (1951), pp. 748-749; Lomax (1960), pp. 340-341.

MUSTANG GRAY

There was a brave old Tex - an;____ They
called him Mus-tang Gray.____ He left his home when
quite a boy____ And went roam - ing far a - way.____

Chorus
He'll go no more a - rang - er - ing Those
sav - ag - es to af - fright;____ He has heard his last
war - whoop;____ He fought his last____ fight.____

1

There was a brave old Texan;
    They called him Mustang Gray.
He left his home when quite a boy
    And went roaming far away.

CHORUS: He'll go no more a-rangering
    Those savages to affright;
He has heard his last war-whoop;
    He fought his last fight.

2

When our country was invaded
    By the Indian warriors' trains,
He used to mount his noble charger
    And scout the hills and plains.

3

He would not sleep within a tent;
    No pleasures did he know;
But like a brave old frontiersman,
    A-scouting he would go.

4

Once he was taken prisoner
    And carried far away,
Had to wear the yoke of bondage
    Through the streets of Monterey.

5

A senorita loved him;
    And with a brave woman's pride,
She opened the gates and gave him
    Her father's horse to ride.

6

And when this gallant life was spent,
    This was his last command:
"Pray bury me in old Texas soil
    On the banks of the Rio Grande."

7

And when the weary traveller
    Is passing by his grave,
He may sometimes shed a farewell tear
    O'er the bravest of the brave.

TEXT: Thorp (1908), pp. 23-24.

MUSIC: Dobie (1932), p. 122. Used by permission of the Texas Folklore Society.

VARIANTS: Lomax (1910), pp. 79-80; Siringo (1919), pp. 12-13; Thorp (1921), pp. 102-104; Dick (1928), pp. 93-94; Dobie (1932), pp. 109-123*; Lomax and Lomax (1934), pp. 395-396, and (1938), pp. 363-364; Botkin (1951), pp. 775-776; Moore and Moore (1964), pp. 311-312; Fife and Fife (1966), pp. 104-111*.

AZARIAH SMITH

THE MORMON BATTALION

TUNE: Hard Times

1

In forty-six we bade adieu
To loving friends and kindred too;
For one year's service, one and all
Enlisted at our country's call,
    In these hard times.

2

We onward marched until we gained
Fort Leavenworth, where we obtained
Our outfit—each a musket drew—
Canteen, knapsack, and money, too,
    In these hard times.

3

Our Colonel died; Smith took his place
And marched us on at rapid pace.
O'er hills and plains, we had to go,
Through herds of deer and buffalo,
    In these hard times.

4

O'er mountains and through valleys too—
We towns and villages went through;
Through forest dense, with mazes twined,
Our tedious step we had to wind,
    In these hard times.

5

At length we came to Santa Fe,
As much fatigued as men could be,
With only ten days there to stay,
When orders came to march away,
    In these hard times.

6

Three days and twenty we march'd down
Rio Del Norte, past many a town;
Then changed our course, resolved to go
Across the mountains, high or low,
    In these hard times.

7

We found the mountains very high,
Our patience and our strength to try;
For, on half rations, day by day,
O'er mountain heights we made our way,
    In these hard times.

8

Some pushed the wagons up the hill;
Some drove the teams, some pack'd the mules;
Some stood on guard by night and day,
Lest haplessly our teams should stray,
    In these hard times.

9

We traveled twenty days or more,
Adown the Gila River's shore—
Crossed o'er the Colorado then,
And marched upon a sandy plain,
    In these hard times.

10

We thirsted much from day to day,
And mules were dying by the way,
When lo! to view, a glad scene burst,
Where all could quench our burning thirst,
    In these hard times.

11

We traveled on without delay,
And quartered at San Luis Rey;
We halted there some thirty days,
And now are quartered in this place,
    In these hard times.

12

A "Mormon" soldier band we are;
May our great Father's watchful care
In safety kindly guide our feet,
Till we again our friends shall meet,
    In these hard times.

13

O yes, we trust to meet our friends
Where truth its light to all extends,
Where love prevails in every breast,
Throughout the province of the blest,
    In these hard times.

TEXT: Daniel Tyler, *A Concise History of the Mormon Battalion in the Mexican War, 1846-1847* (n.p., 1881), pp. 287-289.

VARIANTS: Carter (1944), pp. 511-512; Davidson (1945), p. 285.

LEVI W. HANCOCK   # THE DESERT ROUTE

1

While here, beneath a sultry sky,
Our famished mules and cattle die,
Scarce aught but skin and bones remain
To feed poor soldiers on the plain.

CHORUS: How hard to starve and wear us out,
Upon this sandy, desert route.

2

We sometimes, now, for lack of bread,
Are less than quarter rations fed,
And soon expect, for all of meat,
Naught less than broke-down mules to eat.

3

Now, half-starved oxen, over-drilled,
Too weak to draw, for beef are killed;
And gnawing hunger prompting men
To eat small entrails and the skin.

4

Sometimes we quarter for the day,
While men are sent ten miles away
On our back track, to place in store
An ox, given out the day before.

5

And when an ox is like to die,
The whole camp halts and we lay by;
The greedy wolves and buzzards stay,
Expecting rations for the day.

6

Our hardships reach their rough extremes
When valiant men are roped with teams,
Hour after hour, and day by day,
To wear our strength and lives away.

7

The teams can hardly drag their loads
Along the hilly, sandy roads,
While trav'ling near the Rio Grande,
O'er hills and dales of heated sand.

8

We see some twenty men or more,
With empty stomachs and foot-sore,
Bound to one wagon, plodding on
Thru' sand beneath a burning sun.

9

A Doctor which the Government
Has furnished proves a punishment!
At his rude call of "Jim Along Joe,"
The sick and halt to him must go.

10

Both night and morn, this call is heard;
Our indignation then is stirr'd,
And we sincerely wish to hell
His arsenic and calomel.

11

To take it, if we're not inclined,
We're threatened, "You'll be left behind";
When bored with threat profanely rough,
We swallow down the poisonous stuff.

12

Some stand the journey well, and some
Are by the hardships overcome;
And thus the "Mormons" are worn out
Upon this long and weary route.

———

TEXT: Daniel Tyler, *A Concise History of the Mormon Battalion in the Mexican War,
1846-1847* (n.p., 1881), pp. 182-183.

VARIANT: Davidson (1945), pp. 283-284.

JOHN A. STONE

THE SONORA FILIBUSTERS

N. KNEASS

TUNE: Ben Bolt

Oh don't you re-mem-ber Bill Walk-er, the great, Bill Walk-er, the cap-tain of the band That went to So-no-ra to clean out the State, To take up and fence in the land? They tore down the flag at the En-se-ña-da Camp And hoist-ed the Star-span-gled Ban-ner, Which ter-ri-fied the greas-ers, though no-thing but fun, For Walk-er to scare San-ta An-na.

1

Oh don't you remember Bill Walker, the great,
    Bill Walker, the captain of the band
That went to Sonora to clean out the State,
    To take up and fence in the land?
They tore down the flag at the Ensenada Camp
    And hoisted the Star-spangled Banner.
Which terrified the greasers, though nothing but fun,
    For Walker to scare Santa Anna.

286

2

Oh, don't you remember the town of La Paz,
 Where Walker commenced his career,
And was shot in the back, so Fred Emory says,
 While stealing a poor Spanish steer?
La Paz still is standing, as filibuster dens,
 And each hole and corner is full
Of filibuster thieves that were caught stealing hens,
 And others their backs lined with wood.

3

Oh, don't you remember the ship-loads that went,
 In spite of their friend, Uncle Sam?
With knives, guns and pistols, they started hell-bent;
 For greasers they didn't care a damn.
But warn't they astonish'd when they heard Sam had bought
 Sonora, Chihuahua, and all,
And the "Portsmouth" was coming to hang all she caught,
 So Walker's Republic did fall.

2

TEXT: Stone (1855), p. 50.

MUSIC: Young and Leonard (1855), p. 188.

VARIANTS: *The "Champagne Charlie" and "Coal Oil Tommy" Songster* (San Francisco: Appleton & Co., 1868); Dwyer *et al.* (1964), p. 148.

OUR LEAKY TENTS

GEORGE F. ROOT

TUNE: Tramp, Tramp, Tramp,

1
In our leaky tents we sit, thinking of the good old times
    That in Springville City we had spent so gay;
And our hearts grew sad to think of the long time we'd be gone
    From our dear old home and friends so far away.

CHORUS: Snow, hail, rain, and windy weather
    Pelting our weather-beaten forms
    Till it seemed to us that winter with its white robes had set in,
    And we'd have to bear the brunt of wintry storms.

2

In our leaky tents we sit, thinking of our friends and foes,
    And alternately with love and hate were moved;
For we hate the sneaking red-skins and would like to deal them blows
    That would bring to Sanpete, peace and us, our homes.

3

On the Saturday night we tho't that the morrow we'd start home,
    When the dreadful news from Snow to us arrived:
To remain for forty more, if by him it was required,
    To protect the men of Sanpete and their wives.

4

Tho' the boys they all felt bad, but they never would go home,
    Not until they were released from his command;
And they cheerfully obeyed all the orders that were sent
    To remain and drive the Indians from the land.

TEXT: Daughters of Utah Pioneers (1932), p. 159. Used by permission of Daughters of Utah Pioneers.

MUSIC: "Tramp! Tramp! Tramp! or the Prisoner's Hope," by George F. Root (Chicago: Root & Cady, 1864).

VARIANTS: Briegel (1933), p. 50; Carter (1944), pp. 522-523; Hubbard (1961), p. 444*.

THERE IS NO WORK IN THE ARMY

When leav-ing dear old I-o-way In the first part

of the year,___ My clothes were torn, my feet were

bare, Of hun-ger I had fear.___ An-oth-er

bum ap-proached me, And with a plea-sant sigh,_____

___ He told me he was hun-gry, And I told him

so was I.____ *Chorus* There is no work in the Arm-

y: They call it all fa-tigue.___ If the Pro-vost

catch-es you loaf-ing, He'll make you dance a jig.___

It's eith-er at the saw-mill, Or shov-el-ling up the

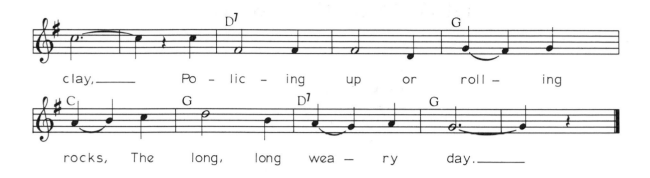

clay,_____ Po - lic - ing up or roll – ing

rocks, The long, long wea — ry day._____

1

When leaving dear old Ioway
In the first part of the year,
My clothes were torn, my feet were bare,
Of hunger I had fear.
Another bum approached me,
And with a pleasant sigh,
He told me he was hungry,
And I told him so was I.

CHORUS: There is no work in the Army;
They call it all fatigue.
If the Provost catches you loafing,
He'll make you dance a jig.
It's either at the saw-mill,
Or shoveling up the clay,
Policing up or rolling rocks,
The long, long weary day.

2

Said he, "Let's join the army
In some Troop of the First;
They'll feed us up on government slum
Until we nearly burst.
They'll give to us a sway-back horse,
And a saber in our hand,
And we'll make right cuts and Moulinets
Out on the burning sand."

3

There were two little soldiers
Just from Ioway.
They came to Arizona
Just the other day.
They thought they'd get a pistol,
A saber and a gun;
But—they gave them a pick and shovel,
And they're having lots of fun.

4

The coast artillery is the place
To soldier—I don't think.
They're doing enough of different drills
To drive a man to drink.
Parade as infantry at seven
And painting guns at nine;
Scrape off again and paint at four;
It's easy and it's fine.

5

So give to me the doughboys,
They're at it all the while;
A-fighting or a-soldiering,
They can do 'em both in style.
They haven't got sixteen drills a day
To keep 'em on the go.
One drill a day's enough for me,
In the regular army, oh!

TEXT AND MUSIC: Dolph (1929), pp. 34-37.

OLD ARIZONA AGAIN

1

Oh, it's old Arizona again.
It's old Arizona again;
It's a place where we all have been.
We have all been there before,
And we're going back once more,
Back to old Arizona again.

2

Oh, it's old Arizona again.
It's old Arizona again
With it's greasers and bad, bad men.
They don't know the Boston dip,
But they shoot you from the hip
Down in old Arizona again.

3

Oh, it's old Arizona again.
It's old Arizona again;
It's a place where we all have been.
With its scenery and fresh air,
They will be your bill of fare
Down in old Arizona again.

4

Oh, it's old Arizona again.
It's old Arizona again;
It's a place where we all have been.
With the bears and rocky ground,
And the rattlers running round,
Round in old Arizona again.

5

Oh, it's old Arizona again.
It's old Arizona again;
It's a place where we all have been.
And if you get away,
They will bring you back to stay,
Down in old Arizona again.

TEXT: Dolph (1929), pp. 552-554.

IT'S A LONG, LONG WAY TO CAPTURE VILLA

TUNE: It's a Long Way to Tipperary

1

It's a long, long way to capture Villa;
    It's a long way to go.
It's a long way across the border
    Where the dirty greasers grow;
So it's good-by to dear old Broadway,
    Hello, Mexico.
It's a long, long way to capture Villa,
    But that's where we'll go.

TEXT: Tracy H. Lewis, *Along the Rio Grande* (New York: Lewis Pub. Co., 1916), p. 190.

WHEN WE GO MARCHING HOME
H. C. WORK

TUNE: Marching Through Georgia

1

We've been upon the border for a couple of months or so;
We're getting mighty tired, and we think it's time to go;
We've dug in the mud and laid the roads, and now we'd like to know
        When we'll go marching home.

CHORUS: To hell, to hell with dear old Texas,
To hell, to hell with all the cactus,
To hell with all the "Mexs."
Three cheers for New York town!
When we'll go marching home.

2

Our home is Camp McAllen, and we're very happy here;
But we haven't any sweethearts, and we haven't any beer;
We haven't any money, and we'd really like to hear
        When we go marching home.

The wop who laid the pavement, the mick who builds the pike,
Both get their union wages—if they don't, they call a strike;
Half a dollar to the soldiers, and no matter what they like,
    They still go marching on.

4

We signed enlistment papers, and they told us with a smile,
"You may go down to Mexico, but only for a while";
They promised us all luxuries and said we'd live in style
    Just the way we do at home.

5

We found the thorny cactus, the scorpion and the toads,
Tarantulas and centipedes and rattlesnakes in loads;
The flies and ants and other bugs infested our abodes.
    Good Lord, let us go home.

TEXT: Tracy H. Lewis, *Along the Rio Grande* (New York: Lewis Pub. Co., 1916), p. 191.
MUSIC: *War Songs* (1883), p. 30.

JOHN CHINAMAN

One of the distortions of the contemporary folk song revival is that, possibly because of the liberal inclinations of the interested parties, discriminatory songs have been slighted. Far from expressing a unanimous togetherness, however, the songs of the people sometimes betray the most violent prejudices, although, more often, these are the products of such bourgeois institutions as the minstrel show. In this connection, we offer some of the Western reflexes of that favorite nineteenth-century stage and literary fetish, the dialect joke. There it took the form of songs about the Chinese.

The Chinese started arriving in San Francisco in 1848, and by 1860 some 35,000 of them lived in the city. Of our first three songs, "John Chinaman," "Josh, John," and "John Chinaman, My Jo," two are from comic songsters of the 1860's. All of them agree in their disappointed observations of the failure of the Chinese immigrants to mix, mingle, and get in step with the White majority:

> I thought of rats and puppies, John,
>   You'd eaten your last fill;
> But on such slimy pot-pies, John,
>   I'm told you dinner still.

Further criticism asserted, "You've left the dress of the land of flowers, And in leaving these, haven't taken ours." And J. W. Conner threw in his Irish tuppence, "Don't abuse the freedom you enjoy, John Chinaman, my jo."

As thousands more, admitted by the Burlingame Treaty of 1868, added experience as railroad laborers to that acquired as miners, servants, and farm hands, the Chinese discovered the limits of that freedom. Replies are put in their mouths by the next four songs, from which we learn that the Chinese could see elephants as well as anyone. Mart Taylor's "John Chinaman's Appeal" recounts John's being fleeced by the Law, blackballed by "Know Nothings," and nearly scalped by an Indian. "Long John, Chineeman," whose tale is sung to the tune of "Brigham Young," is actually scalped, and dies for want of his queue. Ladies also victimized the Chinese. "Cock-eyed Fan . . . was just the cheese for the Chinaman," until "she repudiated rice." And Hay Sing's gin-gin-swilling Irish girl is stolen by a "Melican man."

Whether the prospect of a Chinese running around with his queue cut off made the miners claw themselves with pleasure, we don't know. At least such abuse was comic. But as the immigrants came to outnumber the jobs, depressing wages and remaining aloof; as the agitation of anti-Chinese clubs, Dennis Kearney, and the Workingmen's Party swelled in the 1870's; and as the time of the Chinese Exclusion Act of 1882 approached, the tone of the songs became more bitter and hostile. "Twelve Hundred More," from *The Blue and Gray Songster* of 1871, takes up the unskilled laborers' cry, "Drive out the Chinaman!" The complaint of an Irish washerwoman who lost out to the competition is uttered in "Since the Chinese Ruint the Thrade," and "Get Out, Yellow-Skins, Get Out!," from oral tradition, concludes the case for the persecution.

JOHN CHINAMAN

1

John Chinaman, John Chinaman,
    But five short years ago,
I welcomed you from Canton, John—
    But wish I hadn't though;

2

For then I thought you honest, John,
    Not dreaming but you'd make
A citizen as useful, John,
    As any in the State.

3

I thought you'd open wide your ports
    And let our merchants in
To barter for their crapes and teas,
    Their wares of wood and tin.

4

I thought you'd cut your queue off, John,
    And don a Yankee coat,
And a collar high you'd raise, John,
    Around your dusky throat.

5

I imagined that the truth, John,
    You'd speak when under oath,
But I find you'll lie and steal too—
    Yes, John, you're up to both.

6

I thought of rats and puppies, John,
    You'd eaten your last fill;
But on such slimy pot-pies, John,
    I'm told you dinner still.

7

Oh, John, I've been deceived in you,
    And in all your thieving clan,
For our gold is all you're after, John,
    To get it as you can.

TEXT: Appleton (1855), p. 44.

VARIANTS: Guinn (1906), p. 211; Lengyel (1939), p. 145; Dwyer *et al.* (1964), p. 121.

JOSH, JOHN

1

You have strayed away from your Josh,
    John,
You have strayed away from your Josh;
And between the spot where you stand
And your home in the flowery land,
    The waves of an ocean dash, John,
    The waves of an ocean dash.

2

Your "tail" is severed clean off, John,
    Your pig tail is clean cut off;
I should like to see you, John, set down,
Right in the midst of your native town—
    Yah! wouldn't the Johnnies scoff, John,
    "How can!" they would cry in scoff.

3

The hair now covers your head, John,
    The hair now covers your head;
You have lost your nankin shirt of blue,
And a sorry coat of doubtful hue
    Is seedily worn in its stead, John,
    Is seedily worn in its stead.

4

A boot of at least thirteen, John,
    A boot of a least thirteen,
And made of cowhide, strong and good,
In the place of a sole of solid wood,
    On your elegant foot is seen, John,
    On your elegant foot is seen.

5

You have come, as it were, alone, John,
    You have come, as it were, alone;
And you lead an unhappy kind of life,
Coming without a cheerful wife,
    A cheerful wife of your own, John,
    An almond-eyed wife of your own.

6

You've left your national god, John,
    You've left your god and your land;
You've left the dress of the land of flowers,
And in leaving these, haven't taken ours;
    And you've friends upon neither hand,
        John,
    You have friends upon neither hand.

7

Buffeted, beaten, and cursed, John,
    Buffeted, beaten, and cursed,
I think your life had happier been
As the slave of a nine-tailed Mandarin—
    This last state is worse than the first,
        John,
    This last state is by far the worst!

TEXT: Johnson (1863), pp. 18-19.
VARIANT: Stone (1855), p. 62.

J. W. CONNER   # JOHN CHINAMAN, MY JO   J. WATSON

TUNE: John Anderson, My Jo

John Chi-na-man, my jo, John, You're com-ing pre-cious fast; Each ship that sails from Shang-hai brings An in-crease on the last; And when you'll stop in-vad-ing us, I'm blest, now, if I know. You'll out-num-ber us poor Yan-kees, John Chi-na-man, my jo.

1

John Chinaman, my jo, John,
  You're coming precious fast;
Each ship that sails from Shanghai brings
  An increase on the last;
And when you'll stop invading us,
  I'm blest, now, if I know.
You'll outnumber us poor Yankees,
  John Chinaman, my jo.

2

John Chinaman, my jo, John,
  You not only come in shoals,
But you often shake the washing stuff,
  And spoil the water holes;
And, of course, that riles the miners, John,
  And enrages them, you know,
For they drive you frequently away,
  John Chinaman, my jo.

3

John Chinaman, my jo, John,
  You used to live on rice,
But now you purchase flour, plums,
  And other things that's nice;
And I see a butcher's shop, John,
  At your Chinese place below,
And you like your mutton now and then,
  John Chinaman, my jo.

4

John Chinaman, my jo, John,
  Though folks at you may rail,
Here's blessings on your head, John
  And more power to your tail;
But a bit of good advice, John.
  I'll give you, ere I go—
Don't abuse the freedom you enjoy,
  John Chinaman, my jo.

TEXT: Conner (1868), p. 30.

MUSIC: C. Mackay, J. Pittman and C. Brown, *The Songs of Scotland* (London: Boosey & Co., 1887), p. 72.

VARIANT: Dwyer *et al.* (1964), p. 119.

MART TAYLOR   # JOHN CHINAMAN'S APPEAL

TUNE: Umbrella Courtship

1

American, now mind my song
    If you would but hear *me sing,*
And I will tell you of the wrong
    That happened unto "Gee Sing."
In "fifty-two" I left my home—
    I bid farewell to "Hong Kong"—
I started with Cup Gee to roam
    To the land where they use the "long
       tom."

CHORUS: O ching hi ku tong mo ching ching,
    O ching hi ku tong *chi do,*
Cup Gee hi ku tong mo ching ching,
    Then what could Gee or I do?

2

In forty days I reached the Bay,
    And nearly starved I was, sir.
I cooked and ate a dog one day—
    I didn't know the laws, sir—
But soon I found my dainty meal
    Was against the city order.
The penalty I had to feel—
    Confound the old Recorder.

3

By paying up my cost and fines,
    They freed me from the locker,
And then I started for the mines—
    I got a pick and rocker.
I went to work in an untouched place—
    I'm sure I meant no blame, sir—
But a white man struck me in the face
    And told me to leave his claim, sir.

4

'Twas then I packed my tools away
    And set up in a new place,
But there they would not let me stay—
    They didn't like the *cue* race.
And then I knew not what to do,
    I could not get employ,
The Know Nothings would bid me go—
    'Twas *tu nah mug ahoy.*

5

I started then for Weaverville
    Where Chinamen were thriving,
But found our China agents there
    In ancient feuds were driving.
So I pitched into politics,
    But with the weaker party;
The Canton's with their clubs and bricks
    Did drub us out "right hearty."

6

I started for Yreka then;
    I thought that I would stay there,
But found for even Chinamen
    The "diggings" wouldn't pay there.
So I set up a washing shop,
    But how extremely funny,
The miners all had dirty clothes,
    But not a cent of money.

7

I met a big stout Indian once.
    He stopped me in the trail, sir.
He drew an awful scalping knife,
    And I trembled for my tail, sir.
He caught me by the hair, it's true,
    In a manner quite uncivil,
But when he saw my awful cue,
    He thought I was the devil.

8

Oh, now, my friends, I'm going away
    From this infernal place, sir;
The balance of my days I'll stay
    With the Celestial race, sir.
I'll go to raising rice and tea;
    I'll be a heathen ever,
For Christians all have treated me
    As men should be used never.

TEXT: Taylor (1856), p. 29.

VARIANTS: Johnson (1863), pp. 9-11; Dwyer *et al.* (1964), pp. 112-113.

JOHN CHINAMAN'S MARRIAGE

1

Good people all, give ear, I pray,
To what I'm now about to say:
    I'm giving you, in a song,
    The married life of poor Ching Chong.
This Chinese chap, as I've been told,
At mining saved a lot of gold;
    To get a wife then was his plan,
    Wasn't he a domestic Chinaman!

CHORUS: Good people all, give ear, I pray,
To what I'm now about to say:
    I'm giving you, in a song,
    The married life of poor Ching
        Chong.

2

But the girls would not come out,
And John remained some time in doubt:
    His stock of English words was small,
    And he couldn't tell his wants at all.
Some girls he leered at merely laughed,
While others bantered him and chaffed;
    At length a girl named Cock-eyed Fan,
    Took pity on this Chinaman.

3

To look at her, 'twas hard to say
Exactly where her beauty lay:
    Her complexion was a dirty brown,
    And she lately came from famed
        Hangtown.
Small-pox had left big traces there,
She'd a snub nose and carroty hair;
    But finding fault was not his plan,
    She was just the cheese for the
        Chinaman.

4

They went to church, and John with pride
Surveyed his fat and blooming bride:
    He'd have talked finely if he could,
    But he kept on saying, "Welly good."
At length, quite lushy, home she'd reel,
And for a row she then would peel;
    To play her pranks she then began,
    And she walked into the Chinaman.

5

She put poor John quite in a fright,
For often she'd stay out all night;
    And in the morning home she'd come,
    Smelling delightfully of rum.
She then repudiated rice,
And swore such grub would not suffice;
    At length from him clean off she ran,
    And she left her faithful Chinaman.

6

And after doing John so brown,
She toddled back to her native town;
    But the old folks there knew her go,
    And her doings down at Francisco.
And now whenever she goes out,
The little boys behind her shout:
    "Twig her, Bill, that's Cock-eyed Fan,
    The girl that bamboozled the
        Chinaman!"

LAST CHORUS: Good people all, give ear, I
        pray,
    I've told you all I had to say,
        And stated briefly in my
            song,
        The married *joys* of poor
            Ching Chong.

TEXT: Conner (1868), pp. 60-61.

HAY SING, COME FROM CHINA

My name Hay Sing, come from Chin-a. Me keep a wash-ee shop way down the street. No lik-ee Mel-i-can man, too much chin-chin; No pay wash-ee bill, him a dead beat. Me got an I-rish girl, she well nic-ee. Me mak-ee her some day my wife. We have a nice time, go back Chin-a. Eat much plen-ty rats and mice.

1

My name Hay Sing, come from China.
Me keep a washee shop way down street.
No likee Melican man, too much chin-chin;
No pay washee bill, him a dead beat.

CHORUS: Me got an Irish girl, she well nicee.
Me makee her some day my wife.
We have a nice time, go back China,
Eat much plenty rats and mice.

2

My name Hay Sing, come from China.
Me go away and soon come back.
Me catchee Melican man sittin' on her lapee,
Kissin' my Irish girl—smack, smack smack.

3

Got a little house in Bottle Alley,
Two little rooms on the top side high.
We get married and drink much gin-gin;
She get tight and hit me on the eye.

4

Policeman takee me to the lockee up shop,
Putee me there and makee me stay.
Judge send me up for a very long timee;
My pretty Irish girl she run away.

5

Oh, my name Hay Sing, come from China.
Me likee Irish girl, she likee me.
Me from a Hong Kong, Melican man come
along,
Steal an Irish girl from a poor Chinee.

TEXT: Leland (1947), p. 383. Used by permission of California Folklore Society.

MUSIC: Hubbard (1961), p. 171. Used by permission of University of Utah Press.

VARIANTS: McMullen (1946), pp. 29-30; Green (1947), p. 278; Hubbard (1950), p. 320, and (1961), p. 171.

TWELVE HUNDRED MORE

1

O workingmen dear, and did you hear
The news that's goin' round?
Another China steamer
Has been landed here in town.
Today I read the papers,
And it grieved my heart full sore
To see upon the title page,
O, just "Twelve Hundred More!"

2

O, California's coming down,
As you can plainly see:
They are hiring all the Chinamen
And discharging you and me;
But strife will be in every town
Throughout the Pacific shore,
And the cry of old and young shall be,
"O, damn 'Twelve Hundred More!'"

3

They run their steamer in at night
Upon our lovely bay;
If 'twas a free and honest trade,
They'd land it in the day.
They come here by the hundreds—
The country is overrun—
And go to work at any price—
By them the labor's done.

4

If you meet a workman in the street
And look into his face,
You'll see the signs of sorrow there—
Oh, damn this long-tailed race!
And men today are languishing
Upon a prison floor,
Because they've been supplanted by
This vile "Twelve Hundred More!"

5

Twelve hundred honest laboring men
Thrown out of work today
By the landing of these Chinamen
In San Francisco Bay.
Twelve hundred pure and virtuous girls,
In the papers I have read,
Must barter away their virtue
To get a crust of bread.

6

This state of things can never last
In this, our golden land,
For soon you'll hear the avenging cry,
"Drive out the China man!"
And then we'll have the stirring times
We had in days of yore,
And the devil take those dirty words
They call "Twelve Hundred More!"

TEXT: *The Blue and Gray Songster* (San Francisco: S. S. Green, 1877), pp. 16-17.
VARIANT: Lengyel (1939), p. 143.

LONG JOHN, CHINEEMAN

TUNE: Brigham Young, II

Big Long John was a Chi-nee—man; He came from the land of tea.___ He ped-dled cig-a—reets in the up—per land, Way out in Mil-wau—kee;___ Eat more hash at a free meal a day; Nev-er was late to his meals;___ Had a long tail from the top of his head That hung clear down to his heels.___

Chorus

Ching Ching Chow, Ching-ee ring-ee roo, Ching-ee roo was a Chin—ee—man. He was a bar-ber by birth and a butch-er by trade. I tell you he was oil from the can.___

Big Long John was a Chineeman;
He came from the land of tea.
He peddled cigareets in the upper land,
Way out in Milwaukee;
Eat more hash at a free meal a day;
Never was late to his meals;
Had a long tail from the top of his head
That hung clear down to his heels.

CHORUS: Ching Ching Chow, Chingee ringee
     roo,
Chingee roo was a Chineeman.
He was a barber by birth and a
    butcher by trade.
I tell you he was oil from the can.

2

He went to San Francisco
For a Chinee girl to see.
Feelee very tired he lay down to sleep
In the shade of a huckleberry tree;
Feelee very tired he soon fell asleep
And laid his head on a plank.
Along came an Indian with a big tomahawk
And cut off a piece of his scalp.

3

And when he awoke he felt so bad
That he hollered with all his might;
Put his hand to his head and it made him so
    sick
That he died that very same night.
He was found next day at two P.M.
By the captain of the Hongkong crew,
And he wrote to his sweetheart Chum Chum
    Fee
That he died for the want of his queue.

Used by permission of University of Utah Press.
TEXT: Hubbard (1950), p. 317.
MUSIC: Hubbard (1961), p. 408.
VARIANT: Hubbard (1961), p. 170.

SINCE THE CHINESE RUINT THE THRADE

1

From me shanty down on Sixth Street,
    It's meself have jist kim down;
I've lived there this eighteen year—
    It's in phat they call Cork Town.
I'm on the way to the City Hall
    To get a little aid;
It's meself that has to ax it now
    Since the Chinese ruint the thrade.

CHORUS: For I kin wash an' iron a shirt,
    An' I kin scrub a flure;
An' I kin starch a collar as stiff
    As any Chineseman, I'm shure;
But ther dhirty, pigtailed haythens,
    An' ther prices they are paid
Have brought me to the state you
  see—
    They've ontirely ruint ther
      thrade.

2

I'm a widdy woman, I'd have ye know:
    Poor Mike was kilt at wark.
He got a fall from the City Hall,
    For he was a mason's clark.
An' me daughter Ellen is gone this year
    Wid a Frinch bally troupe, ther jade,
So I find it hard to get along
    Since the Chinese ruint ther thrade.

3

It makes me wild, whin I'm on the street,
    To see those haythens' signs:
Ah Sung, Ah Sing, Sam Lee, Ah Wing,
    An' ther ilegant sprid on ther lines.
If iver I get me hands on Ah Sing,
    I'll make him Ah Sing indade—
On me clothesline I'll pin the leather skin
    Of the haythen that ruint the thrade.

TEXT: *The Poor Little Man and the Man in the Moon Is Looking, Love, Songster* (San Francisco: G. W. Greene, n.d.), p. 11.

GET OUT, YELLOW-SKINS, GET OUT!

The Yel-low-skins here in these hills Now know how it appears To have their gold by oth-ers stole, As we have suf-fered for
years. Get out, Yel-low-skins, get out! Get out, Yel-low-
skins, get out!__ We'll do it a-gain if
you don't go, Get out, Yel-low skins, get out!

1

The Yellow-skins here in these hills
Now know how it appears
To have their gold by others stole,
As we have suffered for years.

CHORUS: Get out, Yellow-skins, get out!
Get out, Yellow-skins, get out!
We'll do it again if you don't go,
Get out, Yellow-skins, get out!

TEXT AND MUSIC: Burt (1958a), p. 157, and (1958b), p. 268. Used by permission of
Olive W. Burt.

WHAT WAS YOUR NAME IN THE STATES?

The jingle "What Was Your Name in the States?" implies that the West gave a sheltering anonymity to such lesser felons as would be named Thompson, Johnson, or Bates, but folk history has brazenly exalted the names of the worst. "Joaquin the Horse-Thief," which has gone from John Stone's songster to the Michigan woods, builds upon the seven-week career of the California bandit, Joaquin Murrieta. After terrorizing Calaveras and Mariposa counties, he was ridden to earth, killed, and allegedly beheaded for evidence by Captain Harry Love's State Rangers near Coalinga in San Joaquin Valley on July 25, 1853.

Lawrence was a center of free-state activity in the Kansas Territory before the Civil War. On August 21, 1863, Confederate forces led by William Clarke Quantrill sacked and burned the town, leaving 150 dead. The song "Quantrell" exists in widely differing versions, the one printed here apparently confusing Quantrill with Robin Hood.

"Sam Bass" was born a Hoosier in 1851. After a life of miscellaneous villainy, he planned to rob the bank at Round Rock, Texas, with his companions Jim Murphy, Seaborn Barnes, and Frank Jackson. Murphy forewarned the Adjutant General of Texas, whose Rangers tried to arrest them the day before the stickup. Barnes was killed outright, but Bass, wounded, fled to a wood, where he died a couple of days later on his twenty-seventh birthday.

Billy the Kid's stock has dropped slightly since research has revealed him to have been an adenoidal psychopath. But the reputation of Sheriff Pat Garret, the man who got him, shows that Westerners had few illusions about the virtues a badge conferred on a gunslinger.

Among the desperados who served an apprenticeship in Quantrill's guerrillas was Cole Younger, a Missourian who became a captain in Shelby's Missouri Cavalry toward the end of the Civil War. With his brothers and the similarly trained James boys, he turned to robbing trains and banks. Captured, as the song relates, during the robbery of a Northfield, Minnesota, bank in 1876, he was imprisoned for twenty-five years. Afterward, he joined Frank James in a Wild West show and survived until 1916.

We include a couple of songs about no-goods who might as well have been nameless. The narrator of "The Portland County Jail" says that the ninety days he spent in the company of Happy Sailor Jack made an honest workingman of him, but nothing is likely to reform the recidivist in "Experience":

> I've been pinched from New York to 'Frisco;
> Now I'm doin' my fourth little "V,"
> So be warned by my lot, which I know you will not,
> An' learn about stone johns from me.

As Woody Guthrie tells it, "Pretty Boy Floyd" was just competing with the government in distributing relief, but probably not all the people he killed needed to be.

WHAT WAS YOUR NAME IN THE STATES?

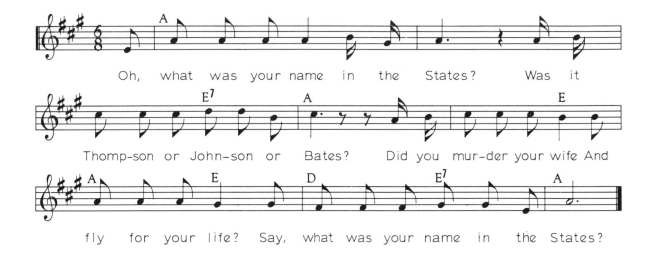

1

Oh, what was your name in the States?
Was it Thompson or Johnson or Bates?
Did you murder your wife
And fly for your life?
Say, what was your name in the States?

TEXT AND MUSIC: Sandburg (1927), p. 106. Used by permission of Harcourt, Brace & World, Inc.

VARIANTS: E Clampus Vitus (1939), p. 6; Lengyel (1939), p. 31A, and (1949), p. 23; Black and Robertson (1940), p. 1.

QUANTRELL

Come all you bold rob—bers and o—pen your ears; Of

Quan—trell the lion heart you quick—ly shall hear With his

band of bold raid—ers in dou—ble—quick time, He

came to lay Law—rence low, o—ver the line.

Chorus

All rout—ing and shout—ing and giv—ing the yell, Like

so man—y de—mons just raised up from hell, The

boys were so drunk—en with pow—der and wine, And

came to burn Law—rence just o—ver the line.

1

Come all you bold robbers and open your ears;
Of Quantrell the lion heart you quickly shall hear.
With his band of bold raiders in double-quick time,
He came to lay Lawrence low, over the line.

CHORUS: All routing and shouting and giving the yell,
Like so many demons just raised up from hell,
The boys they were drunken with powder and wine,
And came to burn Lawrence, just over the line

2

They came to burn Lawrence; they came not to stay.
They rode in one morning at breaking of day
With guns all a-waving and horses all foam,
And Quantrell a-riding his famous big roan.

3

They came to burn Lawrence; they came not to stay.
Jim Lane he was up at the break of the day;
He saw them a-coming and got in a fright,
Then crawled in a corn crib to get out of sight.

4

Oh, Quantrell's a fighter, a bold-hearted boy:
A brave man or woman he'd never annoy.
He'd take from the wealthy and give to the poor,
For brave men there's never a bolt to his door.

TEXT AND MUSIC: Finger (1927), pp. 64-65. Used by permission of Charles J. Finger Estate.

VARIANTS: Lomax and Lomax (1934), pp. 132-133, and (1938), pp. 142-143; Koch and Koch (1961), pp. 22-23.

SAM BASS

Sam Bass was born in In-di-an-a— it was his na-tive home— And at the age of sev-en-teen, young Sam be-gan to roam. He first went down to Tex-as, a cow-boy bold to be; A kind-er-heart-ed fel-low, you'd scarce-ly ev-er see.

1
Sam Bass was born in Indiana—it was his native home—
And at the age of seventeen, young Sam began to roam.
He first went down to Texas, a cowboy bold to be;
A kinder-hearted fellow, you'd scarcely ever see.

2
Sam used to deal in race stock, had one called the Denton mare.
He watched her in scrub races, took her to the County Fair.
She always won the money, wherever she might be.
He always drank good liquor, and spent his money free.

3
Sam left the Collins ranch in the merry month of May
With a herd of Texas cattle, the Black Hills to see;
Sold out in Custer City and all got on a spree—
A harder lot of cowboys you'd scarcely ever see.

4
On the way back to Texas, they robbed the U.P. train,
All split up in couples and started out again.
Joe Collins and his partner were overtaken soon;
With all their hard earned money they had to meet their doom.

5
Sam made it back to Texas all right side up with care,
Rode into the town of Denton, his gold with friends to share.
Sam's life was short in Texas 'count of robberies he'd do.
He'd rob the passengers' coaches, the mail and express, too.

6

Sam had four bold companions, four bold and daring lads:
Underwood and Joe Jackson, Bill Collins and Old Dad.
They were four of the hardest cowboys that Texas ever knew;
They whipped the Texas Rangers and ran the boys in blue.

7

Jonis borrowed of Sam's money and didn't want to pay;
The only way he saw to win was to give poor Sam away.
He turned traitor to his comrades; they were caught one early
    morn.
Oh what a scorching Jonis will get when Gabriel blows his horn.

8

Sam met his fate in Round Rock, July the twenty-first.
They pierced poor Sam with rifle balls and emptied out his purse.
So Sam is a corpse in Round Rock, Jonis is under the clay,
And Joe Jackson in the bushes trying to get away.

TEXT: Thorp (1908), pp. 24-26.

MUSIC: As sung by Lannis F. Sutton, Library of Congress Recording L 30. Transcribed by David Cohen.

VARIANTS: Stanley (1897), p. 25; Lomax (1910), pp. 149-153; Siringo (1919), pp. 16-18; Thorp (1921), pp. 135-138; Pound (1922), pp. 149-152; Barnes (1925), p. 15; Finger (1927), pp. 66-71; Sandburg (1927), pp. 422-424; Dick (1928), p. 93; Larkin (1931), pp. 161-164; Clark (1932), pp. 32-33; Allen (1933), pp. 112-114; Lomax and Lomax (1934), pp. 126-128; Frey (1936), pp. 52-53; Lomax and Lomax (1938), pp. 150-152; Belden (1940), pp. 399-400*; Lomax and Lomax (1947), pp. 298-299; Randolph (1948), pp. 69-72*; Wylder (1949), pp. 70-71; Owens (1950), pp. 122-124; Burt (1958a), pp. 199-200; Moore and Moore (1964), pp. 343-345; Laws (1964), pp. 177-178*; Fife and Fife (1966), p. 112-120*.

JOHN A. STONE   # JOAQUIN THE HORSE-THIEF
TUNE: Now, I Warn All You Darkies Not To Love Her

1

I suppose you have heard all the talkin'
Of the very noted horse-thief Joaquin;
He was caught in Calaveras, but he couldn't stand the joke,
So the rangers cut his head off, and have got it now in soak.

CHORUS: Now I warn every body not to ramble,
Never drink, never fight, never gamble,
For you'll never have a cent, all your money will be spent,
And you to Sacramento to the prison brig be sent.

2

They took three-fingered Jack and cut his hand off;
Then the Rangers drove the rest of the band off;
Then they took the head and the hand, and they had it well
    preserved,
And the Rangers got the credit, which they very much deserved.

3

Joaquin to the mountains was advancing,
When he saw Lola Montez a-dancing;
When she danced the spider dance, he was bound to run her off,
And he'd feed her eggs and chickens, make her cackle, crow, and
    cough.

4

Joaquin, just before he was taken,
Killed a Chinaman, and then stole his bacon;
Then he went to Sonora, where he killed eleven more,
And a big Digger Indian, which made the twenty-four.

5

You have heard of the steel he wore round him;
I will tell you what it was when they found him:
'Twas a long-tom iron, to protect him in his crimes,
And they swore by the holes he'd been shot a thousand times.

6

Now the head it can be seen at Sacramento,
But to have it there, they never did intend to;
For they fought like the devil, while they had half a show,
But the Rangers put an end to the terror of Mexico.

TEXT: Stone (1855), pp. 26-27.

VARIANTS: *Journal of American Folklore*, XXVII (1914), 93; Grant (1924), pp. 146-147;
Lengyel (1939), p. 43, and (1949), p. 34; Dwyer *et al.* (1964), p. 147.

BILLY THE KID

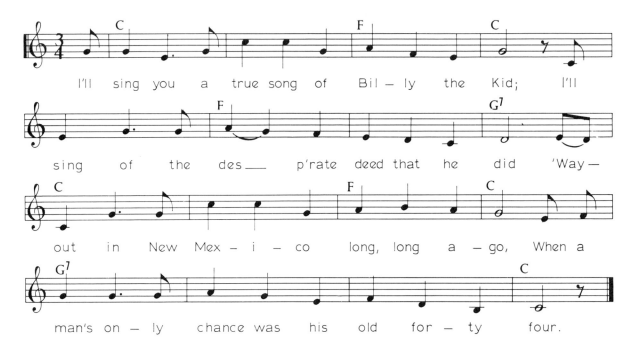

I'll sing you a true song of Bil — ly the Kid; I'll sing of the des — p'rate deed that he did 'Way — out in New Mex — i — co long, long a — go, When a man's on — ly chance was his old for — ty four.

1

I'll sing you a true song of Billy the Kid;
I'll sing of the desp'rate deeds that he did
'Way out in New Mexico long, long ago,
When a man's only chance was his old forty-four.

2

When Billy the Kid was a very young lad,
In old Silver City he went to the bad;
Way out in the West with a gun in his hand,
At the age of twelve years, he killed his first man.

3

Fair Mexican maidens play guitars and sing
A song about Billy, their boy bandit king,
How, ere his young manhood had reached its sad end,
Had a notch on his pistol for twenty-one men.

4

'Twas on the same night that poor Billy died,
He said to his friends, "I'm not satisfied.
There are twenty-one men I've put bullets through,
And Sheriff Pat Garret must make twenty-two."

5

Now this is how Billy the Kid met his fate:
The bright moon was shining, the hour was late;
Shot down by Pat Garret, who once was his friend,
The young outlaw's life had come to its end.

6

There's many a man with face fine and fair,
Who starts out in life with a chance to be square;
But just like poor Billy, he wanders astray,
And loses his life the very same way.

———————

TEXT AND MUSIC: Patterson and Dexter (1932), pp. 6-7.

VARIANTS: Allen (1933), pp. 162-163; Lomax and Lomax (1934), pp. 137-138, and (1938), pp. 141-142; Lomax (1960), p. 387.

COLE YOUNGER

I am one of a band of high — way — men; Cole
Young — er is my name._____ My crimes and
dep — re — da — tions have brought my
friends to shame. The rob — bing of the
North — field Bank, the same I can't de — ny,
For now I am a pris — on —
er; in the Still — wa — ter jail I lie.

1

I am one of a band of highwaymen; Cole Younger is my name.
My crimes and depredations have brought my friends to shame.
The robbing of the Northfield Bank, the same I can't deny,
For now I am a prisoner; in the Stillwater jail I lie.

2

'Tis of a bold, high robbery, a story to you I'll tell,
Of a California miner who unto us befell.
We robbed him of his money and bid him go his way,
For which I will be sorry until my dying day.

And then we started homeward, when brother Bob did say:
"Now, Cole, we will buy fast horses and on them ride away.
We will ride to avenge our father's death and try to win the prize;
We will fight those anti-guerrillas until the day we die."

4

And then we rode towards Texas, that good old Lone Star State;
But on Nebraska's prairies the James boys we did meet.
With knives, guns, and revolvers, we all sat down to play,
A-drinking of good whiskey to pass the time away.

5

A Union Pacific railway train was the next we did surprise,
And the crimes done by our bloody hands bring tears into my eyes.
The engineerman and fireman, killed—the conductor escaped alive—
And now their bones lie mouldering beneath Nebraska's skies.

6

Then we saddled horses; northwestward we did go
To the God-forsaken country called Min-ne-so-te-o.
I had my eye on the Northfield Bank when brother Bob did say:
"Now, Cole, if you undertake the job, you will surely curse the day."

7

But I stationed out my pickets and up to the bank did go,
And there upon the counter I struck my fatal blow.
"Just hand us over your money and make no further delay;
We are the famous Younger brothers, we spare no time to pray."

TEXT: Lomax (1910), pp. 106-107.

MUSIC: "The Texas Cowboy," as sung by Edward L. Crain, Columbia Record 15710-D (1930). Reissued as Folkways Record FA 295. Transcribed by David Cohen.

VARIANTS: Federal Writers' Project (1937a), p. 9; Randolph (1948), pp. 12-16*; Botkin (1951), pp. 776-777; Lomax (1960), pp. 350-351; Moore and Moore (1964), pp. 345-347; Laws (1964), p. 177*.

PORTLAND COUNTY JAIL

I'm a stran-ger in your cit—y; my name is Pad-dy Flynn.

I got drunk the oth—er night, and the cop-pers run me in. I

had no mon—ey to pay my fine, no one to go my bail, So

I got stuck for nine-ty days in the Port-land Count-y Jail____.

1

I'm a stranger in your city ; my name is Paddy Flynn.
I got drunk the other night, and the coppers run me in.
I had no money to pay my fine, no one to go my bail,
So I got stuck for ninety days in the Portland County Jail.

2

Oh, the only friend that I had left was Happy Sailor Jack.
He told me all the lies he knew and all the safes he'd cracked.
He'd cracked them in Seattle ; he'd robbed the Western Mail.
'Twould freeze the blood of an honest man in the Portland County
  Jail.

3

Oh, such a bunch of devils no one ever saw :
Robbers, thieves and highwaymen, breakers of the law.
They sang a song the whole night long ; the curses fell like hail.
I'll bless the day that takes me away from the Portland County
  Jail.

4

Finest friend I ever had was Officer McGurk.
He said I was a lazy bum, a no-good and a shirk.
One Saturday night when I got tight, he trun me in the can,
And now you see he's made of me *A* honest workingman.

TEXT AND MUSIC: Sandburg (1927), pp. 214-215. Used by permission of Harcourt, Brace & World, Inc.

VARIANTS: Anderson (1923), pp. 210-211; Millburn (1930), pp. 176-177; Botkin (1951), pp. 777-778.

EXPERIENCE

1

I've taken my jolts as I got 'em;
I've strong-armed and prowled in my time,
Never passed up a crib as I knows of,
And mostly the pickin's was prime.
My first was a stickup in Portland,
When I was hooched up like a bat;
The beak handed me a hard labor "V,"
And I learned about likker from that.

2

Then I rode the rods down to 'Frisco,
And went back to work for a spell;
But I quit my very first pay-day,
And got all gowed up to beat hell.
Next I met an old con from Chicago
Who said he was Toledo Slim;
He met up with a skunk who had treated him
    punk,
And I learned about shootin' from him.

3

Only once did I fall for a woman,
And she was a cabaret gal,
Who I meets at the old Portola Louvre,
An' I figgered she'd make a good pal.
I asked her an' she seemed to be willin',
So we drinks, an' the rest is a blur;
An' when I awoke, she had blew with me
    poke,
An' I learned about women from her.

4

Next I took a short sleigh ride,
An' felt the wide world was mine,
So I took and sold a young bozo
The Palace Hotel for a dime.
He snitched me away to a gumshoe,
An' did sixty days breakin' rocks,
But I'm not so dead yet that I'll ever forget
The snow, and the habit that mocks.

5

Then I stuck up a grocery in Oakland,
An' most got away in the fog;
They never at all would a nabbed me
If it hadn't a been for a dog.
He grabbed for the seat of me britches
An' hung on to me like a rat—
Yeah, they got me a'right, and locked me up
    tight,
An' I learned about meestles from that.

6

I've taken my jolts as I got 'em;
I've strong-armed an' prowled in my time,
Never passed up a crib as I knows of,
An' mostly the pickin's was prime.
I've been pinched from New York to 'Frisco;
Now I'm doin' my fourth little "V,"
So be warned by my lot, which I know you
    will not,
An' learn about stone johns from me.

TEXT: Irwin (1931), pp. 226-227.

WOODY GUTHRIE

PRETTY BOY FLOYD

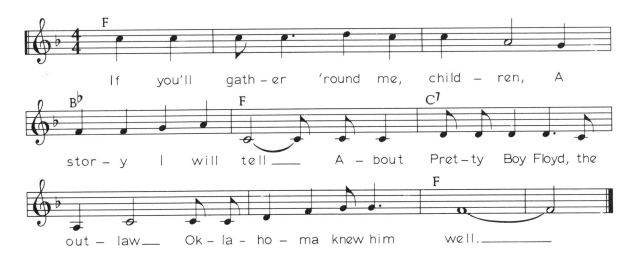

If you'll gath – er 'round me, child – ren, A
stor – y I will tell ___ A – bout Pret – ty Boy Floyd, the
out – law ___ Ok – la – ho – ma knew him well. ___

1
If you'll gather 'round me, children,
A story I will tell
About Pretty Boy Floyd the outlaw—
Oklahoma knew him well.

2
It was in the town of Shawnee;
It was Saturday afternoon;
His wife beside him in his wagon
As into town they rode.

3
There a deputy sheriff approached him
In a manner rather rude
Using vulgar words of language,
And his wife, she overheard.

4
Pretty Boy grabbed a log chain,
And the deputy grabbed a gun;
And in the fight that followed,
He laid that deputy down.

5
He took to the trees and timbers,
And he lived a life of shame;
Every crime in Oklahoma
Was added to his name.

6
Yes, he took to the trees and timbers
On that Canadian River's shore,
And Pretty Boy found a welcome
At a many a farmer's door.

7
There's a many a starving farmer
The same old story told
How this outlaw paid their mortgage
And saved their little home.

8
Others tell you 'bout a stranger
That come to beg a meal
And underneath his napkin,
Left a thousand dollar bill.

9
It was in Oklahoma City;
It was on a Christmas Day;
There come a whole carload of groceries
With a letter that did say:

10
"You say that I'm an outlaw.
You say that I'm a thief.
Here's a Christmas dinner
For the families on relief."

11
Now as through this world I ramble,
I see lots of funny men.
Some will rob you with a six-gun,
And some with a fountain pen.

12
But as through your life you travel,
As through your life you roam,
You won't never see an outlaw
Drive a family from their home.

TEXT AND MUSIC: Guthrie (1947), pp. 27, 49.
VARIANTS: Greenway (1953), pp. 296-297; Lomax (1960), p. 437.

THE TEXAS COWBOY

Six million beasts walked up from Texas and down from Montana to westering railroads in the two decades following the Civil War, and their mounted attendants made one of the firmest and most novel contributions to American folk music. Some two hundred cowboy songs and ballads have survived the last roundup and long drive; the songs that were not wholly new creations at least show the adaptation of traditional and popular materials to the cow pony rhythms of walk, trot, and canter. This first selection of songs suggests the better images the cowboy had of himself. They are about the attractions he insisted were inherent in his trade, and they boast of his skills in pursuing it.

"The Texas Cowboy" anathematizes Montana's consumptive airs, tenderfeet, and lean dogies, Nebraska's easy pastures, and Arizona's sand hills; and implicit in the cowboy's griping is an admiration for the canny, hardworking waddies who rode year-round down in Texas. Montana's indirect reply is given in "I Want To Be a Cowboy," one of six songs we print whose authorship was claimed by D. J. O'Malley, "the Cowboy Poet." In late youth he lived near Fort Keogh, Montana, where his father rode with the 2d Cavalry. In 1881 he struck out on his own, working for a half-dozen spreads in eastern Montana until 1904 when he became a special deputy sheriff in Rosebud. Later he was a guard in the state penitentiary at Deer Lodge, and in 1909 moved to Wisconsin, where he was living at the time John White got out a small pamphlet on him in 1934. He claimed a large output, some of which appeared anonymously or under the initials D. J. W. in the Miles City, Montana, *Stock Grower's Journal* in the 1890's.

"I Want To Be a Cowboy" partly confirms the Texan's accusation. O'Malley says he wrote the song at a stock growers' meeting jammed with milling tenderfeet all dressed up and looking for jobs.

"Yellowstone Flat" makes the case for the good Montana wranglers, although some would say their origins explained their proficiency:

> We come up the trail with the Texas rawhide.
> There is not a bronco that we cannot ride.
> With a quirt we can haze him and ne'er pull the horn,
> For we are the twisters as sure as you're born.

And a ditty of the 1870's called "The Captain of the Cowboys" makes it clear that the Colorado punchers had no use for tenderfeet if beauty was their portion, for on branding day, "A dirty face and a broken nose will likely change your notion."

The "Top Hand" is at the other extreme from the tenderfoot. He has seen it all, knows all the shortcuts and excuses, and is a prima donna:

> When you ship the cattle, he's bound to go along
> To keep the boss from drinking and to see that nothing's wrong.
> Wherever he goes, catch on to his game.
> He likes to be called with a handle to his name.
> He's always primping with a pocket looking glass;
> From the top to the bottom, he's a bold jackass,
>   Waddie cowboy.

From a Cheyenne newspaper of 1883 we print "The Jolly Vaquero," a close look at the language the cowboy used in applauding, and apologizing for, himself.

O'Malley's "The Horse Wrangler," to the tune of something called "The Day I Played Baseball," is an oft-collected narrative on its author's favorite theme of what happens to people who take cow punching lightly:

> Before you try it go kiss your wife,
> Get a heavy insurance on your life;
> Then shoot yourself with a butcher knife.
> It's far the easiest way.

Not about to let the tenderfoot up, the "Old Time Cowboy" makes some mild threats, then praises to the skies the cowboys' generosity, their lack of meanness, and imperviousness to advice. Allen McCandless' "The Cowboy," first printed in the Trinidad, Colorado, *Daily Advertiser* in 1885, was an extraordinarily popular song for one so literary. It mixes wildly different levels of diction, quotes Shakespeare, burlesques the Bible, and makes awful puns. Jacob, for example, "started in business clear down at bed rock, And made quite a fortune by watering stock." Another song called "The Cowboy," printed in 1893 by an itinerant preacher named W. S. James, makes several of the preceding points and adds the touching one that the cowboy's "heart is warm and tender when he sees a friend in pain, Though his education is but to endure."

THE TEXAS COWBOY

Come all you Tex-as cow-boys And warn-ing take of
me: Don't go out in Mon-tan-a For wealth or lib-er—ty.

End of final stanza

Where the cow-boys are all ten-der-feet And the do-gies are all lean.

1
Come all you Texas cowboys
 And warning take of me:
Don't go out in Montana
 For wealth or liberty.

2
But stay home here in Texas,
 Where they work the year around,
And where you'll not get consumption
 From sleeping on the ground.

3
Montana is too cold for me,
 And the winters are too long.
Before the round-ups have begun,
 Your money is all gone.

4
For in Montana the boys get work
 But six months in the year,
And they charge for things three prices
 In that land so bleak and drear.

5
This thin old hen-skin bedding,
 'Twas not enough to shield my form,
For I almost freeze to death
 Whene'er there comes a storm.

6
I've an outfit on the Mussleshell
 Which I expect I'll never see
Unless by chance I'm sent
 To represent this AR and PT.

7

All along these bad lands,
　　And down upon the dry
Where the canons have no bottoms
　　And the mountains reach the sky,

8

Your chuck is bread and bacon
　　And coffee black as ink
And hard old alkali water
　　That's scarcely fit to drink.

9

They'll wake you in the morning
　　Before the break of day
And send you out on circle
　　Full twenty miles away

10

With a "Tenderfoot" to lead you
　　Who never knows the way.
You're pegging in the best of luck
　　If you get two meals a day.

11

I've been over in Colorado
　　And down upon the Platte
Where the cowboys work in pastures
　　And the cattle all are fat;

12

Where they ride silver mounted saddles
　　And spurs and leggin's too,
And their horses are all Normans
　　And only fit to plow.

13

Yes I've traveled lots of country,
　　Arizona's hills of sand
Down through the Indian Nation
　　Plum to the Rio Grande.

14

Montana is the bad land,
　　The worst I've ever seen,
Where the cowboys are all tenderfeet
　　And the dogies are all lean.

TEXT: Thorp (1908), pp. 21-23.

MUSIC: Larkin (1931), pp. 54-55. Used by permission of Alfred A. Knopf, Inc.

VARIANTS: Lomax (1910), pp. 229-232; Thorp (1921), pp. 148-151; Larkin (1931), pp. 54-55; Clark (1932), p. 64; Lomax and Lomax (1938), pp. 22-24; Fife and Fife (1966), pp. 97-103*.

D. J. O'MALLEY

I WANT TO BE A COWBOY

TUNE: I Want To Be an Angel

1

I want to be a cowboy
    And with the cowboys stand,
With leather chaps upon my legs
    And a six-gun in my hand.
And, while the foreman sees me,
    I'll make some Winter plays;
But I will catch a regular
    When the herd's thrown out to graze.

2

I'll have a full-stamped saddle
    And a silver-mounted bit,
With conchos big as dollars,
    And silvered spurs, to wit;
With a long rawhide reata
    And a big Colt's forty-five,
I'll be a model puncher
    As sure as you're alive.

3

I want to be a tough man
    And be so very bad;
With my big white sombrero,
    I'll make the dude look sad.
I'll get plumb full of bug juice
    And shoot up the whole town;
When I start out to have a time,
    You bet I'll do it brown.

4

I want to be a buster
    And ride the bucking horse,
And scratch him in the shoulders
    With my silvered spurs, of course.
I'll rake him up and down the side—
    You bet I'll fan the breeze!
I'll ride him with slick saddle
    And do it with great ease.

5

I want to be a top man
    And work on the outside
So I can ride within the herd
    And cut it high and wide.
Oh, a rep is what I want to be,
    And a rep, you bet, I'll make.
At punching cows, I know I'll shine;
    I'm sure I'll take the cake.

TEXT: *Stock Growers' Journal* (Miles City, Montana), April 7, 1894.
VARIANTS: Pound (1915), p. 106, and (1922), p. 173; O'Malley (1934), p. 14.

YELLOWSTONE FLAT

Here's to the punch-ers on Yel — low — stone Flat, Who wear the high heels, al — so the white hat, Who'd work for the X— 's, al — so the H — S; But as for the C - K, we'd find her the best.

Chorus

We used Col — lins sad — dles, new Miles Cit — y chaps, With our cuffs made of leath — er, al — so the wide hats, With our shirts made of buck — skins__ they're bead — ed all o'er__ With fringe to the el — bow, the cow — boys ga — lore.

1

Here's to the punchers on Yellowstone Flat,
Who wear the high heels, also the white hat,
Who'd work for the X's, also the HS;
But as for the CK, we'd find her the best.
We used Collins saddles, new Miles City chaps,
With our cuffs made of leather, also the wide hats,
With our shirts made of buckskin—they're beaded all o'er—
With fringe to the elbow, the cowboys galore.

2

We come up the trail with the Texas rawhide.
There is not a bronco that we cannot ride.
With a quirt we can haze him and ne'er pull the horn,
For we are the twisters as sure as you're born.

With your foot to the stirrup and hand to the horn,
To ride the wild broncos a cowboy is sworn.
Though he bellows and bawls you can hear him a mile—
His leaps is like lightning; we ride with a smile.

3

So it's ride your wild broncos, to the wagon you'll file.
In pursuit you will hear the cook holler "grub pile."
Then you roll out your bed on the ground cold and hard,
For soon you will have to stand a two-hour guard.
You're woke by a start, by a puncher's loud ring,
"Come alive, you wild cowboys, to the herd you must sing."
Well, the nights are so dark that you can't see at all,
And you ride by the sound of some lost maverick's bawl.

4

So early next morning on a circle you ride,
To round up the mavericks take down your rawhide.
We'll rope them and throw them as in olden day,
And on their left side we will brand a CK.
But the time for the punchers is now growing slim,
So down the old cow trail we'll soon split the wind.
We'll ride to the home ranch, we'll turn the broncs loose;
For the rope on the saddle there's no future use.

5

But as for bronc riding, I've rode broncs enough.
I'm a-going down East and, like Wild Bill, play tough.
My hair will grow long and I'll dance on the stage,
And I'll tell them out West I eat snakes and wild sage.
I'll soon bid adieu to the Yellowstone shore
Where the would-be cowpunchers are there by the score,
Where the steers o'er the trail no longer do come;
The days of the longhorners surely are done.

6

To all you kind cowboys I now bid adieu.
My song is now ended, and I'm parting from you.
I'll hang up my outfit where it'll keep dry;
I'll be at the round-up in the sweet bye and bye.

TEXT AND MUSIC: Wylder (1949), pp. 41-43.

VARIANTS: Craddock (1927), pp. 184-185; Lomax and Lomax (1938), pp. 95-96.

THE CAPTAIN OF THE COWBOYS

TUNE: Captain Jinks

I'm Cap-tain Jack of Kur—ber Creek. I wear good clothes and keep 'em sleek. On What I buy, I ask no "tick," For I'm cap-tain a-mong the cow-boys. I do that work which I think to be, think to be, think to be Con-sis-tent with the dig-ni-ty a cap-tain a-mong the cow-boys.

like—ly change your no—tion.

1

I'm Captain Jack of Kurber Creek.
I wear good clothes and keep 'em sleek.
On what I buy, I ask no "tick,"
For I'm captain among the cowboys.
I do that work which I think to be,
    think to be, think to be
Consistent with the dignity
Of a captain among the cowboys.

2

Twice a year I corral my cattle;
And if he turns to give me battle,
The way I make the fence pole rattle
Would draw a smile from a preacher.
And when I try to rope a calf,
    rope a calf, rope a calf,
My perseverance would make you laugh,
But I mostly catch the creature.

334

3

If a visit to Blackjack Ranch you pay,
By way of advice, just let me say,
You'd better not come on branding day,
If beauty is your portion;
For what with dust and what with blows,
    what with blows, what with blows,
A dirty face and a broken nose
Will likely change your notion.

———————

TEXT: *Gazette* (Colorado Springs, Colo.), Jan. 4, 1873.

MUSIC: *Heart Songs Dear to the American People* (1909), pp. 54-55.

VARIANTS: *Out West,* I (Sept., 1873), 68; Davidson (1943), p. 108; Westermeier (1955), p. 270.

TOP HAND

1

While you're all so frisky, I'll sing a little song—
Think a horn of whiskey will help the thing along—
It's all about the Top Hand when he's busted flat,
Bumming round town in his Mexican hat.
He'd laid up all winter, and his pocket book is flat.
His clothes are all tatters but he don't mind that.

2

See him in town with a crowd that he knows
Rolling cigarettes an' a-smoking through his nose.
First thing he tells you, he owns a certain brand—
Leads you to think he is a daisy hand.
Next thing he tells you 'bout his trip up the trail
All the way to Kansas to finish out his tale.

3

Put him on horse, he's a handy hand to work.
Put him on the branding pen, he's dead sure to shirk.
With his natural leaf tobacco in the pockets of his vest,
He'll tell you his Californy pants are the best.
He's handled lots of cattle—hasn't any fears—
Can draw his sixty dollars for the balance of his years.

4

Put him on herd, he's a cussin all day;
Anything tries, it's sure to get away.
When you have a round-up, he tells it all about:
He's going to do the cuttin' and you can't keep him out.
If anything goes wrong, he lays it on the screws,
Says the lazy devils were trying to take a snooze.

5

When he meets a greener, he ain't afraid to rig,
Stands him on a chuck box and makes him dance a jig;
Waives a loaded cutter, makes him sing and shout—
He's a regular Ben Thompson when the boss ain't about.
When the boss ain't about, he leaves his leggins in camp.
He swears a man who wears them is worse than a tramp.

6

Say's he's not caring for the wages that he earns,
For Dad's rich in Texas'n got wagon loads to burn;
But when he goes to town, he's sure to take it in—
He's always been dreaded, wherever he has been.
He rides a fancy horse, he is a favorite man,
Can get more credit than a common waddie can.

7

When you ship the cattle, he's bound to go along
To keep the boss from drinking and to see that nothing's wrong.
Wherever he goes, catch on to his game.
He likes to be called with a handle to his name.
He's always primping with a pocket looking glass;
From the top to the bottom, he's a bold jackass,
        Waddie cowboy.

TEXT: Thorp (1908), pp. 17-18.

VARIANTS: Lomax (1916), pp. 373-374; Thorp (1921), pp. 156-158; Coolidge (1937), pp. 128-130; Lomax and Lomax (1938), pp. 72-73; Fife and Fife (1966), pp. 61-65*.

THE JOLLY VAQUERO

1

The jolly vaquero is up with the sun,
　　And quick in the saddle, you see;
He swings his quirt and jingles his spurs—
　　A dashing vaquero is he.
He "hangs and rattles" and "hits the high places"
　　That bound the lone prairie;
And woe to the steer when he draws near,
　　For a bold bad roper is he.

CHORUS: Whoop-la! "Set 'em afire!"
Shouts the rider free,
"Give 'em the spurs" and "burn the earth!"
A cowboy's life for me.

2

Over the cow-trail, leaping the sage,
　　His pony can't be beat.
He'll "git that Eli" "Sure's you're born"—
　　See how he "handles his feet!"
The rider "stays with him," and "don't you forget it"—
　　True knight of the saddle is he—
And he "hits the breeze," and rides at ease,
　　And swings the lariat free.

3

"You can bet your life" "he's got the sand,"
　　Whenever there's work to be done;
He "rounds 'em up" and "cuts 'em out,"
　　And "mavericks" just for fun.
In rain or shine, or sleet or hail,
　　He rides the wild prairie—
Oh! who wouldn't envy a life like this
　　Of the cowboy, wild and free!

4

Though often "dead broke"—his saddle "in soak"—
　　He never loses his pluck;
He'll share his "stake" with his partner, too,
　　If he meets him "out of luck."
He'll "wack up" his blankets, or share his "grub"—
　　No need of "calling him down"—
He'll "spend his wealth" in drinking your health,
　　Whenever he comes to town.

TEXT: *Weekly Leader and Stock Journal* (Cheyenne, Wyo.), Aug. 23, 1883.
VARIANT: Westermeier (1955), p. 271.

THE HORSE WRANGLER

TUNE: The Day I Played Baseball

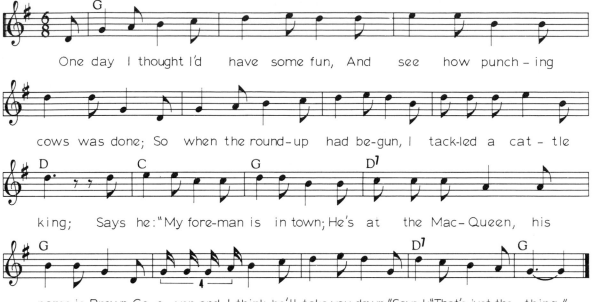

One day I thought I'd have some fun, And see how punch-ing cows was done; So when the round-up had be-gun, I tack-led a cat-tle king; Says he:"My fore-man is in town; He's at the Mac-Queen, his name is Brown;Go o-ver, and I think he'll take you down;"Says I:"That's just the thing."

1

One day I thought I'd have some fun
And see how punching cows was done,
So, when the roundup had begun,
I tackled a cattle king.
Says he: "My foreman is in town;
He's at the MacQueen; his name is Brown.
Go over, and I think he'll take you down.
Says I: "That's just the thing."

2

We started for the ranch next day.
Brown talked to me most all the way.
He said cowpunching was only fun,
It was no work at all,
That all I had to do was ride—
It was just like drifting with the tide—
Geemany crimany, how he lied!
He surely had his gall.

3

He put me in charge of a cavard
And told me not to work too hard,
That all I had to do was guard
The horses from getting away.
I had one hundred and sixty head,
And oft times wished that I was dead.
When one got away, Brown, he turned red.
Now this is the truth, I say.

4

Sometimes a horse would make a break;
Across the prairie he would take
As though he were running for a stake,
For him it was only play.
Sometimes I couldn't head him at all,
And again my saddle horse would fall,
And I'd speed on like a cannon ball
Till the earth came in my way.

5

They led me out an old gray hack
With a great big set fast on his back.
They padded him up with gunny sacks
And used my bedding all.
When I got on he left the ground,
Jumped up in the air and turned around.
I busted the earth as I came down.
It was a terrible fall!

6

They picked me up and carried me in
And rubbed me down with a rolling pin:
"That's the way they all begin;
You are doing well," says Brown.
"And tomorrow morning, if you don't die,
I'll give you another horse to try."
"Oh! won't you let me walk?" says I.
"Yes," says he. "Into town."

7

I've traveled up and I've traveled down.
I've traveled this country all around.
I've lived in city, I've lived in town,
And I have this much to say:
Before you try it go kiss your wife,
Get a heavy insurance on your life;
Then shoot yourself with a butcher knife.
It's far the easiest way.

TEXT: *Stock Growers' Journal* (Miles City, Mont.), Feb. 3, 1894.

MUSIC: Sandburg (1927), pp. 274-275. Used by permission of Harcourt, Brace & World, Inc.

VARIANTS: Thorp (1908), pp. 13-14; Lomax (1910), pp. 136-138; *Montana Cowboy Band Song Book* (1912), p. 13; Will (1913), p. 185; Pound (1915), pp. 29-30, and (1922), pp. 176-178; Thorp (1921), pp. 146-148; Sandburg (1927), pp. 274-275; Sires (1928), pp. 2-3; German (1929); Clark (1932), p. 58; Allen (1933), pp. 89-90; Klickman and Sherman (1933), pp. 38-39; O'Malley (1934), pp. 11-12; Frey (1936), pp. 60-61; Coolidge (1937), pp. 126-127; Lomax and Lomax (1938), pp. 119-122; Pound (1939); pp. 28-29; Wylder (1949), pp. 51-53; Laws (1964), p. 145*; Fife and Fife (1966), pp. 44-57.*

OLD TIME COWBOY

Come all you mel-an-chol-y folks wher-ev-er you may be.___ I'll sing you a-bout the cow-boy whose life is light and free.___ He roams a-bout the prair-ie; and at night when he lies down,___ His heart is as gay as the flow-ers in May in his bed up-on the ground.

1

Come all you melancholy folks wherever you may be.
I'll sing you about the cowboy whose life is light and free.
He roams about the prairie; and at night when he lies down,
His heart is as gay as the flowers in May in his bed upon the ground.

2

They're a little bit rough, I must confess, the most of them at least,
But if you do not hunt a quarrel, you can live with them in peace;
For if you do, you're sure to rue the day you joined their band.
They will follow you up and shoot it out with you just man to man.

3

Did you ever go to any cowboy, whenever hungry or dry,
Asking for a dollar and have him you deny?
He'll just pull out his pocket book and hand you a note.
They are the fellows to help you out whenever you are broke.

4

Go to their ranches and stay awhile, they never ask a cent;
And when they go to town, their money is freely spent.
They walk straight up and take a drink, paying for everyone,
And they never ask your pardon for anything they have done.

When they go to their dances, some dance while others pat.
They ride their bucking broncos and wear their broad brimmed hats,
With their California saddles and their pants inside their boots,
You can hear their spurs a-jingling and perhaps some of them shoot.

6

Come all softhearted tenderfeet, if you want to have some fun,
Go live among the cowboys. They show you how it's done.
They'll treat you like a prince, my boys—about them there's nothing mean—
But don't try to give them too much advice, for all of 'em ain't so green.

TEXT: Thorp (1908), 40-41.

MUSIC: Malone (1961), 158-159. Used by permission of University of Nebraska Press.

VARIANTS: Lomax (1910), 263-264, and (1916), 263-264 & 365-366; Thorp (1921), 121-122; Lomax and Lomax (1938), 220-221; Malone (1961), 158-159; Fife and Fife (1966), 240-243*.

ALLEN MC CANDLESS

THE COWBOY, I

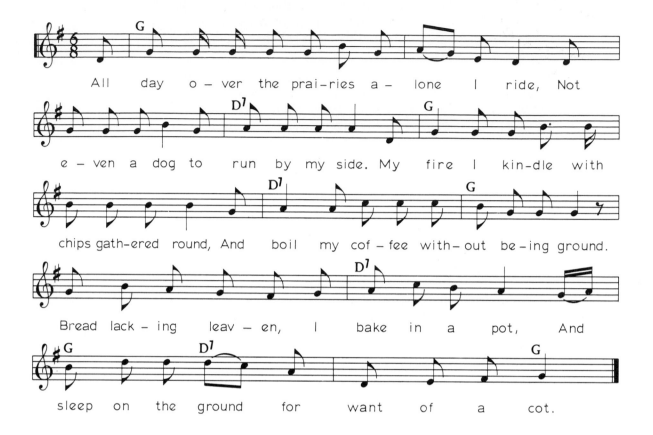

All day o-ver the prai-ries a-lone I ride, Not
e-ven a dog to run by my side. My fire I kin-dle with
chips gath-ered round, And boil my cof-fee with-out be-ing ground.
Bread lack-ing leav-en, I bake in a pot, And
sleep on the ground for want of a cot.

1

All day over the prairies alone I ride,
Not even a dog to run by my side.
My fire I kindle with chips gathered round,
And boil my coffee without being ground.
Bread lacking leaven, I bake in a pot,
And sleep on the ground for want of a cot.

2

I wash in a puddle and wipe on a sack
And carry my wardrobe all on my back.
My ceiling the sky; my carpet, the grass;
My music, the lowing herds as they pass.
My books are the brooks; my sermon, the stones;
My parson, a wolf on a pulpit of bones.

3

But then if my cooking ain't very complete,
Hygienists can't blame me for living to eat;
And where is the man who sleeps more profound
Than the cowboy who stretches himself on the ground.
My books teach me constancy ever to prize;
My sermons, that small things I should not despise,

4

And my parson remarks from his pulpit of bone
That "the Lord favors them who look out for their own."
Between love and me lies a gulf very wide,
And a luckier fellow may call her his bride;
But cupid is always a friend to the bold,
And the best of his arrows are pointed with gold.

5

Friends gently hint I am going to grief,
But men must make money and women have beef.
Society bans me, a savage and dodge,
And Masons would ball me out of their lodge.
If I'd hair on my chin, I might pass for the goat
That bore all sin in ages remote.

6

But why this is thusly, I don't understand;
For each of the Patriarchs owned a big brand.
Abraham emigrated in search of a range,
When water got scarce and he wanted a change.
Isaac had cattle in charge of Esau.
And Jacob "run cows" for his father-in-law.

7

He started in business clear down at bed rock,
And made quite a fortune by watering stock.
David went from night herding and using a sling
To winning a battle and being a king.
And the shepherds, when watching their flocks on the hill,
Heard the message from heaven of peace and good will.

TEXT: *Daily Advertiser* (Trinidad, Colo.), April 9, 1885.

MUSIC: Lomax (1910), 98-99.

VARIANTS: Stanley (1897), 32; Lomax (1910), 96-99; Montana Cowboy Band (1912), 14; Siringo (1919), 14-15; Thorp (1921), 4-6; Larkin (1931), 130-132; Clark (1932), 17; Patterson and Dexter (1932), 12-14; Allen (1933), 69-71; Lomax and Lomax (1938), 67-70; Westermeier (1955), 263-264.

THE COWBOY, II

1

You may call the cowboy horned and may think him hard to tame;
    You may heap vile epithets upon his head;
But to know him is to like him, notwithstanding his hard name,
    For he will divide with you his beef and bread.

2

If you see him on his pony as he scampers o'er the plain,
    You would think him wild and woolly to be sure;
But his heart is warm and tender when he sees a friend in pain,
    Though his education is but to endure.

3

When the storm breaks in its fury and the lightning's vivid flash
    Makes you thank the Lord for shelter and for bed,
Then it is he mounts his pony and away you see him dash,
    No protection but the hat upon his head.

4

Such is life upon a cow ranch, and the half was never told,
    But you never find a kinder hearted set
Than the cattlemen at home; be he young or old,
    "He's a daisy from away back—don't forget."

5

When you fail to find a pony or a cow that's gone astray,
    Be that cow or pony wild or be it tame,
The cowboy, like the drummer (and the bed-bug, too), they say,
    Brings him to you, for he "gets there just the same."

TEXT: James, W. S., *Cowboy Life in Texas, or Twenty-seven Years a Maverick* (Chicago: M. A. Donohue & Co., 1893), 182.

VARIANTS: Lomax (1916), 352-353 Thorp (1921), 34-35.

THE COWBOY'S LIFE

The songs here start out at least by contrasting the romantic ideals of the cowboy's life with the dreary realities of it. Such unvarying miseries could not continue to be wholly absorbing, and so we find these songs moving easily into fantasy. "The Cowboy's Life" and "The Dreary, Dreary Life" make nearly the same point: that cowpunching is, in reality, a fatiguing, mindless succession of cycles—the daily round of sleeping in rain puddles and trailing in hot dust, the seasonal round marked by blind-drunk paydays, and the life round from greenhorn to top hand to derelict—and that all these cycles are made more dreary by the cowhand's inability to connect the misery with its cause. Even his dreams suggest another dreary round:

> I used to run about; now I stay at home,
> Take care of my wife and child,
> Nevermore to roam, always stay at home,
> Take care of my wife and child.

Two other songs here contrast in tone. Larry Chittenden's "The Cowboys' Christmas Ball," a long, giddy reel of names and dialect from his *Ranch Verses* (1893), is pure moonshine compared with D. J. O'Malley's direct parody of it in "A Busted Cowboy's Christmas."

> As soon as Fall work's over,
> We get it in the neck,
> And we get a Christmas present
> On a neatly written check.
> Then come to town to rusticate—
> We've no place else to stay
> When Winter winds are howling,
> Because we can't eat hay.

"Windy Bill" and "Bow-Legged Ike" are mild exaggerations about the confrontation of cowboys with the animals of their profession. The first tells how an old, black outlaw steer sent Windy's "rim-fires driftin' down the draw," while, as if to compensate, Ike masters a mount whose furious sunfishing couldn't "even *in-ter-est* him."

"Tying Knots in the Devil's Tail" by Gail I. Gardener is a full-fledged fantasy about the cowpuncher's prowess; and Charles Badger Clark's poem, "High Chin Bob," given here in the "folk version" anonymously printed in *Poetry* in 1917, lifts the cowboy up to mythic heights as he dreams his glorious way out of that dreary, dreary life.

THE COWBOY'S LIFE

1

The cowboy's life is a dreary old life,
    All out in the sleet and the snow.
When winter time comes, he begins to think
    Where his summer wages go.

2

When the shipping all is over
    And the work all is done,
He hangs up his Frazier saddle
    And starts looking for some fun.

3

He steps up to the boss
    And draws his pay in full.
He says, "Be sure and come back, boy."
    Then he thinks he has a pull.

4

He went into the barroom;
    His little roll he did pull.
He called for drinks for the house,
    And he got pretty full.

5

He told the boys that he had quit
    And that he'd work no more,
And then they got him in a poker game
    And took him to the floor.

6

He got up and looked around.
    He said that he was just that kind:
He'd lose his money in a poker game,
    And he never did mind.

7

Now he's on his way back to the rancho,
    The one he's just quit.
He hits the boss for another job,
    The one he'd made a hit.

Used by permission of the Texas Folklore Society.
TEXT: Dobie (1928), p. 174.

THE DREARY, DREARY LIFE

A cow-boy's life is a drear-y, drear-y life__ Some say it's free from care__ Round-ing up the cat—tle from morn-ing till night in the mid—dle of the prai—rie so bare.

Chorus Half-past four, the noi-sy cook will roar, "Whoop-a — whoop-a — hey!" Slow-ly you will rise with sleep-y feel-ing eyes, The sweet, dream-y night passed a — way.

1

A cowboy's life is a dreary, dreary life—
Some say it's free from care—
Rounding up the cattle from morning till night
In the middle of the prairie so bare.

CHORUS: Half-past four, the noisy cook will roar,
"Whoop-a-whoop-a-hey!"
Slowly you will rise with sleepy-feeling eyes,
The sweet, dreamy night passed away.

2

The greener lad, he thinks it's play.
He'll soon peter out on a cold rainy day.
With his big bell spurs and his Spanish hoss,
He'll swear to you he was once a boss.

3

The cowboy's life is a dreary, dreary life:
He's driven through the heat and cold
While the rich man's a-sleeping on his velvet couch,
Dreaming of his silver and gold.

4

Spring-time sets in; double trouble will begin.
The weather is so fierce and cold.
Clothes are wet and frozen to our necks.
The cattle we can scarcely hold.

5

The cowboy's life is a dreary one:
He works all day to the setting of the sun;
And then his day's work is not done,
For there's his night herd to go on.

6

The wolves and owls with their terrifying howls
Will disturb us in our midnight dream,
As we lie on our slickers on a cold, rainy night
Way over on the Pecos stream.

7

You are speaking of your farms, you are speaking of your charms,
You are speaking of your silver and gold;
But a cowboy's life is a dreary, dreary life—
He's driven through the heat and cold.

8

Some folks say that we are free from care,
Free from all other harm;
But we round up the cattle from morning till night
Way over on the prairie so dry.

9

I used to run about; now I stay at home,
Take care of my wife and child,
Nevermore to roam, always stay at home,
Take care of my wife and child.

LAST CHORUS: Half-past four, the noisy cook will roar,
"Hurrah, boys! She's breaking day!"
Slowly we will rise and wipe our sleepy eyes,
The sweet, dreamy night passed away.

TEXT AND MUSIC: Lomax (1910), pp. 233-236.

VARIANTS: Thorp (1908), pp. 38-39; Lomax (1910), pp. 22-23; Thorp (1921), pp. 61-62; Larkin (1931), pp. 40-43; Clark (1932), p. 25; Patterson and Dexter (1932), pp. 42-43; Frey (1936), p. 54; Lomax and Lomax (1938), pp. 15-17; Lomax (1960), pp. 369-370; Fife and Fife (1966), pp. 228-239*.

LARRY CHITTENDEN # THE COWBOYS' CHRISTMAS BALL

1

'Way out in Western Texas, where the Clear Fork's waters flow;
Where the cattle are "a-browzin'," an' the Spanish ponies grow;
Where the Northers "come a-whistlin' " from beyond the Neutral strip,
And the prairie dogs are sneezin' as if they had "the grip";

2

Where the cayotes come a-howlin' 'round the ranches after dark,
And the mocking-birds are singin' to the lovely "medder lark";
Where the 'possum and the badger, and rattle-snakes abound,
And the monstrous stars are winkin' o'er a wilderness profound;

3

Where lonesome, tawny prairies melt into airy streams,
While the Double Mountains slumber in heavenly kinds of dreams;
Where the antelope is grazin' and the lonely plovers call—
It was there that I attended "The Cowboys' Christmas Ball."

4

The town was Anson City, old Jones's county seat,
Where they raise Polled Angus cattle, and waving whiskered wheat;
Where the air is soft and "bammy," an' dry an' full of health,
And the prairies is explodin' with agricultural wealth;

Where they print the *Texas Western*, that Hec. McCann supplies,
With news and yarns and stories uv most amazin' size;
Where Frank Smith "pulls the badger," on knowin' tenderfeet,
And Democracy's triumphant, and mighty hard to beat;

6

Where lives that good old hunter, John Milsap from Lamar,
Who "used to be the sheriff, back East, in Paris, sah!"
'Twas there, I say, at Anson, with the lively "Widder Wall,"
That I went to that reception, "The Cowboys' Christmas Ball."

7

The boys had left the ranches and come to town in piles;
The ladies—"kinder scattering' "—had gathered in for miles.
And yet the place was crowded, as I remember well,
'Twas got for the occasion at "The Morning Star Hotel."

8

The music was a fiddle an' a lively tambourine,
And a "viol come imported," by the stage from Abilene.
The room was togged out gorgeous—with mistletoe and shawls,
And candles flickered frescoes around the airy walls.

9

The "wimmin folks" looked lovely—the boys looked kinder treed,
Till their leader commenced yellin': "Whoa! fellers, let's stampede."
And the music started sighin' an' a-wailin' through the hall,
As a kind of introduction to "The Cowboys' Christmas Ball."

10

The leader was a feller that came from Swenson's Ranch;
They called him "Windy Billy," from "little Deadman's Branch."
His rig was "kinder keerless," big spurs and highheeled boots;
He had the reputation that comes when "fellers shoots."

11

His voice was like the bugle upon the mountain's height.
His feet were animated, an' a *mighty movin' sight*,
When he commenced to holler, "Neow fellers, stake yer pen!
Lock horns ter all them heifers, an' russle 'em like men.

12

"Saloot yer lovely critters; neow swing an' let 'em go,
Climb the grape vine 'round 'em—all hands do-ce-do!
You Mavericks, jine the round-up—Jest skip her waterfall."
Huh! hit wuz gettin' active—"The Cowboys' Christmas Ball!"

13

The boys were tolerable skittish; the ladies, powerful neat.
That old bass viol's music *just got there with both feet!*
That wailin', frisky fiddle, I never shall forget;
And Windy kept a singin'—I think I hear him yet—

14

"O Xes, chase your squirrels, an' cut 'em to one side,
Spur Treadwell to the center, with Cross P Charley's bride,
Doc. Hollis down the middle, an' twine the ladies' chain,
Varn Andrews pen the fillies in big T Diamond's train.

15

"All pull yer freight tergether, neow swallow fork an' change,
'Big Boston' lead the trail herd, through little Pitchfork's range.
Purr 'round yer gentle pussies, neow rope 'em! Balance all!"
Huh! hit wuz gettin' active—"The Cowboys' Christmas Ball!"

16

The dust riz fast an' furious; we all just galloped 'round
Till the scenery got so giddy, that Z Bar Dick was downed.
We buckled to our partners, an' told 'em to hold on,
Then shook our hoofs like lightning until the early dawn.

17

Don't tell me 'bout cotillions, or germans, no sir'ee!
That whirl at Anson City just takes the cake with me.
I'm sick of lazy shufflin's—of them I've had my fill.
Give me a fronteer break-down, backed up by Windy Bill.

18

McAllister ain't nowhere! when Windy leads the show.
I've seen 'em both in harness, an' so I sorter know.
Oh, Bill, I sha'n't forget yer, and I'll oftentimes recall
That lively gaited sworray, "The Cowboys' Christmas Ball."

TEXT: William Lawrence Chittenden, *Ranch Verses* (New York: G. P. Putnam's Sons, 1893), pp. 12-17.

MUSIC: Clark (1932), pp. 70-71. Used by permission of Shawnee Press Inc.

VARIANTS: *Field and Farm* (Denver), Dec. 25, 1897; Thorp (1908), pp. 33-36; Lomax (1916), pp. 335-339, and (1919), pp. 112-116; Siringo (1919), pp. 27-31; Thorp (1921), pp. 35-39; Clark (1932), pp. 70-71; Lomax and Lomax (1938), pp. 246-249; Westermeier (1955), pp. 279-280; Fife and Fife (1966), pp. 219-224*.

D. J. O'MALLEY   # A BUSTED COWBOY'S CHRISTMAS

TUNE: The Cowboy's Christmas Ball

1

I am a busted cowboy, and I work upon the range.
In Summer time I get some work, but one thing that is strange,
As soon as Fall work's over, we get it in the neck,
And we get a Christmas present on a neatly written check.

2

Then come to town to rusticate—we've no place else to stay
When Winter winds are howling, because we can't eat hay.
A puncher's life's a picnic; it is one continued joke,
But there's none more anxious to see Spring than a cowboy who is broke.

3

The wages that a cowboy earns in Summer go like smoke;
And when the Winter snows have come, you bet your life he's broke.
You can talk about your holiday, your Christmas cheer and joy;
It's all the same to me, my friend, cash gone—I'm a broke cowboy.

4

My saddle and my gun's in soak; my spurs I've long since sold;
My rawhide and my quirt are gone, my chaps—no, they're too old.
My stuff's all gone; I can't even beg a solitary smoke,
For no one cares what becomes of a cowboy who is broke.

5

Now, where I'll eat my dinner this Christmas, I don't know;
But you bet I'm going to have one if they give me half a show.
This Christmas has no charms for me, on good things I'll not choke,
Unless I get a big hand-out—I'm a cowboy who is broke.

———

TEXT: *Stock Growers' Journal* (Miles City, Mont.), Dec. 23, 1893.
VARIANT: O'Malley (1934), p. 17.

WINDY BILL

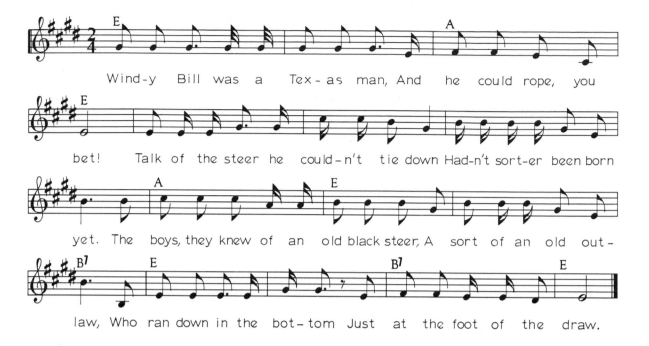

Wind-y Bill was a Tex-as man, And he could rope, you

bet! Talk of the steer he could-n't tie down Had-n't sort-er been born

yet. The boys, they knew of an old black steer, A sort of an old out-

law, Who ran down in the bot-tom Just at the foot of the draw.

1

Windy Bill was a Texas man,
  And he could rope, you bet!
Talk of the steer he couldn't tie down
  Hadn't sorter been born yet.
The boys, they knew of an old black steer,
  A sort of an old outlaw,
Who ran down in the bottom
  Just at the foot of the draw.

2

This slim black steer had stood his ground
  With punchers from everywhere.
The boys bet Bill two to one
  He couldn't quite get there.
So Bill brought up his old cow horse—
  His weathers and back were sore—
Prepared to tackle this old black steer
  Who ran down in the draw.

3

With his grazin' bits and sand stacked tree,
  His chaps and taps to boot,
His old maguey tied hard and fast,
  Went out to tackle the brute.
Bill sorter sauntered around him first;
  The steer began to paw,
Poked up his tail high in the air
  And lit down in the draw.

354

4

The old cow horse flew at him like
 He'd been eatin' corn;
And, Bill, he landed his old maguey
 Around old blackie's horns.
The old time cow horse he stopped dead still;
 The cinches broke like straw.
Both the sand stacked tree and old maguey
 Went driftin' down the draw.

5

Bill landed in a big rock pile.
 His face and hands were scratched.
He 'lowed he always could tie a steer,
 But guessed he'd found his match.
Paid up his bet like a little man
 Without a bit of jaw,
And said old blackie was the boss
 Of all down in the draw.

6

There's a moral to my song, boys,
 Which I hope that you can see:
Whenever you start to tackle a steer,
 Never tie hard your maguey.
Put on your dalebueltas,
 'Cordin' to California law,
And you will never see your old rim-fires
 Driftin' down the draw.

———————

TEXT: Thorp (1908), pp. 11-12.

MUSIC: Larkin (1931), pp. 58-59. Used by permission of Alfred A. Knopf, Inc.

VARIANTS: Lomax (1916), pp. 381-382; Thorp (1921), pp. 168-170; Sires (1928), pp. 28-29; German (1929); Larkin (1931), pp. 58-60; Patterson and Dexter (1932), pp. 40-41; Allen (1933), pp. 140-142; Frey (1936), pp. 74-75; Lomax and Lomax (1938), pp. 113-115; Fife and Fife (1966), pp. 38-43*.

BOW-LEGGED IKE

1

Bow-legged Ike on horseback was sent
From some place, straight down on this broad continent.

2

His father could ride, and his mother could, too.
They straddled the whole way from Kalamazoo.

3

Born on the plains, when he first sniffed the air,
He cried for to mount on the spavined gray mare.

4

And when he got big and could hang to the horn,
'Twas the happiest day since the time he was born.

5

He'd stop his horse loping with one good, strong yank.
He'd rake him on shoulder and rake him on flank.

6

He was only sixteen when he broke "Outlaw Nell,"
The horse that had sent nigh a score of men to Hell.

7

He climbed to the saddle and there sat still,
While she bucked him all day with no sign of a spill.

8

Five years later on, a cayuse struck the trail
Whose record made even old "punchers" turn pale.

9

He was really a terror—could dance on his ear
And sling a man farther than that stump to here!

10

A man heard of Ike, grinned, and bet his whole pile
His sorrel could shake him before one could smile.

11

So the crowd, they came round, and they staked all they had,
While Ike, sorter innocent, said: "Is he *bad?*"

12

And durin' their laugh—for the sorrel, you see,
Had eat up two ropes and was tryin' for me—

13

Ike patted his neck. "Nice pony," says he,
And was into the saddle as quick as a flea.

14

That sorrel, he jumped and he twisted and bucked,
And the men laughed, expectin' that Ike would be chucked.

15

But soon the cayuse was fair swimmin' in sweat
While Ike, looking bored, rolled a neat cigarette.

16

And then from range to range he hunted a cayuse
That could even *in-ter-est* him, but it wasn't any use.

17

So he got quite melancholic, wondering why such an earth,
Where the horses "had no sperrits," should have given himself birth.

TEXT: Russell Doubleday, *Cattle Ranch to College* (New York: Doubleday & McClure, 1899), pp. 227-228.

VARIANT: Dobie (1927), p. 164.

GAIL I. GARDNER

TYING KNOTS IN THE DEVIL'S TAIL

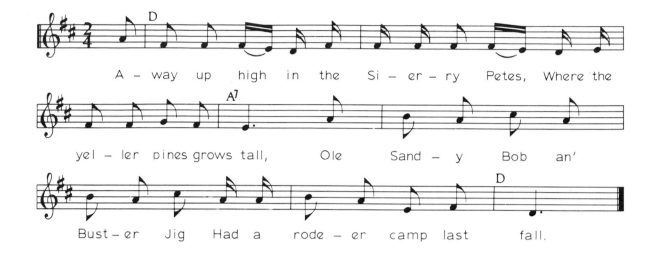

A - way up high in the Si — er — ry Petes, Where the yel — ler pines grows tall, Ole Sand — y Bob an' Bust — er Jig Had a rode — er camp last fall.

1
Away up high in the Sierry Petes,
　　Where the yeller pines grows tall,
Ole Sandy Bob an' Buster Jig
　　Had a rodeer camp last fall.

2
Oh, they taken their hosses and runnin' irons
　　And mabbe a dawg or two,
An' they 'lowed they'd brand all the long-
　　yered calves
　　That come within their view.

3
And any old dogie that flapped long yeres
　　An' didn't bush up by day
Got his long yeres whittled an' his old hide
　　scortched
　　In a most artistic way.

4
Now one fine day, ole Sandy Bob,
　　He throwed his seago down,
"I'm sick of the smell of burnin' hair
　　And I 'lows I'm a-goin' to town."

5
So they saddles up an' hits 'em a lope,
　　Fer it warnt no sight of a ride,
And them was the days when a Buckeroo
　　Could ile up his inside.

6
Oh, they starts her in at the Kaintucky Bar,
　　At the head of Whisky Row,
And they winds up down by the Depot House,
　　Some forty drinks below.

7
They then sets up and turns around,
　　And goes her the other way;
An' to tell you the Gawd-forsaken truth,
　　Them boys got stewed that day.

8
As they was a-ridin' back to camp
　　A-packin' a pretty good load,
Who should they meet but the Devil himself,
　　A-prancin' down the road.

9
Sez he, "You ornery cowboy skunks,
　　You'd better hunt yer holes,
Fer I've come up from Hell's Rim Rock
　　To gather in yer souls."

10

Sez Sandy Bob, "Old Devil, be damned.
  We boys is kinda tight,
But you aint a-goin' to gather no cowboy
  souls
  Thout you has some kind of a fight."

11

So Sandy Bob punched a hole in his rope,
  And he swang her straight and true.
He lapped it on to the Devil's horns,
  An' he taken his dallies too.

12

Now Buster Jig was a riata man,
  With his gut-line coiled up neat,
So he shaken her out an' he built him a loop,
  An' he lassed the Devil's hind feet.

13

Oh, they stretched him out an' they tailed
  him down,
  While the irons was a-gettin' hot.
They cropped and swaller-forked his yeres;
  Then they branded him up a lot.

14

They pruned him up with a de-hornin' saw,
  An' they knotted his tail fer a joke.
They then rid off and left him there,
  Necked to a Black-Jack oak.

15

If you're ever up high in the Sierry Petes,
  An' you hear one Hell of a wail,
You'll know it's that Devil a-bellerin' around
  About them knots in his tail.

© Copyright 1935 by Gail I. Gardner. Used by permission.

TEXT: Gardner (1935), pp. 9-10.

MUSIC: Larkin (1931), p. 66. Used by permission of Alfred A. Knopf, Inc.

VARIANTS: German (1929); Larkin (1931), pp. 66-68; Lomax and Lomax (1934), pp. 407-409; Lomax (1960), pp. 388-389; Toelken (1962), pp. 12-13; Laws (1964), p. 141*.

CHARLES BADGER CLARK # HIGH CHIN BOB

1

Way high up in the Mokiones, among the mountain tops,
A lion cleaned a yearlin's bones and licked his thankful chops,
When who upon the scene should ride, a-trippin' down the slope,
But High Chin Bob of sinful pride and maverick-hungry rope.

"Oh, glory be to me!" says he, "and fame's unfadin' flowers;
I ride my good top hoss today and I'm top hand of Lazy-J,
So, kitty-cat, you're ours!"

2

The lion licked his paws so brown and dreamed soft dreams of veal,
As High Chin's loop come circlin' down and roped him round his meal.
He yowled quick fury to the world and all the hills yelled back;
That top hoss give a snort and whirled, and Bob caught up the slack.

> "Oh, glory be to me," says he, "we'll hit the glory trail.
> No man has looped a lion's head and lived to drag the bugger dead,
> Till I shall tell the tale."

3

'Way high up in the Mokiones that top hoss done his best,
'Mid whippin' brush and rattlin' stones from canon-floor to crest;
Up and down and round and cross, Bob pounded weak and wan,
But pride still glued him to his hoss and glory drove him on.

> "Oh, glory be to me," says he, "this glory trail is rough!
> I'll keep this dally round the horn until the toot of judgment morn,
> Before I'll holler 'nough!'"

4

Three suns had rode their circle home beyond the desert rim,
And turned their star-herds loose to roam the ranges high and dim;
And whenever Bob turned and hoped the limp remains to find,
A red-eyed lion, belly-roped but healthy, loped behind!

> "Oh, glory be to me," says Bob, "he kaint be drug to death!
> These heroes that I've read about were only fools that stuck it out
> To the end of mortal breath."

5

'Way high up in the Mokiones, if you ever come there at night,
You'll hear a ruckus amongst the stones that will lift your hair with fright;
You'll see a cow hoss thunder by and a lion trail along,
And the rider bold, with chin on high sings forth his glory song:

> "Oh, glory be to me," says he, "and to my mighty noose!
> Oh, pardner, tell my friends below I took a ragin' dream in tow,
> And though I never laid him low, I never turned him loose!"

TEXT: *Poetry, X* (1917), pp. 225-227.

MUSIC: As sung by Rudolf Bretz. Transcribed by Ruth Crawford Seeger.

VARIANTS: Charles Badger Clark, *Sun and Saddle Leather* (Boston: Badger, 1915); Lomax (1919), pp. 30-35; Thorp (1921), pp. 81-83; Botkin (1951), pp. 765-766.

GIT ALONG, LITTLE DOGIES

The cattle business on the Great Plains accounted for only about 15 percent of the beef raised in the United States, but its methods were unique. And though the driving of tough, stringy beef over long distances of unoccupied land was only briefly profitable, it was made enduringly memorable in the songs of those trail herds. On the route up from Texas through the Ozarks to the first railhead at Sedalia, Missouri, and on the Goodnight-Loving Trail along the Pecos River and the Rocky Mountain foothills, drivers sang to their herds and themselves.

The famous "Git Along, Little Dogies," to an Irish lullaby, describes the process of fattening—if that's the word—those motherless calves on prickly pears as they moved along toward becoming "soup for Uncle Sam's Injuns." "John Garner's Trail Herd" tells of stampede, the chief danger that drovers feared as they rode up the Dodge City Trail. Anything could set the animals off:

> And then them cattle turned in and dealt us
>   merry hell.
> They stampeded every night that came and did it
>   without fail—
> Oh, you know we had a circus as we all went up
>   the trail.

"The Hills of Mexico," or "Boggy Creek," purports to tell of a real event in the spring of '83, but the Goodnight-Loving Trail is only the latest location of this story of implicit murder. It has been set in Canada, Michigan, and on "The Range of the Buffalo."

Joseph Hanson's "The Railroad Corral," which he had published in the popular *Frank Leslie's Monthly Magazine*, is an excellent song. Among other things, it celebrates the end of the trip:

> Come, strap up the saddle
>   Whose lap you have felt;
> So flap up your holster
>   And snap up your belt;
> Good-bye to the steers and the long chaparral;
> There's a town that's a trump by the railroad corral!

"The Old Chisholm Trail" is a classic—the "Sweet Betsey" of the cowboys—and Lomax asserts that it has hundreds of unprintable couplets. It is a rambling verse, placing one foot after another, and it manages to hit everything:

> Stray in the herd, and the boss said kill it,
> So I shot him in the rump with the handle of
>   the skillet.

"I Ride an Old Paint" and "Goodbye, Old Paint," are different but similar in the affection they show for the dogies. Both are loping, melancholy songs designed to keep the creatures moving, but Harry Stephens' "Night-Herding Song" pleads, with utter fatigue, for them to lie down and

> Snore loud, little dogies, and drown the wild sound—
> They'll all go away when the day rolls 'round.

GIT ALONG, LITTLE DOGIES

TUNE: Rocking the Cradle

As I was a-walk-ing one morn-ing for plea-sure, I spied a cow-punch-er all rid-ing a-lone. His hat was throwed back and his spurs was a-jin-gling, And as he ap-proached he was sing-ing this song:

Chorus

Whoop-ee, ti yi yo, git a-long, lit-tle do-gies! It's your mis-for-tune and none of my own. Whoop-ee, ti yi yo, git a-long, lit-tle do-gies, For you know Wy-o-ming will be your new home!

1

As I was a-walking one morning for pleasure,
I spied a cowpuncher all riding alone.
His hat was throwed back and his spurs was a-jingling,
And as he approached he was singing this song:

CHORUS: Whoopee, ti yi yo, git along, little dogies!
It's your misfortune and none of my own.
Whoopee, ti yi yo, git along, little dogies,
For you know Wyoming will be your new home!

2

Early in the spring, we round up the dogies,
Mark and brand and bob off their tails,
Round up our horses, load up the chuckwagon,
Then throw the dogies up on the trail:

3

It's whooping and yelling and driving the dogies;
O how I wish you would go on!
It's whooping and punching and go on little dogies,
For you know Wyoming will be your new home:

4

When the night comes on, we herd them on the bedground,
These little dogies that roll on so slow;
Roll up the herd and cut out the strays,
And roll the little dogies that never rolled before:

5

Your mother, she was raised way down in Texas,
Where the jimson weed and sand burrs grow.
Now we'll fill you up on prickly pear and cholla
Till you are ready for the trail to Idaho:

6

Oh, you'll be soup for Uncle Sam's Injuns;
It's beef, heap beef," I hear them cry.
Git along, git along, little dogies,
You're going to be beef steers by and by.

TEXT AND MUSIC: Sandburg (1927), pp. 268-270. Used by permission of Harcourt, Brace & World Inc.

VARIANTS: Lomax (1910), pp. 87-91; Thorp (1921), pp. 70-71; Pound (1922), pp. 174-175; Sires (1928), pp. 44-45; Gaines (1928), p. 149; German (1929); Larkin (1931), pp. 92-97; Clark (1932), p. 67; Briegel (1933), pp. 32-33; Allen (1933), pp. 94-95; Klickman and Sherwin (1933), pp. 36-37; Lomax and Lomax (1934), pp. 385-388, and (1938), pp. 4-7; Frey (1936), pp. 20-21; Hull (1939), pp. 41-42; Lomax and Lomax (1947); pp. 204-205; Randolph (1948), p. 174; Wylder (1949), pp. 47-48; Lomax (1960), pp. 372-374; Moore and Moore (1964), pp. 291-293.

THE OLD CHISHOLM TRAIL

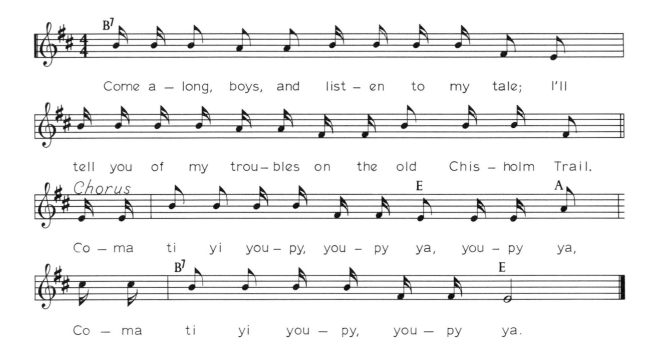

Come a — long, boys, and list — en to my tale; I'll

tell you of my trou — bles on the old Chis — holm Trail.

Chorus

Co — ma ti yi you — py, you — py ya, you — py ya,

Co — ma ti yi you — py, you — py ya.

1
Come along, boys, and listen to my tale;
I'll tell you of my troubles on the old Chisholm Trail.

CHORUS: Coma ti yi youpy, youpy ya, youpy ya,
Coma ti yi youpy, youpy ya.

2
I started up the trail October twenty-third,
I started up the trail with the 2-U herd.

3
Oh, a ten-dollar hoss and a forty-dollar saddle—
And I'm goin' to punchin' Texas cattle.

4
I woke up one morning on the old Chisholm Trail,
Rope in my hand and a cow by the tail.

5
I'm up in the mornin' afore daylight,
And afore I sleep, the moon shines bright.

6
Old Ben Bolt was a blamed good boss,
But he'd go to see the girls on a sore-backed hoss.

7
Old Ben Bolt was a fine old man,
And you'd know there was whiskey wherever he'd land.

8

My hoss throwed me off at the creek called Mud;
My hoss throwed me off round the 2-U herd.

9

Last time I saw him he was going cross the level
A-kicking up his heels and a-running like the devil.

10

It's cloudy in the West, a-looking like rain,
And my damned old slicker's in the wagon again.

11

Crippled my hoss, I don't know how,
Ropin' at the horns of a 2-U cow.

12

We hit Caldwell, and we hit her on the fly;
We bedded down the cattle on the hill close by.

13

No chaps, no slicker, and it's pouring down rain;
And I swear, by god, I'll never night-herd again.

14

Feet in the stirrups and seat in the saddle,
I hung and rattled with them long-horn cattle..

15

Last night I was on guard, and the leader broke the ranks;
I hit my horse down the shoulders and I spurred him in the flanks.

16

The wind commenced to blow, and the rain began to fall;
Hit looked, by grab, like we was goin' to loss 'em all.

17

I jumped in the saddle and grabbed holt the horn—
Best blamed cow-puncher ever was born.

18

I popped my foot in the stirrup and gave a little yell;
The tail cattle broke, and the leaders went to hell.

19

I don't give a damn if they never do stop;
I'll ride as long as an eighty-day clock.

20

Foot in the stirrup and hand on the horn—
Best damned cowboy ever was born.

21

I herded and I hollered and I done very well,
Till the boss said, "Boys, just let 'em go to hell."

22

Stray in the herd, and the boss said kill it,
So I shot him in the rump with the handle of the skillet.

23

We rounded 'em up and put 'em on the cars,
And that was the last of the old Two Bars.

24

Oh it's bacon and beans most every day—
I'd as soon be a-eatin' prairie hay.

25

I'm on my best horse, and I'm goin' at a run;
I'm the quickest shootin' cowboy that ever pulled a gun.

26

I went to the wagon to get my roll
To come back to Texas, dad-burn my soul.

27

I went to the boss to draw my roll;
He had it figgered out I was nine dollars in the hole.

28

I'll sell my outfit just as soon as I can;
I won't punch cattle for no damned man.

29

Goin' back to town to draw my money,
Goin' back home to see my honey.

30

With my knees in the saddle and my seat in the sky,
I'll quit punching cows in the sweet by and by.

TEXT AND MUSIC: Lomax (1910), pp. 58-63.

VARIANTS: Thorp (1921), pp. 109-112; Pound (1922), pp. 167-170; Sandburg (1927), p. 266; Sires (1928), pp. 32-33; Gaines (1928), pp. 150-151; Dobie (1928), pp. 178-180; German (1929); Larkin (1931), pp. 2-8; Clark (1932), p. 47; Patterson and Dexter (1932), pp. 38-39; Allen (1933), pp. 129-131; Klickman and Sherwin (1933), pp. 45-46; Lomax and Lomax (1934), pp. 376-379, and (1938), pp. 28-41; Frey (1936), pp. 42-43; Hull (1939), pp. 38-39; Lomax and Lomax (1947), pp. 200-203; Randolph (1948), pp. 174-175; Lomax (1960), pp. 370-371; Fowke and Glazer (1960), pp. 122-123; Koch and Koch (1961), pp. 18-19; Moore and Moore (1964), pp. 285-287.

JOHN GARNER'S TRAIL HERD

1

Come all you old timers and listen to my song;
I'll make it short as possible and I'll not keep you long;
I'll relate to you about the time you all remember well
When we with old John Garner drove a beef herd up the trail.

2

When we left the ranch, it was early in the spring.
We had as good a corporal as ever rope did swing,
Good hands and good horses, good outfit through and through—
We went well equipped; we were a jolly crew.

3

We had no little herd—two thousand head or more—
And some as wild brush beeves as you ever saw before.
We swung to them all the way and sometimes by the tail—
Oh, you know we had a circus as we all went up the trail.

4

Till we reached the open plains everything went well,
And then them cattle turned in and dealt us merry hell.
They stampeded every night that came and did it without fail—
Oh, you know we had a circus as we all went up the trail.

5

We would round them up at morning, and the boss would make a count
And say, "Look here, old punchers, we are out quite an amount;
You must make all losses good and do it without fail,
Or you'll never get another job of driving up the trail."

6

When we reached Red River, we gave the Inspector the dodge.
He swore by God Almighty in jail old John should lodge.
We told him if he'd taken our boss and had him locked in jail,
We would shore get his scalp as we all came down the trail.

7

When we reached the Reservation, how squirmish we did feel,
Although we had tried old Garner and knew him true as steel;
And if we would follow him and do as he said do,
That old bald-headed cow-thief would surely take us through.

8

When we reached Dodge City, we drew our four months' pay:
Times was better then, boys, than they are to-day.
The way we drank and gambled and threw the girls around—
"Say, a crowd of Texas cowboys has come to take our town."

9

The cowboy sees many hardships, although he takes them well;
The fun we had upon that trip no human tongue can tell.
The cowboy's life is a dreary life, though his mind it is no load,
And he always spends his money like he found it in the road.

10

If ever you meet old Garner, you must meet him on the square,
For he is the biggest cow-thief that ever tramped out there;
But if you want to hear him roar and spin a lively tale,
Just ask him about the time we all went up the trail.

TEXT: Thorp (1921), pp. 84-86. Used by permission of Houghton Mifflin Co.
VARIANTS: Lomax (1910), pp. 114-116; Lomax and Lomax (1938), pp. 25-27.

THE HILLS OF MEXICO

(or Boggy Creek)

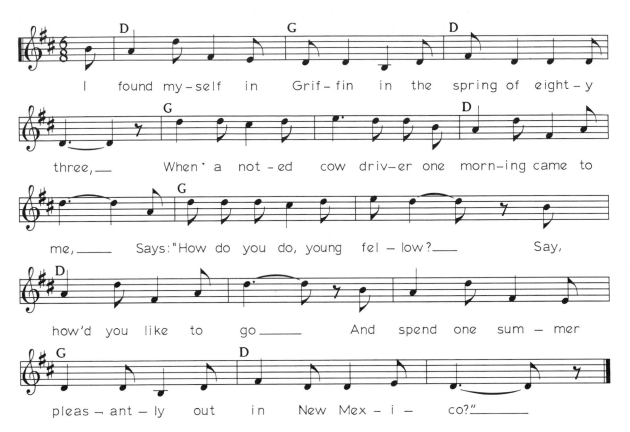

I found my-self in Grif-fin in the spring of eight-y three,__ When a not-ed cow driv-er one morn-ing came to me,__ Says:"How do you do, young fel-low?__ Say, how'd you like to go __ And spend one sum-mer pleas-ant-ly out in New Mex-i-co?"__

1

I found myself in Griffin in the spring of '83,
When a noted cow driver one morning came to me.
Says: "How do you do, young fellow? Say, how'd you like to go
And spend one summer pleasantly out in New Mexico?"

2

I, being out of employment, to the driver thus did say:
"A-going out in New Mexico depends upon the pay.
If you pay to me good wages, transportation to and fro,
I believe I'll go along with you out in New Mexico."

3

"Of course I'll pay good wages, and transportation, too,
Provided that you stay with me the summer season through;
But if you do get homesick and want to Griffin go,
I will even loan you a horse to ride from the hills of Mexico."

4

With all this flattering talk, he enlisted quite a train,
Some ten or twelve in number, strong, able-bodied men.
Our trip was quite a pleasant one, over the road we had to go,
Until we reached old Boggy Creek out in New Mexico.

5

Right there our pleasures ended—our troubles then begun;
The first hailstorm that came on us, Christ, how those cattle run!
In running through thorns and stickers, we had but little show,
And the Indians watched to pick us off the hills of Mexico.

6

The summer season ended, the driver could not pay.
The outfit was so extravagant, he was in debt today.
That's bankrupt law among the cowboys. Christ, this will never do.
That's why we left his bones to bleach out in New Mexico.

7

So, now, we'll cross old Boggy Creek and homeward we are bound;
No more in this cursed country will ever we be found.
Go home to our wives and sweethearts—tell others not to go
To that God-forsaken country they call New Mexico.

TEXT: Haley (1927), pp. 201-202. Used by permission of the Texas Folklore Society.

MUSIC: Larkin (1931), p. 84. Used by permission of Alfred A. Knopf, Inc.

VARIANTS: Webb (1923), p. 45; Lomax and Lomax (1938), pp. 41-42; Lomax (1960), pp. 380-381.

LONE STAR TRAIL

Oh, I am a lone-ly cow-boy And I'm off from the Tex-as trail.____ My trade is cinch-in' sad-dles And pul-lin' brid-le reins,____ But I can twist a las-so With the great-est skill and ease,_ Or rope and ride a bron-cho Most an-y-where I please.

1

Oh, I am a lonely cowboy
And I'm off from the Texas trail.
My trade is cinchin' saddles
And pullin' bridle reins,
But I can twist a lasso
With the greatest skill and ease,
Or rope and ride a broncho
Most anywhere I please.

2

Oh, I love the rolling prairie
That's far from the trail and strife.
'Hind a bunch of longhorns
I'll journey all my life.
But if I had a stake, boys,
Soon married I would be
To the sweetest girl in this wide world
Just fell in love with me.

3

Oh, when we get on the trail, boys,
And the dusty billows ride,
It's fifteen miles from water
And the grass is scorchin' dry.
Oh, the boss is mad and wringy,
You all can plainly see.
I have to follow the longhorns;
I'm a cowboy here to be.

4

But when it comes a-rain, boys,
One of the gentle kind,
When the lakes are full of water
And the grass is wavin' fine,
Oh, the boss will shed his frown, boys,
And a pleasant smile you'll see.
I have to follow the longhorns;
I'm a cowboy here to be.

5

Oh, when we get 'em bedded,
We think, down for the night,
Some horse will shake his saddle;
He will give the herd a fright.
They'll bound to their feet, boys,
And madly they'll beat away.
In one moment's time, boys,
You can hear a cowboy say, (Yodel).

6

Oh, when we get 'em bedded,
We feel most forlorn,
When a cloud'll rise in the west, boys,
And the fire play on their horns.
Oh, the old boss rides around them,
Your pay you'll get in gold.
So I'll have to follow the longhorns
Until I am too old.

TEXT AND MUSIC: As sung by Ken Maynard, Columbia Record 2310D (1930). Transcribed by David Cohen.

VARIANTS: Lomax (1910), pp. 284-289, 310-313; Will (1913), p. 188; Siringo (1919), pp. 38-39; Thorp (1921), pp. 86-88; Sandburg (1927), pp. 266-267; Moore (1927), pp. 196-197; Sires (1928), pp. 8-9; German (1929); Larkin (1931), pp. 140-141, 166-167; Lomax and Lomax (1938), pp. 19-22, 275-278; Lomax (1960), p. 368; Moore and Moore (1964), pp. 287-288.

JOSEPH M. HANSON

THE RAILROAD CORRAL

We are up in the morn-ing ere dawn-ing of day And the
grub-wa-gon's bus-y and flap-jacks in play, While the herd is a-
stir o-ver hill-side and swale With the night-rid-ers round-ing them
in-to the trail. *Chorus.* Come, take up your cin-ches and shake up your
reins; Come, wake up your bron-co and break for the plains; Come,
roust those red steers from the long chap-ar-ral, For the
out-fit is off for the rail-road cor-ral!

1

We are up in the morning ere dawning of day,
And the grub-wagon's busy and flap-jacks in play,
While the herd is astir over hillside and swale
With the night-riders rounding them into the trail.

Come, take up your cinches
    And shake up your reins;
Come, wake up your bronco
    And break for the plains;
Come, roust those red steers from the long chaparral,
For the outfit is off for the railroad corral!

2

The sun circles upward; the steers, as they plod,
Are pounding to powder the hot prairie sod,
And it seems, as the dust turns you dizzy and sick,
That you'll never reach noon and the cool, shady creek.

But tie up your kerchief
And ply up your nag;
Come, dry up your grumbles
And try not to lag;
Come, now for the steers in the long chaparral,
For we're far on the way to the railroad corral!

3

The afternoon shadows are starting to lean
When the grub-wagon sticks in a marshy ravine;
And the herd scatters further than vision can look,
For you bet all true punchers will help out the cook!

So shake out your rawhide
And snake it up fair;
Come, break in your bronco
To taking his share!
Come, now for the steers in the long chaparral,
For it's all in the drive to the railroad corral!

4

But the longest of days must reach evening at last,
When the hills are all climbed and the creeks are all passed,
And the tired herd droops in the yellowing light;
Let them loaf if they will, for the railroad's in sight!

Come, strap up the saddle
Whose lap you have felt;
So flap up your holster
And snap up your belt;
Good-bye to the steers and the long chaparral;
There's a town that's a trump by the railroad corral!

TEXT: *Frank Leslie's Monthly Magazine*, LVIII (1904), 681.

MUSIC: Clark (1932), p. 5. Used by permission of Shawnee Press Inc.

VARIANTS: Joseph M. Hanson, *Frontier Ballads* (Chicago: A. C. McClurg & Co., 1910), pp. 52-53; Lomax (1910), pp. 318-319; Thorp (1921), pp. 132-134; Sires (1928), pp. 22-23; Clark (1932), p. 5; Frey (1936), pp. 92-93; Lomax and Lomax (1938), pp. 42-44; Lomax (1960), p. 367.

I RIDE AN OLD PAINT

I ride an old paint, and I lead an old dam. I'm going to Mon-tan-a for to throw the hou-li-han. They feed in the cou-lees and wat-er in the draw; Their tails are all mat-ted and their backs are all raw. Git a-long, you lit-tle do-gies, git a-long there slow, For the fi—ery and the snuf—fy are a—rar-ing to go.

1
I ride an old paint, and I lead an old dam.
I'm going to Montana for to throw the houlihan.
They feed in the coulees and water in the draw;
Their tails are all matted and their backs are all raw.

CHORUS: Git along, you little dogies, git along there slow,
For the fiery and the snuffy are a-raring to go.

2
Old Bill Jones had two daughters and a song.
One went to Denver and the other went wrong.
His wife, she died in a pool room fight,
But still he sings from morning till night.

3

Oh when I die, take my saddle from the wall,
Put it on my pony, lead him out of his stall,
Tie my bones to his back, turn our faces to the West,
And we'll ride the prairies that we love best.
LAST CHORUS: Ride around the little dogies, ride around 'em slow,
For the fiery and the snuffy are a-raring to go.

TEXT AND MUSIC: Larkin (1931), pp. 18-19. Used by permission of Alfred A. Knopf, Inc.

VARIANTS: Sandburg (1927), pp. 12-13; Clark (1932), p. 39; Patterson and Dexter (1932), pp. 4-5; Klickman and Sherwin (1933), pp. 18-19; Lomax and Lomax (1947), pp. 216-217.

GOODBYE, OLD PAINT

1

Farewell, fair ladies, I'm a-leaving Cheyenne.
Farewell, fair ladies, I'm a-leaving Cheyenne.
By bye, my little Dony, my pony won't stand.

CHORUS: Old Paint, old Paint, I'm a-leaving Cheyenne.
Goodbye, old Paint, I'm a-leaving Cheyenne.
Old Paint's a good pony, and she paces when she can.

2

In the middle of the ocean, there grows a green tree,
But I'll never prove false to the girl that loves me.

3

Oh, we spread down the blanket on the green grassy ground,
And the horses and cattle were a-grazing all 'round.

4

Oh, the last time I saw her, it was late in the fall;
She was riding old Paint and a-leading old Ball.

5

Old Paint had a colt down on the Rio Grande,
And the colt couldn't pace, and they named it Cheyenne.

6

For my feet's in my stirrups, and my bridle's in my hand.
Goodbye, my little Dony, my pony won't stand,

7

Farewell, fair ladies, I'm a-leaving Cheyenne.
Farewell, fair ladies, I'm a-leaving Cheyenne.
Goodbye, my little Dony, my pony won't stand.

TEXT AND MUSIC: As sung by Jess Morris, Library of Congress Recording L 28. Transcribed by David Cohen. The original key was E♭.

VARIANTS: Lomax (1916), pp. 329-330; Thorp (1921), pp. 118-119; Larkin (1931), p. 176; Clark (1932), p. 29; Allen (1933), pp. 121-123; Frey (1936), p. 51; Lomax and Lomax (1938), pp. 12-14; Moore and Moore (1964), pp. 376-377.

HARRY STEPHENS # NIGHT-HERDING SONG

Oh, slow up, do — gies; quit your rov - ing a — round. You've
wan-dered and tramped all o — ver the ground. Oh,
graze a - long, do — gies, and feed kind of slow, And don't for —
ev — er be on the go — Oh, move slow,
do — gies, move ___ slow. Hi yoo, hi
yoo - oo - oo, ___ woo — oo — oo - oo - oo.___
(falsetto)

1

Oh, slow up, dogies; quit your roving around.
You've wandered and tramped all over the ground.
Oh, graze along, dogies, and feed kind of slow,
And don't forever be on the go—
Oh, move slow, dogies, move slow.
    Hi-yoo, hi-yoo-oo-oo,
    Woo-oo-oo-oo-oo.

2

I've circle-herded, trail-herded, cross-herded, too;
But to keep you together, that's what I can't do.
My horse is leg-weary, and I'm awful tired;
But if I let you get away, I'm sure to get fired—
Bunch up, little dogies, bunch up.
    Yoo-oo-oo-oo-oo.
    Hey, cattle! Whoo-oop!

3

Oh, say, little dogies, when you going to lay down
And quit this forever sifting around?
My limbs are weary, my seat is sore;
Oh, lay down, dogies, like you've laid down before—
Lay down, little dogies, lay down.

      Hayyup, cattle! cattle!
      Hi-yoo, hi-yoo-oo-oo.

4

Oh, lay still, dogies, since you have laid down.
Stretch away out on the big open ground.
Snore loud, little dogies, and drown the wild sound—
They'll all go away when the day rolls 'round—
Lay still, little dogies, lay still.

TEXT AND MUSIC: As sung by Harry Stephens, Library of Congress Recording L 28. Transcribed by David Cohen.

VARIANTS: Lomax (1910), pp. 324-325; Thorp (1921), p. 108; Sires (1928), pp. 50-51; German (1929); Larkin (1931), pp. 10-12; Clark (1932), p. 49; Patterson and Dexter (1932), pp. 32-33; Frey (1936), p. 50; Lomax and Lomax (1938), pp. 60-61; Hull (1939), pp. 59-60; Lomax (1960), p. 376.

IF YOUR SADDLE IS GOOD AND TIGHT

In what other being could the common cowboy place his trust, confidence, loyalty, and affection than his horse? Not only were women rare on the Great Plains; those the waddie was likely to meet worked in the Devil's Half Acre across the Kansas Pacific tracks in Abilene. The songs in this selection are about equally divided in subject matter between women and horses, and the emotions the cowboy shows toward each are of some interest. "If Your Saddle Is Good and Tight" makes the initial equation between fillies and fillies, and not in terms of their dependability or big brown eyes:

> For of all the crazy critters
> That you've ever tried to halter,
> A woman is the worst one
> When she's prancing round the altar.

That exuberance is repeated in both the words and the rhythm of "The Gal I Left Behind Me," a delightful song of British origin which assures us that "When I got back, we had a smack, And that was no gol-darned liar." A different, but apparently well-deserved, fate awaited "The Rambling Cowboy," the title of the song referring not only to his travels:

> One day as I was riding across the public square,
> The mail-coach came in, and I met the driver there.
> He handed me a letter which gave me to understand
> That the girl I left in Texas had married another man.
> I turned myself all roundabout, not knowing what to do;
> But I read on down some further, and it proved the
>   words were true.

The narrator in another British import, "The Trail to Mexico," had the same experience, but he also found a way to sublimate:

> The girl has married that I adore,
> I'll stay at home no never more,
> But in the saddle I will ride out
> And throw them longhorns 'round and about.

"Brown-eyed Lee" is an excellent, if sophisticated, song, said by one of its singers to have been based, of course, on a real incident in 1899 down in Bell County, Texas. It introduces into Western song the potential mother-in-law.

> Good fortune fell upon me;
>   My darling proved untrue;
> I gave her back her letters
>   And bid her kind adieu.
>
> I pressed her to my aching heart
>   And kissed her last farewell,
> And prayed a permanent prayer to God
>   To send her Ma to hell.

On the "Careless Love" theme is "The Bucking Bronco," which numbers among the many candidates for its authorship none less probable than Belle Starr, outlawess of the Indian Territory. To conclude the women's side of this collection on the highest possible level, we print Charles Badger Clark's "A Border Affair," sometimes titled after its first line, "Spanish Is the Lovin' Tongue." It is a lovely song about a cowboy who crossed a couple of lines for love.

N. Howard Thorp wrote "Chopo" himself and was so reserved in that pony's praise that he built a false climax.
"Speckles" is his, too; and, although its cussed subject ought to have been more interesting, Thorp had a real gift for letting a story slip away from him. "Sky Ball Paint," from Montana, is a vigorous song about a devilish mount: "Ain't here to brag, but I rode this nag till his blood did fairly boil, And I hit the ground and ate three pounds of good old western soil."

Finally, "Zebra Dun," allegedly composed by a Negro camp cook, is quite interesting, being redolent of allegory and folksay. It starts off in anti-intellectual fashion about a passing dude whose talk just came in herds. To deflate him, the boys saddled him up a bronc that "could paw the white out of the moon for a quarter of a mile," but the tricksters are tricked when:

> He spurred him in the shoulders and whipped him as he whirled,
> Just to show us flunky punchers he was the wolf of the world.

The curiously un-Western moral follows easily.

IF YOUR SADDLE IS GOOD AND TIGHT

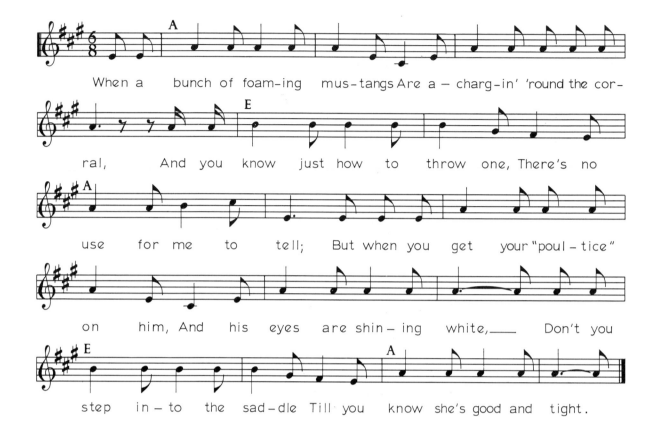

When a bunch of foam-ing mus-tangs Are a — charg-in' 'round the corral, And you know just how to throw one, There's no
use for me to tell; But when you get your "poul — tice"
on him, And his eyes are shin — ing white,____ Don't you
step in — to the sad — dle Till you know she's good and tight.

1
When a bunch of foaming mustangs
Are a-chargin' 'round the corral,
And you know just how to throw one,
There's no use for me to tell;
But when you get your "poultice" on him,
And his eyes are shining white,
Don't you step into the saddle
Till you know she's good and tight.

2
When some outlaw of a mav'rick
Turns the herd up to the hills,
And you're down to just plain runnin'
Without any fancy frills,
When he turns them to the rough rocks,
Don't you let your gills turn white,
But just dig in all the harder
If your saddle's good and tight.

3

When you've got to take the wallop
Out of some long-horned locoed steer,
You'd better take a lookin'
To the hangin' of your gear;
For if your bovine goes length-wise
And your loop goes sailin' right,
Then you get your dally werthas
If your saddle's good and tight.

4

But when you take down your rope
For to catch yourself a bride,
I'll tell you commowadies
That you're going to have a ride;
You will find the range confusing
With no water holes in sight
If you're not very careful
To keep your saddle good and tight.

5

For of all the crazy critters
That you ever tried to halter,
A woman she's the worst one
When she's prancing round the altar.
But when you get the right one
And you're sure that you are right,
Just dally hard and hold her
If your saddle is good and tight.

TEXT AND MUSIC: Sires (1928), pp. 42-43.

N. HOWARD THORP   # CHOPO

1

Through rocky arroyas so dark and so deep,
Down the sides of the mountains so slippery and steep,
You've good judgment, sure footed, wherever you go;
You're a safety conveyance, my little Chopo

CHORUS: Chopo, my pony; Chopo, my pride;
Chopo, my amigo; Chopo I will ride
From Mexico's borders 'cross Texas Llanos
To the salt Pecos river I ride you, Chopo.

2

Whether single or double or in the lead of a team,
Over highways or byways or crossing a stream,
You're always in fix and willing to go
Whenever you're called on, my chico Chopo.

3

You're a good roping horse; you were never jerked down.
When tied to a steer, you will circle him round.
Let him once cross the string, and over he'll go.
You sabe the business, my cow horse Chopo.

4

One day on the Llano, a hail storm began.
The herds were stampeded; the horses all ran.
The lightning, it glittered, a cyclone did blow;
But you faced the sweet music, my little Chopo.

TEXT: Thorp (1908), pp. 30-31.

VARIANTS: Lomax (1916), pp. 371-372; Thorp (1921), pp. 23-24; German (1929); Fife and Fife (1966), pp. 191-194*.

THE GAL I LEFT BEHIND ME

Tune: The Girl I Left Behind Me

1

I struck the trail in seventy-nine,
The herd strung out behind me;
As I jogged along, my mind ran back
For the gal I left behind me.

CHORUS: That sweet little gal, that true little gal,
The gal I left behind me!
That sweet little gal, that true little gal,
The gal I left behind me!

2

If ever I get off the trail
And the Indians they don't find me,
I'll make my way straight back again
To the gal I left behind me.

3

The wind did blow, the rain did flow,
The hail did fall and blind me;
I thought of that gal, that sweet little gal,
That gal I'd left behind me!

4

She wrote ahead to the place I said,
I was always glad to find it;
She says, "I am true, when you get through,
Right back and you will find me."

5

When we sold out, I took the train—
I knew where I would find her—
When I got back, we had a smack,
And that was no gol-darned liar.

TEXT: Thorp (1921), pp. 69-70. Used by permission of Houghton Mifflin Co.

MUSIC: *Most Popular Army and Navy Songs* (1912). Used by permission of Noble and Noble Publishers, Inc.

VARIANTS: Lomax (1916), pp. 342-343; Finger (1927), pp. 63-64; Clark (1932), p. 36; Patterson and Dexter (1932), pp. 19-20; Allen (1933), pp. 127-128; Frey (1936), pp. 94-95; Lomax and Lomax (1934), pp. 282-283, and (1938), pp. 58-60.

THE RAMBLING COWBOY

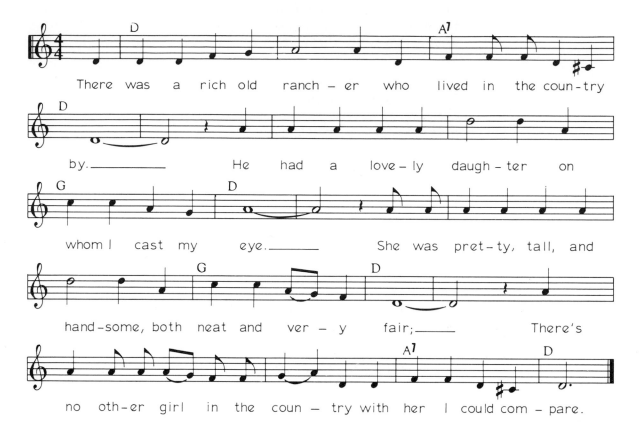

There was a rich old ranch-er who lived in the coun-try by. He had a love-ly daugh-ter on whom I cast my eye. She was pret-ty, tall, and hand-some, both neat and ver-y fair; There's no oth-er girl in the coun - try with her I could com - pare.

1

There was a rich old rancher who lived in the country by.
He had a lovely daughter on whom I cast my eye.
She was pretty, tall, and handsome, both neat and very fair;
There's no other girl in the country with her I could compare.

2

I asked her if she would be willing for me to cross the plains.
She said she would be truthful until I returned again.
She said she would be faithful until death did prove unkind,
So we kissed, shook hands, and parted, and I left my girl behind.

3

I left the state of Texas; for Arizona I was bound.
I landed in Tombstone City; I viewed the place all round.
Money and work were plentiful, and the cowboys they were kind;
But the only thought of my heart was the girl I left behind.

4

One day as I was riding across the public square,
The mail-coach came in, and I met the driver there.
He handed me a letter which gave me to understand
That the girl I left in Texas had married another man.

5

I turned myself all roundabout, not knowing what to do;
But I read on down some further, and it proved the words were
   true.
Hard work I have laid over, it's gambling I have designed.
I'll ramble this wide world over for the girl I left behind.

6

Come, all you reckless and rambling boys, who have listened to
   this song,
If it hasn't done you any good, it hasn't done you any wrong;
But when you court a pretty girl, just marry her while you can,
For if you go across the plains, she'll marry another man.

TEXT: Thorp (1921), pp. 134-135. Used by permission of Houghton Mifflin Co.

MUSIC: "Maggie Walker Blues," as sung by Clint Howard, Fred Price, and Doc Watson on *Old Time Music at Clarence Ashley's*, Folkways Record FA 2355. Transcribed by David Cohen. Used by permission of Folkways Records & Service Corp.

VARIANTS: Lomax (1910), pp. 244-245; German (1929); Lomax and Lomax (1938), pp. 192-194.

THE TRAIL TO MEXICO

TUNE: Early in the Spring

I made up my mind_____ to change my way,_____ To leave my crowd_____ that was so gay,_____ No long-er in Tex_____ as to stay for a while,_____ But trav—el west_____ for man-y a mile._____ Co—ma ti yi yi Com-a ti yi ya Com-a ti yi yoo——pee Ti yi ya!_____

1

I made up my mind to change my way,
To leave my crowd that was so gay,
No longer in Texas to stay for a while,
But travel west for many a mile.

CHORUS: Coma ti yi yi
Coma ti yi ya
Coma ti yi yoopee
Ti yi ya!

2

It was in the fall of '83
That J. P. Stanley hired me.
He said, "Young man, I want you to go
And take a herd to New Mexico."

3

Oh, it was early in the year
When I went on trail to drive those steers,
To leave my darling girl behind
Who had oft-times told me her heart was mine.

4

When I embraced her in my arms,
Seemed she like ten thousand charms
With cheeks so red and lips so sweet,
Sayin', "We'll get married when next we
  meet."

5

It was a long and lonesome go
To take that herd to Mexico,
But the music sweet of the cowboy's song
To New Mexico our herd moved on.

6

When I arrived in New Mexico,
I wanted to see her but I could not go.
I wrote one letter to my love so dear,
But not one word could I ever hear.

7

When I returned to my once loved home
Inquirin' for the darling of my soul,
They said, "She's married to a richer life;
Therefore, young man, seek another wife."

8

O! curse to gold and silver, too!
What account is a girl who won't prove true?
I'll cut my way to the far off land
And go back to the cowboy band.

9

Oh, buddy, oh, buddy, please stay at home,
Don't be forever on the roam.
There's many a girl much truer than she;
Oh, buddy, don't go where the bullets fly.

10

The girl has married that I adore.
I'll stay at home no never more,
But in my saddle I will ride out
And throw them longhorns 'round and about.

Used by permission of the Texas Folklore Society.

TEXT AND MUSIC: Gaines (1928), pp. 151-152.

VARIANTS: Lomax (1910), pp. 132-135; Sandburg (1927), pp. 285-286; Larkin (1931), pp. 50-51; Clark (1932), pp. 62-63; Briegel (1933), p. 28; Allen (1933), pp. 72-73; Frey (1936), pp. 68-69; Hendren (1938), pp. 270-279*; Lomax and Lomax (1938), pp 52-56; Moore and Moore (1964), pp. 288-289; Laws (1964), p. 139*.

BROWN-EYED LEE

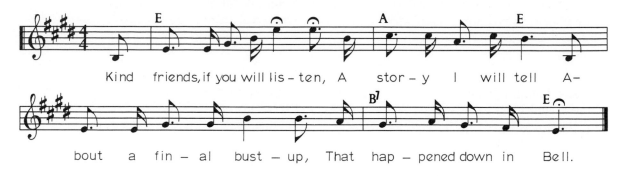

Kind friends, if you will lis-ten, A stor-y I will tell A-
bout a fin-al bust—up, That hap—pened down in Bell.

1

Kind friends, if you will listen,
    A story I will tell
About a final bust-up
    That happened down in Bell.

2

I courted a brown-eyed angel
    That goes by the name of Lee;
And when I popped the question,
    She said she would marry me.

3

She told me that she loved me,
    And loved no one but me;
And I pressed a kiss upon the lips
    Of my darling angel, Lee.

4

My rapture at that moment
    No human could explain,
To know that I had loved her
    And had not loved in vain.

5

I went and bought my license,
    March, eighteen ninety-nine,
Expecting in a few more days
    That darling would be mine.

6

Her mother grew quite angry
    And said it could not be;
She said she had picked another man out
    For brown-eyed Lee.

7

She talked to friends and neighbors,
    And said that she would fight;
She said she'd get her old six-shooter
    And put old Red to flight.

8

But lovers laughed at shooters
    And the old she-devil, too;
I said I would have my darling
    If she didn't prove untrue.

9

I borrowed Dad's old buggy
    And got Jim's forty-one;
I started down to Kerns's,
    Thinking I would have some fun.

10

And passing Mr. O'Dell's,
    Out came Frankie's son
To bring a letter from the old folks,
    Saying, "Harry, don't you come."

11

I thought the matter over,
    Not knowing what to do,
When something seemed to whisper,
    "Are you going to prove untrue?"

12

I am not one to craw-fish
    When I am in a tight;
I said, "I will have my angel
    And not be put to flight."

13

I went on down to Kerns's
    With the devil in my head;
I said I'd have my darling
    Or leave the old folks dead.

14

Good fortune fell upon me;
    My darling proved untrue;
I gave her back her letters
    And bid her kind adieu.

15

I pressed her to my aching heart
    And kissed her last farewell,
And prayed a permanent prayer to God
    To send her Ma to hell.

16

She stood and gazed upon us,
    As if she thought it were fun;
I caught myself a time or two
    A-reaching for my gun.

17

I went back home all broken-hearted
    And almost wished I was dead,
Till something seemed to whisper,
    "It was best for you, Old Red."

18

I sold my cows to J. M. G.,
    My corn to K. M. P.,
And cursed the day that I first met
    That darling angel, Lee.

19

I sold my horse and saddle
    And caught a north-bound train,
Leaving the darling girl behind
    That I had loved in vain.

20

I landed in Paul's Valley,
    All right-side-up-with-care,
And dreamed of the girl I loved that night
    With dark brown eyes and hair.

21

When I got up next morning
    To see what I could see,
And every sound that I could hear
    Would speak the name of Lee.

22

I stepped into a billiard hall,
    Thinks, "I'll have a game,"
And every ball that I would knock
    Would speak the same dear name.

23

I drank two glasses of whiskey
    And emptied a bottle of wine,
And cursed the very day that I first met
    That darling girl of mine.

24

I hopped a freighter's wagon,
    Went to Midland town,
And hired to a man by the name of Smith
    And quietly settled down.

25

Although I am broken-hearted,
    There is one thing I know well,
That the one that caused this bust-up
    Will some day scorch in Hell.

26

She will cast her eyes to heaven,
    To Jesus on His throne,
And ask for a drop of water
    To cool her scorching tongue.

27

But Jesus will answer her:
    "Go to the old Scratch;
You are the very hypocrite
    That busted up this match.

28

"Depart from me, you cursed;
    You are the devil's own.
Old Red shall find a resting place
    On the right hand of my throne."

29

Now, kind friends, remember
    The H. M. P.
I could not help but love the girl
    That wore the name of Lee.

30

I loved her, oh, I loved her,
    Yes, more than tongue can tell;
I know that there is no other
    That I could love so well.

31

And in my dreams at night,
    My darling's face I see;
And it seems to whisper,
    "Dear one, remember me."

32

And every night I go to bed,
    I pray a permanent prayer
For the girl I loved so well
    With dark brown eyes and hair.

Used by permission of the Texas Folklore Society.

TEXT AND MUSIC: Payne (1927), pp. 217-220.

VARIANTS: Larkin (1931), pp. 62-64; Clark (1932), p. 8; Frey (1936), pp. 80-81; Lomax and Lomax (1938), pp. 214-217.

SKY BALL PAINT

1

Old Sky Ball Paint was a devil saint, and his eyes were fiery red.
Many a man had tried this nag to ride, but all of them are dead.
Ain't here to brag, but I rode this nag till his blood did fairly boil,
And I hit the ground and ate three pounds of good old western soil.

CHORUS: Singing hi ho, whoopee ti yo, ride him high and down you go,
Sons of the western soil.

2

I swore by heck I'd break his neck for the jolt that he give my pride,
So I threw my noose on the old cayuse, and I once more took a ride.
He turned around and soon I found his head where his tail should be,
So, says I, perhaps he's shy or he just don't care for me.

3

Down town one day I chanced to stray upon old Sheriff Jim,
With a whoop and a holler and a counterfeit dollar and I swapped that
    nag to him.
When old Jim plants the seat of his pants in Sky Ball's leather chair,
I'll bet four bits when Sky Ball quits old Jim will not be there.

———————

TEXT AND MUSIC: Wylder (1949), pp. 39-40.

N. HOWARD THORP   # SPECKLES

1

He was little en peaked en thin en narr'y a no account horse—
Least that's the way you'd describe him in case that the beast had been
    lost—
But for single and double cussedness en double fired sin,
The horse never come out o' Texas that was half way knee-high to him.

2

The first time that ever I saw him was nineteen year ago last spring.
'Twas the year we had grasshoppers that come en et up everything
That a feller rode up here one evening en wanted to pen overnight
A small bunch of horses he said, en I told him I guessed 'twas all right.

3

Well the feller was busted, the horses was thin en the grass around here,
    kind of good;
En he said if I'd let him hold here a few days he'd settle with me when he
    could.
So I told him all right, turn them loose down the draw, that the latch
    string was always untied.
He was welcome to stop a few days if he liked en rest from his weary ride.

4

Well, the cuss stay'd around for two or three weeks till at last he decided
    to go,
And that horse away yonder being too poor to move, he gimme—the cuss
    had no dough.
Well, at first the darn brute was as wild as a deer en would snort when he
    came to the branch,
En it took two cowpunchers on good horses too to handle him here at the
    ranch.

5

Well, winter came on and the range it got hard and my mustang commenced
    to get thin,
So I fed him along and rode him round some and found out old Freckles
    was game.
For that was what the other cuss called him—just Freckles, no more or no
    less.
His color, couldn't describe it—something like a paintshop in distress.

6

Them was Indian times, young feller, that I'm a tellin' about,
And oft's the time I've seen the red men fight and put the boys in blue to
    route.
A good horse in them days, young feller, would save your life,
One that in any race could hold the pace when the redskin bands were rife.

TEXT: Thorp (1908), pp. 48-50.
VARIANTS: Lomax (1916), pp. 360-361; Thorp (1921), pp. 142-145.

BUCKING BRONCO

My love is a rid-er, wild bronch-os he breaks, Though he's

prom-ised to quit it, just for my sake, He

ties up one foot, the sad-dle puts on; With a

swing and a jump he is mount-ed and gone.

1
My love is a rider; wild broncos he breaks,
Though he's promised to quit it, just for my sake.
He ties up one foot, the saddle puts on;
With a swing and a jump, he is mounted and gone.

2
The first time I met him 'twas early one spring
Riding a bronco, a high headed thing.
He tipped me a wink as he gaily did go,
For he wished me to look at his bucking bronco.

3
The next time I saw him 'twas late in the fall
Swinging the girls at Tomlinson's ball.
He laughed and he talked, as we danced to and fro,
Promised never to ride on another bronco.

4
He made me some presents, among them a ring.
The return that I made him was a far better thing.
'Twas a young maiden's heart; I'd have you all know
He'd won it by riding his bucking bronco.

5
Now all you young maidens, where'er you reside,
Beware of the cow-boy who swings the rawhide.
He'll court you and pet you and leave you and go
In the spring up the trail on his bucking bronco.

TEXT: Thorp (1908), pp. 26-27.
MUSIC: Larkin (1931), pp. 46-47. Used by permission of Alfred A. Knopf, Inc.
VARIANTS: *McClure's Magazine*, XXIV (Dec., 1904), 175-176; Lomax (1910), p. 251; Lomax (1916), pp. 251, 367-368; Thorp (1921), pp. 14-15; Barnes (1925), p. 16; Sires (1928), pp. 40-41; Dobie (1928), pp. 170-172; Larkin (1931), pp. 46-47; Clark (1932), p. 7; Allen (1933), pp. 157-158; Frey (1936), pp. 82-83; Lomax and Lomax (1934), pp. 417-418, and (1938), pp. 267-268; Randolph (1948), pp. 228-230; Lomax (1960), pp. 383-384; Laws (1964), p. 140*; Fife and Fife (1966), pp. 121-134.*

THE ZEBRA DUN

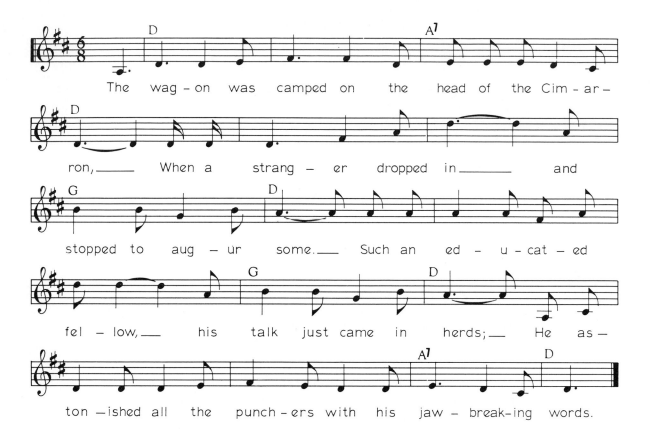

The wag - on was camped on the head of the Cim - ar -
ron,_____ When a strang - er dropped in _____ and
stopped to aug - ur some.___ Such an ed - u - cat - ed
fel - low,___ his talk just came in herds;___ He as -
ton -ished all the punch -ers with his jaw - break-ing words.

1

The wagon was camped on the head of the Cimarron,
When a stranger dropped in and stopped to augur some.
Such an educated fellow, his talk just came in herds;
He astonished all the punchers with his jaw-breaking words.

2

We asked him if he'd had his breakfast and he hadn't had a sniff,
So we opened up the chuck-box and bid him help himself.
He helped himself to beefsteak, a biscuit and some beans,
And then began to talk about the foreign kings and queens.

3

He talked about the Spanish war and fighting on the sea
With guns as big as beef-steers and ramrods big as trees.
He spoke about old Dewey, that fighting son-of-a-gun,
And said he was the bravest cuss that ever pulled a gun.

4

He kept on talking till he made the boys all sick,
And they tried to figure up some way to play a trick.
He said he'd lost his job up close to Santa Fe,
And was cutting across the country to strike the 7 Ds.

5

Didn't say what was the matter, but some trouble with the boss
And wanted to know if he could borrow a fresh, fat saddle horse.
That tickled all the boys—they laughed down in their sleeves;
We told him he could have one as fresh and fat as he pleased.

6

Shorty grabbed the lasso and roped old Zebra Dun,
Turned him over to the stranger and stepped back to see the fun.
Old Dun, he was a rocky outlaw that had grown so awful wild,
He could paw the white out of the moon for a quarter of a mile.

7

Old Dunny stood quite gentle as if he didn't know
That the stranger had him saddled and was fixing for to go.
When the stranger hit the saddle, old Dunny quit the earth,
Traveled up towards the moon for everything he was worth.

8

We could see the tops of all the trees under old Dunny's belly every
    jump,
But the stranger he was growed there just like a camel's hump.
He spurred him in the shoulders and whipped him as he whirled,
Just to show us flunky punchers he was the wolf of the world.

9

He sat up on old Dunny and curled his long mustache
Just like a summer boarder a-waiting for his hash.
When his hind feet were perpendicular and fore ones on the bits,
He spurred him in the shoulders till old Dunny had wall-eyed fits.

10

When old Dunny was all through pitching and the stranger was on the
    ground,
The rest of us punchers were gathered close around.
The boss said, "If you can throw the lasso like you can ride old Dun,
You are the man I've been looking for ever since the year of one."

11

Well, I can throw the lasso, neither do I do it slow,
I can catch their fore pins nine times out of ten for any kind of dough;
But there's one thing sure and certain I've learned since I've been
    born,
The educated follows ain't all green horns.

TEXT: Coolidge (1912), pp. 509-510.

MUSIC: Larkin (1931), pp. 36-37. Used by permission of Alfred A. Knopf, Inc.

VARIANTS: Thorp (1908), pp. 27-29; Lomax (1910), pp. 154-157; Thorp (1921), pp. 171-174; Barnes (1925), pp. 125-128; German (1929); Larkin (1931), pp. 36-38; Clark (1932), pp. 68-69; Patterson and Dexter (1932), pp. 56-57; Allen (1933), pp. 159-161; Frey (1936), pp. 62-63; Lomax and Lomax (1938), pp. 78-81; Pound (1939), pp. 29-30; Randolph (1948), pp. 244-245; Laws (1964), pp. 140-141*; Fife and Fife (1966), pp. 135-147*.

CHARLES BADGER CLARK   # A BORDER AFFAIR

1

Spanish is the lovin' tongue,
Soft as music, light as spray.
'Twas a girl I learnt it from
    Livin' down Sonora way.
I don't look much like a lover,
Yet I say her love words over
    Often, when I'm all alone—
    "Mi amor, mi corazón."

2

Nights when she knew where I'd ride
    She would listen for my spurs,
Fling the big door open wide,
    Raise them laughin' eyes of hers;
And my heart would nigh stop beatin'
When I heard her tender greetin'
    Whispered soft for me alone—
    "Mi amor! mi corazón!"

3

Moonlight in the patio,
    Old Senora noddin' near,
Me and Juana talkin' low
    So the Madre couldn't hear.
How those hours would go a-flyin'!
And too soon I'd hear her sighin'
    In her little sorry tone—
    "Adios, mi corazón!"

4

But one time I had to fly
    For a foolish gamblin' fight,
And we said a swift goodbye
    In that black, unlucky night.
When I'd loosed her arms from clingin'
With her words the hoofs kep' ringin',
    As I galloped north alone—
    "Adios, mi corazón!"

5

Never seen her since that night;
    I kaint cross the Line, you know.
She was Mex and I was white;
    Like as not it's better so.
Yet I've always sort of missed her
Since that last wild night I kissed her,
    Left her heart and lost my own—
    "Adiós, mi corazón!"

TEXT: Charles Badger Clark, *Sun and Saddle Leather* (Boston: Badger, 1915).
VARIANTS: Lomax (1919), pp. 67-68; Thorp (1921), pp. 10-11.

THE CAMPFIRE HAS GONE OUT

Long-range cattle droving and oxteaming in the West were enterprises living on borrowed time from the beginning. "Through progress of the railroads, our occupation's gone," says an insightful song from a clipping in E. F. Piper's ballad collection. "The cowboy and the freighter soon will hear the angel shout: 'Here they have come to heaven, and the campfire has gone out.' "

Other inescapable forces, both technological and legal, conspired to push the cowboy off the public domain. Homesteaders preempted the land, water, and manpower for more profitable uses. "The Wyoming Nester" puts it in human terms:

> "The cattle are still getting thinner,
> And the ranchers are shorter on men;
> But I've got me a full quart of whiskey
> And nearly a full quart of gin."

One desperate alternative to cowpunching was buffalo hunting. The Plains Indians, of course, had erected whole cultures around the vast herds of American bison, while the cowboys shot them for hides until the railroads cut into that activity, too. "The Range of the Buffalo" and "The Buffalo Hunters" tell rather different stories, but they agree on the dangerousness of the occupation.

Charlie Johnson wrote a good song called "The Old Cowboy," printed in the Bandera, Texas, *Frontier Times* in 1925. Having turned stampedes by the lightning on the cattle's horns and gratefully drunk water from their tracks, the cowboy begins to feel as obsolete as the buffalo at the sight of the granger's mules and hoes, whereas in "Cowboy Reverie" D. J. O'Malley sketches the psychologically realistic musings of a wrangler who was weary of it all anyway:

> No more will I ride on the night guard
> When loud Heaven's thunders do roar.
> No. I'll pound my ear down on a goose hair
> And think me of third guard no more.

All these gentle songs notwithstanding, there was a great deal of violence in the transition from the open to the closed range. Some of the worst of it was within the cattle industry itself. "The Invasion Song" recounts another of those Western vigilance stories in which large vested interests try force before law in removing irritations. A powerful group of Wyoming ranchers had gotten that state to recognize their Live Stock Commission as the authority to supervise all roundups. In the spring of 1892, however, various lesser cattlemen and rustlers formed the Northern Wyoming Farmers and Stock Growers Association and arranged to hold their own roundup on May 1, a month early. The commission listed seventy of these rustlers to be exterminated, and a group of stockmen and "deputy marshals" traveled by train and horseback from Cheyenne up to Johnson County to fight. As the song relates, at the K. C. Ranch they killed Nick Rae and Nate Champion, while Jack Flagg and Alonzo Taylor escaped to notify Sheriff Red Angus. The regulators holed up but were taken prisoner by United States troopers from Fort McKinney on April 13, 1892. They were never convicted, and rustling was largely eliminated by legal means.

In spite of its title, "Home, Sweet Home," is a bloody story. It refers to the Kansas dugout fled by the survivor of a knife fight over a girl. If its story has a significance in this context, it is possibly that the songs people sing agree, in their perceptions of the forces that move men, alternately with the historian and with the psychologist.

THE CAMPFIRE HAS GONE OUT

1

Through progress of the railroads, our occupation's gone.
We put our ideas into words, our words into song.
First comes the cowboy—he's headed for the west.
Of all the pioneers, I claim the cowboy is the best.
We miss him on the roundup, gone is his merry shout.
The cowboy's left the country, and the campfire's going out.

2

No railroads nor grangers, nor anything to mar
Our happiness in camping out or traveling with a star.
Oh, when I think of the good old times, my eyes do sometimes fill.
When I think of the camping out and the coyote on the hill,
Imagination takes me back, I hear their merry shout.
The cowboy's left the sand hills, and the campfire's going out.

3

You freighters and companions will have to leave the land.
You cannot have your loads for nothing through gumbo and through
    sand.
The railroad's bound to beat us, so do your level best;
We'll sell out to the granger and pull out for the west.
Shake hands before you leave us, and give your merry shout.
The cowboy's left the country, and the campfire's going out.

4

In times when freight was higher, old timers had a show.
Their pockets full of money, no sorrow did they know.
But, oh! how times have changed since then, we are poorly clothed
    and fed,
Our wagons are all broken down, our ponies are all dead.
The cowboy and the freighter soon will hear the angel shout:
"Here they have come to heaven, and the campfire has gone out."

TEXT: Unidentified newspaper clipping in the Ballad Collection of Edwin Ford Piper at the Library of the State University of Iowa, Iowa City.

VARIANTS: Lomax (1910), pp. 322-323; Thorp (1921), pp. 20-21.

THE WYOMING NESTER

(or The Dry-Landers)

"Here's luck to all you home-stead-ers._____ You've
tak-en this coun-try at last,__ And I hope you'll suc-ceed in the
fu — ture____ As the cow — boys done in the past."__

1

"Here's luck to all you homesteaders.
You've taken this country at last,
And I hope you succeed in the future
As the cowboys done in the past.

2

"You've homesteaded all of this country,
Where the slicks and the mavericks did
roam;
You've driven me far from my country,
Far from my birthplace and home.

3

"The cattle are still getting thinner,
And the ranches are shorter on men;
But I've got me a full quart of whisky
And nearly a full quart of gin.

4

"You have taken up all of the water
And all of the land that's near by"—
And he took a big drink from his bottle
Of good old '99 rye.

5

He rode far into the evening;
His limbs at last had grown tired.
He shifted himself in his saddle
And he slowly hung down his head.

6

His saddle he used for a pillow;
His blanket he used for a bed.
As he lay himself down for a night's slumber,
These words he to himself then said:

7

"I'm leaving this grand state forever,
This land and the home of my birth.
It fills my heart with sorrow,
But it fills your heart with mirth."

Used by permission of the Texas Folklore Society.

TEXT AND MUSIC: Dobie (1928), pp. 175-176.

VARIANTS: Patterson and Dexter (1932), pp. 15-16; Federal Writers' Project (1938a),
p. 6; Lomax and Lomax (1938), pp. 306-307; Wylder (1949), pp. 61-62; Botkin (1951),
p. 762.

CHARLIE JOHNSON   # THE OLD COWBOY

1

I rode a line on the open range
    When cowpunching wasn't slow;
I've turned the longhorned cow one way,
    And the other the buffalo.

2

I went up the trail in the eighties—
    Oh, the hardships I have stood!
I've drank water from cow tracks, boys,
    When you bet it tasted good.

3

I've stood night guard many a night
    In the face of a driving storm,
And sang to them a doleful song,
    While they rattled their hocks and horns.

4

I've been in many a stampede, too;
    I've heard the rumbling noise;
And the light we had to turn them by
    Was the lightning on their horns.

5

But many a boy I worked with then
    Is sleeping on old Boot Hill,
For his last cow drive was made to Dodge
    Over the Jones and Plummer Trail.

6

They're building towns and railroads now
    Where we used to bed our cows;
And the man with the mule, the plow, and the
      hoe
    Is digging up our old bed grounds.

7

The old cowboy has watched the change,
    Has seen the good times come and go;
But the old cowboy will soon be gone
    Just like the buffalo.

TEXT: *Frontier Times* (Bandera, Tex.), Nov., 1925, p. 35. Used by permission.
VARIANTS: Dobie (1928), pp. 164-165; Lomax and Lomax (1938), pp. 93-94.

THE RANGE OF THE BUFFALO

(or The Buffalo Skinners)

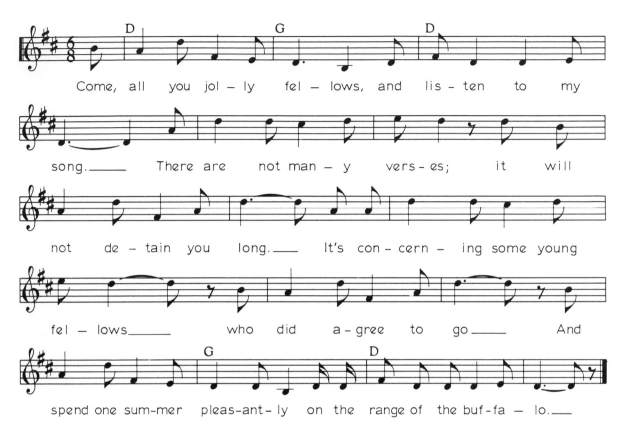

Come, all you jol - ly fel - lows, and lis - ten to my
song.___ There are not man - y vers - es; it will
not de - tain you long.___ It's con - cern - ing some young
fel - lows___ who did a - gree to go___ And
spend one sum-mer pleas-ant-ly on the range of the buf-fa - lo.___

1

Come, all you jolly fellows, and listen to my song.
There are not many verses; it will not detain you long.
It's concerning some young fellows who did agree to go
And spend one summer pleasantly on the range of the buffalo.

2

It happened in Jacksboro in the spring of seventy-three,
A man by the name of Crego came stepping up to me
Saying, "How do you do, young fellow, and how would you like to go
And spend one summer pleasantly on the range of the buffalo?"

3

"It's me being out of employment," this to Crego I did say,
"This going out on the buffalo range depends upon the pay.
But if you will pay good wages and transportation too,
I think, sir, I will go with you to the range of the buffalo."

4

"Yes, I will pay good wages, give transportation too,
Provided you will go with me and stay the summer through;
But if you should grow homesick, come back to Jacksboro,
I won't pay transportation from the range of the buffalo."

5

It's now our outfit was complete—seven able-bodied men,
With navy six and needle gun—our troubles did begin;
Our way it was a pleasant one, the route we had to go,
Until we crossed Pease River on the range of the buffalo.

6

It's now we've crossed Pease River, our troubles have begun.
The first damned tail I went to rip, Christ! how I cut my thumb!
While skinning the damned old stinkers, our lives wasn't a show,
For the Indians watched to pick us off while skinning the buffalo.

7

He fed us on such sorry chuck I wished myself most dead.
It was old jerked beef, croton coffee, and sour bread.
Pease River's as salty as hell fire, the water I could never go—
O God! I wished I had never come to the range of the buffalo.

8

Our meat it was buffalo hump and iron wedge bread,
And all we had to sleep on was a buffalo robe for a bed.
The fleas and gray-backs worked on us—O boys, it was not slow—
I'll tell you there's no worse hell on earth than the range of the
    buffalo.

9

Our hearts were cased with buffalo hocks, our souls were cased
    with steel,
And the hardships of that summer would nearly make us reel.
While skinning the damned old stinkers, our lives they had no show,
For the Indians waited to pick us off on the hills of Mexico.

10

The season being near over, old Crego he did say
The crowd had been extravagant, was in debt to him that day.
We coaxed him and we begged him and still it was no go—
We left old Crego's bones to bleach on the range of the buffalo.

11

Oh, it's now we've crossed Pease River and homeward we are bound,
No more in that hell-fired country shall ever we be found.
Go home to our wives and sweethearts, tell others not to go,
For God's forsaken the buffalo range and the damned old buffalo.

TEXT: Lomax (1910), pp. 158-161.

MUSIC: Larkin (1931), p. 84. Used by permission of Alfred A. Knopf, Inc.

VARIANTS: Thorp (1908), pp. 31-33; Pound (1922), pp. 181-183; Sandburg (1927), pp. 270-272; Sires (1928), pp. 34-35; Larkin (1931), pp. 84-86; Clark (1932), pp. 9-10; Allen (1933), pp. 109-111; Frey (1936), pp. 70-71; Lomax and Lomax (1934), pp. 390-392, (1938), pp. 335-338, and (1947), pp. 174-175; Dobie (1943), pp. 5-6; Wylder (1949), pp. 78-79; Fowke and Glazer (1960), pp. 120-121; Moore and Moore (1964), pp. 289-291; Laws (1964), pp. 137-138*; Fife and Fife (1966), pp. 195-218*.

THE BUFFALO HUNTERS

TUNE: Sam Bass

Come, all you pret-ty girls, to you these lines I'll write: We are go-ing to the range in which we take de — light; We are go-ing on the range,— as we poor hunt-ers do, And the ten — der — foot — ed fel — lows can stay at home with you.

1

Come, all you pretty girls, to you these lines I'll write:
We are going to the range in which we take delight;
We are going on the range, as we poor hunters do,
And the tender-footed fellows can stay at home with you.

2

It's all of the day long, as we go tramping round
In search of the buffalo that we may shoot him down,
Our guns upon our shoulders, our belts of forty rounds.
We send them up Salt River to some happy hunting grounds.

3

Our game, it is the antelope, the buffalo, wolf, and deer,
Who roam the wide prairies without a single fear;
We rob him of his robe, and think it is no harm,
To buy us food and clothing to keep our bodies warm.

4

The buffalo, he is the noblest of the band.
He sometimes rejects in throwing up his hand.
His shaggy main thrown forward, his head raised to the sky,
He seems to say, "We're coming, boys, so hunter, mind your eye."

5

Our fires are made of mesquite roots, our beds are on the ground;
Our houses made of buffalo hides, we make them tall and round;
Our furniture is the camp kettle, the coffee pot, and pan;
Our chuck it is both bread and meat, mingled well with sand.

6

Our neighbors are the Cheyennes, the 'Rapahoes, and Sioux.
Their mode of navigation is a buffalo-hide canoe.
And when they come upon you, they take you unaware,
And such a peculiar way they have of raising hunter's hair.

TEXT: Siringo (1919), pp. 19-20.

MUSIC: As sung by Lannis F. Sutton, Library of Congress Recording L 30. Transcribed by David Cohen.

VARIANTS: Lomax (1910), pp. 185-186; Haley (1927), p. 203; Lomax and Lomax (1938), pp. 343-344.

D. J. O'MALLEY # COWBOY REVERIE

1

Tonight as I rode 'round my cattle,
    I thought of my once cozy home,
So full of the little one's prattle,
    And wondered how I came to roam.

2

To leave the dear home of my childhood
    Cost my poor heart a great deal of pain,
But now my mind's fixed on one happy thought:
    I'll soon see my dear ones again.

3

No more will I be a wild cowboy,
    But I'll live like a man ought to do,
And sit by the stove when the chilly winds blow
    And not freeze myself through and through.

4

No more will I ride on the night guard
    When loud Heaven's thunders do roar.
No. I'll pound my ear down on a goose hair
    And think me of third guard no more.

5

No more will the cook's call to "grub pile"
    Cause me from my hard bed to creep.
No. I'll wait till the gong sounds at seven
    To rouse from my innocent sleep.

6

No more festive calves will I wrestle
    So close by the hot branding fire.
I'll have no hide knocked off my knuckles,
    For that always did rouse my ire.

7

When the rain's coming down, my slicker I'll have
    And not leave it lying in camp,
For in herding without one when Fall rains are here,
    A cowboy most always feels damp.

8

Now look at that long-horned son-of-a-gun,
    Up that draw now he's going to sneak.
I wish I could run him plumb off that cut-bank
    And break his blamed neck in the creek.

9

Get back in the bunch, blame your trifling hide,
    Or with you it will go mighty hard.
What's that, Jim? Ten minutes of twelve did you say?
    Well, go in and call up the third guard.

TEXT: *Stock Growers' Journal* (Miles City, Mont.), May 14, 1892.

VARIANT: O'Malley (1934), p. 16.

THE INVASION SONG

1

Sad and dismal is the tale
    I now relate to you.
'Tis all about the cattlemen,
    Them and their murderous crew.
They started out on their man hunt,
    Precious blood to spill,
With a gang of hired assassins
    To murder at their will.

CHORUS: God bless poor Nate and Nick
    Who gave their precious lives
To save the town of Buffalo,
    Its brave men and their wives.
If it hadn't been for Nate and Nick,
    What would we have come to?
We would have all been murdered
    by
    Frank Canton and his crew.

2

Poor Nate Champion is no more.
    He lost his precious life.
He lies down in the valley
    Freed from all care and strife.
He tried to run the gantlet
    When they had burned his home,
And Nick was lying lifeless,
    Lips wet with bloody foam.

3

The run was made; his doom was sealed,
    A fact you all know well.
They left his lifeless body there
    On the slope, above the dell.
No kindred near to care for him,
    To grasp his nerveless hand;
A braver man was never faced
    By Canton's bloody band.

4

The very next name upon the list
    Was that of brave Jack Flagg.
Frank Canton must have surely thought
    That he would "fill his bag."
Jack and his stepson came in view
    A-riding round the curve;
"Throw up your hands! By God they're off!"
    Frank Canton lost his nerve.

5

"Red Angus" next, the "Canny Scot,"
    Was marked for Canton's lead;
But Angus, warned by bold Jack Flagg,
    For aid and succor, sped.
The countryside now swarmed to life;
    The settlers armed in haste.
Soon Red had hundreds at his back
    Who Canton's minions faced.

6

To Crazy Woman's winding bank,
    The cowed invaders fled
With K.C. blazing in their rear,
    And Ray and Champion dead.
Here, held at bay the cravens halt
    Till soldiers come to aid;
And now secure in jail they rest,
    The debt of blood, unpaid.

TEXT: Davidson (1947), pp. 115-118. Used by permission of California Folklore Society.
VARIANTS: Davidson (1951), pp. 59-61; Burt (1958a), pp. 173-174.

HOME, SWEET HOME

HENRY BISHOP

TUNE: Home, Sweet Home

We were ly - ing on a prair - ie On Slaugh-ter's ranch one night, With our heads up - on our sad - dles While the fire was burn - ing bright. Some were tel - ling stor — ies, And some were sing - ing songs, While oth - ers were id — ly smok - ing As the long hours rolled a — long.

1

We were lying on a prairie
    On Slaughter's ranch one night,
With our heads upon our saddles
    While the fire was burning bright.
Some were telling stories,
    And some were singing songs,
While others were idly smoking
    As the long hours rolled along.

2

At last we fell to talking
    Of distant friends so dear,
When a boy raised up in his saddle
    And brushed away a tear.
"Now, though it's only a Kansas dugout
    I left behind to roam,
I'd give my saddle and my pony
    To be at home, sweet home."

416

3

We all asked why he had left his home,
  If it was so dear to him.
He looked the rough crowd over
  And spoke in a voice that was dim.
"I fell in love with a neighbor girl,
  Her cheeks were soft and white.
Another feller loved her too;
  It ended in a fight.

4

"This feller his name was Thomas Jones—
  We'd known each other from boys;
We had rode each other's horses;
  We had shared each other's joys.
Tom was tall and slender;
  His face was young and fair;
His eyes were the color of heaven;
  He had dark curly hair.

5

"Oh now it makes me shudder
  To think of that awful night.
When Tom and I began fighting,
  I stuck him with my knife.
I fell right down on my knees
  And tried to stop the blood
That from his side came spurting
  All in a crimson flood.

6

"And now whenever I sleep,
  I dream I hear him say:
'Bob, old boy, you'll be sorry—
  I'll be gone before it's day.'
Now, boys, you can see the reason
  Why I am compelled to roam;
But I'd give my pony and saddle
  To be at home, sweet home."

Used by permission of the Texas Folklore Society.

TEXT: Dobie (1927), pp. 165-166.

MUSIC: *Most Popular College Songs* (1904), p. 89.

VARIANTS: Larkin (1931), pp. 144-145; Lomax and Lomax (1938), pp. 124-125; Randolph (1948), pp. 204-207; Laws (1964), p. 136*.

THE DYING COWBOY

As on many other matters, the cowboy's songs and Hollywood's films do not agree on the most common manner of the cowboy's going out. Being crushed by his own horse was a far more common conclusion to the cowboy's average working life of seven years than being gunslung. The threat to his mount of chuckholes, stampedes, and things in the night was permanent, and he sang about it. We begin, however, with the most familiar, albeit exceptional, dirges. "The Dying Cowboy" is an adaptation of "The Ocean Burial." The older song appeared in the *Southern Literary Messenger* in 1839 and is still current in the East. The cowboy version appeared in the 1870's and has survived many candidates for its authorship. The song is not specific about the cause of the cowboy's death; it implies that he just wasted away. "The Cowboy's Lament," one of dozens of wild Irish oats sown by the "Unfortunate Rake," is more specific about what killed him, and it turns out to have been a long series of things.

A shorter version than we print of "The Cowboy's Dream" was claimed by D. J. O'Malley. It was astonishingly popular and very effective in its governing metaphor:

> The trail to that bright, mystic region
> Is narrow and dim, so they say;
> But the broad road that leads to perdition
> Is staked and is blazed all the way.

Beginning here with O'Malley's "Charlie Rutledge," we encounter a spate of songs about that fatal fall beneath a horse. Before he saw the shining throne of grace, Charlie worked for the huge XIT in the Panhandle which ran cattle on 3 million fenced acres. The same author's "When Work Is Done This Fall" tells a similar story of a puncher who swore to give it up and go home. "That very night this cowboy went on guard"— the rest is foregone.

Thorp's "Little Joe, the Wrangler," is his best effort. The *remuda* accompanying a trail herd was often tended by a youth, and we can see Thorp's hand in the irrelevant interest in the boy's upbringing. The actual story begins when Little Joe tries to turn a stampede, and ends: "Beneath his horse mashed to a pulp; his horse had rung the knell." The line reminds us of the follow-up song called "Little Joe the Wrangler's Sister Nell."

"They're all alike at the bottom" mutters the narrator of "I've Got No Use for the Women." One of these women may have turned his young pal into a gunman and gambler, but it was normal Western chivalry that instructed him to fill with lead the rascal who insulted her picture. Better evidence of his alienation is his uncommon wish to be buried on the lone prairie:

> Wrap me up in my blankets,
> And bury me deep in the ground.
> Cover me over with boulders
> Of granite gray and round.

"Utah Carroll" is another death-by-stampede story, but it increases the heroic factor by Utah's rescue of a little girl in the cattle's path. Being a cowboy required that kind of courage and evoked that sort of sentimental fantasy. "Blood on the Saddle" reduces the cowboy to nothing but a "big blob of gore":

> Our friend, the brave cowboy,
> Is cold now and dead,
> For his sure-footed pinto
> Has fell on his head.

THE DYING COWBOY

TUNE: The Ocean Burial

"Oh! bur-y me not on the lone prai-rie!" These words came low and mourn-ful-ly From the pal-lied lips of a youth who lay On his dy-ing bed at the close of day.

Chorus

Oh! bur-y me not on the lone prai-rie Where the wild coy-otes will howl o'er me, Where the rat-tle-snakes hiss and the crow sports free! Oh bur-y me not on the lone prair—ie.

1
"Oh! bury me not on the lone prairie!"
These words came low and mournfully
From the pallid lips of a youth who lay
On his dying bed at the close of day.

CHORUS: Oh! bury me not on the lone prairie
Where the wild coyotes will howl o'er me,
Where the rattlesnakes hiss and the crow sports free—
Oh! bury me not on the lone prairie.

2
He had wasted and pined till o'er his brow
Death's shadows were gathering thickly now;
And he thought of his home as the end drew nigh
And the cowboys gathered to see him die.

CHORUS: Oh! bury me not on the lone prairie
In a narrow grave just six by three,
Where the buzzard waits and the wind blows free—
Oh! bury me not on the lone prairie.

3

It matters not, so I've been told,
Where the body lies when the heart grows cold;
Yet grant, oh! grant this boon to me,
And bury me not on the lone prairie.

CHORUS: Oh! bury me not on the lone prairie,
Where the wild coyotes will howl o'er me;
In a narrow grave just six by three—
Oh! bury me not on the lone prairie.

4

I had always hoped to be laid when I died
In the old churchyard on the green hillside.
By my father's grave, oh! bury me,
And bury me not on the lone prairie.

CHORUS: Oh! bury me not on the lone prairie
Where the wild coyotes will howl o'er me,
Where the blizzard beats and the wind goes free—
Oh! bury me not on the lone prairie.

5

Oh! bury me where a mother's prayer
And a sister's tears may mingle there,
Where my friends may come and weep o'er me—
And bury me not on the lone prairie.

CHORUS: Oh! bury me not on the lone prairie.
In a lonely grave just six by three;
For the sake of those who will mourn for me,
Oh! bury me not on the lone prairie.

6

Oh! bury me not—but his voice failed there,
And they took no heed of his dying prayer;
In a narrow grave just six by three,
They buried him there on the lone prairie.

CHORUS: They buried him there on the lone prairie,
Where the owl all night hoots mournfully;
And the blizzard beats and the wind blows free
O'er his lowly grave on the lone prairie.

TEXT: Hall (1908), pp. 219-220.

MUSIC: As sung by Sloan Matthews, Library of Congress Recording L28. Transcribed by David Cohen.

VARIANTS: Stanley (1897), p. 25; Owen Wister, *Lin McLean* (New York: Harper & Bros., 1898), p. 217; Ellis, (1901), p. 186; Lomax (1910), pp. 3-8; Coolidge (1912), p. 506; Pound (1915), p. 27; Siringo (1919), pp. 5-8; Thorp (1921), pp. 62-63; Pound (1922), pp. 171-172; Barnes (1925), p. 125; Sandburg (1927), p. 20; Dobie (1927), pp. 173-183*; Sires (1928), pp. 52-55; Dick (1928), p. 94; Larkin (1931), pp. 22-23; Clark (1932), pp. 24, 53; Allen (1933), pp. 115-117; Klickman and Sherwin (1933), p. 42; Frey (1936), pp. 88-89; Lomax and Lomax (1938), pp. 48-51; Hull (1939), pp. 47-48; Belden (1940), pp. 387-392*; McMullen (1946), pp. 97-98; Lomax and Lomax (1947), pp. 208-209; Randolph (1948), pp. 184-187*; Wylder (1949), pp. 32-33; Paredes (1959), pp. 88-92*; Hubbard (1961), pp. 313-314; Moore and Moore (1964), pp. 307-309; Laws (1964), p. 134*.

LITTLE JOE, THE WRANGLER

TUNE: Little Old Log Cabin in the Lane

1. Lit – tle Joe, the wran – gler, will nev – er wran – gle more; His days with the "re – mu – da," they are done. 'Twas a year a – go last A – pril he joined the out – fit here, A lit – tle "Tex – as Stray" and all a – lone.

2. 'Twas long late in the eve – ning he rode up to the herd On a lit – tle old brown po – ny he called Chaw; With his bro – gan shoes and o – ver-alls, a hard – er – look – ing kid You nev – er in your life had seen be – fore.

1

Little Joe, the wrangler, will never wrangle more;
 His days with the "remuda," they are done.
'Twas a year ago last April he joined the outfit here,
 A little "Texas Stray" and all alone.

2

'Twas long late in the evening he rode up to the herd
 On a little old brown pony he called Chaw;
With his brogan shoes and overalls, a harder-looking kid
 You never in your life had seen before.

3

His saddle, 'twas a southern kack built many years ago;
 An O. K. spur on one foot idly hung,
While his "hot roll" in a cotton sack was loosely tied behind,
 And a canteen from the saddle horn he'd slung.

4

He said he'd had to leave his home—his daddy'd married twice,
 And his new ma beat him every day or two—
So he saddled up old Chaw one night and "lit a shuck" this way,
 Thought he'd try and paddle now his own canoe.

5

Said he'd try and do the best he could if we'd only give him work,
 Though he didn't know "straight" up about a cow,
So the boss, he cut him out a mount and kinder put him on,
 For he sorter liked the little stray somehow.

6

Taught him how to herd the horses and to learn to know them all,
 To round 'em up by daylight if he could,
To follow the chuck-wagon, and to always hitch the team
 And help the "cosinero" rustle wood.

7

We'd driven to Red River and the weather had been fine;
 We were camped down on the south side in a bend
When a norther commenced blowing and we doubled up our guards
 For it took all hands to hold the cattle then.

8

Little Joe, the wrangler, was called out with the rest
 And scarcely had the kid got to the herd
When the cattle they stampeded. Like a hail storm, long they flew,
 And all of us were riding for the lead.

9

'Tween the streaks of lightning, we could see a horse far out ahead;
 'Twas little Joe the wrangler in the lead.
He was riding "old Blue Rocket" with his sticker 'bove his head
 Trying to check the leaders in their speed.

10

At last we got them milling and kinder quieted down,
    And the extra guard back to the camp did go;
But one of them was missin', and we all knew at a glance
    'Twas our little Texas stray, poor wrangler Joe.

11

Next morning, just at sunup, we found where Rocket fell
    Down in a washout twenty feet below.
Beneath his horse mashed to a pulp; his horse had rung the knell
    For our little Texas stray, poor wrangler Joe.

TEXT: Thorp (1908), pp. 9-11.

MUSIC: "Little Joe, the Wrangler," as sung by Jules Allen, Victor Record 21470 (1928). Transcribed by David Cohen.

VARIANTS: Lomax (1910), pp. 167-171; Thorp (1921), pp. 96-99; Sires (1928), pp. 48-49; German (1929); Larkin (1931), pp. 120-122; Clark (1932), pp. 44-45; Patterson and and Dexter (1932), pp. 27-29; Allen (1933), pp. 65-68; Lomax and Lomax (1938), pp. 91-93; Randolph (1948), pp. 234-237*; Wylder (1949), pp. 27-29; Laws (1964), p. 135*; Fife and Fife (1966), pp. 28-37*.

THE COWBOY'S LAMENT

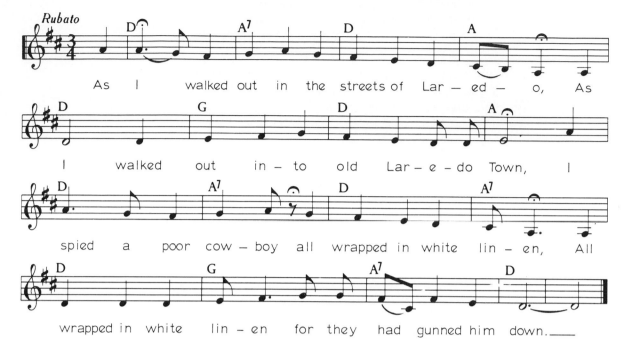

1

As I walked out in the streets of Laredo,
As I walked out into old Laredo Town,
I spied a poor cowboy all wrapped in white linen,
All wrapped in white linen, for they had gunned him down.

2

"Oh, I see by your outfit you are a cowpuncher,"
This poor boy said from his lips of flame red,
"They done gunned me down, boys, and run off and left me
Here in the back street just like I was dead."

3

"Well, I see by your outfit you are a cowpuncher,"
This poor boy says as I boldly step by,
"Come sit down beside me, my story I'll tell you,
Cause I'm a poor cowboy and I'm going to die.

4

"Well, I was born in Southeast Texas,
Where the jimson weed and the lilac does bloom;
I went to go live there for to go far a-ranging,
And I've trailed from Canady down to old Mexico.

5

"'Twas once in the saddle I used to go dashing,
'Twas once in the saddle I used to go gay;
'Twas first down to the dram house and then down to Maisy's,
I'se shot in the breast and I'm dying today.

6

"Well, go write a letter to my grey-haired mother;
Go pen me a note to my sister so dear;
But there is another more dear than a mother,
Who'll bitterly weep when she knows that I'm hurt.

7

"Get sixteen cowboys to carry my coffin.
Get sixteen pretty ladies to bear up my pall.
Put roses all over the top of my coffin
To deaden the smell as they bear me along.

8

"Oh, swing the rope slowly and ring your spurs lowly,
And play the dead march as you bear me along.
Take me to the green valley; there lay the sod o'er me
'Cause I'm a poor cowboy and I know I've done wrong."

TEXT AND MUSIC: As sung by Harry Jackson, *The Cowboy: His Songs, Ballads and Brag Talk*, Folkways Record FH 5723. Transcribed by David Cohen.

VARIANTS: Thorp (1908), p. 29; Hall (1908), p. 217; Will (1909), p. 259; Lomax (1910), pp. 74-76; Pound (1915), p. 26; Thorp (1921), pp. 41-44; Pound (1922), pp. 170-171; Barnes (1925), p. 125; Sandburg (1927), p. 263; Sires (1928), pp. 4-5; German (1929); Larkin (1931), pp. 14-15; Clark (1932), pp. 10-11; Patterson and Dexter (1932), pp. 10-11; Allen (1933), pp. 118-120; Klickman and Sherwin (1933), pp. 27-28; Frey (1936), p. 55; Federal Writers' Project (1937a), pp. 3-4; Coolidge (1937), pp. 130-132; Lomax and Lomax (1938), pp. 417-420; Hull (1939), pp. 49-50; Belden (1940), pp. 392-397*; McMullen (1946), p. 98; Lomax and Lomax (1947), pp. 206-207; Randolph (1948), pp. 179-181*; Botkin (1951), pp. 766-767; Lodewick (1955), pp. 98-109*; Lomax (1960), pp. 384-385; Hubbard (1961), p. 310*; Moore and Moore (1964), pp. 309-310; Laws (1964), p. 133*; Fife and Fife (1966), pp. 148-190*.

THE COWBOY'S DREAM

H. J. FULLER

TUNE: My Bonnie Lies over the Ocean

1

Last night as I lay on the prairie
   And looked up to the stars in the sky,
I wondered if ever a cowboy
   Would drift to that Sweet Bye and Bye.

CHORUS: Roll on, roll on;
   Roll on, little dogies, roll on, roll on;
   Roll on, roll on;
   Roll on, little dogies, roll on.

2

The trail to that bright, mystic region
   Is narrow and dim, so they say;
But the broad road that leads to perdition
   Is staked and is blazed all the way.

3

They say there will be a great round-up,
    And the cowboys like dogies will stand
To be marked by the Riders of Judgment,
    Who are posted and know every brand.

4

I wonder was there ever a cowboy
    All right for that great judgment day,
Who could say to the Boss of the Riders,
    "I'm ready, come drive me away?"

5

For they're all like the cows that are locoed,
    That stampede at the sight of a hand,
And are dragged with a rope to the round-up,
    Or get marked with some crooked man's brand.

6

I know there's many a stray cowboy
    Who'll be lost at that great final sale,
When he might have gone in to green pasture
    If he'd heard of that bright, mystic trail.

7

And I'm scared I will be a stray yearling,
    A maverick, unbranded on high,
And get cut in the bunch with the "rusties,"
    When the Boss of the Riders goes by.

8

For they tell of another big owner,
    Who is ne'er over-stocked, so they say,
But who always makes room for the sinner
    Who drifts from that straight, narrow way.

9

And they say he will never forget you,
    That he knows every action and look;
So for safety you'd better get branded—
    Have your name in the big Tally Book.

TEXT: Hall (1908), p. 218.

MUSIC: *Most Popular College Songs* (1904), p. 11.

VARIANTS: E. D. Smith, "The Passing of the Cattle-Trail," *Kansas Historical Collection*, X, (1908), 583; Thorp (1908), p. 19; Lomax (1910), pp. 18-19; Pound (1915), p. 27, and (1922), pp. 166-167; Thorp (1921), pp. 40-41; Barnes (1925), p. 125; Finger (1927), pp. 101-103; Sires (1928), pp. 24-25; Dick (1928), pp. 94-95; Larkin (1931), pp. 100-102; Clark (1932), pp. 20-21; Allen (1933), pp. 91-93; Klickman and Sherwin (1933), pp. 43-45; O'Malley (1934), p. 10; Frey (1936), pp. 84-85; Pound (1939), p. 26; Lomax and Lomax (1938), pp. 45-48, and (1947), pp. 210-211; Koch and Koch (1961), pp. 20-21; Moore and Moore (1964), pp. 305-307; Fife and Fife (1966), pp. 66-86*.

D. J. O'MALLEY

CHARLIE RUTLEDGE

TUNE: Lake Pontchartrain

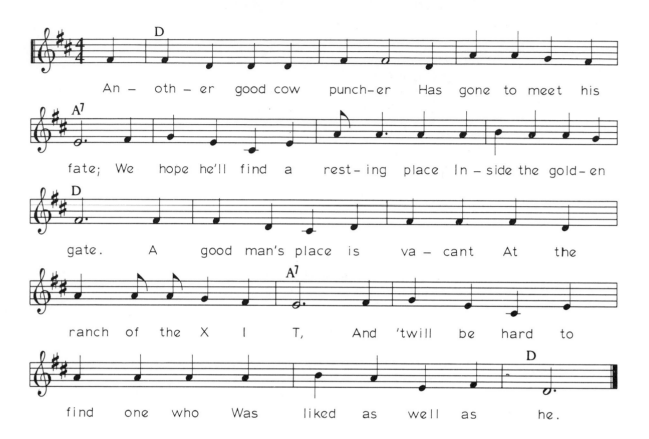

An — oth — er good cow punch—er Has gone to meet his
fate; We hope he'll find a rest—ing place In — side the gold—en
gate. A good man's place is va — cant At the
ranch of the X I T, And 'twill be hard to
find one who Was liked as well as he.

1

Another good cow puncher
 Has gone to meet his fate;
We hope he'll find a resting place
 Inside the golden gate.
A good man's place is vacant
 At the ranch of the X I T,
And 'twill be hard to find one who
 Was liked as well as he.

2

First "Kid" White of the Flying E;
 Then Preller, young and brave;
Now Charlie Rutledge makes the third
 That has been sent to his grave
By a cow-horse falling on him
 Whils't running after stock
This spring, while on the round-up
 Where death a man does mock.

3

How blithely he went forth that morn
    On the circle through the hills,
Happy, gay and full of life
    And free from earthly ills;
And when they came to clean the bunch,
    To work it he was sent,
Not thinking that his time on earth
    Was very nearly spent.

4

But one X I T would not go
    And turned back in the herd,
So Charlie shoved him out again—
    His cutting horse he spurred.
Another started to come back;
    To head him off he hied.
  The creature fell, the horse was thrown,
    And 'neath him Charlie died.

5

'Twas a sad death for man to meet
    Out on that lonely lea.
His relatives in Texas live—
    No more his face they'll see;
But we hope the Father greets him
    With a smile upon his face,
And seats him by His right hand
    Near the shining throne of grace.

TEXT: *Stock Growers' Journal* (Miles City, Mont.), July 11, 1891.

MUSIC: "Bayou Bluegrass," as sung by the Louisiana Honeydrippers, Folk-Lyric Record FL 122. Transcribed by David Cohen.

VARIANTS: Lomax (1910), pp. 267-268; Sires (1928), pp. 16-17; Clark (1932), p. 13; O'Malley (1934), p. 9; Lomax and Lomax (1938), p. 82; Wylder (1949), pp. 22-23.

D. J. O'MALLEY

WHEN WORK IS DONE THIS FALL

A group of jol-ly cow-boys dis - cussed their plans at

ease. Said one, "I'll tell some - thing, boys,

if___ you___ please. See, I'm a punch-er,

dressed most in rags. I used to be a wild one and

took on big jags. I have a home, boys, a

good one, you know; But I have-n't seen it since

long, long a - go. But I'm go - ing home, boys, once

more to see them all; Yes, I'll go back

home when work is done this fall."_____

1

A group of jolly cowboys discussed their plans at ease.
Said one, "I'll tell something, boys, if you listen please.
See, I'm a puncher, dressed most in rags.
I used to be a wild one and took on big jags.

I have a home, boys, a good one, you know;
But I haven't seen it since long, long ago.
But I'm going home, boys, once more to see them all;
Yes, I'll go back home when work is done this fall.

CHORUS: "After the roundup's over, after the shipping's done,
I'm going straight back home, boys, ere all my money's gone.
My mother's dear heart is breaking, breaking for me, that all;
But, with God's help I'll see her, when work is done this fall.

2

"When I left my home, boys, for me she cried,
Begged me to stay, boys, for me she'd have died.
I haven't used her right, boys; my hard-earned cash I've spent
When I should have saved it and it to my mother sent.
But, I've changed my course, boys, I'll be a better man
And help my poor old mother; I'm sure that I can.
I'll walk in the straight path; no more will I fall;
And I'll see my mother when work's done this fall."

3

That very night this cowboy went on guard.
The night, it was dark and 'twas storming very hard.
The cattle got frightened and rushed in mad stampede.
He tried to check them, riding full speed;
Riding in the darkness, loud he did shout,
Doing his utmost to turn the herd about.
His saddle horse stumbled, on him did fall;
He'll not see his mother when work's done this fall.

4

They picked him up gently and laid him on a bed.
The poor boy was mangled; they thought he was dead.
He opened his blue eyes and gazed all around;
Then motioned his comrades to sit near him on the ground:
"Send her the wages that I have earned.
Boys, I'm afraid that my last steer I've turned.
I'm going to a new range. I hear the Master call.
I'll not see my mother when work's done this fall.

5

"Bill, take my saddle; George, take my bed;
Fred, take my pistol after I am dead.
Think of me kindly when on them you look"—
His voice then grew fainter, with anguish he shook.
His friends gathered closer and on them he gazed,
His breath coming fainter, his eyes growing glazed.
He uttered a few words, heard by them all:
"I'll see my mother when work's done this fall."

TEXT: *Stock Growers' Journal* (Miles City, Mont.), Oct. 6, 1893.
MUSIC: This song was originally written to the tune of "After the Ball," but the tune given here is more common in oral tradition and is sung without the chorus. "When the Work's All Done This Fall," as sung by Carl T. Sprague, Victor Record 19747 (1925). Transcribed by David Cohen.
VARIANTS: Lomax (1910), pp. 53-55; Sandburg (1927), pp. 260-262; Clark (1932), p. 66; Allen (1933), pp. 154-156; Klickman and Sherwin (1933), pp. 40-41; O'Malley (1934), p. 8; Frey (1936), pp. 72-73; Coolidge (1937), pp. 123-125; Federal Writers' Project (1937b), pp. 11-12; Lomax and Lomax (1938), pp. 74-76; Pound (1939), p. 27; Wylder (1949), pp. 19-20; Moore and Moore (1964), pp. 297-300; Laws (1964), pp. 134-135*.

I'VE GOT NO USE FOR THE WOMEN

(or, Bury Me Out on the Prairie)

Now, I've got no use for the wom-en;_____ A
true one may sel-dom be found._____ They
use a man for his mon-ey;_____ When it's
gone, they'll turn him down._____ They're all a-
like at the bot-tom,_____ Self-ish and
grasp-ing for all._____ They'll stay by a
man while he's win-ning,_____ And
laugh in his face at his fall._____

1

Now, I've got no use for the women;
A true one may seldom be found.
They use a man for his money;
When it's gone, they'll turn him down.
They're all alike at the bottom,
Selfish and grasping for all.
They'll stay by a man while he's winning,
And laugh in his face at his fall.

2

My pal was an honest young puncher,
Honest and upright and true;
But he turned to a hard-shooting gun-man
On account of a girl named Lou.
He fell in with evil companions,
The kind that are better off dead;
When a gambler insulted her picture,
He filled him full of lead.

3

All through the long night they trailed him,
Through mesquite and thick chaparral;
And I couldn't help think of that woman
As I saw him pitch and fall.
If she'd been the pal that she should have,
He might have been raising a son
Instead of out there on the prairie
To die by the ranger's gun.

4

Death's sharp sting did not trouble;
His chances for life were too slim;
But where they were putting his body
Was all that worried him.
He lifted his head on his elbow;
The blood from his wounds flowed red.
He gazed at his pals grouped about him,
As he whispered to them and said:

5

"Oh, bury me out on the prairie,
Where the coyotes may howl o'er my grave.
Bury me out on the prairie,
But from them my bones please save.
Wrap me up in my blankets,
And bury me deep in the ground.
Cover me over with boulders
Of granite gray and round."

6

So we buried him out on the prairie,
Where the coyotes can howl o'er his grave;
And his soul is now a-resting
From the unkind cut she gave.
And many another young puncher,
As he rides past that pile of stone,
Recalls some similar woman
And thinks of his mouldering bones.

TEXT AND MUSIC: Clark (1932), pp. 42-43. Used by permission of Shawnee Press Inc.

VARIANTS: Federal Writers' Project (1938*b*), pp. 10-12; Lomax and Lomax (1938), pp. 300-302; Hull (1939), pp. 50-51; Federal Writers' Project (1940), pp. 7-8; Hendrix (1944), pp. 29-33*; Wylder (1949), pp. 65-66.

UTAH CARROLL

Oh,   kind friend, you may   ask me what makes me sad and

still, And   why   my brow is   dark-ened like clouds up-on   a

hill.   Run   in   your po — ny   clos-er, and   I'll tell you the

tale Of U - tah Car-roll, my part-ner, and his last ride on the   trail.

1

Oh, kind friend, you may ask me what makes me sad and still,
And why my brow is darkened like clouds upon a hill.
Run in your pony closer, and I'll tell you the tale
Of Utah Carroll, my partner, and his last ride on the trail.

2

In a grave without a headstone, without a date or name,
Quietly lies my partner in the land from which I came.
Long, long we rode together, had ridden side by side;
I loved him as a brother; I wept when Utah died.

3

While rounding up one morning—our work was almost done—
The cattle quickly started on a wild and maddening run.
The boss's little daughter, who was riding on that side,
Rushed in to stop the stampede; 'twas there poor Utah died.

4

Lenore upon her pony tried to turn the cattle right.
Her blanket slipped beneath her, but she caught and held on tight;
But when we saw that blanket, each cowboy held his breath,
For should her pony fail her, none could save the girl from death.

5

When the cattle saw the blanket almost dragging on the ground,
They were maddened in a moment and charged with deafening sound.
The girl soon saw her danger; she turned her pony's face,
And bending in her saddle tried the blanket to replace.

6

Just then she lost her balance in front of that wild tide.
Carroll's voice controlled the round-up; "Lie still, little girl," he cried.
And then close up beside her came Utah riding fast,
But little did the poor boy know that ride would be his last.

7

Full often from the saddle had he caught the trailing rope;
To pick her up at full speed was now his only hope.
He swung low from his saddle to take her to his arm;
We thought that he'd succeeded, that the girl was safe from harm.

8

Such a strain upon his saddle had never been put before;
The cinches gave beneath him and he fell beside Lenore.
When the girl fell from her pony, she had dragged the blanket down;
It lay there close beside her where she lay upon the ground.

9

Utah took it up again and to Lenore he said,
"Lie still," and quickly running waved the red thing o'er his head.
He turned the maddened cattle from Lenore, his little friend.
As the mighty herd rushed toward him, he turned to meet his end.

10

And as the herd came on him, his weapon quickly drew—
He was bound to die defended as all brave cowboys do.
The weapon flashed like lightning; it sounded loud and clear.
As the cattle rushed and killed him, he dropped the leading steer.

11

When I broke through that wide circle to where poor Utah lay—
With a thousand wounds and bruises his life blood ebbed away—
I knelt down close beside him and I knew that all was o'er
As I heard him faintly whisper, "Goodbye, my sweet Lenore."

12

Next morning at the church yard I heard the preacher say,
"Don't think our kind friend Utah was lost on that great day.
He was a much-loved cowboy and not afraid to die,
And we'll meet him at the round-up on the plains beyond the sky."

TEXT AND MUSIC: Larkin (1931), pp. 116-118. Used by permission of Alfred A. Knopf. Inc.

VARIANTS: Lomax (1910), pp. 66-68; Sires (1928), pp. 6-7; German (1929); Clark (1932), pp 48-49; Patterson and Dexter (1932), pp. 52-53; Allen (1933), pp. 96-98; Frey (1936), pp. 86-87; Lomax and Lomax (1938), pp. 125-128; Randolph (1948), pp. 239-241; Wylder (1949), pp. 16-17; Botkin (1951), pp. 760-761; Fife and Fife (1956), pp. 333-336; Moore and Moore (1964), pp. 325-327; Laws (1964), p. 135*.

ONLY A COWBOY

Way out in old Tex-as, that great Lone Star state, Where the
mock-ing bird whis-tles both ear-ly and late; It was in wes-tern
Tex-as, on the old N. A. range, That the boy fell a vic-tim on the
old stak-ed plains. *Chorus* He was on-ly a cow-boy that's gone on be-fore; He was
on-ly a cow-boy we'll nev-er see more. He was do-ing his dut-y on the
old N. A. range, But now he is sleep-ing on the old stak-ed plains.

1

'Way out in old Texas, that great Lone Star State,
Where the mocking bird whistles both early and late;
It was in western Texas, on the old NA range,
That the boy fell a victim on the old staked plains.

CHORUS: He was only a cowboy that's gone on before.
He was only a cowboy we'll never see more.
He was doing his duty on the old NA range,
But now he is sleeping on the old staked plains.

2

His crew, they were numbered twenty seven or eight;
The boys were like brothers; their friendship was great.
When "O God have mercy!" was heard from behind,
The cattle were left to drift on the line.

3

He leaves a dear wife and the little ones too,
To earn them a living, as fathers oft do;
For while he was working for the loved ones so dear,
He was took without warning or one word of cheer.

———————

TEXT AND MUSIC: Clark (1932), p. 50. Used by permission of Shawnee Press Inc.

VARIANTS: Lomax (1910), pp. 124-125; Sires (1928), pp. 10-11; Frey (1936), p. 42; Lomax and Lomax (1938), p. 116; Randolph (1950), p. 126.

BLOOD ON THE SADDLE

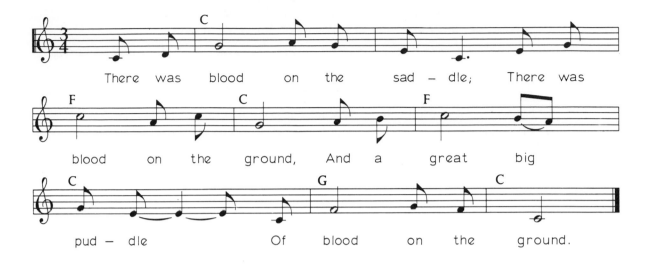

There was blood on the sad-dle; There was
blood on the ground, And a great big
pud-dle Of blood on the ground.

1

There was blood on the saddle;
There was blood on the ground,
And a great big puddle
Of blood on the ground.

2

Now our friend, the brave cowboy,
Will ride never more,
For his head it is nothing
But a big blob of gore.

3

He was born here in Texas,
The best in the land.
Now he's gone to the angels
In the Promised Land.

4

O he had a young sweetheart
He loved once so well,
Whose grief o'er his dying
No tongue e'er can tell.

5

He asked her to marry
One fine night in June;
Now he's left her all lonely
And covered with gloom.

6

Our friend, the brave cowboy,
Is cold now and dead,
For his sure-footed pinto
Has fell on his head.

7

There was blood on the saddle;
There was blood all around,
And a great big puddle
Of blood on the ground.

TEXT AND MUSIC: E. E. Chickering and G. J. Chickering, *Ballads and Songs of Southern Michigan* (Ann Arbor: University of Michigan, 1939), pp. 253-254.

VARIANTS: German (1929); Lomax and Lomax (1938), p. 288; Hull (1939), p. 46.

THE KANSAS EMIGRANT

Farmers were finally able to make the Great Plains productive as the result of a technological efflorescence in the late 1870's. Barbed wire, metal windmills, gangplows, disc harrows, seed drills, binders, and threshing machines made the single-family farm in the West seem as attractive for a while as gold mining and cowpunching had been; but for it to be so, men had to recognize that, as Walter Prescott Webb said, "The salient truth, the essential truth, is that the West cannot be understood as a mere extension of things eastern." That militant pacifist, John Greenleaf Whittier, seems not to have grasped this distinction in his "The Kansas Emigrant," which calls on these emigrant farmers "to make the West, as they [the pilgrims had], the East, The homestead of the free." His notion of freedom was inadequate, too. That it did not include economic emancipation was shown the year after the song text was printed in a Kansas newspaper, when Whittier condemned the nationwide railroad strikes of 1877, dismissing the leaders as demagogues.

Seeking a kind of freedom the East clearly could not give him, Dr. Brewster Higley had fled from his Hoosier home and his scolding wife to Smith County, Kansas. There in the early 1870's he composed "Western Home," now generally recognized as the original of the famous "Home on the Range." The transformation has usually been in the direction of commonsense dilution, most folk versions having pruned verse like

> Oh! give me a gale of the Solomon vale,
> Where the life streams with buoyancy flow;
> Or the banks of the Beaver, where seldom if ever,
> Any poisonous herbage doth grow.

"Immigration Song," composed in 1891 to the tune of "Charles Guiteau," is far more realistic boosting: "The soil is rich and loamy, From three to ten feet deep." But the "Kansas Jayhawker," while equally enthusiastic, begins to locate the real resources in the people: "Neither Jayhawker winds, nor Jayhawker drought Stops the Jayhawker's heart, nor the Jayhawker's mouth."

With the "Kansas Boys," which has Mormon, Texas, and other variants, we begin to get impressions of the hardships attending plains life, particularly in terms of the exactions placed on marriage. It warns all young girls:

> They'll take you out on the jet black hill,
> Take you there so much against your will,
> Leave you there to perish on the plains,
> For that is the way with the Kansas range.

A. L. Stokesberry composed "The Old Bachelor," a favorite still sung by the Carter family, for an Independence Day celebration in Farnsworth, Kansas, in 1887. It combines old Higley's yearn for freedom with a recognition of the difficulties ladies faced in Kansas.

> On Sunday morn I go to church
> Without a wife to storm;
> My latest paper is not rolled up
> To beautify her form.

Finally, "In Kansas" lets the gloom down over all prairie life:

> They say that drink's a sin
> So they guzzle all they kin,
> And they throw it up again
> In Kansas.

JOHN GREENLEAF WHITTIER

THE KANSAS EMIGRANT

TUNE: Auld Lang Syne

1

We cross the prairies as of old
The pilgrims crossed the sea,
To make the West, as they, the East,
The homestead of the free.

CHORUS: The homestead of the free, my boys,
The homestead of the free;
To make the West, as they, the East,
The homestead of the free.

2

We go to rear a wall of men
On Freedom's Southern line,
And plant beside the cotton tree,
The rugged Northern pine!

3

We're flowing from our native hills,
As our free rivers flow;
The blessing of our mother-land
Is on us as we go.

443

4

We go to plant our common schools
　　On distant prairie swells,
And give the Sabbaths of the wild
　　The music of its bells.

5

Upbearing like the ark of old,
　　The Bible in our van,
We go to test the truth of God
　　Against the fraud of man.

6

No pause, nor rest, save where the streams
　　That feed the Kansas run,
Save where our pilgrim gonfalon
　　Shall flout the setting sun.

7

We'll sweep the prairies as of old
　　Our fathers swept the sea,
And make the West, as they, the East,
　　The homestead of the free.

TEXT: *Kirwin Chief* (Kirwin, Kans.), Feb. 26, 1876.
MUSIC: *The Good Old Songs We Used To Sing* (1887), p. 113.
VARIANT: Koch and Koch (1961), p. 8.

DANIEL E. KELLEY   # WESTERN HOME   BREWSTER HIGLEY

1

Oh! give me a home where the buffalo roam,
Where the deer and the antelope play;
Where never is heard a discouraging word,
And the sky is not clouded all day.

CHORUS: A home! A home!
Where the deer and the antelope play,
Where seldom is heard a discouraging word,
And the sky is not clouded all day.

2

Oh! give me land where the bright diamond sand
Throws its light from the glittering streams,
Where glideth along the graceful white swan,
Like the maid in her heavenly dreams.

3

Oh! give me a gale of the Solomon vale,
Where the life streams with bouyancy flow;
Or the banks of the Beaver, where seldom if ever,
Any poisonous herbage doth grow.

4

How often at night, when the heavens were bright
With the light of the twinkling stars,
Have I stood here amazed, and asked as I gazed,
If their glory exceed that of ours.

5

I love the wild flowers in this bright land of ours;
I love the wild curlew's shrill scream;
The bluffs and white rocks, and antelope flocks
That graze on the mountains so green.

6

The air is so pure and the breezes so free,
The zephyrs so balmy and light,
That I would not exchange my home here to range
Forever in azures so bright.

TEXT: *Kirwin Chief* (Kirwin, Kans.), Feb. 26, 1876, reprinted from issue of March 21, 1874.

VARIANTS: Will (1909), pp. 257-258; *Smith County Pioneer* (Smith Center, Kans.), Feb. 19, 1914; McMullen (1946), pp. 82-83; Mechem (1949), pp. 313-339*; Koch and Koch (1961), pp. 8-9; Malone (1961), pp. 141-142. *See also* "Home on the Range."

HOME ON THE RANGE

1

Oh, give me a home where the buffalo roam,
Where the deer and the antelope play;
Where seldom is heard a discouraging word,
And the skies are not cloudy all day.

CHORUS: Home, home on the range,
Where the deer and the antelope play;
Where seldom is heard a discouraging word,
And the skies are not cloudy all day.

2

Where the air is so pure, the zephyrs so free,
The breezes so balmy and light,
That I would not exchange my home on the range
For all of the cities so bright.

3

The red man was pressed from this part of the West;
He's likely no more to return
To the banks of Red River where seldom if ever
Their flickering camp-fires burn.

4

How often at night when the heavens are bright
With the light from the glittering stars,
Have I stood here amazed and asked as I gazed
If their glory exceeds that of ours.

5

Oh, I love these wild flowers in this dear land of ours,
The curlew I love to hear scream,
And I love the white rocks and the antelope flocks
That graze on the mountain-tops green.

6

Oh, give me a land where the bright diamond sand
Flows leisurely down the stream;
Where the graceful white swan goes gliding along
Like a maid in a heavenly dream.

7

Then I would not exchange my home on the range,
Where the deer and the antelope play;
Where seldom is heard a discouraging word,
And the skies are not cloudy all day.

TEXT AND MUSIC: Lomax (1910), pp. 39-43.

VARIANTS: Siringo (1919), pp. 32-33; Sires (1928), pp. 46-47; Larkin (1931), pp. 171-173; Briegel (1933), p. 18; Klickman and Sherwin (1933), pp. 16-17; Allen (1933), pp. 107-108; Frey (1936), pp. 22-23; Lomax and Lomax (1938), pp. 424-428; McMullen (1946), p. 83; Lomax and Lomax (1947), pp. 212-213; Randolph (1948), pp. 210-213; Mechem (1949), pp. 313-339*. *See also* "Western Home."

IMMIGRATION SONG

TUNE: Charlie Guiteau

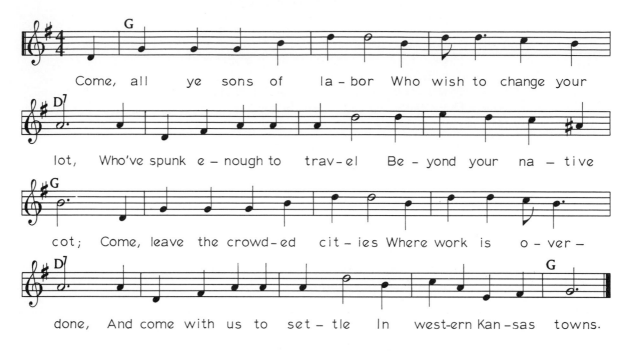

Come, all ye sons of la — bor Who wish to change your

lot, Who've spunk e — nough to trav-el Be — yond your na — tive

cot; Come, leave the crowd-ed cit — ies Where work is o — ver —

done, And come with us to set — tle In west-ern Kan —sas towns.

1

Come, all ye sons of labor
Who wish to change your lot,
Who've spunk enough to travel
Beyond your native cot;
Come, leave the crowded cities
Where work is overdone,
And come with us to settle
In western Kansas towns.

2

The soil is rich and loamy,
From three to ten feet deep;
The subsoil is cement and clay
That will the moisture keep.
'Tis the bed of an inland sea
Drained off a long time ago,
And rich for grain and fruit and vines,
Where ever you may go.

3

What more, ye sons of labor,
Than these can you desire:
Good health, good soil, good neighbors,
A climate all admire?
Two railroads now have we;
Free land is now all gone,
So come with us and settle
In peerless Lane County.

TEXT: *Lane County Farmer* (Dighton, Kans.), Feb. 20, 1891.
MUSIC: "Charles Guiteau," as sung by Kelly Harrell, Victor Record 20797B (1927).
Reissued on Folkways Record FA 2951. Transcribed by David Cohen.

A. L. STOKESBERRY

THE OLD BACHELOR

TUNE: Pure Cold Water

I am a stern old bache-lor; My age is for-ty four. I
do de-clare I'll nev-er live With wom-en an-y more.
Chorus Oh, lit-tle sod shan-ty,_____ Sod shan-ty give to
me, For I'm a stern old bache-lor, From mat-ri-mo-ny free.

1
I am a stern old bachelor;
   My age is forty-four.
I do declare I'll never live
   With women any more.

CHORUS: Oh, little sod shanty,
   Sod shanty give to me,
For I'm a stern old bachelor,
   From matrimony free.

2
I live upon a homestead claim;
   From women I am hid;
I do not have to dress a wife,
   Or take care of a kid.

3
I cook my little dirty bite
   Three times or less a day;
I lick my plates to keep them clean,
   And just shove things away.

4
I have a stove that's worth ten cents,
   A table worth fifteen;
I cook my grub in oyster cans,
   And always have things clean.

5
On Sunday morn I go to church
   Without a wife to storm;
My latest paper is not rolled up
   To beautify her form.

6
I go to bed whene'er I please,
   And get up just the same;
I change my socks three times a year,
   With no one to complain.

7
And when I die and go to heaven
   As all old bachelors do,
I will not have to grieve for fear
   My wife won't get there too.

TEXT: *Dighton Republican* (Dighton, Kans.), July 6, 1887.

MUSIC: "Stern Old Bachelor," as sung by the Carter Family, Decca Record LP 4404. Transcribed by David Cohen.

VARIANTS: Lomax and Lomax (1934), pp. 354-355; Randolph (1949), pp. 246; A. C. Morris, *Folksongs of Florida* (Gainesville: University of Florida, 1950), p. 159.

KANSAS JAYHAWKER
T. A. METZ

TUNE: There'll Be a Hot Time in the Old Town Tonight

I'm a Jay-hawk-er girl from a Jay-hawk-er State; I wear

Jay-hawk-er flow-ers with Jay-hawk-er grace; I sing

Jay-hawk-er songs with a Jay-hawk-er voice, And the

Jay-hawk-er State is___ my own free choice.

Chorus

Don't you hear the voic-es from the West? The

bells, they ring the song that we love best. They

tell of life on that free and hap-py

plain__ There will be a hot time in the old town to-

nite, Jay-hawk-er! Hear it! hear it! So___

strong and so clear! The bells, they ring and the wild prai-ries

450

sing, For the Jay—hawk-er girls and the Jay___ hawk-er

boys All find a warm heart in the old home to—night.

1
I'm a Jayhawker girl from a Jayhawker State;
I wear Jayhawker flowers with Jayhawker grace;
I sing Jayhawker songs with a Jayhawker voice,
And the Jayhawker State is my own free choice.

CHORUS: Don't you hear the voice from the West?
The bells, they ring the song that we love best.
They tell of life on that free and happy plain—
There will be a hot time in the old town tonight, Jayhawker!
Hear it! hear it! So strong and so clear!
The bells, they ring and the wild prairies sing,
For the Jayhawker girls and the Jayhawker boys
All find a warm heart in the old home tonight.

2
I'm a Jayhawker boy from the Jayhawker state;
I wear a Jayhawker hat on a Jayhawker pate;
I ride a Jayhawker horse in a Jayhawker way;
In the Jayhawker state, I am bound for to stay.

3
Oh, the Jayhawker's skies and the Jayhawker's days
Are the Jayhawker's pride and the Jayhawker's praise,
For the Jayhawker knows that the Jayhawker's rains
Fill the Jayhawker's barns with the Jayhawker's grains.

4
So the Jayhawker sows, and the Jayhawker reaps,
And the Jayhawker sings, and the Jayhawker sleeps;
While the Jayhawker's cows and the Jayhawker's shoats
Grow into Jayhawker gold and the Jayhawker notes.

5
Neither Jayhawker winds, nor Jayhawker drought
Stops the Jayhawker's heart, nor the Jayhawker's mouth,
For the Jayhawker's faith is always first rate—
He has Jayhawker's pride in his Jayhawker State!

TEXT: Malone (1961), pp. 142-143. Used by permission of University of Nebraska Press.

MUSIC: *Most Popular Army and Navy Songs* (1912), pp. 43-45. Used by permission of Noble and Noble Publishers Inc.

KANSAS BOYS

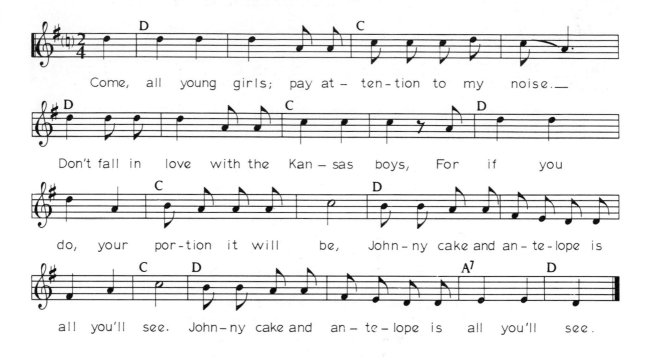

Come, all young girls; pay at - ten-tion to my noise.—

Don't fall in love with the Kan — sas boys, For if you

do, your por-tion it will be, John — ny cake and an - te-lope is

all you'll see. John — ny cake and an — te-lope is all you'll see.

1

Come, all young girls; pay attention to my noise.
Don't fall in love with the Kansas boys,
For if you do, your portion it will be,
Johnny cake and antelope is all you'll see.

2

They'll take you out on the jet black hill,
Take you there so much against your will,
Leave you there to perish on the plains,
For that is the way with the Kansas range.

3

Some live in a cabin with a huge log wall,
Nary a window in it at all,
Sand stone chimney and a puncheon floor,
Clapboard roof and a button door.

4

When they get hungry and go to make bread,
They kindle a fire as high as your head,
Bake around the ashes and in they throw—
The name they give it is "doughboys' dough."

5

When they go to milk, they milk in a gourd,
Heave it in the corner and cover with a board;
Some get plenty and some get none—
That is the way with the Kansas run.

6

When they go to meeting, the clothes that they wear
Is an old brown coat all picked and bare,
An old white hat more rim than crown,
A pair of cotton socks they wore the week around.

7

When they go to farming, you needn't be alarmed!
In February they plant their corn.
The way they tend it. I'll tell you now,
With a Texas pony and a grasshopper plow.

8

When they go a-fishing, they take along a worm,
Put it on the hook just to see it squirm.
The first thing they say when they get a bite
Is, "I caught a fish as big as Johnny White."

9

When they go courting, they take along a chair.
The first thing they say is, "Has your daddy killed a bear?"
The second thing they say, when they sit down,
Is, "Madam, your Johnny cake is baking brown."

TEXT: Sandburg (1927), p. 129. Used by permission of Harcourt, Brace & World, Inc.

MUSIC: *The Lilly Brothers*, Folkways Record FA 2433. Transcribed by David Cohen. Used by permission of Folkways Records & Service Corp.

VARIANTS: Lomax (1910), pp. 108-109; Pound (1915), p. 25, and (1922), pp. 175-176; Federal Writers' Project (1938*a*), pp. 4-5; Lomax and Lomax (1938), pp. 339-342; Belden (1940), pp. 426-428*; Lomax and Lomax (1947), pp. 44-45; Porter (1947), pp. 299-301; Botkin (1951), pp. 783-784; Koch and Koch (1961), pp. 12-13; Moore and Moore (1964), pp. 300-302.

IN KANSAS

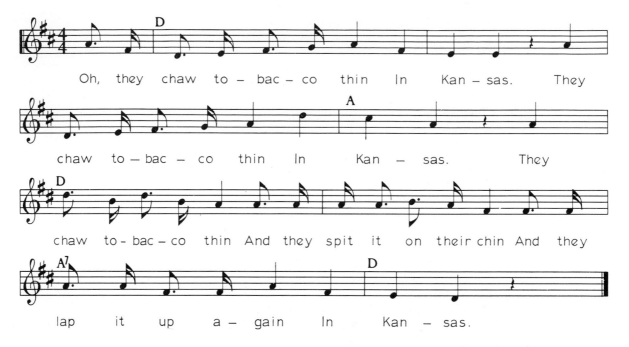

Oh, they chaw to-bac-co thin In Kan-sas. They chaw to-bac-co thin In Kan-sas. They chaw to-bac-co thin And they spit it on their chin And they lap it up a-gain In Kan-sas.

1

Oh, they chaw tobacco thin
    In Kansas.
They chaw tobacco thin
    In Kansas.
They chaw tobacco thin
And they spit it on their chin
And they lap it up agin
    In Kansas.

2

Oh, they churn the butter well
    In Kansas.
They churn the butter well
    In Kansas.
They churn the butter well
And the buttermilk they sell
And they get as lean as hell
    In Kansas.

3

Oh, potatoes, they grow small
    In Kansas.
Potatoes, they grow small
    In Kansas.

Oh, potatoes, they grow small
And they dig 'em in the fall
And they eat 'em hides and all
    In Kansas.

4

Oh, they say that drink's a sin
    In Kansas.
They say that drink's a sin
    In Kansas.
They say that drink's a sin
So they guzzle all they kin,
And they throw it up again
    In Kansas.

5

Come, all who want to roam
    To Kansas.
Come, all who want to roam
    To Kansas.
Come all who want to roam
And seek yourself a home
And be happy with your doom
    In Kansas.

TEXT: Federal Writers' Project (1938a), pp. 3-4.

MUSIC: Belden (1940), p. 429. Used by permission of University of Missouri Press.

VARIANTS: Belden (1940), pp. 428-429; Federal Writers' Project (1941), pp. 11-12; Randolph (1949), pp. 18-19; Botkin (1951), p. 741; Greenway (1953), pp. 212-213; Lomax (1960), pp. 395-396.

STARVING TO DEATH
ON A GOVERNMENT CLAIM

Reactions to sod house realities were by no means exclusively petulant. We offer here a selection of remarkably gritty and determined musical responses to hardship. Frank Baker's "Starving to Death on a Government Claim," or "The Lane County Bachelor," from an 1891 manuscript, was a very popular criticism of both the land and the various federal land acts. The original Homestead Act of 1862 had made available parcels that were too small, given the nature of the Great Plains, and the terms of the later modifications encouraged large speculators. By the time Frank got there, anyway, the land was of such quality as to justify these comments:

> How happy I am on my government claim,
> For I've nothing to lose nor I've nothing to gain.
> I've nothing to eat, and I've nothing to wear,
> And nothing from nothing is honest and fair.

One of a series of parodies of the hymn "Beulah Land," a place appropriately inaccessible, is "Nebraska Land" from the *Alliance and Labor Songster* (1891). In it one can read of the spirits broken by wind, heat, and drought: "We do not live—we only stay, And are too poor to get away." From an 1888 issue of the *Stanton Telegram*, "Kansas Land, I," exhibits a jubilation:

> I got my land from Uncle Sam,
> And I'm as happy as a clam.

answered later by "Kansas Land, II," from oral tradition:

> The hot wind blows the livelong day,
> And all my cash has passed away.

Such differing views about the conditions on the plains, coupled with the convenience of local newspapers, prompted a number of these sequences of parody answering parody. "The Little Old Sod Shanty on the Claim, I," itself a parody, was answered, and the answer was answered, in a string of songs composed in the mid-1880's. The basic story is of an anxious, but potentially prosperous, bachelor who would like to interest a girl in his tribulations. The "answerer" is a woman enjoying a lengthening engagement in the East while her seedy Sam works his claim out West. She sees his desertion as good riddance: "He says he'll make his fortune, but I'm afraid he'll lose his hair." The answer to the answer presents the original narrator as having made good and being ready to crow a bit. There are two other parodies of the original "The Little Old Log Cabin in the Lane." "The Little Old Sod Shanty on the Claim, II," is good and, ultimately, optimistic:

> Our hogs, they died of cholera; our chickens had the pip;
> The baby swallowed buttons like a chain;
> Our wife was married thirteen years before she saw a dime
> When we lived in that sod shanty on the claim.

And Tom Beasley's "Little Adobe Casa," which Thorp collected, serves the lament stirred up in chili sauce.

For the sodbuster's side in those fencing disputes with the cattlemen, we give "The Kansas Farmer's Lament," to the tune of "The Disheartened Ranger."

> From my bunch, they'll cut cows,
> And run over plows,
> Crippling a chicken or killing a hog.
> 'Way off in the dark
> There is heard a bark,
> When crack goes a pistol and down goes a dog.

But with all these hazards, hardships, and distractions, Kansas reclaimed her migratory crowd, if for no other reason than, as "Comin' Back to Kansas" tells it:

> ... they found that other sections
> Had their tales of woe to sing,
> So they're humpin' now for Kansas
> At the breakin' forth of spring.

One of those "other sections," incidentally, was Canada, where American emigrants carried "Starving to Death on a Government Claim" and "Nebraska Land," squaring the debt incurred when "Red River Valley" was adapted to various American locations, including "The Bright Mohawk Valley."

FRANK BAKER

STARVING TO DEATH
ON A GOVERNMENT CLAIM

(or The Lane County Bachelor)

TUNE: The Irish Washerwoman

Frank Bak-er's my name, and a bach-e-lor I am; I'm

keep-ing old batch on an el-e-gant plan. You'll

find me out west in the coun-ty of Lane __ I'm

starv-ing to death on a gov-ern-ment claim. My

house, it is built of the nat-u-ral soil; The

walls are e-rec-ted ac-cord-ing to Hoyle. The

roof has no pitch, but is lev-el and plain, And I

al-ways get wet when it hap-pens to rain.

Hur-rah for Lane Coun-ty, the land of the free, The

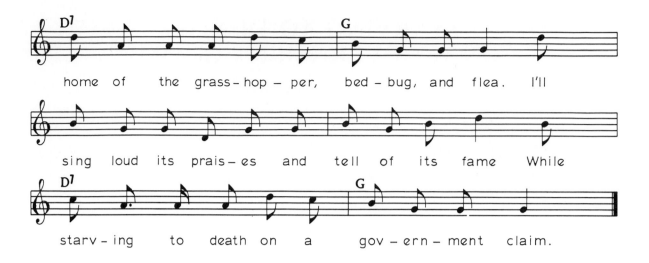

home of the grass-hop — per, bed - bug, and flea. I'll

sing loud its prais—es and tell of its fame While

starv - ing to death on a gov—ern—ment claim.

1

Frank Baker's my name, and a bachelor I am;
I'm keeping old batch on an elegant plan.
You'll find me out west in the county of Lane—
I'm starving to death on a government claim.
My house, it is built of the natural soil;
The walls are erected according to Hoyle.
The roof has no pitch, but is level and plain,
And I always get wet when it happens to rain.

> Hurrah for Lane County, the land of the free,
> The home of the grasshopper, bedbug and flea.
> I'll sing loud its praises and tell of its fame
> While starving to death on a government claim.

2

My clothes, they are ragged; my language is rough;
My bread is case-hardened both solid and tough.
The dough is scattered all over the room,
And the floor, it gets scared at the sight of a broom.
My dishes are scattered all over the bed;
They are covered with sorghum and Government bread.
Still I have a good time and live at my ease
On common sop-sorghum, old bacon, and grease.

> Then come to Lane County. Here is a home for you all
> Where the winds never cease and the rains never fall,
> And the sun never sets but will always remain
> Till it burns you all up on a Government claim.

3

How happy I feel when I crawl into bed,
And a rattlesnake rattles a tune at my head,
And the gay little centipede, void of all fear,
Crawls over my neck and down into my ear,
And the little bed bugs so cheerful and bright,
They keep me a-laughing two-thirds of the night,
And the gay little flea with sharp tacks in his toes
Plays "why don't you catch me" all over my nose.

Hurrah for Lane County, hurrah for the West,
Where farmers and laborers are ever at rest,
For there's nothing to do but to sweetly remain
And starve like a man on a Government claim.

4

How happy am I on my government claim,
For I've nothing to lose nor I've nothing to gain.
I've nothing to eat, and I've nothing to wear,
And nothing from nothing is honest and fair.
Oh, it is here I am solid and here I will stay,
For my money is all gone and I can't get away.
There is nothing that makes a man hard and profane
Like starving to death on a Government claim.

Hurrah for Lane County, where blizzards arise,
Where the winds never cease and the flea never dies.
Come join in the chorus and sing of its fame,
You poor hungry hoboes that's starved on the claim.

5

No, don't get discouraged, you poor hungry men,
For we are all here as free as a pig in a pen.
Just stick to your homestead and battle the fleas
And look to your Maker to send you a breeze.
Now, all you claim holders, I hope you will stay
And chew your hardtack till you are toothless and grey;
But, as for myself, I'll no longer remain
And starve like a dog on a Government claim.

Farewell to Lane County, farewell to the West.
I'll travel back East to the girl I love best.
I'll stop in Topeka and get me a wife,
And there shall I stay the rest of my life.

TEXT: "The Lane County Bachelor," MS by Ed Kepner, dated March 8, 1891, in Forsyth Library, Fort Hays Kansas State College.

MUSIC: As sung by Vance Randolph, Library of Congress Recording L 30. Transcribed by David Cohen.

VARIANTS: Lomax (1910), pp. 278-279; Pound (1915), pp. 30-31, and (1922), pp. 178-180; Sandburg (1927), pp. 120-122; Clark (1932), p. 71; Lomax and Lomax (1934), p. 434, and (1938), pp. 407-408; Hull (1939), pp. 52-53; McMullen (1946), pp. 133-135; Lomax and Lomax (1947), pp. 238-239; Randolph (1948), pp. 190-191; Koch and Koch (1961), p. 10; Malone (1961), pp. 146-149; Moore and Moore (1964), pp. 282-285.

JOHN A. DEAN # NEBRASKA LAND

TUNE: Beulah Land

We're in a land of drouth and heat, Where no - thing grows for man to eat: The winds that blow with burn - ing heat O'er all this land is hard to beat. O Ne - bras - ka land, sweet Ne - bras - ka land! As on its burn - ing soil I stand And look a-way a - cross the plains, And won-der why it nev - er rains; But Ga - bri-el calls with trum-pet sound, And says the rain has passed a — round.

1

We're in a land of drouth and heat,
    Where nothing grows for man to eat:
The winds that blow with burning heat
    O'er all this land is hard to beat.

CHORUS: O Nebraska land, sweet Nebraska land!
    As on its burning soil I stand
    And look away across the plains,
    And wonder why it never rains;
    But Gabriel calls with trumpet sound
    And says the rain has passed around.

2

The farmers go into their corn,
    And there they stand and look around;
They look and then they are so shocked
    To find the shoot has missed the stalk.

3

We have no wheat; we have no oats;
    We have no corn to feed our shoats.
Our chickens are too poor to eat,
    And pigs go squealing through the
        streets.

4

Our horses are the broncho race—
    Starvation stares them in the face;
We do not live—we only stay,
    And are too poor to get away.

———————

TEXT AND MUSIC: Vincent (1891), p. 41 (music, p. 28).

VARIANTS: Pound (1915), p. 28, and (1922), p. 185; Sandburg (1927), pp. 280-281; Federal Writers' Project (1938a), pp. 7-8; Lomax and Lomax (1938), pp. 410-412; Federal Writers' Project (1941), pp. 12-13; McMullen (1946), p. 129; Brunvand (1965), pp. 245-246.

KANSAS LAND, I

TUNE: Beulah Land

1

I've reached the land of corn and wheat,
Of pumpkin pies and taters sweet.
I got my land from Uncle Sam,
And I am happy as a clam.

CHORUS: O, Kansas land, sweet Kansas land!
As on my dugout roof I stand,
I look away across the plains
And wonder if it never rains;
But as I turn and view my corn,
I think I'll never sell my farm.

2

When first I came to get my start,
My neighbors they were miles apart;
But now there's one on every claim,
And sometimes three all want the same.

3

My horses, Clydesdale-Norman stock,
My chickens are all Plymouth Rock,
My cattle, Jersey—very fine—
And Poland-China are my swine.

4

And now at last the cars are here!
We've waited for them many a year.
And won't you with me take a smile?
For I have "freighted" many a mile.

LAST CHORUS: O Kansas girls, sweet Kansas girls!
With sky-blue eyes and teeth like pearls!
They sing and at the organ play
Until some dudlet comes that way.
They fly to meet him at the door
And skip with him for evermore.

TEXT: *Stanton Telegram* (Johnson City and Gognac, Kans.), July 13, 1888.

VARIANTS: Vincent (1891), p. 29; Pound (1939), pp. 30-31; Koch and Koch (1961), p. 14; Malone (1961), pp. 143-144.

KANSAS LAND, II

TUNE: Beulah Land

1

I've reached the land of short-grass fine
And sought to make a homestead mine.
The hot wind blows the livelong day,
And all my cash has passed away.

CHORUS: Oh, Kansas Land! My Kansas Land!
As on the dugout roof I stand,
I look away across the plain
And see the corn is needing rain.
I see the 'hoppers flying low,
And feel the burning hot wind blow.

2

The dust clouds float upon the breeze,
Through drooping corn and wilting trees.
The wheatfields all are lifeless brown;
The sunflower leaves hang limply down.

3

The 'hoppers come and camp on me.
I know no place from them to flee.
They eat my crops, they eat my shirt;
They leave me nought but sun-dried dirt.

4

In Kansas Land I'm going to stay,
For all these things shall pass away.
Sure, pleasure follows after pain;
Next spring it's going to rain again.

———————————

TEXT: Koch and Koch (1961), pp. 13-14. Used by permission of William Koch.

THE LITTLE OLD SOD SHANTY
ON THE CLAIM, I

WILL S. HAYS

TUNE: The Little Old Log Cabin in the Lane

I am look-ing rath-er seed-y now, while
Yet, I rath-er like the nov-el-ty of

hold-ing down my claim, And my vict-uals are not
liv-ing in this way, Though my bill of fare is

al-ways served the best; And the mice play sly-ly
al-ways rath-er tame; But I'm hap-py as a

'round me as I nes-tle down to sleep, In my
clam__ on this land of Un-cle Sam's, In my

lit-tle old sod shan-ty on the claim.
lit-tle old sod shan-ty on the claim.

Chorus

The hing-es are of leath-er, and the win-dows have no

glass, While the board roof lets the howl-ing bliz-zard in;

And I hear the hun-gry coy-ote, as he sneaks up through the

grass, 'Round my lit-tle old sod shant-y on the claim.__

1

I am looking rather seedy now, while holding down my claim,
And my victuals are not always served the best;
And the mice play slyly 'round me as I nestle down to sleep,
In my little old sod shanty on the claim.
Yet, I rather like the novelty of living in this way,
Though my bill of fare is always rather tame;
But I'm happy as a clam on this land of Uncle Sam's,
In my little old sod shanty on the claim.

CHORUS: The hinges are of leather, and the windows have no glass,
While the board roof lets the howling blizzard in;
And I hear the hungry coyote, as he sneaks up through the grass,
'Round my little old sod shanty on the claim.

2

But when I left my Eastern home, a bachelor so gay,
To try to win my way to wealth and fame,
I little thought that I'd come down to burning twisted hay,
In my little old sod shanty on the claim.
My clothes are plastered o'er with dough, and I'm looking like a fright,
And everything is scattered 'round the room;
But I wouldn't give the freedom that I have out in the West,
For the bauble of an Eastern mansard house.

3

Still I wish that some kind hearted girl would pity on me take
And relieve me of the mess that I am in;
The angel—how I'd bless her, if this her home she'd make,
In my little old sod shanty on the claim.
And when we made our fortune on the prairies of the West,
Just as happy as two lovers we'd remain;
We'd forget the trials and the troubles which we endured at first,
In our little old sod shanty on the claim.

4

And if the fates should bless us with now and then an heir
To cheer our hearts with honest pride to flame,
O then we'd be content for the toil that we have spent,
In our little old sod shanty in the claim.
When time enough had lapsed, and all those little brats
To man and modest woman hood have grown,
It won't seem half so lonely when around us we shall look,
And see other old sod shanties on the claim.

TEXT: *Clark County Clipper* (Ashland, Kans.), Sept. 25, 1884.

MUSIC: "Little Old Log Cabin in the Lane," as sung by Riley Puckett, Columbia Record 107 (1924). Transcribed by David Cohen.

VARIANTS: *Lane County Herald* (Dighton, Kans.), Aug. 14, 1885; Lomax (1910), pp. 187-189; Pound (1915), pp. 24-25, and (1922), p. 165; Sandburg (1927), pp. 89-91; Allen (1933), pp. 103-106; Frey (1936), pp. 40-41; Lomax and Lomax (1938), pp. 405-406; McMullen (1946), pp. 57-58; Randolph (1948), pp. 219-221; Botkin (1951), pp. 742-743; Fowke and Johnston (1954), pp. 90-91; Lomax (1960), pp. 397-398; Moore and Moore (1964), pp. 293-295.

ANSWER TO THE LITTLE OLD SOD SHANTY ON THE CLAIM

TUNE: The Little Old Log Cabin In the Lane

1

My Sam is getting seedy now, while holding down his claim,
And his flap-jacks (so he writes) are not the best,
So I'll put my hair in papers ere I lay me down to rest,
While my Sam is in his shanty on the claim.
Yet I rather like the novelty of living in this way,
For such long engagements now are rather tame,
And I'm happy as a clam since I said good-bye to Sam,
When he went to seek his shanty on the claim.

CHORUS: The dances are so pleasant, so delightful, I should say.
There I have as many beaus as I could name,
Oh! the buggy rides I'll take when my Sam is far away,
In his little old sod shanty on the claim.

2

Since he left his eastern home, I'm happy and I'm gay,
For, of course, I've so't me out another flame;
No doubt he thought I'd come down to burning twisted hay,
In his filthy old sod shanty on the claim.
Oh, let him dabble in the dough. I'm sure it serves him right
For leaving me for Kansas, there to roam;
Does he think me such a mummy as to marry such a fright,
To be a slave in his dirty cabin home.

3

No doubt some tawny Indian Miss would pity on him take,
And help extricate him from the fix he's in;
He need not think a city belle the sacrifice will make,
For there's many men to wed with lots of tin.
He says he'll make his fortune, but I'm afraid he'll lose his hair,
'Way out among the Indians, frogs and sloughs.
He'd better get some other lass to be the mother of his heir,
For I'm determined some other man to choose.

4

He dreams his early bliss scene, when in wedlock he is bound,
And living with his fair and buxom dame;
But when his cash she's spent until he's not a cent,
She may leave him and his shanty on the claim.
And if she's a vixen, she will make him toe the mark,
And thrash and thump and pound him till he's lame.
I think I'll wed the owner of the stone front near the park,
And leave Sam in his shanty on the claim.

TEXT: "Answer to the Little Old Sod Shanty on the Claim" (McCracken, Kans.: A. A. Forbes, *ca.* 1885-1888), in the Kansas Collection (Sodhouse Section) of Kenneth W. Porter, University of Oregon.

VARIANT: McMullen (1946), pp. 58-59.

ANSWER TO THE ANSWER
TO THE LITTLE OLD SOD SHANTY
ON THE CLAIM

1

I'm not looking half so seedy, since I made my final proof,
And my bill of fare is now not quite so tame;
And though Sal gave me the "mitten," I'm more than satisfied
With my little old sod shanty and my claim.
I read her letter o'er and o'er; it made me feel quite sad,
For I never thought she was up to such a game;
But I'm happy now as ever as I lay me down to rest,
In my little old sod shanty on the claim.

CHORUS: O, I've made my final proof, I'm as happy as a clam,
And I'm on the road to wealth if not to fame.
And I wonder if Miss Sally doesn't wish she'd stuck to Sam,
And his little old sod shanty on the claim.

2

The other day a railroad man came looking 'round this way,
And in private shyly took me by the arm.
"We are going to run a line across the country here," said he,
"And we want to build a town upon your farm."
The bargain is completed and lots are selling fast,
And the place is not now looking just the same.
I've lots of tin, and soon will build a splendid brown stone front,
Just beside my little old sod shanty on the claim.

3

No doubt she would be happy now to make the sacrifice,
Since she finds these wealthy men do not propose,
And the buggy rides grow scarcer as she's growing up in years,
And her cheeks their wonted tint begin to lose.
But since I've commuted I'm happy and I'm gay,
And of course I've sought me out another flame,
And she's not afraid of coming down to burning twisted hay,
In my little old sod shanty on the claim.

4

Although my new found treasure may spend my ready cash
And make me toe the mark when she gets mad,
Yet an Indian Miss would hardly suit my elevated views,
And I'd hate to have a half-breed call me "dad."
Now if Sal don't want to be the mother of my heir,
She will have no one but herself to blame,
For the prairies are prolific and she'd better stay away,
And leave Sam in his shanty on the claim.

TEXT: "Answer to the Answer of the Little Old Sod Shanty on the Claim" (McCracken, Kans.: A. A. Forbes, *ca.* 1885-1888), in the Kansas Collection (Sodhouse Section) of Kenneth W. Porter, University of Oregon.

VARIANT: McMullen (1946), pp. 59-60.

THE LITTLE OLD SOD SHANTY
ON THE CLAIM, II

1

A bumper crop of corn we raised in eighteen ninety-two;
To dress our wife in silk we thought was plain;
But we sold our corn for thirteen cents, three cents beside a share,
So the wife stayed in the shanty on the claim.

2

Our hogs, they died of cholera; our chickens had the pip;
The baby swallowed buttons like a chain;
Our wife was married thirteen years before she saw a dime
When we lived in that sod shanty on the claim.

3

Yet for all the hardships we went through, we never gave up hope,
But plugged the harder till we made it gain,
For love was close beside us in all our ups and downs
In that little old sod shanty on the claim.

TEXT: Federal Writers' Project (1938a), p. 8.
VARIANT: Federal Writers' Project (1941), p. 13.

TOM BEASLEY ## LITTLE ADOBE CASA

TUNE: Little Old Log Cabin in the Lane

1

Just one year ago to-day, I left my eastern home
Hunting for a fortune and for fame.
Little did I think that now, I'd be in Mexico
In this little adobe casa on the plains.

CHORUS: The roof is ocateo; the coyotes, far and near;
The Greaser roams about the place all day;
Centipedes and tarantulas crawl o'er me while I sleep
In my little adobe casa on the plains.

2

Alacranies on the ceiling, cockroaches on the wall.
My bill-of-fare is always just the same:
Frijoles and tortillas stirred up in chili sauce,
In my little adobe casa on the plains.

3

But if some dark eyed mujer would consent to be my wife,
I would try to be contented and remain
'Til fate should show a better place to settle down for life
Than this little adobe casa on the plains.

TEXT: Thorp (1908), p. 20.
VARIANT: Thorp (1921), pp. 93-94; Fife and Fife (1966), pp. 87-96*.

WILL HOWELL # THE KANSAS FARMER'S LAMENT

TUNE: Texas Ranger's Lament

Come, lis-ten to a gran-ger, You soft-head-ed rang-er, And a
ver-y sad stor-y you're wel-come to hear. I left a good farm, And
mean-ing no harm, I em-i-grat-ed my fam-i-ly to this Kan-sas fron-tier.

Chorus

No corn or tom-at-oes; No cab-bage, pot-at-oes But
soup boiled from boot-tops I saved last year. Cow-punch-ers rid-ing 'Crat
where I'm res-id-ing. Go, take me a-way from this Kan-sas fron-tier.

1

Come, listen to a granger,
You soft-headed ranger,
And a very sad story you're welcome to hear.
I left a good farm,
And, meaning no harm,
I emigrated my family to this Kansas frontier.

CHORUS: No corn nor tomatoes;
No cabbage, potatoes,
But soup boiled from boot-tops I saved last year.
Cowpunchers riding
'Crost where I'm residing.
Go, take me away from this Kansas frontier.

470

2

'Crost crops they'll drive cattle,
Then turn to fight a battle,
Their rein in their hand, their guns by their side.
With quirt they'll make gestures
And mimic winchesters,
Then, quirting and rowling, on through they ride.

3

From my bunch, they'll cut cows,
And run over plows,
Crippling a chicken or killing a hog.
'Way off in the dark
There is heard a bark,
When crack goes a pistol and down goes a dog.

4

My only objection
To the through-herded Texan:
He drinks up my water and beds on my farm.
When I tell him to leave,
He rolls up his sleeves
And says, "Go on, you old nester. We'll do you no harm."

5

When I go to town,
First a blacksmith be found;
From a narrow-gauged wagon, my wheels are all sprung.
The town folks are mocking
The way my wife's walking;
Her apron strings flying, her shoes all unstrung.

6

I'll pick up my knapsack
And strap on my wife's back,
And on to the railroad count ties far away.
My wife and I trudging,
Our children on budging;
When we get to Boston, you bet we will stay.

TEXT: *Dighton Journal* (Dighton, Kans.), Jan. 28, 1892.

MUSIC: As sung by Carl T. Sprague, Victor Record V-40066. Transcribed by David Cohen.

COMIN' BACK TO KANSAS

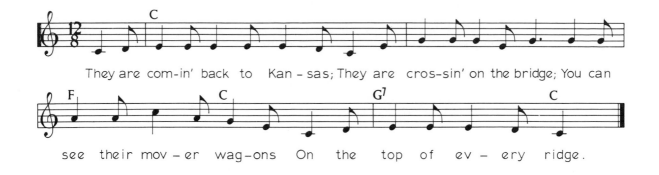

They are com-in' back to Kan-sas; They are cros-sin' on the bridge; You can

see their mov — er wag-ons On the top of ev — ery ridge.

1
They are comin' back to Kansas;
They are crossin' on the bridge;
You can see their mover wagons
On the top of every ridge.

2
On the highways and the turnpikes,
You can see their wagons come,
For they're comin' back to Kansas,
And they're comin' on the run.

3
Who's a comin' back to Kansas?
Why, the migratory crowd
That left the state some months ago
With curses long and loud,

4
And they swore by the eternal
They would never more return
To this Kansas land infernal
Where the hot winds blast and burn.

5
Where the rivers run in riot
When you want it to be dry,
Where the sun so fiercely scorches
When you want a cloudy sky.

6
So they loaded up the children
And they whistled for the dog,
Tied a cow behind the wagon,
To the butcher sold the hog.

7
Hitched the ponies to the schooner,
Turned her prow toward the east,
Left this beastly state of Kansas
For a land of fat and feast.

8
Did they find it? No, they didn't,
Though they roamed the country o'er,
From the lakes up in the northland
To the far off ocean shore.

9
And they found that other sections
Had their tales of woe to sing,
So they're humpin' now for Kansas
At the breakin' forth of spring.

TEXT AND MUSIC: O'Bryant (1961), pp. 180-181. Used by permission of University of Nebraska Press.

BUT THE MORTGAGE
WORKED THE HARDEST

John Greenway has observed that, compared with the sharecropper and the plantation and migratory farm worker, the independent midwestern farmer has produced very little of value in the way of protest songs. The comparison may be odious, for there is stuff of emotional and intellectual interest in such songs as those of the Nebraska Farmers Alliance of the 1890's. Will Carleton's "But the Mortgage Worked the Hardest" and several of the following songs show that Western economics was a worse enemy than the elements, for the latter at least changed with the seasons:

> We worked through spring and winter, through summer and
>   through fall;
> But the mortgage worked the hardest and the steadiest of them all.
> It worked on nights and Sundays; it worked each holiday;
> It settled down among us and never went away.

"The Farmer" tells of his suffering under middlemen and the credit system, and "The Kansas Fool," another of those "Beulah Land" parodies, regrets his stupidity in thinking that the way to make the land produce was to plow and plant it:

> The bankers followed us out west,
>   And did in mortgages invest;
> They looked ahead and shrewdly planned,
>   And soon they'll have our Kansas land.

A Mrs. J. T. Kellie contributed a couple of songs to the Alliance songsters. In one, "Dear Prairie Home," she blames her loss of hair, home, and faith on the banks and the railroads, and begins to hint at a political solution; "But my neighbors all around me then were in a party dream. And they voted to rob my home from me." The 1890's song "There Comes a Reckoning Day" joins H. F. Johnson's "Come, All Ye Toiling Millions" in its cry for greenbacks as a solution, the one favored by the National Farmers Alliance and the Knights of Labor:

> We're fighting old monopoly and the gigantic trust.
> They've taken all the corn and oil, left us cob
>   and husk;
> But when we get our ballots in, you'll hear their
>   bubble burst.

"The Hayseed," used also by the miners and the Wobblies, is Marxist jargon ("I was once a tool of oppression"), but it does look to the vote as a remedy. And Mrs. Kellie's other song here, "Vote for Me," to a temperance tune, sees great hope in the rejection of the railroads' candidates:

> Dear Father, that's right. Oh, what a glad sight!
>   That old railroad ticket thrown down.
> Now Ma will be hopeful; her heart will be light;
>   I'll have clothes like rich boys in town.

BUT THE MORTGAGE WORKED THE HARDEST

WILL CARLETON

1

We worked through spring and winter, through summer and through
  fall;
But the mortgage worked the hardest and the steadiest of them all.
It worked on nights and Sundays; it worked each holiday;
It settled down among us and never went away.

2

Whatever we kept from it seemed almost as a theft;
It watched us every minute; it ruled us right and left.
The rust and blight were with us sometimes, and sometimes not;
The dark-browed, scowling mortgage was forever on the spot.

3

The weevil and cut worm, they went as well as came;
The mortgage stayed forever, eating hearty all the same.
It nailed up every window, stood guard at every door,
And happiness and sunshine, made their home with us no more.

4

Till with failing crops and sickness we got stalled upon the grade,
And there came a dark day on us, when the interest wasn't paid;
And there came a sharp foreclosure, and I kind o' lost my hold,
And grew weary and discouraged, and the farm was cheaply sold.

5

The children left and scattered, when they hardly yet were grown:
My wife, she pined and perished, and I found myself alone.
What she died of was a "mystery"—the doctors never knew;
But I knew she died of mortgage just as well as I wanted to.

6

If to trace the hidden arrow was within the doctor's art,
They'd ha' found a mortgage lying on that woman's broken heart.
Worm or beetle, drouth or tempest on a farmer's land may fall;
But for first-class ruination, trust a mortgage 'gainst them all.

TEXT: Federal Writers' Project (1938a), pp. 12-13.
VARIANT: Federal Writers' Project (1940), p. 9.

C. S. WHITNEY

THE KANSAS FOOL

TUNE: Beulah Land

We have the land to raise the wheat, And ev—ery-thing that's good to eat; And when we had no bonds or debt, We were a jol—ly, hap—py set. Oh! Kan—sas fool! poor Kan—sas fool! The bank—er makes of you a tool. I look a—cross the fer—tile plain, Big crops made so by gen—tle rain; But twelve-cent corn gives me a-larm, And makes me want to sell my farm.

1

We have the land to raise the wheat,
    And everything that's good to eat;
And when we had no bonds or debt,
    We were a jolly, happy set.
CHORUS: Oh! Kansas fool! poor Kansas fool!
The banker makes of you a tool.
I look across the fertile plain,
Big crops—made so by gentle rain;
But twelve-cent corn gives me alarm,
And makes me want to sell my farm.

476

2

With abundant crops raised everywhere,
'Tis a mystery, I do declare,
Why, farmers all should fume and fret,
And why we are so deep in debt.

3

At first we made some money here,
With drouth and grasshoppers each
year;
But now the interest that we pay
Soon takes our money all away.

4

The bankers followed us out west,
And did in mortgages invest;
They looked ahead and shrewdly planned,
And soon they'll have our Kansas land.

———————

TEXT AND MUSIC: Vincent (1891), pp. 28-29.

DEAR PRAIRIE HOME

TUNE: Darling Nellie Gray

There's a dear old home-stead on Ne - bras-ka's fer-tile plain, Where I toiled my man-hood's strength a — way; All that la — bor now is lost to me, but it is Shy-lock's gain, For that dear old home he claims to - day. Oh my dear prai-rie home! Nev -er - more in years to come Can I call what I made by toil my own; The rail — roads and the banks com-bined, the law-yers paid to find Out a way to rob me of my home.

1

There's a dear old homestead on Nebraska's fertile plain,
Where I toiled my manhood's strength away;
All that labor now is lost to me, but it is Shylock's gain,
For that dear old home he claims today.

CHORUS: Oh my dear prairie home! Nevermore in years to come
Can I call what I made by toil my own;
The railroads and the banks combined, the lawyers paid to find
Out a way to rob me of my home.

2

When first I took that prairie home, my heart was free and light,
And I sang as I turned the prairie sod;
My hair that then was thick and brown today is thin and white,
And I've lost all faith in man or God.

3

It was many years ago that I first saw through this scheme,
And I struggled from their meshes to get free;
But my neighbors all around me then were in a party dream,
And they voted to rob my home from me.

4

Now their homes are gone as well as mine, and they're awake at last,
And they see now the great injustice done;
While some few their homes may save, yet the greater part, alas!
Must be homeless for all time to come.

5

We must now the robbers pay for a chance to fill the soil,
And when God calls us over the great range,
All Heaven will be owned, I s'pose, by men who never toil,
So I doubt if we notice the exchange.

TEXT: *Farmers' Alliance* (Lincoln, Neb.), Sept. 27, 1890.
MUSIC: *Minstrel Songs, Old and New* (1882), pp. 27-29.
VARIANT: Federal Writers' Project (1938*a*), pp. 13-14.

THERE COMES A RECKONING DAY

S. C. FOSTER

TUNE: Oh! Susannah

1

I had a dream the other night when every thing was still.
I dreamt I saw the lab'ring men all going down the hill.
Their clothes were rags; their feet were bare; a tear was in their eye.
Said I, "My friend, what grieves you so, and causes you to cry?"

CHORUS: Oh! Bondholders, take pity, now, we pray.
We're out of food and out of clothes—
There comes a reckoning day.

2

We have to work to earn our bread, and our children cry for food;
Have scarce a place to lay our heads—complaining does no good.
We hate to beg. We will not steal. Pray, tell us what to do.
We cannot starve—what shall we do?—we leave the case to you.

480

3

Our greenbacks're gone. You've made us poor, reduced us all to slaves.
You took our means; you took our homes; you've treated us as knaves.
We fought your battles, saved your homes, took greenbacks as our pay.
Now, when we ask for work or bread, you boldly answer, nay.

4

Bring in your bonds and get the cash the same you gave to us;
'Twas greenbacks then, 'tis greenbacks now; we'll end this little muss.
We must have money through the land, and business lively, too;
We'll feed the hungry, clothe the poor, with work for all to do.

5

You own the bonds but pay no tax; for justice now we cry.
You bought with greenbacks, now ask for gold; pray tell us how and
  why?
Who promised you to pay in gold? the people now inquire.
We'll keep our contract, you keep yours, as honest men admire.

TEXT: Vincent (1891), p. 37.
MUSIC: Turner *et al.* (1858), p. 18.

COME, ALL YE TOILING MILLIONS

TUNE: Marching Through Georgia

1

Come, all ye toiling millions that labor for your life
To support yourselves and familes, your children and your wife;
Come, rally to our standard now in this gigantic strife,
   Then we'll go marching to victory.

CHORUS: Hurrah! Hurrah! Our banner is unfurled.
   Hurrah! Hurrah! It's waving proudly o'er the world.
   The tyrants and the robbers from their places will be hurled
   As we go marching to victory.

2

Come, join the brave Alliance, boys, and help the cause along;
Our battle is for freedom now, against a giant wrong.
We never will give up our homes to such a thieving throng,
    As we go marching to victory.

3

We're fighting old monopoly and the gigantic trust.
They've taken all the corn and oil, left us the cob and husk;
But when we get our ballots in, you'll hear their bubble burst,
    As we go marching to victory.

4

The promises they made us, not one was ever kept;
But 'round the tree of liberty the sneaking tyrants crept.
They sought to blight our heritage while quietly we slept,
    But we'll go marching to victory.

5

They gobbled up our greenbacks then issued out their bond;
Then made us pay the interest to support the thieving throng.
And when we made objection, they told us we were wrong,
    But we'll go marching to victory.

6

They've taken all our land estate and claim it as their own,
While husbands, wives and children are left without a home;
And willing hands to foreign lands in search of work must roam,
    But we'll go marching to victory.

7

The bankers rob the farmers, and the railroads steal the land,
And in their cursed robbing schemes, they both go hand in hand.
They think our business is to obey while theirs is to command,
    But we'll go marching to victory.

8

We've trusted the Republicans and failed to take a trick;
We've leaned upon the Democrats and found a broken stick;
We'll try the Knights and Farmers now and then you'll see how
    quick
    That we'll go marching to victory.

9

And now we stand united, the bosses best look out;
With faith and honor plighted, we'll put them all to rout.
And with an honest ballot now we'll put the rascals out
    As we go marching to victory.

TEXT: Hannibal F. Johnson, *Poems of Idaho* (Weiser, Idaho: Signal Job House, 1895), pp. 123-125.

MUSIC: *War Songs* (1883), p. 30.

VARIANT: Vincent (1891), p. 19.

THE HAYSEED

TUNE: Save a Poor Sinner Like Me

1

I was once a tool of oppression,
And as green as a sucker could be,
And monopolies banded together
To beat a poor hayseed like me.

2

The railroads and old party bosses
Together did sweetly agree;
And they thought there would be little trouble
In working a hayseed like me.

3

But now I've roused up a little,
And their greed and corruption I see.
And the ticket we vote next November
Will be made up of hayseeds like me.

TEXT: Federal Writers' Project (1938*b*), p. 1.

VARIANTS: *Miners' Magazine* (Denver), Oct. 29, 1908; Federal Writers' Project (1941), p. 19; Greenway (1953), p. 60.

THE FARMER

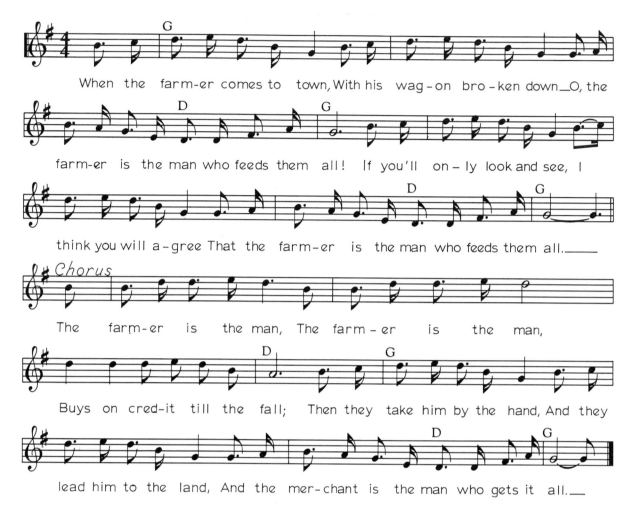

When the farm-er comes to town, With his wag-on bro-ken down—O, the farm-er is the man who feeds them all! If you'll on-ly look and see, I think you will a-gree That the farm-er is the man who feeds them all.——

Chorus

The farm-er is the man, The farm-er is the man, Buys on cred-it till the fall; Then they take him by the hand, And they lead him to the land, And the mer-chant is the man who gets it all.——

1

When the farmer comes to town,
With his wagon broken down—
O, the farmer is the man who feeds them all!
If you'll only look and see,
I think you will agree
That the farmer is the man who feeds them
  all.

  The farmer is the man,
  The farmer is the man,
  Buys on credit till the fall;
  Then they take him by the hand,
  And they lead him to the land,
  And the merchant is the man who
    gets it all.

2

The doctor hangs around
While the blacksmith heats his iron—
O, the farmer is the man who feeds them all!
The preacher and the cook
Go strolling by the brook,
And the farmer is the man who feeds them
  all.

  The farmer is the man,
  The farmer is the man,
  Buys on credit till the fall.
  Tho' his family comes to town
  With a wagon broken down,
  O, the farmer is the man who
    feeds them all!

TEXT AND MUSIC: Sandburg (1927), pp. 282-283. Used by permission of Harcourt, Brace & World, Inc.

VARIANTS: Greenway (1953), p. 213; Fowke and Glazer (1960), pp. 96-97.

VOTE FOR ME

MRS. J. T. KELLIE

HENRY C. WORK

TUNE: Father, Come Home

Oh fa-ther, dear fa-ther, come vote for me now: My clothes are so worn out and old. You said you would get me some new ones this fall; But now wheat and corn all are sold, The roads took the best, the banks get the rest, And noth-ing is left us at all; We thought if we worked through the heat and the cold, We'd have lots of new things this fall.

Chorus

Be free, be free, for me; Come, fa-ther, please vote for me now.

1

Oh father, dear father, come vote for me now:
    My clothes are so worn out and old.
You said you would get me some new ones this fall;
    But now wheat and corn are all sold.
The roads took the best, the banks get the rest,
    And nothing is left us at all;
We thought if we worked through the heat and the cold,
    We'd have lots of new things this fall.

CHORUS: Be free, be free, for me;
Come, father, please vote for me now.

2

Oh father, dear father, come vote for me now;
    Heed not what the railroad men say.
Of course they will tell you they love you the best;
    You know that was always the way.
Yet our sod house is old and lets in the cold,
    And Ma's always patching, you see;
The rest of the children, their shoes are so old—
    There's no one can bring cobs but me.

3

Oh father, dear father, come vote for me now;
    You know that I can't go to school,
For summer or winter, year round I must work,
    And when I am grown be a fool.
Oh what can I do when grown up like you,
    And nothing I know but to save,
Free land will be gone and naught else can I do
    But be to the rich men a slave.

4

Oh father, dear father, come vote for me now:
    Let money men threaten or pray.
They told you last summer we all worked too hard;
    This year we are lazy, they say.
Dear father, that's right. Oh, what a glad sight!
    That old railroad ticket thrown down.
Now Ma will be hopeful; her heart will be light;
    I'll have clothes like rich boys in town.

TEXT: Federal Writers' Project (1938b), pp. 7-8.

MUSIC: "Come Home, Father!," words and music by Henry Clay Work (Chicago: Root and Clay, 1864).

VARIANT: Federal Writers' Project (1941), pp. 20-21.

HARVEST LAND

As soon as they begin to hire, and grind the faces of, others, the farmers found themselves the objects of protest more vigorous and effective than their own. The Wobblies' own parody of "Beulah Land," called "Harvest Land," struck out at the farmers' policy of advertising for more hands than they needed and paying the minimum going wage. That kind of treatment made "The Swede from North Dakota" want to "Yump on the tail of a Yim Hill wagon."

Pat Brennan's "The Harvest War Song" complains, not only of such mistreatment, but of being called names for taking it: "We have sent your kids to college, but still you rave and shout, And call us tramps and hoboes, and pesky go-abouts." Joe Hill's answer to such nonsense was unambiguous: "Ta-Ra-Ra BOOM Dee-Ay" is almost a manual of guerrilla warfare when it describes how to drop the pitchfork "accidentally" into the threshing machine and "forget" to put the hub nut back on the greased wagon wheel.

The fear of such violence always worked against attempts to organize workers in the West. The song "Overalls and Snuff" is the product of one violent confrontation between the workers and an panicky press, police force, and citizenry. The Wheatland Hop Riot, at the California hop ranch of E. B. Durst in August, 1913, was the first nationally publicized migratory labor riot. Having attracted more workers than he needed, Durst massed them in squalid bunkhouses; under such conditions it was easy to organize the workers overnight. The ranchers resorted to deputies rather than negotiation, and violence ensued. The IWW grievance committee members mentioned in the song served ten years of their life sentences.

Woody Guthrie's songs both reflect these common attitudes and refract them into a personal vision. His "Tom Joad" was based on the movie version of Steinbeck's *Grapes of Wrath*, but his own experience, told in *Bound for Glory*, could have confirmed every indictment. Through all such miseries, however, Guthrie has resisted alienation. His position is best stated in the moving "Pastures of Plenty": "Every state in this nation us migrants has been. We'll work in your fight and we'll fight till we win."

HARVEST LAND

TUNE: Beulah Land

The har-vest drive is on a-gain. John Farm-er needs a

lot of men To work be-neath the Kan-sas heat And

Chorus

shock and stack and thresh his wheat. Oh, Farm-er John, poor

Farm-er John, Our faith in you is o-ver-drawn. Old

Fos-sil of the Feu-dal Age, Your on-ly creed is

Go-ing Wage. "Bull Dur-ham" will not

buy our brawn—You're out of luck, poor Farm-er John.

1

The harvest drive is on again.
John Farmer needs a lot of men
To work beneath the Kansas heat
And shock and stack and thresh his wheat.

CHORUS: Oh, Farmer John, poor Farmer John,
Our faith in you is overdrawn.
Old Fossil of the Feudal Age,
Your only creed is Going Wage.
"Bull Durham" will not buy our brawn—
You're out of luck, poor Farmer John.

2

You advertise in Omaha,
"Come, leave the Valley of the Kaw."
Nebraska calls, "Don't be misled,"
"We'll furnish you a feather bed!"

3

Then South Dakota "lets a roar,"
"We need ten thousand men—or more;
Our grain is turning—prices drop!
For God's sake, save our bumper crop."

4

In North Dakota (I'll be darn),
The "wise guy" sleeps in "hoosier's" barn.
Then hoosier breaks into his snore
And yells, "It's quarter after four."

LAST CHORUS: Oh, Harvest Land, Sweet Burning Sand!
As on the sun-kissed field I stand,
I look away across the plain
And wonder if it's going to rain.
I vow, by all the Brands of Cain,
That I will not be here again.

TEXT: IWW (1921*b*), pp. 61-62.

MUSIC: Vincent (1891), p. 28.

VARIANTS: IWW (1922?–1932); Kornbluh (1964), p. 247.

THE SWEDE FROM NORTH DAKOTA

TUNE: Reuben, Reuben, I've Been Thinking

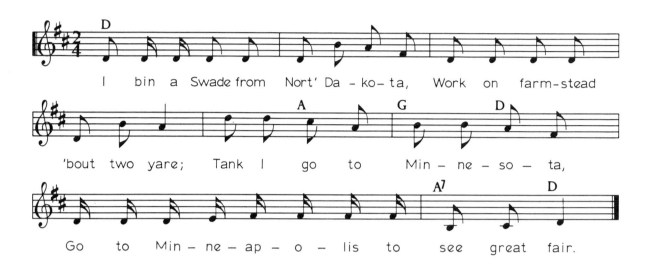

I bin a Swade from Nort' Da-ko-ta, Work on farm-stead 'bout two yare; Tank I go to Min — ne — so — ta, Go to Min — ne — ap — o — lis to see great fair.

1
I bin a Swade from Nort' Dakota,
Work on farmstead 'bout two yare;
Tank I go to Minnesota,
Go to Minneapolis to see great fair.

2
I buy me a suit, I buy me a bottle,
Dress me up way out of sight;
Yump on the tail of a Yim Hill wagon—
Yesus Chreest, I feel for fight!

3
I go down to Seven Corners
Where Salvation Army play.
One dem vomans come to me;
This is what dat voman say.

4
She say, "Will you work for Yesus?"
I say, "How much Yesus pay?"
She say, "Yesus don't pay nothing."
I say, "I won't work today."

TEXT: Milburn (1930), p. 139. Used by permission of Ives Washburn, Inc.

MUSIC: *Treasury of Song for the Home Circle* (Philadelphia: Hubbard Bros., 1882), pp. 85-86.

VARIANTS: E. C. Beck, *Lore of the Lumber Camps* (Ann Arbor: University of Michigan, 1948), p. 182.

JOE HILL   # TA-RA-RA BOOM DEE-AY

TUNE: Ta-Ra-Ra Boom De-Ay

1

I had a job once threshing wheat, worked sixteen hours with hands and
    feet;
And when the moon was shining bright, they kept me working all the
    night.
One moonlight night, I hate to tell, I accidentally slipped and fell;
My pitchfork went right in between some cog wheels of that thresh-ma-
    chine.

> Ta-ra-ra BOOM dee-ay,
> It made a noise that way,
> And wheels and bolts and hay
> Went flying every way.
> That stingy rube said, "Well,
> A thousand gone to Hell."
> But I did sleep that night—
> I needed it all right.

2

Next day that stingy Rube did say, "I'll bring my eggs to town today;
You grease my wagon up, you mutt, but don't forget to screw your nut."
I greased his wagon for him, but I plumb forgot to screw the nut;
And when he started on that trip, a wheel slipped off and broke his hip.

> Ta-ra-ra BOOM dee-ay
> It made a noise that way.
> That Rube was sure a sight,
> And mad enough to fight.
> His whiskers and his legs
> Were full of scrambled eggs:
> I told him, "That's too bad,
> I'm feeling very sad."

3

And then that farmer said, "You Turk; I'll bet you are an I Won't Work."
He paid me off right there, by gum, and I went home and told my chum.
Next day when threshing did commence, my chum was "Johnny on the
    fence,"
And on my word, that awkward kid, he dropped his pitchfork like I did.

> Ta-ra-ra BOOM dee-ay,
> It made a noise that way,
> And part of that machine
> Hit Reuben on the bean.
> He cried, "Oh me, Oh my,
> I nearly lost my eye."
> My partner said, "You're right—
> It's bedtime now, good-night."

But still that Rube was pretty wise; those things did open up his eyes.
He said, "There must be something wrong; I think I work my men too
   long."
He cut the hours and raised the pay, gave ham and eggs for every day.
Now gets his men from Union Hall, and has no "acidents" at all.

    Ta-ra-ra BOOM dee-ay,
    That Rube is feeling gay.
    He learned his lesson quick,
    Just through a simple trick.
    For fixing rotten jobs,
    And fixing greedy slobs,
    This is the only way—
    TA-RA-RA BOOM DEE-AY!

TEXT: IWW (1912*a*), pp. 3-4.

VARIANTS: *Industrial Worker* (Spokane, Wash.), March 27, 1913; IWW (1916-1917*d*);
Stavis and Harmon (1955), pp. 22-23; Kornbluh (1964), pp. 143-144.

OVERALLS AND SNUFF

TUNE: Wearing of the Green

1

One day as I was walking along the railroad track,
I met a man in Wheatland with his blankets on his back.
He was an old-time hop picker—I'd seen his face before—
I knew he was a Wobbly by the button that he wore.
By the button that he wore, by the button that he wore—
I knew he was a Wobbly by the button that he wore.

2

He took his blankets off his back and sat down on the rail
And told us some sad stories 'bout the workers down in jail.
He said the way they treat them there, he never saw the like,
For they're putting men in prison just for going out on strike.
Just for going out on strike, just for going out on strike—
They're putting men in prison just for going out on strike.

496

3

They have sentenced Ford and Suhr, and they've got them in the pen.
If they catch a Wobbly in their burg, they vag him there and then.
There is one thing I can tell you, and it makes the bosses sore,
As fast as they can pinch us, we can always get some more.
We can always get some more, we can always get some more—
As fast as they can pinch us, we can always get some more.

4

Oh, Horst and Durst are mad as hell—they don't know what to do;
And the rest of those hop barons are all feeling mighty blue.
Oh, we've tied up all their hop fields, and the scabs refuse to come,
And we're going to keep on striking till we put them on the bum.
Till we put them on the bum, till we put them on the bum—
We're going to keep on striking till we put them on the bum.

5

Now we've got to stick together, boys, and strive with all our might.
We must free Ford and Suhr, boys; we've got to win this fight.
From these scissorbill hop barons, we are taking no more bluff.
We'll pick no more damned hops for them for overalls and snuff.
For our overalls and snuff, for our overalls and snuff—
We'll pick no more damned hops for them for overalls and snuff.

TEXT: Solidarity (Cleveland), Aug. 1, 1914.
MUSIC: Johnson (1881), pp. 488-490.
VARIANTS: IWW (1914b-1921a); Kornbluh (1964), pp. 238-240.

PAT BRENNAN

THE HARVEST WAR SONG

TUNE: It's a Long Way to Tipperary

1

We are coming home, John Farmer; we are coming back to stay.
For nigh on fifty years or more, we've gathered up your hay.
We have slept out in your hayfields; we have heard your morning
    shout;
We've heard you wondering, where in hell's them pesky go-abouts?

CHORUS: It's a long way, now understand me, it's a long way to town;
It's a long way across the prairie, and to hell with Farmer John.
Up goes machine or wages, and the hours must come down,
For we're out for a winter's stake this summer, and we want no
    scabs around.

2

You've paid the going wages; that's what's kept us on the bum.
You say you've done your duty, you chin-whiskered son-of-a-gun.
We have sent your kids to college, but still you rave and shout,
And call us tramps and hoboes, and pesky go-abouts.

3

But now the wintry breezes are a-shaking our poor frames,
And the long-drawn days of hunger try to drive us boes insane.
It is driving us to action—we are organized today;
Us pesky tramps and hoboes are coming back to stay.

TEXT: IWW (1916), p. 7.

VARIANTS: *Solidarity* (Cleveland), April 3, 1915; IWW (1917*a*-1932); Anderson (1923),
p. 208; Milburn (1930), pp. 104-105; Greenway (1953), p. 211; Kornbluh (1964), pp.
240-241.

TOM JOAD

WOODY GUTHRIE   WOODY GUTHRIE

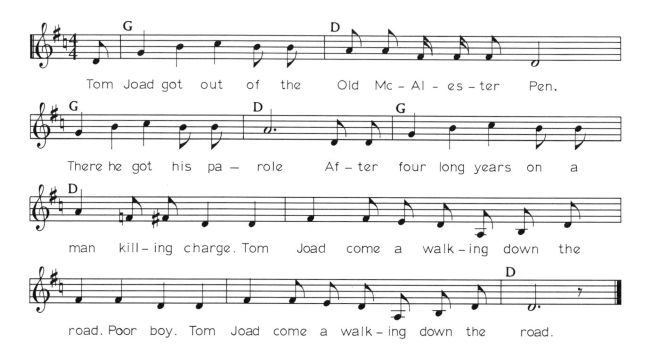

Tom Joad got out of the Old Mc-Al-es-ter Pen. There he got his pa-role Af-ter four long years on a man kill-ing charge. Tom Joad come a walk-ing down the road. Poor boy. Tom Joad come a walk-ing down the road.

1

Tom Joad got out of the Old McAlester Pen.
There he got his parole
After four long years on a man killing charge.
Tom Joad come a-walking down the road. Poor boy.
Tom Joad come a-walking down the road.

2

It was there that he found him a truck driving man,
There that he caught him a ride;
Said, "I just got a loose from McAlester's Pen
On a charge called homicide. Great God.
A charge called homicide."

3

That Truck rolled away in a big cloud of dust,
And Tommy turned his face towards home.
He met Preacher Casey, and they had a little drink,
And he found that his family, they was gone. Tom Joad.
He found that his family, they was gone.

4

He found his mother's old fashion shoe,
And he found his daddy's hat.
He found Little Muley, and Little Muley said,
"They been tractored out by th' cats, Tom.
They been tractored out by th' cats."

5

Well Tom, he walked over to the neighboring farm,
And he found his family,
And they took Preacher Casey, and they loaded in a car,
And his mammy said, "We got to git away, Tom."
His mammy said, "We got to get away."

6

The twelve of the Joads made a might heavy load,
And Grandpa Joad he cried.
He picked up a handful of land in his hand
And said, "I'm stickin' with my farm till I die.
I'm stickin' with my farm till I die."

7

They fed him spare ribs and coffee and soothing syrup,
And Grandpa Joad he died.
We buried Grandpa Joad on the Oklahoma road
And Grandma on the California side—
And Grandma on the California side.

8

We stood on a mountain, and we looked to the West,
And it looked like the Promised Land—
Was a big green valley with a river running through,
And there was work for every single hand. We thought.
There was work for every single hand.

9

Now the Joads rolled into a jungle camp.
It was there that they cooked them a stew,
And the hungry little kids in the jungle camp
Said, "We'd like to have some, too. Yes.
We'd like to have some, too."

10

A deputy sheriff fired loose at a man,
And he shot a woman in the back;
But before he could take his aim again,
It was Preacher Casey dropped him in his tracks. Good boy.
Preacher Casey dropped him in his tracks.

11

Well, they handcuffed Casey, and they took him to jail,
And then he got away;
And he met Tom Joad by the old river bridge,
And these few words he did say. Preacher Casey.
These few words he did say:

12

"Well, I preached for the Lord a mighty long time.
I preached about the rich and the poor;
But us workin' folks has got to stick together
Or we ain't got a chance anymore. God knows.
We ain't got a chance any more.

13

Then the deputies come, and Tom and Casey run
To a place where the water run down;
And a vigilante thug hit Casey with a club,
And he laid Preacher Casey on the ground.
And he laid Preacher Casey on the ground.

14

Tom Joad, he grabbed that deputy's club,
And he brung it down on his head.
When Tommy took flight that dark and rainy night,
Was a preacher and a deputy lying dead. Two men.
A preacher and a deputy lying dead.

15

Tommy run back where his mama was asleep,
And he woke her up out of bed;
And he kissed goodbye to the mother that he loved,
And he said what Preacher Casey said. Tom Joad.
He said what Preacher Casey said.

16

Ever'body might be just one big soul—
Well, it looks that a way to me—
So everywhere you look in th' day or th' night,
That's where I'm a gonna be. Ma.
That's where I'm a gonna be.

17

Wherever little kids are hungry and cry,
Wherever people ain't free,
Wherever men are fightin' for their rights,
That's where I'm a gonna be. Ma.
That's where I'm a gonna be.

TEXT AND MUSIC: Guthrie (1947), pp. 24-25, 48.

VARIANT: Greenway (1953), pp. 289-291.

WOODY GUTHRIE # PASTURES OF PLENTY WOODY GUTHRIE

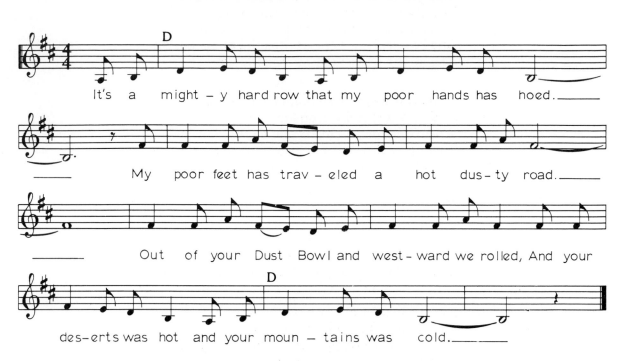

It's a might-y hard row that my poor hands has hoed._____

_____ My poor feet has trav-eled a hot dus-ty road._____

_____ Out of your Dust Bowl and west-ward we rolled, And your

des-erts was hot and your moun-tains was cold._____

1

It's a mighty hard road that my poor hands has hoed.
My poor feet has traveled a hot dusty road.
Out of your Dust Bowl and westward we rolled,
And your deserts was hot and your mountains was cold.

2

I work in your orchards of peaches and prunes,
And I sleep on the ground 'neath the light of your moon.
On the edge of your city you'll see us, and then
We come with the dust and we go with the wind.

3

California, Arizona, I make all your crops.
Then it's north up to Oregon to gather your hops.
Dig beets from your ground, cut the grapes from your vine
To set on your table your light sparkling wine.

4

Green Pastures of Plently from dry desert ground
From the Grand Coulee Dam where the waters run down
Every state in this union us migrants has been.
We'll work in your fight and we'll fight till we win.

5

It's always we ramble, that river and I.
All along your green valley I'll work till I die.
My land I'll defend with my life if needs be,
'Cause my Pastures of Plenty must always be free.

TEXT AND MUSIC: Guthrie (1947), pp. 44, 53.
VARIANT: Greenway (1953), 293-294.

FIFTY THOUSAND LUMBERJACKS

Although the logging industry has been the subject of more songs than have such industries as sheepherding and salmon fishing, the loggers of the American West have not been prolific song makers. Unlike the cowboys and hard-rock miners, they inherited a large body of topical music from their Mackinaw predecessors, and most of their new musical matter was provided for them by the professional composers of the labor organizations. As an illustration of what folk process was applied to such ready-made material, we begin with a pair of songs entitled "Fifty Thousand Lumberjacks." The first, to the tune of "Portland County Jail," was an IWW composition promoting the strike of 1917 which paralyzed the lumber industry in western Washington. It is hard to imagine anyone singing such detailed demands to an employer:

> Take a tip and start right in—plan some cozy rooms,
> Six or eight spring beds in each, with towels, sheets
>   and brooms;
> Shower baths for men who work keeps them well and fit.
> A laundry, too, and drying room, would help a little bit.

The memorable part—the chanted title—was worked into a song of protest which has entered oral tradition to the tune of "A Son of a Gamboleer;"

> Fifty thousand lumberjacks
>   Goin' in to eat
> Fifty thousand plates of slum
>   Made from tainted meat.
> Fifty thousand lumberjacks
>   All settin' up a yell
> To kill the bellyrobbers
>   An' damn their souls to hell.

Who would not sing that?

Another consequence of having propagandists rather than people make songs is that such a piece as Loren Roberts' "The Tragedy of Sunset Land," about the martyrdom of Wesley Everest, misses all the grim drama of that event. As elsewhere during World War I, the Pacific Northwest company owners had charged most organized appeals for better wages and working conditions with pro-Hunism. In the course of an Armistice Day parade of American Legionnaires in Centralia, Washington, in 1919, the troops unwisely halted before the IWW headquarters. A volley fired in panic from the building killed four legionnaires, and the rest of the veterans poured through the office and cornered Everest out back. He offered to turn himself over to any legal authority, but they castrated him and lynched him from a trestle over the Chehalis River.

For comic relief at this point, James Stevens' recent "The Frozen Logger" will do very well. And O. L. Ufavise's "Them Days Is Gone Forever," collected by WPA archivists in Oregon, is a good blend of humorous detail and protest:

> But nowadays timber is sold by the feet,
>   And they count every sliver and stick;
> They figure the snags and the windfalls to boot,
> And the fallers go down on their knees by the root,
>   And they chop down the tree with a pick.

FIFTY THOUSAND LUMBERJACKS, I

TUNE: Portland County Jail

Fif - ty thou-sand lum - ber jacks, fif - ty thou-sand packs,

Fif - ty thou-sand dir - ty rolls of blan - kets on their backs,

Fif - ty thou-sand minds made up to strike and strike like men; For

fif - ty years they've "packed" a bed, but nev - er will a - gain.

Chorus

"Such a lot of dev - ils," that's what the pap - ers say__ They've

gone on strike for short - er hours and some in-crease in pay, They

left the camps, the laz - y tramps, they walked all out as one; They

say they'll win the strike or put the bos - ses on the bum.

1

Fifty thousand lumberjacks, fifty thousand packs,
Fifty thousand dirty rolls of blankets on their backs,
Fifty thousand minds made up to strike and strike like men;
For fifty years they've "packed" a bed, but never will again.

CHORUS: "Such a lot of devils," that's what the papers say—
"They've gone on strike for shorter hours and some increase in pay.
They left the camps, the lazy tramps, they all walked out as one;
They say they'll win the strike or put the bosses on the bum."

2

Fifty thousand wooden bunks full of things that crawl;
Fifty thousand restless men have left them once for all.
One by one they dared not say, "Fat, the hours are long."
If they did, they'd hike—but now they're fifty thousand strong.

3

Fatty Rich, we know you're game, know your pride is pricked.
Say—but why not be a man, and own when you are licked?
They've joined the One Big Union—Gee! For goodness sake, "Get wise!"
The more you try to buck them now, the more they organize.

4

Take a tip and start right in—plan some cozy rooms,
Six or eight spring beds in each, with towels, sheets and brooms;
Shower baths for men who work keeps them well and fit.
A laundry, too, and drying room, would help a little bit.

5

Get some dishes, white and clean; good pure food to eat.
See that cook has help enough to keep the table neat.
Tap the bell for eight hours' work; treat the boys like men,
And fifty thousand lumberjacks may come to work again.

6

Men who work should be well paid. "A man's a man for a' that."
Many a man has a home to keep same as yourself, Old Fat.
Mothers, sisters, sweethearts, wives, children, too, galore,
Stand behind the men to win this bread and butter war.

TEXT: IWW (1918), pp. 55-56.

MUSIC: Sandburg (1927), p. 214. Used by permission of Harcourt, Brace & World Inc.

VARIANTS: *Solidarity* (Chicago), Aug. 4, 1917; IWW (1919-1932); Kornbluh (1964), p. 267.

FIFTY THOUSAND LUMBERJACKS, II

TUNE: A Son of a Gamboleer

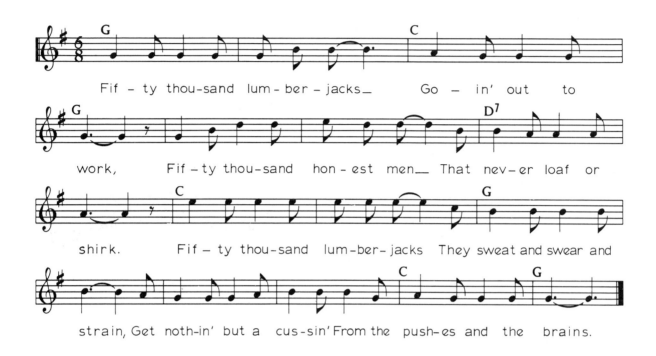

Fif - ty thou-sand lum - ber - jacks_ Go - in' out to work, Fif - ty thou-sand hon - est men_ That nev - er loaf or shirk. Fif - ty thou-sand lum - ber - jacks They sweat and swear and strain, Get noth-in' but a cus-sin' From the push-es and the brains.

1	3
Fifty thousand lumberjacks	Fifty thousand lumberjacks
Goin' out to work,	Sleepin' in pole bunks,
Fifty thousand honest men	Fifty thousand odors
That never loaf or shirk.	From dirty socks to skunks.
Fifty thousand lumberjacks,	Fifty thousand lumberjacks
They sweat and swear and strain,	Who snore and moan and groan
Get nothin' but a cussin'	While fifty million graybacks
From the pushes and the brains.	Are pickin' at their bones.

2	4
Fifty thousand lumberjacks	Fifty thousand lumberjacks,
Goin' in to eat	Fifty thousand packs,
Fifty thousand plates of slum	Fifty thousand dirty rolls
Made from tainted meat.	Upon their dirty backs.
Fifty thousand lumberjacks	Fifty thousand lumberjacks
All settin' up a yell	Strike and strike like men;
To kill the bellyrobbers	For fifty years we packed our rolls,
An' damn their souls to hell.	But never will again.

TEXT: Alderson (1942), p. 376. Used by permission of California Folklore Society.

MUSIC: *Most Popular College Songs* (1904), pp. 56-57.

VARIANT: Kornbluh (1964), pp. 267-268.

THE FROZEN LOGGER

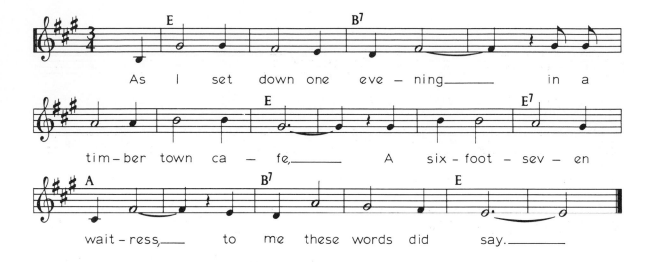

As I set down one eve-ning_____ in a tim-ber town ca-fe,_____ A six-foot-sev-en wait-ress,_____ to me these words did say._____

1

As I set down one evening in a timber town cafe,
A six-foot-seven waitress, to me these words did say:

2

"I see you are a logger, and not a common bum,
For no one but a logger, stirs his coffee with his thumb.

3

"My lover was a logger—there's none like him today—
If you'd sprinkle whisky on it, he'd eat a bale of hay;

4

"He never shaved the whiskers from off his horny hide,
But he'd pound 'em in with a hammer, then bite 'm off inside.

5

"My lover came to see me one freezing winter day.
He held me in a fond embrace that broke three vertebrae.

6

"He kissed me when we parted so hard he broke my jaw,
And I could not speak to tell him he'd forgot his mackinaw.

7

"I watched my logger lover going through the snow,
A sauntering gaily homeward at forty-eight below.

8

"The weather tried to freeze him, it tried its level best—
At a hundred degrees below zero, he buttoned up his vest.

9

"It froze clean down to China, it froze to the stars above.
At ONE THOUSAND DEGREES BELOW ZERO, it froze my logger love.

10

"They tried in vain to thaw him, and if you'll believe me, sir,
They made him into ax blades, to chop the Douglas fir.

11

"That's how I lost my lover, and to this caffay I come,
And here I wait till someone stirs his coffee with his thumb.

12

"And then I tell my story, of my love they could not thaw,
Who kissed me when we parted, so hard he broke my jaw."

TEXT: James Stevens, "Bunk-Shanty Ballads and Tales," *Oregon Historical Quarterly,* L (1949), 241.

MUSIC: As sung by James F. Stevens. Transcribed by Ruth Crawford Seeger.

VARIANT: Botkin. (1951), p. 769.

LOREN ROBERTS   # THE TRAGEDY OF SUNSET LAND

TUNE: Where the Silvery Colorado Wends Its Way

1

There's a little Western city in the shadow of the hills
    Where sleeps a brave young rebel 'neath the dew;
Now he's free from life's long struggle, his name is with us still;
    We know that he was fearless, tried and true.
In a homely pine-board coffin, our warrior lies at rest.
    Those henchmen turned loose on him one day.
These parting words were spoken: "Boys, I did my best!"
    Where the old Chehalis River flows its way.

CHORUS: Now the moonbeams in the dell linger there in sad farewell,
    In memory of that fateful autumn day;
And some day we are coming home, in the Sunset Land to roam,
    Where the old Chehalis River flows its way.

2

The monarchs of the forest were secure in their regime
    When they took brave Wesley Everest's life away.
His name will be a memory in the workers' high esteem
    Where the old Chehalis River flows its way.
When the sunlight floods the hilltops and the birds will sing once more,
    In that valley we will settle down to stay,
There to organize the workers on that lonely woodland shore
    Where the old Chehalis River flows its way.

TEXT: "The Tragedy of Sunset Land" (Los Angeles: IWW Local Prison Comfort Club, ca. 1920).

VARIANTS: IWW (1925-1932).

O. L. UFAVISE # THEM DAYS IS GONE FOREVER

1

Come, all you old loggers, and list to my tale,
  As I weep on the shoulder of time,
And sob out a story to make you turn pale
And the sin of the new-fangled notions bewail,
  With pity and shame for the crime.

2

Once timber was common and plenty and cheap,
  And logging was easy as pie;
Then a man had a chance where the side-hill was steep
And the trees had a lean and the river ran deep
  And the sawmill lay handily by.

3

Once the fallers went up with their springboards to where
  It was easy to saw and to chop;
And if ten feet or twenty, then who was to care,
For the height of the stump was the faller's affair—
  He knew where he wanted to stop!

4

But nowadays timber is sold by the feet,
  And they count every sliver and stick;
They figure the snags and the windfalls to boot,
And the fallers go down on their knees by the root,
  And they chop down the tree with a pick.

5

Once you might borrow a "forty" or two,
  And no one be any the wiser;
And rustle a donkey, a line and a crew,
And maybe some rigging—a "Tommy" would do—
  And go logging, as proud as the Kaiser.

6

No fussing with figures or plans and such truck,
  A-mapping to south and to north;
You stuck in some fellows to fall and to buck,
And pick out a "setting," and if you had luck,
  You pulled out a stake by the "Fourth."

7

There wasn't no high-collar experts to chin
  Of investment and product and cost;
You tackled the layout and gambled to win,
And took any grief that was yours with a grin,
  And cussed out the "show" if you lost.

8

But the days of the shoe-string adventure are dead,
    And the romance has gone to the hogs;
The spirit of happy-go-lucky has fled,
For the woods-boss has taken to system instead,
    And the glamour has gone to the dogs.

TEXT: WPA Oregon Folklore Archive, Folder 2, Salem, Ore.

A DOLLAR A DAY WITHOUT BOARD

During the railroad strikes of 1877, Henry Ward Beecher, a preacher and quondam encomiast of the West, said: "It was true that $1 a day was not enough to support a man and five children, if a man would insist on smoking and drinking beer. Was not a dollar a day enough to buy bread? Water costs nothing. Men cannot live by bread, it is true; but the man who cannot live on bread and water is not fit to live." Beecher was noted for his liberal views. These songs record Western replies to this attitude from that largely voiceless number, the miscellaneous, urban poor. Frustrated and unskilled, they sometimes fell for such shabby attractions as that offered by Denis Kearney's Workingmen's Party. Established in 1877, its fight to save the Irish washerwoman from the emigrant Chinese was won in 1882. Paradise did not, however, follow immediately upon that remedy to such complaints as that of Harry Norcross in "A Dollar a Day Without Board":

> The coolie, you'll find, will get plenty of work,
> And get fat! Oh! The miserable horde!
> While a man has to work in the mud and the mire
> For a dollar a day without board.

"The San Francisco Rag-Picker" brings the seeing-the-elephant theme up to skid row modernity:

> As the last resort left me, I got out these old bags,
> Also this 'ere hook to "snake out" the rags;
> But t'other day I picked up a pair of old socks,
> And now, blast my luck! I'm broke out with small pox!

Had that unfortunate tried San Francisco's infamous waterfront, the Barbary Coast, he might have fared far worse. The narrator of "Go to Sea No More" tells of being rolled while blind-drunk there, and then shanghaied for San Francisco's whale fleet, the only one surviving in America, though it now spears leviathan for pet food.

"Ship Out," from an early Western edition of the "Little Red Songbook," holds out the promise of job stability, of respite from wandering. And Richard Brazier's "The Suckers Sadly Gather" muses on those who reject the brotherhood:

> The Hoboes quietly gather 'round a distant water tank,
> While the Bulls are safely resting home in bed;
> And they sadly sit and ponder on the days when they ate pie
> And occasionally some moldy punk instead.

There was considerable unemployment in the Golden State in the decade before World War I; therefore, when extensive labor was called for in the construction of the lavish, plaster of paris buildings of the Pan Pacific International Exposition in San Francisco in 1915, frustration was also invited. Joe Hill composed "It's a Long Way Down to the Soup Line" in protest against the situation.

One of the consequences of strikebreaking in densely populated urban areas is incidentally related in "The Ballad of Bloody Thursday." This ballad commemorates the battle between 1,000 San Francisco police and 5,000 striking longshoremen and their sympathizers on the Embarcadero on July 5, 1934. The state insisted on operating its waterfront railroad in spite of the strike, curious citizens insisted on getting a closer look, and the strikers insisted on hurling bricks through the tear gas. The results were two shot to death, 31 wounded by gunfire, seventy-eight seriously injured by bricks, clubs, and tear gas, and the establishment of a hiring hall system that has kept the docks free of serious strife since.

HARRY NORCROSS

A DOLLAR A DAY WITHOUT BOARD

TUNE: Jim Fisk

I've trav-eled this wide world o'er and o'er, And have

lived in man-y a clime;__ But pov-er-ty

seems to have hold of me now, For I'm left__ a-

lone with-out a dime.__ The coo-lie, you'll

find, will get plen-ty of work, And get fat! Oh! The

mis-er-a-ble horde!__ While a man has to

work in the mud and the mire For a dol-lar a

day with-out board.__ Then strike out, ye he-roes of

la-bor,__ The sin-ew and bone of our

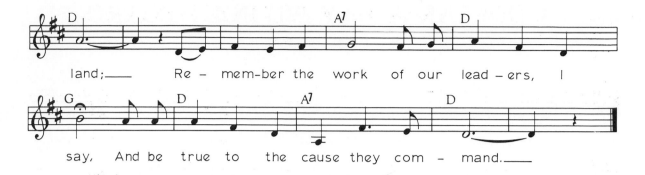

land;___ Re - mem-ber the work of our lead – ers, I

say, And be true to the cause they com - mand.___

1

I've traveled this wide world o'er and o'er,
And have lived in many a clime;
But poverty seems to have hold of me now,
For I'm left alone without a dime.
The coolie, you'll find, will get plenty of work,
And get fat! Oh! The miserable horde!
While a man has to work in the mud and the mire
For a dollar a day without board.

CHORUS: Then strike out, ye heroes of labor,
The sinew and bone of our land;
Remember the work of our leaders, I say,
And be true to the cause they command.

2

I got up just before daybreak,
For I heard that Crocker would give
A thousand men work in the morning
To buy "grub" enough so they could live.
I've got a good wife and two children—
There's bright little Freddie and Maud—
So I'm compelled to look out for my dear family
On a dollar a day without board.

3

We must not forget Mr. Kearney,
Our Leader, so brave and so true,
Who so nobly fought every battle;
To him alone honor is due.
When workingmen rule our grand country
And wipe out this "political fraud,"
We won't work for cruel corporations, I know,
For a dollar a day without board.

TEXT: *The Blue and Gray Songster* (San Francisco: S. T. & S. S. Greene, 1877), pp. 44-45.

MUSIC: Sandburg (1927), pp. 416-418. Used by permission of Harcourt, Brace & World, Inc.

VARIANT: Lengyel (1939), p. 145a.

FRED WOODHULL # THE SAN FRANCISCO RAG-PICKER

TUNE: Lather and Shave

1

O, ladies and gentlemen, list to my song!
It's about a poor devil who can't get along,
For whenever some promising business I try,
I'm sure to get "diddled" and "burst up sky-high."

CHORUS: I can't get along, and I've got "nixey" cash;
So I have to go picking up rags for my "hash."

2

When first I went trading upon my own hook,
I started down South to sell a new book;
But I got tarred and feathered the very first day,
Because folks thought I came to run niggers away.

3

Then I went back down East and opened a shop
To sell candy and cakes, "likewise ginger-pop";
And I hired but one clerk—not to go it too brash—
But he eat up my stock and run off with my cash.

4

I thought I'd turn farmer, and went way Out West,
Where I squatted on land of the richest and best;
But for three long years I shooks with the "chills,"
And mortgaged my farm to buy quinine and pills.

5

Then I thought I'd turn Mormon and went to Salt Lake;
But that was a trip that about "cooked my cake,"
For "Old Young" gave me ninety big women to keep—
And how can a man stand it without any sleep?

6

So I ran off and drove an ox-team to Washoe,
Found a "rich silver lead," and Lord! didn't I blow?
But I soon saw 'twouldn't make me rich in a hurry,
As 'twas claimed as a "spur" by the "Gould & Curry."

7

Then I came down to Frisco and went on the Stage;
I made my debut in announcing a carriage;
But I "stuck," and the "boys" sung out "Supe, Get, You Guy,"
And one chap hove a big Irish "spud" in my eye.

8

I've tried everything else other people make pay;
I've been Methodist preacher, and I've worked by the day;
Taught school, made bricks, played poker, wrote rhymes,
But whatever I do, it's always "hard times!"

9

As the last resort left me, I got these old bags,
Also this 'ere hook to "snake out" the rags;
But t'other day I picked up a pair of old socks,
And now, blast my luck! I'm broke out with small pox!

———————

TEXT: "The San Francisco Rag-Picker," as sung by Fred Woodhull (San Francisco: T. C. Boyd, n.d.).

VARIANTS: *Novelty Songster, No. 1* (San Francisco: LaMalfa & Co., n.d.); Lengyel (1939), p. 142.

WALQUIST # SHIP OUT

TUNE: School Days

1

Nothing to do, sucker darling.
Nothing to do today.
Come take a trip to Oregon—
Fat shark will ship you there.
Erickson and Peterson are wanting men
To come and work for them,
So, if you will go, we'll give you a show—
Two dollars you'll have to pay.

CHORUS: Ship out, ship out,
Ship out to a master;
They give you a poor wage
And feed you on peas.
The bunks they are plumb full
Of crums and fleas.
No wonder a worker becomes a "Bo"—
You knock on back doors till your
knuckles are sore—
Whenever you ship to a job.

2

Don't you remember the driver
Who worked you so hard, you know?
He'll make you work fast as long as you last,
And then you will have to go
Hike along the railroad
With your blankets upon your back.
So come and get wise—
Come, now, organize and never ship out any
more.

TEXT: IWW (1910), p. 37.
VARIANTS: IWW (1912b-1914a).

RICHARD BRAZIER

THE SUCKERS SADLY GATHER

TUNE: Where the Silvery Colorado Wends Its Way

1

Oh! The suckers sadly gather around the Red Cross office door,
    And at the job signs longingly they gaze;
They think it's time they shipped out to a job once more,
    For they haven't bought a job for several days.
So inside they go and they put down their dough—
    "We have come to buy a job from you," they say.
The employment shark says: "Right. I will ship you out tonight,
    Where the silvery Colorado wends its way."

CHORUS: Now those suckers by the score
  Are hiking back once more,
    For they didn't get no job out there, they say;
  So to town they're hiking back
  O'er that bum old railroad track,
    Where the silvery Colorado wends its way.

2

The Hoboes quietly gather 'round a distant water tank,
    While the Bulls are safely resting home in bed;
And they sadly sit and ponder on the days when they ate pie
    And occasionally some moldy punk instead.
But now they're living high when a chicken coop is nigh,
    For the ranchers send them chicken every day,
So to the jungles they skidoo to dine on chicken stew,
    Where the silvery Colorado wends its way.

CHORUS: There's a Bo 'neath every tree,
  And they are happy as can be,
    For the chewings 'round that place are good, they say,
  For they have chicken galore,
  And they know where there is more,
    Where the silvery Colorado wends its way.

TEXT: IWW (1909*b*), p. 21.
VARIANTS: IWW (1910, 1912*b*); Kornbluh (1964), p. 73.

JOE HILL   # IT'S A LONG WAY DOWN TO THE SOUP LINE

TUNE: Its a Long Way to Tipperary

1

Bill Brown came a thousand miles to work on Frisco Fair.
 All the papers said a million men were wanted there.
Bill Brown hung around and asked for work three times a day,
 'Till finally he went busted flat, then he did sadly say:

CHORUS: It's a long way down to the soup line,
 It's a long way to go.
It's a long way down to the soup line,
 And the soup is weak I know.
Good-bye, good old pork chops,
 Fare-well beefsteak rare.
It's a long way down to the soup line
 But my soup is there.

2

Bill Brown saw a big fine house; he knocked upon the door;
 But they told him that they only helped the "worthy poor."
"Guess I'll have to live on sunshine in the Golden West,"
 Said Billy Brown, and then he joined the chorus with the rest.

3

There's a whisper round the town among "the men of means"
 That they would be glad to give the Fair to New Orleans;
And when all is over, many sharks with faces long
 Will line up at the Ferry and then sadly hum this song.

———————

TEXT: "It's a Long Way Down to the Soup Line," by Joe Hill (San Francisco: IWW Locals, 1915), 4 pp.

VARIANTS: Glazer and Friedland (1953), p. 5; Stavis and Harmon (1955), pp. 34-35; Kornbluh (1964), p. 145.

GO TO SEA NO MORE

When first I went to Fris-co, I went up-on the spree. Me hard-earned cash I spent it fast, got drunk as drunk could be. Be-fore me mon-ey was all gone, or spent wi' some ol' whore, I wuz ful-ly in-clined, made up me mind, to go to sea no more.

Chorus

No more, no more, No more, no more, no more! There goes Jack Rack, poor sail-or boy, Who's go-in' to sea no more!

1

When first I went to Frisco, I went upon the spree.
Me hard-earned cash I spent it fast, got drunk as drunk could be.
Before me money was all gone, or spent wi' some ol' whore,
I wuz fully inclined, made up me mind, to go to sea no more.

CHORUS: No more, no more, no more, no more, no more!
There goes Jack Rack, poor sailor boy, who's goin' to sea no more!

That night I slept wid Mary Ann, too drunk to turn in bed.
Me clothes wuz new, me money wuz too, next morn wid them she'd fled.
A-feelin' sick I left the house an' went down by the shore.
Oh, an' then as I went, me head all bent, the crimps, they all did roar.

3

The first chap I ran foul of wuz Mister Shanghai Brown.
I axed him neat for to stand treat; he looked me up an' down.
Sez he, "Last time yiz wuz paid off, wi' me yiz chalked no score,
But I'll give ye a chance, an' I'll take yer advance, for to go to sea once
     more!"

4

Oh, he shipped me aboard of a whalin'-ship, bound for the Arctic Seas,
Where the cold winds blow an' the frost an' the snow makes even hot rum
     freeze.
I had no clothes, I had no gear, me cash spent on a whore.
Oh, 'twas then that I swore when once on shore I'd go to sea no more.

5

Some days we caught our sparm whales, boys; some days we did catch
     none.
Wid a twenty-foot oar stuck in yer paw, we pulled the whole day long,
And when the night it came along, an' ye nod upon yer oar.
Oh, a man must be blind fer ter make up his mind fer ter go ter sea once
     more.

6

Come, all ye bully sailormen, an' listen to me song.
O, I hope ye just will listen till I tell yiz what went wrong.
Take my advice, don't drink strong rum, nor go sleepin' wid a whore,
But just git spliced, that's my advice, and go ter sea no more!

TEXT AND MUSIC: Hugill (1961), pp. 582-583.

VARIANTS: Lomax and Lomax (1934), pp. 495-496; Doerflinger (1951), pp. 107-109,
346*; Hugill (1961), pp. 583-585.

THE BALLAD OF BLOODY THURSDAY

TUNE: The Cowboy's Lament

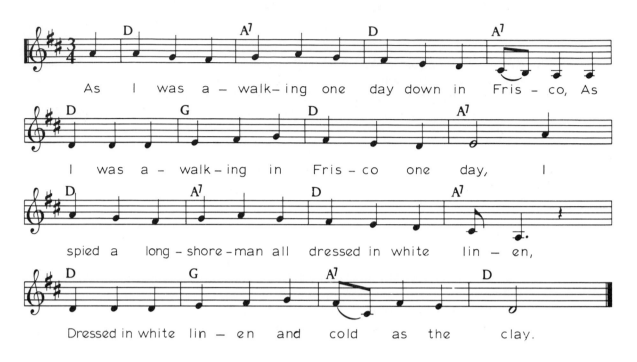

As I was a-walk-ing one day down in Fris - co, As

I was a-walk-ing in Fris - co one day, I

spied a long-shore-man all dressed in white lin - en,

Dressed in white lin - en and cold as the clay.

1

As I was a-walking one day down in Frisco,
As I was a-walking in Frisco one day,
I spied a longshoreman all dressed in white linen,
Dressed in white linen and cold as the clay.

2

"I see by your outfit that you are a worker,"
These words he did say as I slowly passed by;
"Sit down beside me and hear my sad story,
For I'm shot in the breast and I know I must die.

3

"It was down on the Front where I worked on the cargoes,
Worked on the cargoes ten hours a day;
I lost my right fingers because of the speedup,
The speedup that killed many a man in my day.

4

"With too much of a sling load on old rusty cable,
The boss saved ten dollars, ten dollars, I say.
That old rusty sling broke and fell on my buddy;
Ten lousy bucks carried Jimmie away.

5

"Those were the days when the Boss owned the union;
We poor working stiffs—we had nothing to say.
Ours was to work and to keep our big traps shut;
We stood in the shape-up for a dollar a day.

6

"But our children were hungry; their clothing was tattered.
It's then that we workers began to get wise.
We tore up our fink books and listened to Bridges,
Saying, 'Look at your kids, brother, let's organize.'

7

"Strong and united we went to the bosses
For better conditions and a decent day's pay;
The bosses just laughed—we all had a meeting,
That's why we're hitting the bricks here today.

8

"Our struggles were many; our struggles were bloody.
We fought the shipowners with all that we had.
With thousands of dollars, they tempted our leaders;
But our guys were honest—they couldn't be had.

9

"It was there on the line that I marched with my brothers.
It was there on the line, as we proudly passed by,
The cops and the soldiers they brought up their rifles—
I'm shot in the breast and I know I must die.

10

"Four hundred strikers were brutally wounded,
Four hundred workers and I left there to die.
Remember the day, sir, to all of your children,
This bloody Thursday—the fifth of July.

11

"Don't beat the drums slowly, don't play the pipes lowly;
Don't play the dead march as they carry me along.
There's wrongs that need righting, so keep right on fighting
And lift your proud voices in proud union songs."

12

Fight on together, you organized workers.
Fight on together; there's nothing to fear.
Remember the martyrs of this bloody Thursday.
Let nothing divide you, and victory is near.

TEXT: Greenway (1953), pp. 237-238. Used by permission of John Greenway.

MUSIC: As sung by Harry Jackson, *The Cowboy: His Songs, Ballads and Brag Talk*, Folkways Record FH 5723. Transcribed by David Cohen.

HALLELUJAH, ON THE BUM

Aggressively idle, at least as he pictured himself in some of his songs, the "Great American Bum" was our answer to Europe's gypsies. He sought his freedom along the path of least resistance, singing as he went. Others, lumped together under the various titles of hobo, migrant, tramp, bum, vagrant, and moocher, were the tragic products of such different forces as a seasonal labor market and strong drink. There are songs about all these men who divided their time among rides on the rods, work, the jungles outside towns, and the main stems in their cities.

Harry McClintock claimed to have composed "Hallelujah, On the Bum," and printed it broadside in 1906. It also appeared in the first edition of the "Little Red Songbook," and in the Chicago *I.W.W. Industrial Union Bulletin* in 1908. At any rate, it became an anthem of both the Wobs and hobos, generally, as it mingled humor and frustration:

> Whenever I get
> All the money I earn,
> The boss will be broke,
> And to work he must turn!

For the connection between the IWW and hobos, we may quote the authority, Nels Anderson: "Since so many boys and young men are attracted into the class and since the promise of adventure generally proves a delusion there is naturally considerable unrest, which may explain the zeal with which hobos often turn to syndicalism."

"The Bum on the Stem," from George Milburn's *Hobo's Hornbook*, exhibits more strongly the freedom first discussed, although, depending on the singer, it could reek of sour grapes:

> My clothes are gettin' ragged,
> My shoes are gettin' thin—
> What do I care?—I get the air—
> I'm on the bum again.

Milburn's rich collection also supplies "The Great American Bum," a song that stresses the migrant's experience at a wide variety of menial jobs and his unlimited knowledge of the hard types that turn him down: cops, railroad bulls, stingy housewives, and scab hirers.

We give two quite different versions of the famous "The Big Rock Candy Mountains." The longer version, the second one here, is a modern hobo's Land of Cockaigne, the fool's paradise, ingeniously adapted to a narrator who, even in his remotest dreams, cannot imagine a life without cops and jails:

> The shacks all have to tip their hats,
> And the railroad bulls are blind.
> There's a lake of stew and of whisky, too—
> You can paddle all around in a big canoe—
> In the Big Rock Candy Mountains.

A shorter version is more poignant, for it restricts the paradisal vision to a refrain chanted by an old bum to his young protégé—gunsel, if you will. The narrative portion reveals the youth's disillusionment:

> "I've hiked and hiked till my feet are sore.
> I'll be God damned if I hike any more
> To be a home guard with a lemonade card
> In the Big Rock Candy Mountains."

Woody Guthrie's "Hard Travelin'" is a recent and original expression of the migrant's life and hazards, while "The Dying Hobo," from a 1917 copy of the *Hobo News*, is a tear-jerking mixture of fantasy and dirge:

> "I am going to a better land,
> Where everything is bright,
> Where beef-stews grow on bushes
> And you sleep out every night."

"The Hobo's Last Ride" is an interesting catalogue of railroad names woven into a litany for the hobo's dying pal.

HARRY MC CLINTOCK

HALLELUJAH, ON THE BUM

TUNE: Revive Us Again

O, why don't you work As oth-er men do? How in
hell can I work When there's no work to do? Hal-le-
lu-jah, I'm a bum! Hal-le-lu-jah, bum a-gain! Hal-le-
lu-jah, give us a hand-out To re-vive us a-gain.

1
O, why don't you work
As other men do?
How in hell can I work
When there's no work to do?

CHORUS: Hallelujah, I'm a bum!
Hallelujah, bum again!
Hallelujah, give us a handout
To revive us again.

2
O, why don't you save
All the money you earn?
If I did not eat,
I'd have money to burn!

3
O, I like my boss—
He's a good friend of mine;
That's why I'm starving
Out in the bread-line!

4
I can't buy a job,
For I ain't got the dough,
So I ride in a box-car,
For I'm a hobo!

5
Whenever I get
All the money I earn,
The boss will be broke,
And to work he must turn!

TEXT: IWW (1909a), p. 2.

MUSIC: Milburn (1930), p. 98. Used by permission of Ives Washburn, Inc.

VARIANTS: *I.W.W. Industrial Union Bulletin* (Chicago), April 4, 1908; IWW (1909b-1914b); *Industrial Worker* (Spokane, Wash.), May 1, 1912; Webb (1923), p. 39; Sandburg (1927), pp. 184-185; Milburn (1930), pp. 97-101; Clark (1932), p. 77; Lomax and Lomax (1934), pp. 26-27; Glazer and Friedland (1953), p. 6; Greenway (1953), pp. 197-202; Fowke and Glazer (1960), pp. 126-127; Toelken (1962), p. 15; Kornbluh (1964), pp. 71-72.

THE BUM ON THE STEM

On the high-ways and the rail—road tracks,You'll find bums ev - ery-

where. They're shoot - in' snipes, they're smok - in' pipes, They're

mooch - in' for a square. Oh, some birds like their

high - class grab With lots of ser - vice, too;___ But

give me a sha - dy jun - gle And a can of mul - li - gan stew.

1

On the highways and the railroad tracks,
    You'll find bums everywhere.
They're shootin' snipes, they're smokin' pipes,
    They're moochin' for a square.
Oh, some birds like their highclass grub,
    With lots of service, too;
But give me a shady jungle
    And a can of mulligan stew.

2

There's lots of joy and sunshine,
    Wherever you chance to roam,
But how are you going to see them
    If you always stay at home?
Oh, plinging down the highway,
    Going to be gone so long;
If you don't think I'm goin',
    Just you count the days I'm gone.

3

Once I met John Farmer;
  He stopped me on my way.
He said, "I've got some 'taters,
  And I want them dug today."
"Naw, I can't dig no 'taters,
  Because I'm gettin' fat;
Go get the guy that planted them,
  'Cause he knows where they're at!"

4

While I was sleeping in the shade,
  Just to pass the time away,
A man came up and asked me,
  To help him pitch some hay.
He said his land was rollin'.
  I said, "Now is that true?
Just roll it past this shady spot—
  I'll see what I can do!"

5

Oh, sleeping among the daisies
  After hiking all the day—
Some folks like a foldin' bed,
  But give me the new mown hay.
My clothes are gettin' ragged,
  My shoes are gettin' thin—
What do I care?—I get the air—
  I'm on the bum again.

6

The nights are gettin' colder,
  And soon we'll all be froze;
I'm going to a sunny state
  Where the weather fits me clothes.
Oh, waiting at the water-tank
  For a rattler passin' by—
If she don't stop here,
  I'll catch her on the fly.

7

I hear her whistle blowin'
  And yonder comes the train—
I'll see you all in 'Frisco.
  I'm on the bum again!

TEXT AND MUSIC: Milburn (1930), pp. 124-127. Used by permission of Ives Washburn, Inc.

THE GREAT AMERICAN BUM

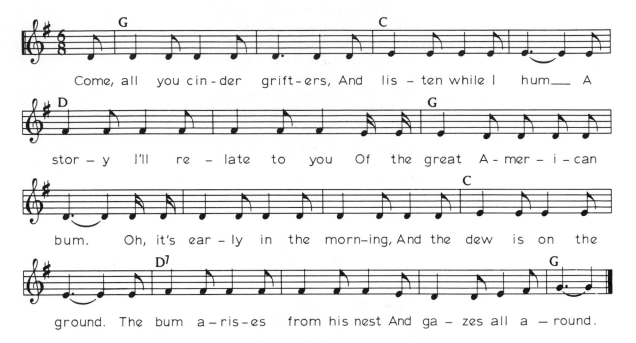

Come, all you cin-der grift-ers, And lis-ten while I hum___ A
stor-y I'll re-late to you Of the great A-mer-i-can
bum. Oh, it's ear-ly in the morn-ing, And the dew is on the
ground. The bum a-ris-es from his nest And ga-zes all a-round.

1

Come, all you cinder grifters,
    And listen while I hum—
A story I'll relate to you
    Of the great American bum.
Oh, it's early in the morning,
    And the dew is on the ground.
The bum arises from his nest
    And gazes all around.

2

From the boxcar and the haystack,
    He gazes everywhere.
He never turns back upon his track
    Until he gets a square.
I've beat my way from 'Frisco Bay
    To the rockbound coast of Maine,
To Canada and Mexico,
    And wandered back again.

3

I've met town clowns and harness bulls
    As tough as cops can be.
I've been in ev'ry calaboose
    In this land of liberty.
I've topped the spruce and worked the sluice,
    And I've taken a turn at the plow;
I've searched for gold in the rain and cold,
    And I've worked on a river scow.

4

I've dug the clam and built the dam,
    And packed the elusive prune;
But my troubles pale when I hit the trail
    A-packing my old balloon!
Oh, a-standing in the railroad yards
    A-waiting for a train—
Waiting for a westbound freight,
    But I think it's all in vain.

5

Going east they're loaded—
    Going west, sealed tight.
I think we'll have to get aboard
    A fast express tonight.
O, lady, would you be kind enough
    To appease my appetite,
For really I'm so hungry
    I don't know where to sleep tonight.

6

We are four bums, four doozy old bums.
    We live like dukes and oils.
We're having good luck in bumming our
    chuck—
    God bless the man who toils.
Oh, sleeping against the tool-house,
    And sleeping against the station—
Plenty of running water
    Is the only recommendation.

7

I met a man the other day
    I never had met before.
He asked me if I wanted a job
    A-shovelin' iron ore.
I asked him what the wages was,
    And he says, "Two bits a ton."
I says, "Old man, go chase yourself,
    I'd rather be a bum!"

TEXT AND MUSIC: Milburn (1930), pp. 70-73. Used by permission of Ives Washburn, Inc.

THE BIG ROCK
CANDY MOUNTAINS, I

HARRY MC CLINTOCK

One sum-mer day in the month of May, A jock-er, he came hik-ing. He came to a tree and "Ah," says he, "This is just to my lik-ing." In the ver-y same month on the ver-y same day, A Hoo-sier boy came hik-ing.__ Said the bum to the son, "Oh will you come To the Big Rock Can-dy Moun-tains?" I'll show you the bees in the cig-a-rette trees, and the so-da wa-ter foun-tain, And the lem-on-ade springs where the blue bird sings In the Big Rock Can-dy Moun-tains.

1

One summer day in the month of May,
A jocker, he came hiking.
He came to a tree and "Ah," says he,
"This is just to my liking."
In the very same month on the very same day,
A Hoosier boy came hiking.
Said the bum to the son, "Oh will you come
To the Big Rock Candy Mountains?"

CHORUS: I'll show you the bees in the cigarette trees,
And the soda water fountain,
And the lemonade springs where the blue bird sings
In the Big Rock Candy Mountains.

2

So they started away on the very same day,
The bum and the kid together,
To romp and to rove in the cigarette grove
In the land of the sunny weather.
They danced and they hiked for many a day,
The mile posts they were counting;
But they never arrived at the lemonade tide
Or the Big Rock Candy Mountains.

3

The punk rolled up his big blue eyes
And said to the jocker, "Sandy,
I've hiked and hiked and wandered too,
But I ain't seen any candy.
I've hiked and hiked till my feet are sore.
I'll be God damned if I hike any more
To be a home guard with a lemonade card
In the Big Rock Candy Mountains."

TEXT: Greenway (1953), pp. 203-204. Used by permission of John Greenway.

MUSIC: Clark (1932), p. 79. Used by permission of Shawnee Press, Inc.

VARIANTS: Milburn (1930), pp. 61-62; Clark (1932), p. 79; Briegel (1933), pp. 8-9; Frey (1936), pp. 34-35.

THE BIG ROCK CANDY MOUNTAINS, II

One eve-ning as the sun went down And the

jun-gle fire was burn-ing, Down the track came a ho — bo,

hum-ming, And he said, "Boys, I'm not turn-ing. I'm

head-ed for a land that's far a-way Be-side the crys — tal

foun-tains. I'll see you all this com-ing fall In the

Chorus

Big Rock Can-dy Moun-tains. In the Big Rock Can-dy

Moun-tains, There's a land that's fair and bright, Where the

hand-outs grow on bush-es And you sleep out eve-ry

night, Where the box-cars all are emp-ty And the sun shines eve-ry

day_ Oh, the birds and the bees and the cig-a-rette trees, The

rock and rye springs where the whang-doo-dle sings, In   the Big   Rock Can-dy Moun-tains.

1

One evening as the sun went down
And the jungle fire was burning,
Down the track came a hobo, humming,
And he said, "Boys, I'm not turning.
I'm headed for a land that's far away
Beside the crystal fountains.
I'll see you all this coming fall
In the Big Rock Candy Mountains.

CHORUS: "In the Big Rock Candy Mountains,
There's a land that's fair and
    bright,
Where the handouts grow on bushes
And you sleep out every night,
Where the boxcars all are empty
And the sun shines every day—
Oh, the birds and the bees and the
    cigarette trees,
The rock and rye springs where the
    whangdoodle sings,
In the Big Rock Candy Mountains.

2

"In the Big Rock Candy Mountains,
All the cops have wooden legs,
And the bulldogs all have rubber teeth,
And the hens lay softboiled eggs.
The farmers' trees are full of fruit,
And the barns are full of hay.
Oh, I'm bound to go where there ain't no
    snow,
Where the sleet don't fall and the wind don't
    blow,
In the Big Rock Candy Mountains.

3

"In the Big Rock Candy Mountains,
You never change your socks,
And the little streams of alkyhol
Come trickling down the rocks.
The shacks all have to tip their hats,
And the railroad bulls are blind.
There's a lake of stew and of whisky, too—
You can paddle all around in a big canoe—
In the Big Rock Candy Mountains.

4

"In the Big Rock Candy Mountains,
The jails are made of tin,
And you can bust right out again
As soon as they put you in.
There ain't no shorthandled shovels,
No axes, saws or picks.
I'm a-going to stay where you sleep all day—
Oh, they boiled in oil the inventor of toil—
In the Big Rock Candy Mountains.
"Oh, come with me, and we'll go see
The Big Rock Candy Mountains."

TEXT AND MUSIC: Milburn (1930), pp. 86-89. Used by permission of Ives Washburn, Inc.
VARIANTS: Lomax and Lomax (1947), pp. 278-281; Lomax (1960), pp. 422-423.

WOODY GUTHRIE # HARD TRAVELIN' WOODY GUTHRIE

1

I been havin' some hard travelin', I thought you knowed;
I been havin' some hard travelin' way down the road.
I been havin' some hard travelin', hard ramblin', hard gamblin';
I been havin' some hard travelin', Lord.

2

I been ridin' in fast rattlers, I thought you knowed;
I been ridin' in flat wheelers, way down the road.
I been ridin' in blind passengers, dead enders, pickin' up cinders;
I been havin' some hard travelin', Lord.

3

I been hittin' some hard-rock mining, I thought you knowed,
North of Dakota to Kansas city, way down the road.
Cuttin' that wheat, stackin' that hay, and I'm tryin' to make about a dollar a day;
An' I been havin' some hard travelin', Lord.

4

I been workin' that Pittsburg steel, I thought you knowed;
I been dumpin' that red hot slag, way down the road.
I been blastin', I been firin', I been pourin' that red hot iron;
An I been hittin' some hard travelin', Lord.

5

I been layin' in a hard-rock jail, I thought you knowed;
I been layin' out ninety days, way down the road.
Damned old judge he said to me "Ninety days for vagrancy";
I been hittin' some hard travelin', Lord.

TEXT AND MUSIC: As sung by Woody Guthrie, Folkways Record FA 2483. Transcribed by David Cohen.

VARIANTS: Fowke and Glazer (1960), pp. 124-125; Lomax (1960), pp. 435-436.

THE DYING HOBO

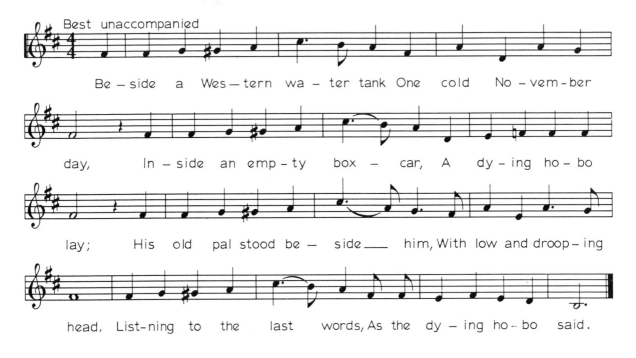

Best unaccompanied

Be—side a Wes—tern wa—ter tank One cold No—vem—ber day, In—side an emp—ty box— car, A dy—ing ho—bo lay; His old pal stood be— side___ him, With low and droop—ing head, List—ning to the last words, As the dy—ing ho—bo said.

1
Beside a Western water tank
    One cold November day,
Inside an empty boxcar,
    A dying hobo lay;
His old pal stood beside him,
    With low and drooping head,
Listening to the last words,
    As the dying hobo said:

2
"I am going to a better land,
    Where everything is bright,
Where beef-stews grow on bushes
    And you sleep out every night;
And you do not have to work at all,
    And never change your socks,
And streams of goodly whiskey
    Come trickling down the rocks.

3
"Tell the bunch around Market street
    That my face, no more, they'll view;
Tell them I've caught a fast freight,
    And that I'm going straight on through.
Tell them not to weep for me—
    No tears in their eyes must lurk—
For I'm going to a better land,
    Where they hate the word called 'work.'

4
"Hark! I hear her whistling,
    I must catch her on the fly;
I would like one scoop of beer
    Once more before I die."
The hobo stopped, his head fell back,
    He'd sung his last refrain;
His old pal stole his coat and hat
    And caught an East-bound train.

TEXT: *Hobo News* (St. Louis), June, 1917.

MUSIC: Milburn (1930), p. 66. Used by permission of Ives Washburn, Inc.

VARIANTS: Webb (1923), pp. 40-41; Anderson (1923), p. 212; Finger (1927), pp. 106-107; Milburn (1930), pp. 66-69; Irwin (1931), p. 222; Porter (1943), pp. 42-43; Randolph (1950), pp. 360-361; Botkin (1951), p. 773; Hubbard (1961), p. 309*; Laws (1964), p. 231*.

THE HOBO'S LAST RIDE

1

In the Dodge City yards of the Santa Fe
    Stood a freight made up for the East;
The engineer, with oil and waste,
    Was grooming his iron beast.
While ten cars back, in the murky dusk,
    A boxcar door slid wide,
And a hobo lifted his dying pal
    To start on his last long ride.

2

A lantern swung and the freight pulled out,
    The engine gathered speed;
The engineer pulled his throttle wide,
    And nursed his snorting steed.
While ten cars back, in the empty box,
    The hobo rolled a pill,
And the flaring match showed his partner's face,
    Stark white and deathly still.

3

The train wheels clicked the joints away,
    A song for a rambler's ears,
And the hobo talked to the lifeless form
    Of his pal through a score of years:
"For a long, long stretch we've travelled, Jack,
    With the luck of the men that roam,
A backdoor step for a dining-room,
    And a boxcar for a home.

4

"We've dodged the bulls on the Monon Route,
    And the shacks on the Chesapeake.
We've bummed the Leadville narrow gauge
    In the days of Cripple Creek.
We've coasted down through sunny Cal.,
    On the rails of the old S.P.,
And of all you had, through good and bad,
    The half belonged to me.

5

"One day you made me promise, Jack,
    If I lived when you cashed in,
That I'd take you home and bury you
    In the churchyard with your kin.
You seemed to know I'd keep my word,
    For you'd found that I was white;
And so I'm true to my promise, pal,
    And I'm keeping it to-night.

6

"I knew the fever had you right,
    And the croaker wouldn't come—
Too busy treating the decent folks
    To doctor a worn-out bum.
And I hadn't the dough to send you back,
    So I'm taking you on the fly;
It's a fitting way for a 'bo to ride
    To the sweet bye and bye."

7

The rattler rolled on its ribbons of steel,
    Straight through to the East it sped;
The engineer on his high cab seat
    Kept his eyes on the rail ahead.
While ten cars back, in an empty box,
    A lonely hobo sighed,
For the days of old with his faithful pal,
    Who was taking his last, long ride.

TEXT: Irwin (1931), pp. 223-224.
VARIANT: Milburn (1930), pp. 131-133.

OH, YOU WOBBLIES!

The unskilled worker's songs prove that, whether mucker, logger, hop picker, or hay baler, he was not an entirely forgotten man in the West. The job sharks were keenly interested in selling him a spurious job, and the Red Cross generously provided them the floor space from which to do so; the police of every town were concerned that he move on yet refrain from migrating; the Holy Rollers urged him to load his diseases on Jesus; and the scissorbills were satisfied if he was not a Nigger, Jap, Dutchman, Swede, Mick, Hottentot, Bushman, or the man in the moon.

From 1905 until World War I, the Industrial Workers of the World, unlike these others, wanted only a dime from the unskilled worker, for which he would get a little red card, lectures on the evils of the capitalist system, and a sense of fellowship and purpose, which had been denied him since the first Mr. Block let someone else take the credit for, and the profits from, his labor. Scottie's "Oh, You Wobblies!" was printed for the Butte miners' local. It puts a finger on the chief Wobbly activity: organizing on the job, where the grievances were.

For the Los Angeles local's edition of the IWW songbook, Joe Hill wrote his most famous song, "The Preacher and the Slave," attacking all millenarian promises: "'Work and pray, live on hay, You'll get pie in the sky when you die." And in "Scissor Bill," he faced one of the problems that organizers of heterogeneous masses of mistreated, angry men still encounter—blind prejudice. Big Bill Haywood had been outraged when he found that a Wobbly organizational meeting he visited in Louisiana was all white. The fact that outrage was possible at that time and place proves the depth of the Wobblies' belief in total proletarian brotherhood. Hill's song insists that the lines of loyalty be redrawn: "He'll say, 'This is my country,' with an honest face, while all the cops they chase him out of every place." Richard Brazier's "When You Wear That Button," written for the 1915 harvest drive of the IWW Agricultural Workers' Organization, gives us a glimpse of one of the regulars at his recruiting work.

Violence, however, is the activity most often associated with the Wobblies. The first vigorous attribution of an incident of violence to them came in 1907. Big Bill Haywood and other officers of the Wobbly-affiliated Western Federation of Miners were accused of conspiracy in the murder of ex-Governor Steunenberg of Idaho. The Governor had been bombed by a creature calling himself Harry Orchard, and under sufficient encouragement he admitted to dozens of other atrocities. After defense lawyer Clarence Darrow made a shambles of his testimony, Orchard got religion:

Harry blamed the Wobblies,
And maybe he spoke true,
For no one on this earth can tell
What such a band will do.

Beginning in Missoula, Montana, and Spokane, Washington, in 1909, continuing in Fresno and San Diego, California, in 1911 and 1912, and ending in Everett, Washington, in 1916, local business organizations formed vigilance committees and enlisted police forces and the press in the job of preventing labor organizers—primarily those of the IWW—from holding public meetings and making speeches in their efforts to increase membership. Out of this suppression grew the free speech fights, one of which is the subject of "We're Bound for San Diego." The chief tactic employed in these fights was the massive testing of *ad hoc* ordinances and the subsequent overcrowding of jails with migrant sympathizers. The Wobblies' own propaganda worked strongly against them, for, while no member was ever convicted of a single act of sabotage, the IWW press widely advocated it in this period, and businessmen and the police reacted accordingly.

Another victim of Western violence was the Wobbly poet, Joe Hill. As Joel Emmanuel Haaglund, he had come to the United States from Sweden in 1901 at the age of nineteen. Before 1913 he had participated in a variety of radical activities, including a filibuster expedition attempting to annex Tijuana, Mexico. The story of how he came to be executed by a Utah firing squad on November 19, 1915, is admirably told in Woody Guthrie's "Joe Hillstrom."

SCOTTIE   # OH, YOU WOBBLIES!

1
I've traveled north, I've traveled south.
I've traveled east and west,
And every place I've set my foot
I've met the same old pest.

2
It's Wobblies, Wobblies, everywhere.
It's Wobblies night and day.
Week in, week out, they're on the job,
And always in the fray.

3
You'll find them in the harvest fields
Of North and South Dakota,
And picking fruit in Yakima,
In prisons picking okum.

4
You'll find them in the frozen North,
In Yukon and Alaska.
They're mushing on the dreary trails
From Nome to Athabaska.

5
They're in the jails thruout the land,
From New York state to 'Frisco,
And sailing on the seven seas
Where breezes blow so briskly.

6
The lumber-jacks are Wobblies all,
Right thru this western country.
They're picking hops in sunny Cal,
And tobacco in Kentucky.

7
They're in old Spokane and Cheyenne.
You'll find them in the jungle,
Beating their way by night and day,
And on their backs a bundle.

8
They're organizing on the job,
From heaven to hell right thru.
The angels and the shovel-stiffs
Have joined the O.B.U.

TEXT: *New Songs for Butte Mining Camp* (Butte: Century Printing Co., *ca.* 1918), p. 20.

543

THE PREACHER AND THE SLAVE

TUNE: Sweet Bye and Bye

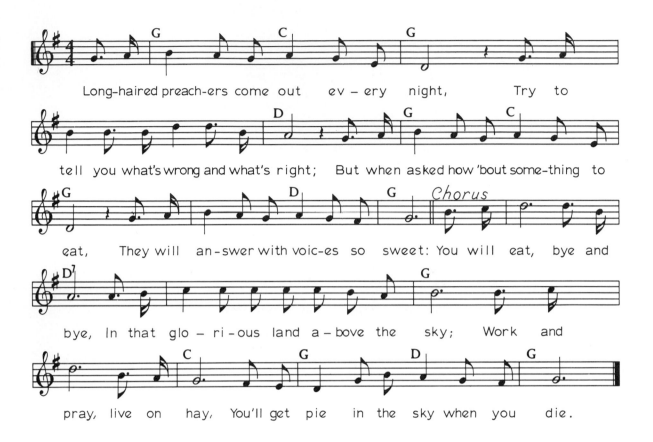

Long-haired preach-ers come out ev — ery night, Try to

tell you what's wrong and what's right; But when asked how 'bout some-thing to

eat, They will an-swer with voic-es so sweet: *Chorus* You will eat, bye and

bye, In that glo — ri-ous land a — bove the sky; Work and

pray, live on hay, You'll get pie in the sky when you die.

1

Long-haired preachers come out every night,
Try to tell you what's wrong and what's
   right;
But when asked how 'bout something to eat,
They will answer with voices so sweet:

CHORUS: You will eat, bye and bye,
In that glorious land above the sky;
Work and pray, live on hay,
You'll get pie in the sky when you die.

2

And the starvation army they play,
And they sing and they clap and they pray
Till they get all your coin on the drum,
Then they'll tell you when you're on the bum:

3

Holy Rollers and Jumpers come out,
And they holler, they jump and they shout.
"Give your money to Jesus," they say,
"He will cure all diseases today."

4

If you fight hard for children and wife—
Try to get something good in this life—
You're a sinner and bad man, they tell,
When you die you will sure go to hell.

5

Workingmen of all countries, unite.
Side by side we for freedom will fight.
When the world and its wealth we have
    gained,
To the grafters we'll sing this refrain:
LAST CHORUS: You will eat, bye and bye,
    When you've learned how to cook and to fry.
    Chop some wood, 'twill do you good,
    And you'll eat in the sweet bye and bye.

TEXT: IWW (1910), p. 26.

MUSIC: *Treasury of Song for the Home Circle* (Philadelphia: Hubbard Bros., 1882), p. 509.

VARIANTS: IWW (1912a-1932); Webb (1923), pp. 39-40; Anderson (1923), p. 210; Sandburg (1927), p. 222; Milburn (1930), pp. 83-85; Irwin (1931), p. 250; Glazer and Friedland (1953), p. 9; Greenway (1953), p. 185; Stavis and Harmon (1955), pp. 10-11; Fowke and Glazer (1960), pp. 155-157; Lomax (1960), pp. 423-424; Toelken (1962), pp. 14-15; Kornbluh (1964), p. 133.

RICHARD BRAZIER # WHEN YOU WEAR THAT BUTTON

TUNE: When You Wore a Tulip

1

I met him in Dakota when the harvesting was o'er.
A "Wob" he was, I saw by the button that he wore.
He was talking to a bunch of slaves in the jungles near the tracks.
He said, "You guys whose homes are on your backs,
Why don't you stick together with the "Wobblies" in one band
And fight to change conditions for the workers in this land."

CHORUS: When you wear that button, the "Wobblies" red button
And carry their red, red card,
No need to hike, boys, along these old pikes, boys,
Every "Wobbly" will be your pard.
The boss will be leery, the "stiffs" will be cheery
When we hit John Farmer hard.
They'll all be affrighted, when we stand united
And carry that Red, Red Card.

2

The "stiffs" all seemed delighted, when they heard him talk that way.
They said, "We need more pay, and a shorter working day."
The "Wobbly" said, "You'll get these things without the slightest
    doubt
If you'll organize to knock the bosses out.
If you'll join the One Big Union, and wear their badge of liberty,
You'll strike that blow all slaves must strike if they would be free.

———

TEXT: IWW (1918), p. 31.
VARIANTS: IWW (1919-1932); Kornbluh (1964), p. 240.

JOE HILL   # SCISSOR BILL   LEIGHTON BROS.

TUNE: Steamboat Bill

1

You may ramble 'round the country anywhere you will,
You'll always run across that same old Scissor Bill.
He's found upon the desert, he is on the hill;
He's found in every mining camp and lumber mill.
He looks just like a human, he can eat and walk;
But you will find he isn't when he starts to talk.
He'll say, "This is my country," with an honest face,
While all the cops they chase him out of every place.

> Scissor Bill, he is a little dippy.
> Scissor Bill, he has a funny face.
> Scissor Bill should drown in Mississippi.
> He is the missing link that Darwin tried to trace.

2

And Scissor Bill, he couldn't live without the booze.
He sits around all day and spits tobacco juice.
He takes a deck of cards and tries to beat the Chink!
Yes, Bill would be a smart guy if he only could think.
And Scissor Bill, he says: "The country must be freed
From Niggers, Japs and Dutchmen and the gol durn Swede."
He says that every cop would be a native son
If it wasn't for the Irishman, the sonna fur gun.

> Scissor Bill, the "foreigners" is cussin.
> Scissor Bill, he says: "I hate a Coon."
> Scissor Bill is down on everybody—
> The Hottentots, the bushmen, and the man in the
>   moon.

3

Don't try to talk your union dope to Scissor Bill.
He says he never organized and never will.
He always will be satisfied until he's dead
With coffee and a doughnut and a lousy old bed.
And Bill, he says he gets rewarded a thousand fold
When he gets up to Heaven on the streets of gold;
But I don't care who knows it, and right here I'll tell,
If Scissor Bill is goin to Heaven, I'll go to Hell.

> Scissor Bill, he wouldn't join the union.
> Scissor Bill, he says, "Not me, by Heck!"
> Scissor Bill gets his reward in Heaven—
> Oh! Sure, he'll get it, but he'll get it in the neck.

TEXT: IWW (1913a), p. 17.

VARIANTS: *Industrial Worker* (Spokane, Wash.), Feb. 6, 1913; IWW (1913b-1932); Irwin (1931), pp. 246-247; Glazer and Friedland (1953), p. 10; Stavis and Harmon (1955), p. 29; Kornbluh (1964), p. 136.

WE'RE BOUND FOR SAN DIEGO

TUNE: Wearing of the Green

In that town called San Di — e — go when the

work — ers try to talk, The cops will smash them

with a sap and tell 'em "take a walk." They

throw them in a bull pen, and they feed them rot — ten

beans, And they call that "law and or — der" in that

Chorus

cit — y, so it seems. So we're bound for San Di —

e — go, you bet — ter join us now. If

they don't quit, you bet your life there'll be an aw — ful

row. We're com — ing by the hun — dreds, will be

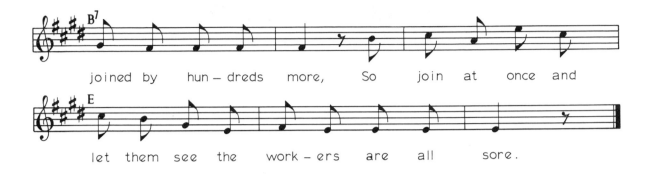

joined by hun—dreds more, So join at once and

let them see the work—ers are all sore.

1

In that town called San Diego when the workers try to talk,
The cops will smash them with a sap and tell 'em "take a walk."
They throw them in a bull pen, and they feed them rotten beans,
And they call that "law and order" in that city, so it seems.

CHORUS: So we're bound for San Diego, you better join us now.
If they don't quit, you bet your life there'll be an awful row.
We're coming by the hundreds, will be joined by hundreds more,
So join at once and let them see the workers are all sore.

2

They're clubbing fellow working men who dare their thoughts
    express;
And if old Otis has his way, there's sure to be a mess.
So swell this army, working men, and show them what we'll do
When all the sons of toil unite in ONE BIG UNION true.

3

We have put the town of Aberdeen with others on our map;
And the brass bound thugs of all of them were handy with the
    "sap";
But the IWW's are boys who have no fears,
And we'll whip old San Diego if it takes us twenty years.

———————

TEXT: *Industrial Worker* (Spokane, Wash.), May 1, 1912.

MUSIC: Johnson (1881), pp. 488-490.

VARIANT: Kornbluh (1964), p. 104.

HARRY ORCHARD

1

Harry Orchard is in prison.
The reason you all know:
He killed Frank Steunenberg
Right here in Idyho.

2

He set his bomb out carefully—
He did not hesitate.
It blew poor Frank to Kingdom Come
When he tried to shut the gate.

3

Harry says he has killed others.
For them my heart it bleeds.
He should pray for God's forgiveness
For his terrible misdeeds.

4

Harry blamed the Wobblies,
And maybe he spoke true,
For no one on this earth can tell
What such a band will do.

5

The chiefs were brought from Denver.
They were shanghaied, as you know.
Bill Haywood and George Pettibone
Were brought to Idyho.

6

Clarence Darrow stood to shield them.
The result, it was so sure.
Bill Haywood and his comrades,
Free men, walked out the door.

7

Now listen, all you young men,
The lesson, it is plain.
Just be prepared to pay the cost
When you set a bomb for gain.

TEXT: Burt (1958*a*), pp. 93-95, and (1958*b*), p. 270. Used by permission of Olive W. Burt.

WOODY GUTHRIE # JOE HILLSTROM

1

On January Tenth, Nineteen Fourteen,
Two men fixed some masks of red handkerchiefs,
Walked into the Temple and South Street Store,
Laid Morrison and his son dead on the floor.
> Before he died, Merlin Morrison
> Reached under his counter and pulled his gun.
> The fellows tried to run back out the door again.
> Morrison put a bullet in one of the men.

2

Just three days later you arrested me
At the Eselius home on Seventeenth South Street.
Just because I've got a fresh bullet hole,
You claim that I killed the Morrisons in their store.
> I was courting a woman and had a fight with a man.
> He fired a pistol that lodged in me.
> Old Prosecutor Leatherwood can beat out his brains,
> But I'm not going to tell you this lady's name.

3

Take away these attorneys you picked for me.
My own lawyer now I'm going to be.
It's because I'm a union organizer in the copper mines
You've got me on your killing floor to die.
> My labor friends sent Judge Hilton and Christensen
> To prove I did not kill the Morrisons,
> But I cannot drag my lady's honor down.
> I can't tell where I got my gunshot wound.

4

It was in June you convicted me.
You said I was guilty in the worst degree.
I don't want your pardon, but an honest trial;
If I can't get a fair trial I will die.
> President Wilson wired the Governor Spry
> Saying please don't let Joe Hillstrom die.
> Several thousand letters and telegrams
> Piled up on the governor's desk from workers hands.

5

The governor wired to Wilson, Nothing I can do.
The Pardon Board and Supreme Court, too,
Both did uphold the frame up trial.
They all want to see me walk my last long mile.
> The death watch is set. It's November Eighteenth.
> My comrades are marching up and down the streets
> Of all of the cities and the towns around.
> They can sing Joe Hillstrom never let them down.

6

The Nineteenth Day of November is here,
A frosty old morning with winter in the air.
Two telegrams that I got to send
To Elizabeth Gurley Flynn and Bill Haywood.
    It's a hundred miles to the Wyoming line.
    Could you arrange to have my body hauled
    Past that old state line before you bury me at all?
    I just don't want to be found dead here in Utah.

7

Hey, Gurley Flynn, I wrote you a song
To the dove of peace. It's coming along.
I lived like a rebel, like a rebel I die.
Forget me. Organize these copper mines.
    They march me now out to the baseball park,
    Tie me down in a chair, and the Doctor marks my heart
    With a little white rag against this black robe.
    Goodbye, Joe Hillstrom, you done a pretty good job.

TEXT: Guthrie (1947), pp. 22-23.

THE OLD SETTLER

These songs add a postscript to the tale of the West told up to now. Usually in the form of reminiscences, they serve to summarize, befog, distort, and update earlier facts and feelings. They provide one solution, for example, to the affliction of seeing the elephant, which is to go blind, as did the narrator of "The Old Settler." On the skids from the mining region, he found Washington's Puget Sound to be the next thing to the jumping-off place, but he adjusted:

> No longer the slave of ambition,
> I laugh at the world and its shams
> As I think of my pleasant condition,
> Surrounded by acres of clams.

Another way out of miseries was to gang up and get sentimental about them. This route was taken in 1876 by the fellows in Charles Rhoades's reminiscence, "The Days of '49." Their spokesman has concluded that things have gotten steadily worse since those clearly superior times:

> Since that time how things have changed
>   In this land of liberty.
> Darkies didn't vote nor plead in court
>   Nor rule this country;
> But the Chinese question, the worst of all,
>   In those days did not shine,
> For the country was right and the boys all white
>   In the days of '49.

J. Riley Mains called his "The Good Old Days of '50, '1, and '2" an answer to Rhoades's nonsense, but sighs and tears choked him up as he patted his own back, and before he got very specific.

Another way to look back on the past was found by Myron Crandall in "This Is the Place." It is an excellent summary, touching upon several major incidents in Mormon history without sacrificing the convincing detail:

> Forty years a-building a Temple in Salt Lake,
> Another one down in Manti, one in the Logan Stake,
> Another down in Dixie—now there's eight all told—
> And we all work diligently, young and old.

Although there are many reminiscent songs about the cowboys and their lost era, we have gone afield for a skewed view of them. The great Negro folk singer Huddie Ledbetter—Leadbelly—sang a song called "When I Was a Cowboy," and it gave, among other things, a strong blues wrench to those tunes about the forsaken, self-pitying horseman:

> If your house catches on fire and there ain't no water 'round,
> If your house catches on fire and there ain't no water 'round,
> Throw your jelly out the window, let the doggone shack burn down.
> Come a cow cow yicky, come a cow cow yicky yicky ay.

O. E. Murray published his "The Little Old Sod Shanty in the West" in a South Dakota newspaper in 1909, but that was apparently just long enough after the facts to blur the details with clichés:

> For then the wildest red skins came down like wolves in packs
> To drive us from the homes that we had made.
> Ah! Those were the times that tried men souls and sifted out the chaff.

The song "Great-Grand-Dad," on the other hand, picks out the telling details while looking ahead to the genetic consequences of pioneer resolution with a pleasantly positive aura of sentimentality. But for a more justifiable tone on which to end this volume, we resort to Woody Guthrie's "Do Re Mi." It is a depression song, but its theme remains as true today as it was also a hundred years ago: that the Gilded West is still the most perilously attractive, alluringly hostile, region in America.

FRANCIS D. HENRY

THE OLD SETTLER

TUNE: Old Rosin the Beau

I'd wan-dered all o-ver the count-ry, Pros-
pect-ing a dig-ging for gold. I'd
tun-neled, hy-drau-licked, and cra-dled, And
I had been fre-quent-ly sold.

Chorus

And I had been fre-quent-ly sold,___ And
I had been fre-quent-ly sold.___ I'd
tun-neled, hy-drau-licked, and cra-dled, And
I had been fre-quent-ly sold.___

1

I'd wandered all over the country,
Prospecting and digging for gold.
I'd tunneled, hydraulicked, and cradled,
And I had been frequently sold.

CHORUS: And I had been frequently sold,
          And I had been frequently sold.
          I'd tunneled, hydraulicked, and
              cradled,
          And I had been frequently sold.

2

For one who gets riches by mining,
Perceiving that hundreds grow poor—
I made up my mind to try farming,
The only pursuit that is sure.

CHORUS: The only pursuit that is sure, etc.

3

So rolling my grub in my blankets,
I left all my tools on the ground,
And started one morning to shank it
For a country they called Puget Sound.

CHORUS: For a country they called Puget Sound, etc.

4

Arriving flat broke in mid-winter,
I found it enveloped in fog,
And covered all over with timber,
Thick as hair on the back of a dog.

CHORUS: Thick as hair on the back of a dog, etc.

5

As I looked on the prospect so gloomy
The tears trickled over my face,
For I felt that my travels had brought me
To the edge of the jumping-off place.

CHORUS: To the edge of the jumping-off place, etc.

6

I took up a claim in the forest,
And sat myself down to hard toil;
For two years I chopped and I niggered,
But I never got down to the soil.

CHORUS: But I never got down to the soil, etc.

7

I tried to get out of the country,
But poverty forced me to stay
Until I became an Old Settler—
Then nothing could drive me away.

CHORUS: Then nothing could drive me away, etc.

8

And now that I'm used to the climate
I think that if man ever found
A spot to live easy and happy
That Eden is on Puget Sound.

CHORUS: That Eden is on Puget Sound, etc.

9

No longer the slave of ambition,
I laugh at the world and its shams
As I think of my pleasant condition,
Surrounded by acres of clams.

CHORUS: Surrounded by acres of clams, etc.

TEXT AND MUSIC: "The Old Settler," by Francis D. Henry (Olympia, Wash.: 1902 [sheet music]).

VARIANTS: Lomax and Lomax (1947), pp. 184-187; Botkin (1951), pp. 747-748; Fowke and Glazer (1960), pp. 138-140; Toelken (1962), pp. 17-18*.

GREAT-GRAND-DAD

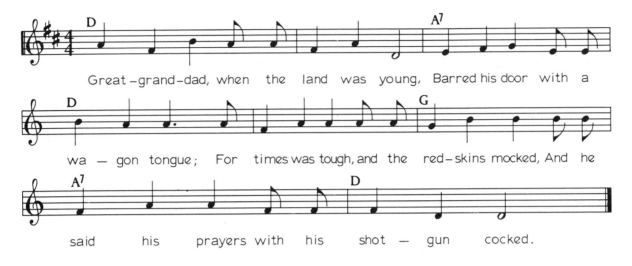

Great-grand-dad, when the land was young, Barred his door with a
wa—gon tongue; For times was tough, and the red—skins mocked, And he
said his prayers with his shot—gun cocked.

1

Great-grand-dad, when the land was young,
Barred his door with a wagon tongue;
For times was tough, and the redskins
    mocked,
And he said his prayers with his shotgun
    cocked.

2

Great-grand-dad was a lusty man,
Cooked his grub in a frying pan,
Picked his teeth with his hunting knife,
And wore the same suit all his life.

3

Twenty-one children came to bless
The old man's home in the wilderness.
Doubt this statement if you can
That great-grand-dad was a busy man.

4

Twenty-one boys and not one bad.
They never got fresh with their great-grand-
    dad!
If they had, he'd been right glad
To tan their hides with a hickory gad.

5

He raised them rough, but he raised them strong.
    strong.
When their feet took hold on the road to
    wrong,
He straightened them out with the old ramrod
And filled them full of the fear of God.

6

They grew strong in heart and hand,
A firm foundation of our land.
They made the best citizens we ever had.
We need more men like great-grand-dad.

7

Grand-dad died at eighty-nine;
Twenty-one boys he left behind.
Times have changed, but you never can tell;
You might yet do half as well.

Used by permission of Duke University Press.

TEXT: Brown (1952a), p. 621.

MUSIC: Brown (1957), p. 297.

VARIANTS: German (1929); Larkin (1931), pp. 73-75; Clark (1932), p. 37; Frey (1936),
p. 59; Lomax and Lomax (1938), pp. 302-304; Randolph (1949), p. 248; Fowke and
Johnston (1954), "Great Grand-Ma."

CHARLES RHOADES (BENSELL) # THE DAYS OF '49 # ARR. E. ZIMMER

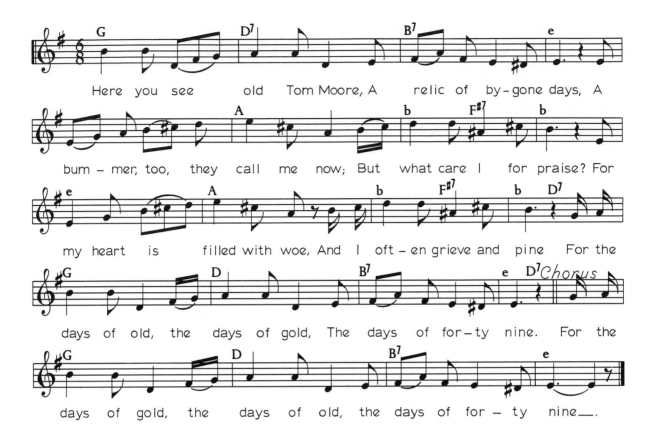

Here you see old Tom Moore, A relic of by-gone days, A bum-mer, too, they call me now; But what care I for praise? For my heart is filled with woe, And I oft-en grieve and pine For the days of old, the days of gold, The days of for-ty nine. For the days of gold, the days of old, the days of for-ty nine—.

1

Here you see old Tom Moore,
    A relic of bygone days,
A bummer, too, they call me now;
    But what care I for praise?
For my heart is filled with woe,
    And I often grieve and pine
For the days of old, the days of gold,
    The days of '49.

CHORUS: For the days of gold, the days of old,
        The days of '49.

2

I had comrades then, a saucy set.
    They were rough, I must confess,
But staunch and brave, as true as steel,
    Like hunters from the west.
But they, like many another fish,
    Have now run out their line;
But like good old bricks, they stood the kicks
    Of the days of '49.

3

There was Monte Pete—I'll ne'er forget
    The luck that he always had.
He'd deal for you both night and day,
    Or as long as you had a scad.
One night a pistol laid him out—
    'Twas his last lay out in fine.
It caught Pete sure, right bang in the door,
    In the days of '49.

4

There was another chap from New Orleans—
    Big Reuben was his name.
On the plaza there with a sardine box
    He opened a faro game.
He dealt so fair that a millionaire
    He became in course of time,
Till death stept in and called the turn
    In the days of '49.

5

There was Kentuck Bill, one of the boys
 Who was always in for a game;
No matter whether he lost or won,
 To him 'twas all the same.
He'd ante a slug; he'd pass the buck;
 He'd go a hat full blind.
In the game of death, Bill lost his breath
 In the days of '49.

6

There was New York Jake, the butcher boy,
 So fond of getting tight;
Whenever Jake got full of gin,
 He was looking for a fight.
One night he ran against a knife
 In the hands of old Bob Kline,
And over Jake we had a wake
 In the days of '49.

7

There was North Carolina Jess, a hard old
  case
 Who never would repent.
Jess was never known to miss a meal,
 Or ever pay a cent.
But poor old Jess like all the rest,
 To death did at last resign,
And in his bloom he went up the flume
 In the days of '49.

8

There was Rackensack Jim who could out
  roar
 A buffalo bull, you bet!
He roared all night; he roared all day;
 He may be roaring yet.
One night he fell in a prospect hole—
 'Twas a roaring bad design—
And in that hole Jim roared out his soul
 In the days of '49.

9

Of all the comrades I had then,
 There's none left now but me,
And the only thing I'm fitting for
 Is a Senator to be.
The people cry as I pass by,
 "There goes a traveling sign;
That's old Tom Moore, a bummer sure,
 Of the days of '49."

10

Since that time how things have changed
 In this land of liberty.
Darkies didn't vote nor plead in court
 Nor rule this country;
But the Chinese question, the worst of all,
 In those days did not shine.
For the country was right and the boys all
  white
 In the days of '49.

TEXT AND MUSIC: "The Days of '49," arr. by E. Zimmer (San Francisco: Sherman & Hyde, 1876).

VARIANTS: *The Great Emerson New Popular Songster* (San Francisco: Blake & Sharp, 1872); *Miner* (Havilah, Calif.), Nov. 22, 1873; Nicholas Ball, *Pioneers of '49* (Boston: Lee and Shepard, 1891); Lummis (1903), pp. 203-204; Lomax (1910), pp. 9-14; Grant (1924), pp. 52-55; Drury (1931); Sherwin and Katzman (1932), pp. 12-13; Clark (1932), pp. 26-27; Allen (1933), pp. 151-153; Frey (1936), pp. 76-77; Lomax and Lomax (1938), pp. 378-381; E Clampus Vitus (1939), pp. 20-21; Lengyel (1939), pp. 58-59; Black and Robertson (1940), pp. 53-55; Lomax and Lomax (1947), pp. 180-183; Randolph (1948), pp. 221-222; Lengyel (1949), pp. 44-45; Botkin (1951), pp. 735-736; Hubbard (1961), pp. 297-299; Fowke (1962), pp. 253-254; Dwyer *et al.* (1964), pp. 189-190.

J. RILEY MAINS

THE GOOD OLD DAYS
OF '50, '1, AND '2

TUNE: The Days of '49

1

Tom Moore has sung of '49,
    And the Pioneers who came
Across the plains and 'round the horn
    In search of gold and fame;
But in his song he tells us not
    One word of those we knew,
Those pioneers of the good old days
    Of '50, '1, and '2.

2

There's "Kentuck Bill" and "Monte Pete,"
    He holds them up to fame,
New York Jake and Ransack Jim
    And old lame Jess the same;
But men like these were not the boys
    So hardy, tough and true,
That flumed the streams and worked the
      mines
    In '50, '1, and '2.

3

There's Captain Love and gallant Burns,
    Dave Buell tall and brave,
Likewise Bob Fall, and also Thorn,
    Were the dread of Robber's Cave.
They would trace them over the mountain
      steep,
    Ravines and canons through,
Those men of pluck in the good old days
    Of '50, '1, and '2.

4

There was Joaquin and three-fingered Jack—
    To catch them seemed in vain—
Though followed on their bloody track
    O'er mountain, hill and plain;
But they at last were forced to yield
    To men whom well I knew,
Those gallant souls who knew no fear
    Of '50, '1, and '2.

5

Where are they now, that gallant band,
    Those friends that once were mine?
Some sleep beneath the willow's shade;
    Some 'neath the lofty pine,
Whilst some have sank beneath the wave
    Deep in the ocean's blue,
Those cherished friends of bygone years
    Of '50, '1, and '2.

6

I once had wealth. It brought new friends.
    I thought them true, I'll own,
But when kind fortune ceased to smile,
    Those summer friends had flown;
And now I wander on alone
    Life's thorny pathways through,
But I'll ne'er forget those dear old friends
    Of '50, '1, and '2.

7

'Tis true there's some old pioneers
    That unto wealth have grown,
But there are many that are poor,
    And I am one, I'll own;
But never shun a ragged coat
    If the heart beneath is true,
Of a pioneer of the good old days
    Of '50, '1, and '2.

8

And now, kind friends, I've sung my song,
    "I've had my little speak,"
But when I think of those good old days,
    Tears ofttimes wet my cheek.
We opened then the Golden Gate
    And its treasures unto you,
We boys who came in '49,
    And in '50, '1, and '2.

TEXT: "The Good Old Days of '50, '1, and '2: Answer to 'The Days of '49,'" by J. Riley Mains (n.p., n.d. [broadside]).

VARIANTS: J. W. Sullivan, *Popular California Songs* (San Francisco: Sullivan, n.d.); Dwyer *et al.* (1964), pp. 191-192.

MYRON CRANDALL

THIS IS THE PLACE

Come, all ye peo-ple, if you want to hear A stor-y a-bout a brave pi-o-neer. Brig-ham Young is the pi-o-neer's name, In the Salt Lake Val-ley's where he won his fame. He told his peop-le on the Mis-sis-sip-pi Riv-er, You bet-ter get read-y, we are leav-ing for-ev-er. We'll turn our fac-es out to West. Do not get dis-cour-aged for we'll do our best.

Chorus

Brig-ham Young, the West-ern pi-o-neer, Brig-ham Young won a no-ble race. Brig-ham Young made a broad state-ment When he raised up-on his el-bow and said,"This is the Place."

1

Come, all ye people, if you want to hear
A story about a brave pioneer.
Brigham Young is the pioneer's name.
In the Salt Lake Valley's where he won his fame.
He told his people on the Mississippi River,
"You better get ready, we are leaving forever.
We'll turn our faces out to the West.
Do not get discouraged for we'll do our best."

CHORUS: Brigham Young, the Western pioneer,
Brigham Young won a noble race.
Brigham Young made a broad statement
When he raised upon his elbow and said, "This is the
    Place."

2

From Germany and Holland, Denmark, Sweden, France and Wales,
Johnny Bull and Scotch and Irish with their clever Irish tales,
He put them in a melting pot—I give him many thanks—
When he stirred 'em up a little bit, they all were Yanks.
He says, "Repair your wagons, your carriages and carts;
Shoe your horses, mules and oxen, we are about to start.
Make roads through the valleys and bridges o'er the rivers,"
And they had to travel slow because they never had a flivver.

3

They reached Salt Lake Valley on July the twenty-fourth.
A thousand miles they traveled; they were very tired, of course.
Their leader was sick, weariness was on his face,
But he raised upon his elbow and said, "This is the Place."
Some went to California—they wouldn't heed advice.
They didn't seem to prosper, were as poor as church mice.
Some joined the other churches, and I have a little hunch
They wish the heck they'd never quit the Brigham Young bunch.

4

They met old Jim Bridger in the country of Wyoming.
He would give a thousand dollars for an ear of corn a-growing.
They instituted irrigation, had fine crops,
'Til along came the crickets and the old grass-hops.
The crickets and the grasshoppers, they got so awful bad
The saints tried to kill 'em. They fought 'til they were mad.
The Lord sent the sea gulls, in about two shakes—
How they heaved them over in the Great Salt Lake!

5

Before they left the Middlewest, a message came from Uncle Sam:
"We want five hundred volunteers to fight the Mexican!"
"We're loyal to the Stars and Stripes, want everyone to know
If we haven't got five hundred men our women, they will go."
The old stage coach, the Pony Express
Carried mail and passengers from East to the West.
They moved the best they could before the days of the rail
Along the Emigrant Road and the Oregon Trail.

6

They built wagon roads and railroads and irrigation ditches,
Woolen mills to manufacture dresses and britches.
They dug for gold and silver and a little copper, too,
And soon they were better off than back in Nauvoo.
Forty years a-building a Temple in Salt Lake,
Another one in Manti, one in the Logan Stake,
Another down in Dixie—now there's eight all told—
And we all work diligently, young and old.

7

Once they had a celebration up in old Cottonwood.
They were happy and doing the very best they could.
Hard news came to Brigham, Johnston's Army on the wing,
"Before we let them enter we'll destroy everything!"
He built Salt Lake Theatre, erected many schools
To educate the kiddies 'cause they wanted no fools.
He called 'em his busy bees—they built a lot of hives—
And he ought to go to Heaven with his nineteen wives.

TEXT AND MUSIC: Fife and Fife (1956), pp. 327-329. Used by permission of Indiana University Press.

THE LITTLE OLD
SOD SHANTY IN THE WEST

O. E. MURRAY

TUNE: The Little Old Log Cabin in the Lane

You may sing a-bout the lit-tle old log cab-in in the lane Or of lit-tle Ger-man homes a-cross the sea,___ But my lit-tle old sod shan-ty that I built up on my claim Has be-come the dear-est spot on earth to me.___ I built it in my pov-er-ty up-on my prai-rie claim, And af-ter toil it gave me sweet-est rest;___ Safe-ly shel-tered from the bliz-zards and all the storms that came In my lit-tle old sod shan-ty in the West.

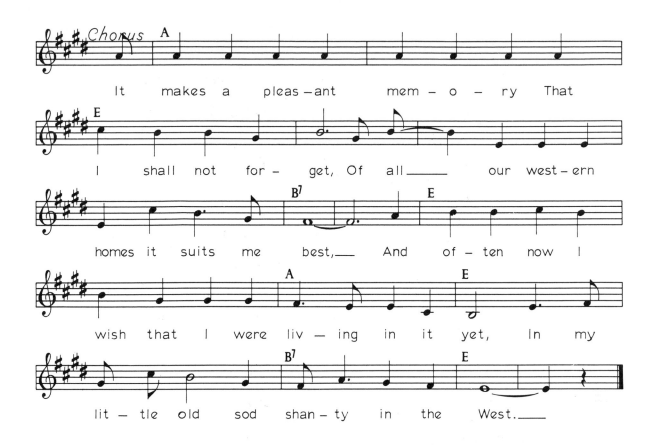

It makes a pleas—ant mem—o—ry That I shall not for—get, Of all_____ our west—ern homes it suits me best,_____ And of—ten now I wish that I were liv—ing in it yet, In my lit—tle old sod shan—ty in the West._____

1

You may sing about the little old log cabin in the lane
Or of little German homes across the sea,
But my little old sod shanty that I built upon my claim
Has become the dearest spot on earth to me.
I built it in my poverty upon my prairie claim,
And after toil it gave me sweetest rest;
Safely sheltered from the blizzards and all the storms that came
In my little old sod shanty in the West.

CHORUS: It makes a pleasant memory that I shall not forget,
Of all our western homes it suits me best,
And often now I wish that I were living in it yet,
In my little old sod shanty in the West.

2

We had hungry wolves and coyotes for our nearest neighbors then,
The buffalo and deer supplied our meat;
And where the black and prowling bear would fall before our men,
We would live like kings upon the game so sweet.
The only town we knew for miles, by prairie dogs was made.
They yelped and sported 'round our little nest,
And sometimes they took a tumble before the rifle's raid,
And such we thought was sport out in the West.

Our path was full of troubles, nor were they little ones,
For sure the pioneers were single boys.
Then every man's own body guard was two good shooting guns
With ropes and lariats to use as toys.
We sometimes hunted down the thief who stole from us a horse,
A little neck-tie party did the rest;
The morning sun shone grimly as its rays fell on the corpse
Near my little old sod shanty in the West.

4

The miners built their cabins, the ranchers lived in "shacks,"
And some were forced to make a log stockade,
For then the wildest red skins came like wolves in packs
To drive us from the homes that we had made.
Ah! Those were times that tried men's souls and sifted out the
     chaff.
Each fight would mark the man we called the best,
And some proved weak and left us—it must be more than half;
The others held their shanties in the West.

5

But all things change; those stirring times have long since passed
     away,
And churches, schools and cities followed on,
Along the trail we tracked with blood back in that early day,
And others hold the fields that we have won.
But we have saved a little cash, so we will not complain,
Tho' others of our fruits shall reap the best;
But we hope they will remember not to treat us with disdain,
Because we built the shanties in the West.

6

Where once the cabin graced the gulch or shanties marked the
     plain,
With signs of wealth the homes and mansions rise.
The wigwam, too, has passed away. The braves are with the slain
In happy hunting grounds beyond the skies.
When 'round our winter fires we meet, not made of twisted hay,
We recount the past before we seek our rest.
The stories of our struggles will hush the childen's play,
And their dreams will be the shanties in the West.

TEXT: *Dakota Farmer* (Aberdeen, S.D.), Dec. 15, 1909. Clipping in the Ballad Collection of Edwin Ford Piper at the Library of the State University of Iowa, Iowa City.

MUSIC: "Little Old Log Cabin in the Lane," as sung by Riley Puckett, Columbia Record 107 (1924). Transcribed by David Cohen.

LEADBELLY # WHEN I WAS A COWBOY

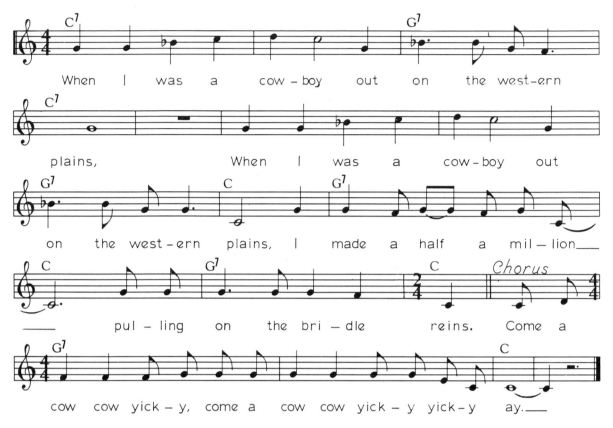

cow cow yick – y, come a cow cow yick – y yick – y ay. ___

1

When I was a cowboy out on the western plains,
When I was a cowboy out on the western plains,
I made a half a million pulling on the bridle reins.

CHORUS: Come a cow cow yicky, come a cow cow yicky yicky ay.

2

I rode up to my gal's house, she was rocking in her rocking chair,
I rode up to my gal's house, she was rocking in her rocking chair,
"Oh, western cowboy, please don't you leave me here."

3

Oh the hardest battle was ever on the western plains,
Oh the hardest battle was ever on the western plains,
When me and a bunch of cowboys run into Jesse James.

4

When me and a bunch of cowboys run into Jesse James,
When me and a bunch of cowboys run into Jesse James,
All the bullets was a-falling just like a shower of rain.

5

Oh the hardest battle was ever on Bunker's Hill,
Oh the hardest battle was ever on Bunker's Hill,
When me and a bunch of cowboys run into Buffalo Bill.

SPOKEN: The boys had it in for a man on the outskirts of town. All around that man's house them horses was a-walking, and them forty-fives was a-talking. They done made the horses drunk, and they was already drunk, and the forty-fives were drunk. So they said best regards to the man's house.

6

If your house catches on fire and there ain't no water 'round,
If your house catches on fire and there ain't no water 'round,
Throw your jelly out the window, let the doggone shack burn down.

TEXT AND MUSIC: As sung by "Leadbelly," Capital Record LP T1821 (1944. Transcribed by David Cohen.

VARIANTS: Lomax and Lomax (1938), p. 39; Lomax (1960), p. 381.

DO RE MI

WOODY GUTHRIE   WOODY GUTHRIE

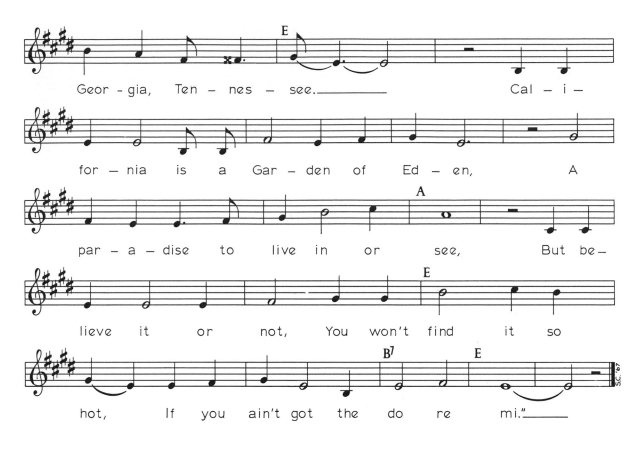

Geor – gia, Ten – nes – see._____ Cal – i –

for – nia is a Gar – den of Ed – en, A

par – a – dise to live in or see, But be –

lieve it or not, You won't find it so

hot, If you ain't got the do re mi."_____

S.C. '67

1

Lots of folks back East, they say,
Is leaving home every day,
Beating the hot old dusty way
To the California line.
'Cross the desert sands they roll,
Gittin' out of that old dust bowl.
They think they're goin' to a sugar bowl.
But here's what they find:
Now the police at the port of entry say,
"You're number fourteen thousand for today—

2

If you want to buy you a home or farm,
That cain't deal nobody harm,
Or take your vacations by the mountains or the sea,
Don't swap your old cow for a car,
You'd better stay right where you are.
You'd better take this little tip from me,
'Cause I look through the want ads every day,
But the headlines on the papers always say—

CHORUS: "Oh, if you ain't got the do re mi, folks,
If you ain't got the do re mi,
Why you'd better go back to beautiful Texas,
Oklahoma, Kansas, Georgia, Tennessee.
California is a Garden of Eden,
A paradise to live in or see,
But believe it or not,
You won't find it so hot,
If you ain't got the do re mi."

───────────────

TEXT AND MUSIC: As sung by Woodie Guthrie, *Dust Bowl Ballads*, Folkways Record FH
5212. Transcribed by David Cohen.

REFERENCE MATERIAL

BIBLIOGRAPHY

Abbreviations

CFQ   *California Folklore Quarterly*
JAF   *Journal of the American Folklore Society*
SFQ   *Southern Folklore Quarterly*
TFSP   *Texas Folklore Society Publication*
UHR   *Utah Humanities Review*
WF   *Western Folklore*

Anonymous

N.d.   *Utah Indian War Veterans' Songster.* N.p.

Ca. 1850   *The Violin Primer.* Cover and title page missing. In the collection of William Broderson, Sutter's Fort, Sacramento.

1850-1870   "Ballads and Songs Collected in Ghost Towns of California, 1850-1870." Broadside Collection in Los Angeles Public Library.

1860   *Bella Union Melodeon Songster, No. 1.* San Francisco: Appleton & Co.

1863   *John Brown and the Union Right or Wrong Songster.* San Francisco: Appleton & Co.

1864   *Sally Come Up Songster.* San Francisco: Clark & Fisher.

1867   *Marching Through Georgia and the Wearing of the Green Songster.* San Francisco: Appleton & Co.

1868   *Bee Hive Songster.* Salt Lake City: Daily Telegraph.

1877   *Blue and Gray Songster.* San Francisco: S. T. & S. S. Greene.

1882   *Minstrel Songs, Old and New.* Boston: Oliver Ditson & Co.

1883   *War Songs.* Boston: Oliver Ditson & Co.

1887   *The Good Old Songs We Used To Sing.* Vol. I. Boston: Oliver Ditson & Co.

1888   *Division and Admission: Dakota Campaign Song Book for 1888.* Huron, Dak. Terr.: Dakota Farmer Job Printing House.

1900   "Days of 'Forty-nine," *Land of Sunshine,* XIII, 271-272.

1900   "Two Argonaut Songs," *Land of Sunshine,* XIII, 165-167.

1904   *Most Popular College Songs.* New York: Hinds, Noble & Eldredge.

1909   *Heart Songs Dear to the American People.* Boston: Chapple Publishing Co.

1912   *Montana Cowboy Band Song Book at Minneapolis Land Products Exposition, November 12 to 23, 1912.* N.p.

1912   *Most Popular Army and Navy Songs.* New York: Hinds, Noble & Eldredge.

1914   "Folk-song of Recent Origin," *Literary Digest,* XLVIII, 985.

1918   *New Songs for Butte Mining Camp* (by Home Talent). Butte, Mont.: Century Printing Co.

1918   *Original Songs of the Old Settlers Quartette of Jefferson County.* Fairfield, Iowa.

Alderson, William L.
1942   "On the Wobbly 'Casey Jones' and Other Songs," *CFQ*, I, 373-376.
1945   "The Comical History of Baldy Green," *SFQ*, IX, 1-11.
Allan, Francis D.
1874   *Lone Star Ballads*. Galveston, Tex.: J. D. Sawyer.
Allen, Jules Verne
1933   *Cowboy Lore*. San Antonio, Tex.: Naylor Co.
Anderson, M. F.
1947   "The Mormon Car," *UHR*, I, 187-188.
Anderson, Nels
1923   *The Hobo*. Chicago: University of Chicago Press.
Appleton, David E.
1855   *California Songster*. San Francisco: Appleton & Co.
Barnes, Will C.
1925   "The Cowboy and His Songs," *Saturday Evening Post*, CXCVII (June 27), 14-15, 122, 125, 128.
Belden, Henry M.
1940   *Ballads and Songs Collected by the Missouri Folk-lore Society*. Columbia: University of Missouri.
Benjamin, Harold
1953   "Case Study in Folksong Making," *Tennessee Folklore Society Bulletin*, XIX, 27-30.
Bingham, Seth
1930   *Five Cowboy Songs*. New York: H. W. Gray Co.
Black, Eleanora, and Sidney Robertson
1940   *The Gold Rush Song Book*. San Francisco: Colt Press.
Boatright, Mody C.
1944   "More About 'Hell in Texas,'" *TFSP*, XIX, 134-138.
Booth, Sam
1872   *Local Lyrics*. San Francisco: Bruce's Printing House.
Botkin, B. A. (ed.)
1944   *A Treasury of American Folklore*. New York: Crown Publications.
1951   *A Treasury of Western Folklore*. New York: Crown Publications.
Botkin, B. A., and A. F. Harlow (eds.)
1953   *A Treasury of Railroad Folklore*. New York: Crown Publications.
Branch, Douglas
1926   *The Cowboy and His Interpreters*. New York: Appleton.
Briegel, George F.
1933   *44 Old Time Mormon and Far West Songs*. New York: Briegel.
Brown, Frank C.
1952a   *Folk Ballads from North Carolina*. Vol. II of *The Frank C. Brown Collection of North Carolina Folklore*. Ed. H. M. Belden and A. P. Hudson. Durham, N.C.: Duke University Press.
1952b   *Folk Songs from North Carolina*. Vol. III of *The Frank C. Brown Collection of North Carolina Folklore*. Ed. H. M.

Belden and A. P. Hudson. Durham, N.C.: Duke University Press.

1957   *The Music of the Ballads.* Vol. IV of *The Frank C. Brown Collection of North Carolina Folklore.* Ed. A. P. Shinhan. Durham, N.C.: Duke University Press.

1962   *The Music of the Folk Songs.* Vol. V of *The Frank C. Brown Collection of North Carolina Folklore.* Ed. A. P. Shinhan. Durham, N.C.: Duke University Press.

Brunvand, Jan Harold
1965   "Folk Song Studies in Idaho," *WF,* XXIV, 231-248.

Burt, Olive W.
1958a   *American Murder Ballads.* New York: Oxford Press.
1958b   "The Minstrelsy of Murder," *WF,* XVII, 263-272.
1959   "Murder Ballads of Mormondom," *WF,* XVIII, 141-156.

Carlisle, Cliff
1932   *Cliff Carlisle's World's Greatest Collection of Hobo Songs.* Chicago: M. M. Cole Publications.

Carter, Kate B.
1944   "Songs Composed and Sung by the Western Pioneers." In *Heart Throbs of the West.* V, 493-532. Salt Lake City: Daughters of Utah Pioneers.

Clark, Kenneth S.
1932   *The Cowboy Sings: Traditional Songs of the Western Frontier.* New York: Paull-Pioneer Music Corp.

Clifford, John
1955   "Range Ballads," *Kansas Historical Quarterly,* XXI, 588-597.

Combs, Josiah H.
1925   *Folk-Songs du Midi des Etats-Unis.* Paris: Les Presses Universite de France.

Conner, J.W.
1868   *Conner's Irish Song Book.* San Francisco: Appleton & Co.

Coolidge, Dane
1912   "Cowboy Songs," *Sunset,* XXIX, 503-510.
1932   *Texas Cowboys.* New York: Dutton. Pp. 97-132.

Craddock, John R.
1927   "Songs the Cowboys Sing," *TFSP,* VI, 184-191.

Damon, S. Foster
1936   *Series of Old American Songs, Reproduced in Facsimile from Original or Early Editions in the Harris Collection of American Poetry and Plays.* Providence: Brown University.

Daughters of Utah Pioneers
1932   *Pioneer Songs.* Cincinnati.
1940   *Pioneer Songs.* 2d ed., enl. Cincinnati.

Davidson, Levette J.
1941a   "Rocky Mountain Folklore" *SFQ,* V, 205-219.
1941b   "Colorado Folklore," *Colorado Magazine,* XVIII, 1-13.
1943   "Songs of the Rocky Mountain Frontier," *CFQ,* II, 89-112.
1944   "Home on the Range Again," *CFQ,* III, 208-211.
1945   "Mormon Songs," *JAF,* LVIII, 273-300.

1947   "A Ballad of the Wyoming 'Rustler War,'" *WF*, VI, 115-118.

1951   *Poems of the Old West.* Denver: University of Denver Press.

Dean, Michael C.

1922   *Flying Cloud, and One Hundred and Fifty Other Old Time Songs and Ballads of Outdoor Men, Sailors, Lumber Jacks, Soldiers, Men of the Great Lakes, Railroadmen, Miners, etc.* Virginia, Minn.: The Quickprint.

Dick, Everett

1928   "The Long Drive," *Kansas State Historical Society Collection,* XVII, 27-97.

Dobie, J. Frank

1920   "The Cowboy and His Songs," *Texas Review,* V, 163-169.

1927   "Ballads and Songs of the Frontier Folk," *TFSP*, VI, 121-183.

1928   "More Ballads and Songs of the Frontier Folk," *TFSP*, VII, 155-180.

1932   "Mustang Gray: Fact, Tradition and Song," *TFSP*, X, 109-123.

1943   "A Buffalo Hunter and His Song," *TFSP*, XVIII, 1-10.

Doerflinger, William M.

1951   *Shantymen and Shantyboys.* New York: Macmillan.

Dolph, E.A.

1929   *Sound Off!* New York: Cosmopolitan Book.

Drury, Wells

1931   *Three Pioneer Ballads.* San Francisco: privately printed.

Dwyer, Richard A., Richard E. Lingenfelter, and David Cohen

1964   *The Songs of the Gold Rush.* Berkeley and Los Angeles: University of California Press.

E Clampus Vitus

1939   *What Was Your Name in the States?* Yerba Buena (San Francisco).

Ellis, A. L.

1901   "Oh, Bury Me Not on the Lone Prairie," *JAF*, XIV, 186.

Emerson, L. O.

1857   *The Golden Wreath: A Choice Collection of Favorite Melodies.* Boston: Oliver Ditson & Co.

Emrich, Duncan

1942*a*   "The Song Prospector," *Mines Magazine* (Jan.-Aug.).

1942*b*   "Mining Songs," *SFQ*, VI, 103-106.

1942*c*   "Songs of the Western Miners," *CFQ*, I, 213-232.

1942*d*   *Casey Jones and Other Ballads of the Mining West.* Denver: Emrich.

1942*e*   "Casey Jones, Union Scab," *CFQ*, I, 292-293.

Farwell, Arthur

1905   *Folk-songs of the West and South.* Newton Center, Mass.: Wa-Wan Press.

Federal Writers' Project

1937*a*   *Cowboy Songs (Part I). Nebraska Folklore Pamphlet No. 1.* Lincoln, Nebr.: WPA.

1937*b*   *Cowboy Songs (Part II). Nebraska Folklore Pamphlet No. 11.* Lincoln, Nebr.: WPA.

1938*a*   *Ballads. Nebraska Folklore Pamphlet No. 16.* Lincoln, Nebr.: WPA.

1938*b*   *Farmers' Alliance Songs of the 1890's. Nebraska Folklore Pamphlet No. 18.* Lincoln, Nebr.: WPA.

1939   *More Farmers' Alliance Songs of the 1890's. Nebraska Folklore Pamphlet No. 20.* Lincoln, Nebr.: WPA.

1940   *Nebraska Folklore.* Book 2. Lincoln, Nebr.: Woodruff.

1941   *Nebraska Folklore.* Book 3. Lincoln, Nebr.: Woodruff.

Fife, Austin E.

1947   "The Mormon Car," *UHR*, I, 298-299.

1953   "Ballad of the Mountain Meadows Massacre," *WF*, XII, 229-241.

Fife, Austin E., and Alta S. Fife

1947   "Folk Songs of Mormon Inspiration," *WF*, VI, 42-52.

1956   *Saints of Sage and Saddle.* Bloomington: University of Indiana Press.

1966   *Songs of the Cowboys by N. Howard Thorp.* New York: Clarkson N. Potter, Inc.

Finger, Charles J.

1923   *Sailor Chanties and Cowboy Songs.* Girard, Kans.: Haldeman-Julius Co.

1927   *Frontier Ballads.* Garden City, N.Y.: Doubleday, Page.

Flander, H. H., E. F. Ballard, G. Brown, and P. Barry

1939   *The New Green Mountain Songster.* New Haven: Yale University Press.

Fowke, Edith F.

1962   "American Cowboy and Western Pioneer Songs in Canada," *WF*, XXI, 247-256.

1964   "The Red River Valley, Re-examined," *WF*, XXIII, 163-171.

Fowke, Edith F., and Joe Glazer

1960   *Songs of Work and Freedom.* Chicago: Roosevelt University.

Fowke, Edith F., and Richard Johnston.

1954   *Folk Songs of Canada.* Waterloo Publishing Co.

Frey, Hugo

1936   *American Cowboy Songs.* New York: Robbins Music Corp.

Frothingham, Robert

1922–23   "Old Songs That Men Have Sung," *Adventure Magazine* (June 20, 1922–June 20, 1923).

Gaines, Newton

1928   "Some Characteristics of Cowboy Songs," *TFSP*, VII, 145-154.

Gardner, Gail I.

1935   *Orejana Bull for Cowboys Only.* Phoenix, Ariz.: Messenger Printing Co.

German, George B.

1929   *Cowboy Campfire Ballads.* Yankton, S. D.: privately printed.

Gillis, Everett A.

1954   "Literary Origins of Some Western Ballads," *WF*, XIII, 101-106.

Glazer, Joe, and Bill Friedland
    1953   *Songs of the Wobblies.* New York: Labor Arts.
Gordon, Robert W.
    1923-1927 "Old Songs That Men Have Sung," *Adventure Magazine*
                (July 10, 1923–Sept. 15, 1927).
    1938   *Folk-Songs of America.* NewYork: National Service Bureau.
Grant, Phil S.
    1924   "The Songs of the Forty-Niners." Unpublished M.A. thesis,
                University of California, Berkeley.
Green, J. W.
    1947   "Sing Ha Ha, Come from China," *WF*, VI, 278.
Greenway, John
    1953   *American Folksongs of Protest.* Philadelphia: University of
                Pennsylvania Press.
Guinn, J. M.
    1906   "Songs from a California Songsters," *Annual Publication
                of the Historical Society of Southern California*, VII, 207-
                215.
Guthrie, Woody
    1947   *American Folksong.* New York: Disc Company of America.
Haley, J. Evetts
    1927   "Cowboy Songs Again," *TFSP*, VI, 198-204.
Hall, Sharlot M.
    1908   "Songs of the Old Cattle Trails," *Out West*, XXVIII, 216-
                221.
Hand, Wayland D.
    1942   "California Miners' Folklore," *CFQ*, I, 24-46, 127-153.
    1946   "The Folklore, Customs and Traditions of the Butte Miners,"
                CFQ, V, 1-25, 153-178.
Hand, Wayland D., Charles Cutts, Robert C. Wylder, and Betty Wylder
    1950   "Songs of the Butte Miners," *WF*, IX, 1-49.
Handy, W. J.
    1908   "Some Early California Songs," *Out West*, XXIX, 430-437.
Harrison, Russell M.
    1952   "Folksongs from Oregon," *WF*, XI, 174-184.
Hastings, George E.
    1931   "Hell in Texas," *TFSP*, IX, 175-182.
Hendren, J. W.
    1938   "An English Source of 'The Trail to Mexico.' " *TFSP*, XIII,
                270-279.
Hendrix, William S.
    1944   "The Source of 'Oh Bury Me Out on the Lone Prairie,' "
                Hispania, XXVII, 29-33.
Holliday, Walter H.
    1924   *Mining-Camp Melodies.* Butte, Mont. Oates & Roberts.
Howay, F. W.
    1928   "Memorandum on the Ballads of the Northwest Fur Trade,"
                New England Quarterly, I, 71-79.
Hubbard, Lester A.
    1947   "Songs and Ballads of the Utah Pioneers," *UHR*, I, 74-96.
    1950   "John Chinaman in the West," *UHR*, IV, 311-321.

1959   "Militant Songs of the Mormons," *WF*, XVIII, 121-130.

1961   *Ballads and Songs from Utah.* Salt Lake City: University of Utah.

Hugill, Stan
1961   *Shanties from the Seven Seas.* New York: Dutton.

Hull, Myra E.
1938   "Kansas Play-Party Songs," *Kansas Historical Quarterly*, VII, 258-286.

1939   "Cowboy Ballads," *Kansas Historical Quarterly*, VIII, 35-60.

Industrial Workers of the World
1909*a*   *I.W.W. Songs.* 1st ed. Spokane: IWW.

1909*b*   *I.W.W. Songs.* 2d ed. Spokane: IWW.

1910   *I.W.W. Songs.* 3d ed. Spokane: IWW.

1912*a*   *I.W.W. Songs.* Los Angeles ed. Los Angeles: Los Angeles Local IWW.

1912*b*   *I.W.W. Songs.* 4th ed. Spokane: IWW.

1913*a*   *I.W.W. Songs.* 5th ed. Spokane: IWW.

1913*b*   *I.W.W. Songs.* 6th ed. Spokane: IWW.

1914*a*   *I.W.W. Songs.* 7th ed. Cleveland: IWW.

1914*b*   *I.W.W. Songs.* 8th ed. Cleveland: IWW.

1916   *I.W.W. Songs.* 9th ed. Cleveland: IWW.

1917*a*   *I.W.W. Songs.* 10th ed. Chicago: IWW.

1917*b*   *I.W.W. Songs.* 11th ed. Chicago: IWW.

1917*c*   *I.W.W. Songs.* 12th ed. Chicago: IWW.

1917*d*   *I.W.W. Songs.* 13th ed. Chicago: IWW.

1918   *I.W.W. Songs.* 14th ed. Chicago: IWW.

1919   *I.W.W. Songs.* 15th ed. Chicago: IWW.

1921*a*   *I.W.W. Songs.* 16th ed. Chicago: IWW.

1921*b*   *I.W.W. Songs.* 17th ed. Chicago: IWW.

1922?   *I.W.W. Songs.* 18th ed. Chicago: IWW.

1923?   *I.W.W. Songs.* 19th ed. Chicago: IWW.

1924?   *I.W.W. Songs.* 20th ed. Chicago: IWW.

1925   *I.W.W. Songs.* 21st ed. Chicago: IWW.

1926   *I.W.W. Songs.* 22d ed. Chicago: IWW.

1927   *I.W.W. Songs.* 23d ed. Chicago: IWW.

1930-1932 *I.W.W. Songs.* 24th ed. Chicago: IWW.

1933   *I.W.W. Songs.* 25th ed. Chicago: IWW.

1936   *I.W.W. Songs.* 26th ed. Chicago: IWW.

1939   *I.W.W. Songs.* 27th ed. Chicago: IWW.

1945   *I.W.W. Songs.* 28th ed. Chicago: IWW.

1956   *I.W.W. Songs.* 29th ed. Chicago: IWW.

Irwin, Godfrey
1931   *American Tramp and Underworld Slang.* London: Partridge. Pp. 199-252.

Ives, Ronald L.
1941   "Folklore of Eastern Middle Park, Colorado," *JAF*, LIV, 24-43.

Johnson, Helen K.
1881   *Our Familiar Songs and Those Who Made Them.* New York: Holt & Co.

Johnson, J. E.
1858   *Johnson's Original Comic Songs.* San Francisco: Presho & Appleton.
1863   *Johnson's New Comic Songs, No. 2.* San Francisco: Appleton & Co.
1864   *Johnson's Original Comic Songs, No. 3.* San Francisco: Appleton & Co.

Jordan, Philip D., and Lillian Kessler
1941   *Songs of Yesterday.* Garden City, N.Y.: Doubleday, Doran.

Klickman, F. Henri, and Sterling Sherwin
1933   *Songs of the Saddle.* New York: Sam Fox Publishing Co.

Koch, William, and Mary Koch
1956   "Beat the Drum Slowly Boys," *Kansas Magazine*, pp. 8-12.
1961   "Kansas History and Folksong," *Heritage of Kansas*, V, 3-32.

Kornbluh, Joyce L. (ed.)
1964   *Rebel Voices: An I.W.W. Anthology.* Ann Arbor: University of Michigan Press.

Larkin, Margaret
1931   *Singing Cowboy: A book of Western Songs.* New York: Knopf.

Laws, G. Malcolm, Jr.
1964   *Native American Balladry: A Descriptive Study and a Bibliographical Syllabus.* Rev. ed. Philadelphia: American Folklore Society.

Lee, Jack H.
1938   *Powder River Jack and Kitty Lee's Cowboy Song Book.* Butte, Mont.: McKee Printing Co.

Leland, J. A. C.
1947   "Hay Sing Come from China," *WF*, VI, 383.

Lengyel, Cornel (ed.)
1939   *A San Francisco Songster, 1849-1939.* Vol. 2 of *History of Music in San Francisco Series.* San Francisco: Northern California WPA.
1949   *Hangtown Ballads.* Georgetown, Calif.; The Forty-niner.

Library of Congress
1942   *Check List of Recorded Songs in the English Language in the Archive of American Folk Song to July, 1940.* Washington, D.C. 2 vols.

Lodewick, Kenneth
1955   " 'The Unfortunate Rake' and his Descendants," *WF*, XIV, 98-109.

Lomax, Alan
1960   *Folk Songs of North America.* Garden City, N.Y.: Doubleday.

Lomax, John A.
1910   *Cowboy Songs and Other Frontier Ballads.* New York: Sturgis & Walton Co.
1911   "Cowboy Songs of the Mexican Border," *Sewanee Review*, XIX, 1-18.
1915   "Some Types of American Folk-Songs," *JAF*, XXVIII, 1-17.

1916	*Cowboy Songs and Other Frontier Ballads.* 2d ed., rev. and enl. New York: Sturgis & Walton Co.
1919	*Songs of the Cattle Trail and Cow Camp.* New York: Macmillan.
1934	"The Story of 'Good-Bye Old Paint,'" *Wild West Weekly* (Feb. 10), pp. 133-134.
1937	"'Home on the Range': Story of a Famous Song," *Scholastic*, XXXI (Dec. 11), 17.

Lomax, John A., and Alan Lomax

1934	*American Ballads and Folk Songs.* New York: Macmillan.
1938	*Cowboy Songs and Other Frontier Ballads.* Rev. and enl. New York: Macmillan.
1941	*Our Singing Country.* New York: Macmillan.
1947	*Folk Song U.S.A.* New York: Duell, Sloan & Pearce.

Lummis, Charles F.

| 1903 | "The Days of 'Forty-Nine," *Out West*, XVIII, 202-205. |
| 1904 | "Oh, Susanna" (California version), *Out West*, XXI, 272-273. |

Lumpkin, Ben Gray

| 1959 | "Pioneer Colorado Sings," *Colorado Adventure*, I, 13-15. |
| 1960 | "Colorado Folk Songs," *WF*, XIX, 77-97. |

McMullen, Mildred M.

| 1946 | "The Prairie Songs: Northwest Kansas Folksongs." Unpublished M.A. thesis, University of Kansas, Lawrence. |

Malone, Henry H.

| 1961 | "Folksongs and Ballads, Part I." In *Kansas Folklore.* Ed. S. J. Sackett and William E. Koch. Lincoln: University of Nebraska Press. |

Marshall, W. G.

| 1882 | *Through America, or Nine Months in the United States.* London. Pp. 207-213. |

Mechem, Kirke

| 1949 | "Home on the Range," *Kansas Historical Quarterly*, XVII, 313-339. |

Milburn, George

| 1930 | *Hobo's Hornbook.* New York: Ives Washburn. |

Miller, Jeannette

| 1937 | "Folks Songs of California." Unpublished M.A. thesis, University of California, Berkeley. |

Moore, Arbie

| 1927 | "The Texas Cowboy," *TFSP*, VI, 196-197. |

Moore, Chauncy O., and Ethel Moore

| 1964 | *Ballads and Folksongs of the Southwest.* Norman: University of Oklahoma Press. |

Murray, James

| 1946 | "Sailors' Songs with California Significance," *CFQ*, V, 143-152. |

O'Bryant, Joan

| 1961 | "Folksongs and Ballads, Part II." In *Kansas Folklore.* Ed. S. J. Sackett and William E. Koch. Lincoln: University of Nebraska Press. |

O'Malley, Dominick J.
    1934   *D. J. O'Malley: Cowboy Poet.* Ed. John Irwin White. West-field, N.J.: Westfield Leader.

Owens, William A.
    1950   "Texas Folk Songs," *TFSP*, XXIII.

Paredes, A.
    1959   "The 'Bury Me Not' Theme in the Southwest," *TFSP*, XXIX, 88-92.

Patterson, Patt, and Lois Dexter
    1932   *Songs of the Roundup Rangers.* New York: George T. Worth & Co.

Payne, L. W., Jr.
    1927   "Songs and Ballads—Grave and Gay," *TFSP*, VI, 209-237.

Peterson, Harold D.
    1934   "A Syllabus of the Ballad Collection of Edwin Ford Piper." Unpublished M.A. thesis, State University of Iowa, Iowa City.

Porter, John E.
    1943   "Wobbly and Other Songs," *CFQ*, II, 42-44.

Porter, Kenneth W.
    1947   "Kansas Song," *JAF*, LX, 299-301.

Pound, Louise
    1913–14   "The Southwestern Cowboy Songs and the English and Scottish Popular Ballads," *Modern Philology*, XI, 195-207.
    1915   *Folk-Songs of Nebraska and the Central West: A Syllabus.* Nebraska Academy of Science Publications, IX, no. 3.
    1922   *American Ballads and Songs.* New York: Scribners.
    1937   "Joe Bowers Again," *SFQ*, I, 13-15.
    1939   "Some Texts of Western Songs," *SFQ*, III, 25-31.
    1942   "Baldy Green," *SFQ*, VI, 121-122.
    1957   "Yet Another Joe Bowers," *WF*, XVI, 111-120.

Randolph, Vance
    1946   *Ozark Folksongs.* Vol. I. Columbia: State Historical Society of Missouri.
    1948   *Ozark Folksongs.* Vol. II. Columbia: State Historical Society of Missouri.
    1949   *Ozark Folksongs.* Vol. III. Columbia: State Historical Society of Missouri.
    1950   *Ozark Folksongs.* Vol. IV. Columbia: State Historical Society of Missouri.

Rice, Claton S.
    1930   *Songs of the Mormon Way.* Billings, Mont.: privately printed.

Rickaby, Franz L.
    1926   *Ballads and Songs of the Shanty-Boy.* Cambridge: Harvard University Press.

Robertson, Sidney H.
    1940   *Check List of California Songs.* Berkeley: University of California Music Department.

Robinson, D. G.
    1853   *Comic Songs, or Hits at San Francisco.* San Francisco: San Francisco Commercial & Job Office.

Sackett, S. J., and William E. Koch (eds.)
    1961   *Kansas Folklore*. Lincoln: University of Nebraska Press.

Sandburg, Carl
    1927   *The American Songbag*. New York: Harcourt, Brace.

Sherwin, Sterling, and Louis Katzman
    1932   *Songs of the Gold Miners*. New York: C. Fisher & Son.

Sherwin, Sterling, and F. Henri Klickman
    1934   *Songs of the Round-Up*. New York: Robbins Music Corp.

Sherwin, Sterling, and Harry K. McClintock
    1943   *Railroad Songs of Yesterday*. New York: Shapiro, Berstein.

Sires, Ina
    1927   "Songs of the Open Range," *TFSP*, VI, 192-195.
    1928   *Songs of the Open Range*. Boston and New York: C. C. Birchard & Co.

Siringo, Charles A.
    1919   *The Song Companion of a Lone Star Cowboy*. Santa Fe: privately printed.

Smith, C. Fox
    1927   *A Book of Shanties*. Boston: Houghton Mifflin.

Speck, Ernest
    1944   "Song of the Little Llano," *TFSP*, XIX, 165-166.

Stanley, Clark
    1897   *The Life and Adventures of the American Cow-boy*. Providence: Clark Stanley. Pp. 24-36.

Stavis, Barrie, and Frank Harmon
    1955   *The Songs of Joe Hill*. New York: People's Artists Inc.

Stone, John A.
    1855   *Put's Original California Songster*. 1st ed. San Francisco: Appleton & Co.
    1857   *Put's Mountain Songster*. San Francisco: Appleton & Co.
    1858a   *Put's Golden Songster*. 1st ed. San Francisco: Appleton & Co.
    1858b   *Put's Golden Songster*. 2d ed. San Francisco: Appleton & Co.
    1861   *Pacific Song Book*. San Francisco: Appleton & Co.
    1868   *Put's Original California Songster*. 4th ed. San Francisco: Appleton & Co.

Swan, Howard
    1952   *Music in the Southwest, 1825-1950*. San Marino, Calif.: Huntington Library.

Taylor, Mart
    1856   *The Gold Diggers' Song Book*. Marysville, Calif.: Marysville Daily Herald Printer.
    1858   *Local Lyrics and Miscellaneous Poems*. San Francisco: Hutchings & Rosenfeld.

Thompson, Harold W.
    1958   *A Pioneer Songster: Texts from the Stevens-Douglas Manuscripts of Western New York, 1841-1856*. Ithaca, N.Y.: Cornell University Press.

Thorp, N. Howard
    1908   *Songs of the Cowboys*. Estancia, N.M.: News Print Shop.

1921   *Songs of the Cowboys*. Boston and New York: Houghton Mifflin.

Toelken, J. Barre
1959   "The Ballad of the Mountain Meadows Massacre," *WF*, XVIII, 169-172.
1962   "Northwest Traditional Ballads: A Collector's Dilemma," *Northwest Review*, V, 9-18.

Turner, J. W., E. T. Bates, *et al.*
1858   *100 Comic Songs*. San Francisco: A. Kohler.

Vernon, Grenville
1927   *Yankee Doodle Doo: A Collection of Songs of the Early American Stage*. New York: Payson & Clark.

Vincent, Leopold
1891   *The Alliance and Labor Songster: A Collection of Labor and Comic Songs*. Winfield, Kans.: H. & L. Vincent.

Webb, W. P.
1923   "Miscellany of Texas Folk-lore," *TFSP*, II, 38-49.

Westermeier, Clifford P.
1955   *Trailing the Cowboy*. Caldwell, Idaho: Caxton. Pp. 259-281.

Wiley, Mildred M.
N.d.   "Bar-Room Ballads of the Fifties." Unpublished collection in Bancroft Library, University of California, Berkeley.

Will, G. F.
1909   "Songs of Western Cowboys," *JAF*, XXII, 256-261.
1913   "Four Cowboy Songs," *JAF*, XXVI, 185-188.

Willes, William
1872   *The Mountain Warbler: Being a Collection of Original Songs and Recitations*. Salt Lake City: Deseret News, Book & Job Establishment.

Wolf, Edwin, II
1963   *American Song Sheets, Slip Ballads and Poetical Broadsides, 1850-1870*. Philadelphia: Library Company of Philadelphia.

Wylder, Robert C.
1949   "A Comparative Analysis of Some Montana Folksongs." Unpublished M.A. thesis, Montana State University, Missoula.

Young, James, and S. W. Leonard
1855   *The National Temperance Songster*. Cincinnati: Applegate & Co.

MUSICAL AFTERWORD

Because many of the sources for this volume provided texts without music or, occasionally, music that was unusable for one reason or another, much of the musical editing consisted of securing and adapting tunes to couple with texts. One approach would have been to gather the tunes exclusively from authentic sources so that this book could have served as a regional reference volume of Western American melody. It is my feeling, however, that the transcriptions in published collections are not sufficiently reliable. In the few instances where field recordings were available for comparison with the transcriptions, the discrepancies were often distressing; in many more instances the tunes as published were so preposterous as to be nearly useless to the critical reader. Thus the compiler of a scholarly compendium of authentic Western tunes will need at hand the field tapes of private collectors, university archives, and the Library of Congress, on which the music is stored. I have used, rather, *singability* of a tune as my general criterion of selection. Such a rule is not only far more manageable than a scholarly one, but better suited to the needs of the majority of readers, who will use this collection, I trust, for singing.

Broadsides were to be sung to the tunes of familiar popular songs of the day. For these tunes I either went to the sheet music, in one form or another, or made use of field recordings, commercial phonograph recordings, and published field collections. For example, for the texts written to be sung to the tune of "Marching Through Georgia," I used the tune as originally composed by Henry C. Work. On the other hand, the ubiquitous parodies of "Little Old Log Cabin in the Lane" have been set to the tune recorded in 1924 by Riley Puckett. For "Little Joe, the Wrangler," basically the same melody, I used the 1928 commercial recording of Jules Allen, an authentic cowboy singer. "The Old Bachelor" comes from a recording by the Carter Family. On one occasion I followed both practices. "The Scab's Lament" and "When Work Is Done This Fall" were both written to be sung to the tune of "After the Ball." The former was set to that tune as composed by Charles K. Harris; for the latter, I used a far better tune sung in 1925 by the first commercially recorded cowboy singer, Carl T. Sprague.

Where the tunes called for were folk tunes, I used the standard collections, supplemented by recorded material. "Goodbye, Old Paint" and "Night-Herding Song," for example, appear in many collections of folk music. Because of this, I felt it more

585

worthwhile to transcribe the previously unpublished (and very beautiful) versions of these songs as recorded by the Library of Congress, than to reprint others more readily available.

Because of my basic distrust of printed music in the entire area of folk song, published sources were not treated as sacrosanct. Confronted not a few times with the work of previous musical editors who eschewed the simplest dictates of common sense, I fearlessly denuded many tunes of notational curiosities that would have confounded the most zealous of readers. The alterations, aside from transposition, consisted mainly of changing meter and rhythmic notation. I do not share the affinity of many of my colleagues for eighth and sixteenth notes, and, in many cases, changed a time signature from 2/4 to 4/4 so that the melody could move in more easily read quarter and eighth notes. A slow 6/8 has occasionally been changed to 3/4 to make the guitar accompaniment more obvious. *Fermatas*, a device used by some editors apparently to enshroud a tune in mystery, have been replaced, where it seemed appropriate, by longer note values.

Judging from the material available on the Library of Congress recordings, Western songs were sung *a capella* more often than not. Such guitar accompaniment as there was, if it is possible to generalize from the playing of Sprague, Allen, and Glenn Ohrlin, consisted of a very simple style in which a single bass note was plucked by the thumb on the downbeat of the measure and then the treble strings were brushed or plucked once or twice, depending upon the meter of the song.

The guitar chords indicated conform generally to the harmonic vocabulary of traditional American folk guitar: tonic, subdominant, and dominant triads; dominant sevenths; occasional applied dominants; and the relative minor when a phrase of the melody cadences on the sixth degree of the scale and the subdominant chord does not seem to fit. Despite the social and musical intercourse between the South and the West, there seemed to be no compelling reason, in a book of Western songs, to follow the Southern tradition of harmonizing minor tunes with major chords, so I often used minor chords when it seemed that the general character of a melody was Anglo-Irish rather than old-time Southern. Where a tune was transcribed from Southern musicians, such as the Lilly Brothers ("Kansas Boys") or Clint Howard, Doc Watson, and Fred Price ("The Rambling Cowboy"), I remained faithful to the recorded accompaniments.

D. C.

CHORD CHART

Capital letters indicate major chords. Lowercase letters indicate minor chords. The open (nonbarred) chords are given first: majors, sevenths, then minors. These are followed by barred chords and clutch chords.

The double horizontal line at the top of each diagram represents the nut of the guitar. The lines below and parallel to the nut represent the frets. The vertical lines represent the strings.

The dots indicate the placement of the fingers. If there is no dot on a string, it is to be played open, unless there is an X above it, in which case it is not to be played under any circumstances.

The letters below the diagrams indicate which finger is to be used. I = index; M = middle; R = ring; L = little; and T = thumb.

Most chords in the book will be found among the open chords. Others can be made with the barred or clutch chords, by moving them to the appropriate fret. For each fret the barred chord is moved up the chord is raised a half step. For example, F barred on the 2d fret is F$^\#$; f barred on the 3d fret is g; B^b barred on the 5th fret is D; b^b barred on the 7th fret is e; and so on. Remember that there is a whole step (two frets) between every note except between E and F, and B and C.

Barred chords are made by laying the index finger across all the strings on one fret and making a chord position with the other fingers. The index functions as a capo, and raises the chord in the same way.

Clutch chords involve the use of the thumb to hold down the 6th, and sometimes the 5th, strings to eliminate having to use a bar. It is difficult to make, especially on a wide-neck or classical guitar, but less fatiguing than a barred chord. It has the same advantage of movability which a barred chord has, because there are no open strings.

MAJOR CHORDS:

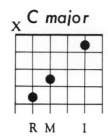

C major

R M   I

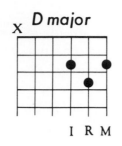

D major

I R M

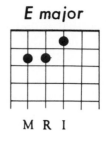

E major

M R   I

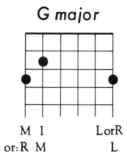

G major

M   I   L or R
or: R M   L

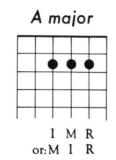

A major

I   M   R
or: M   I   R

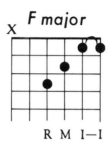

F major

R   M   I—I

7ᵗʰ CHORDS:

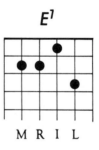

C⁷

R M L I

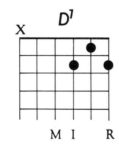

D⁷

M   I   R

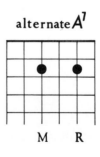

E⁷

M R I L

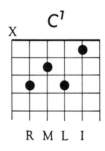

G⁷

R M   I

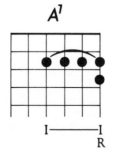

A⁷

I———I
     R

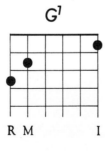

alternate A⁷

M   R

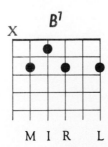

B⁷

M I R   L

MINOR CHORDS:

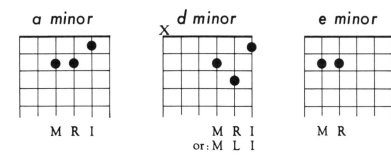

a minor
M R I

d minor
X
M R I
or: M L I

e minor
M R

BARRED CHORDS:*

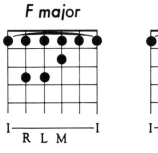

F major
I ——— I
R L M

f minor
I ——— I
R L

CLUTCH CHORDS:*

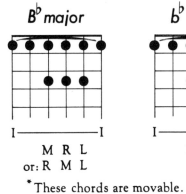

B♭ major
I ——— I
M R L
or: R M L

b♭ minor
I ——— I
R L M

*These chords are movable.

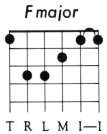

F major
T R L M I — I

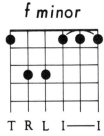

f minor
T R L I — I

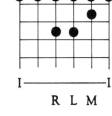

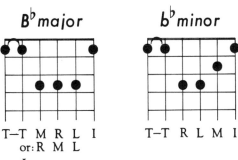

B♭ major
T—T M R L I
or: R M L

b♭ minor
T—T R L M I

*These chords are movable in the same manner as barred chords.

INDEX OF TITLES
AND FIRST LINES

(Titles are in *italics*; first lines are in roman type)